ASPEN PUBLISHERS

Blond's
LAW GUIDES

MULTISTATE BAR EXAM

NEIL C. BLOND, Esq.

Fifth Edition revised by
Tania N. Shah, Esq.,
and Melissa A. Gill, Esq.

Wolters Kluwer
Law & Business

AUSTIN   BOSTON   CHICAGO   NEW YORK   THE NETHERLANDS

To contact Customer Care, e-mail customer.care@aspenpublishers.com,
call 1-800-234-1660, fax 1-800-901-9075, or mail correspondence to:

Aspen Publishers
Attn: Order Department
PO Box 990
Frederick, MD 21705

Printed in the United States of America.

1 2 3 4 5 6 7 8 9 0

ISBN 978-07355-7795-4

About Wolters Kluwer Law & Business

Wolters Kluwer Law & Business is a leading provider of research information and workflow solutions in key specialty areas. The strengths of the individual brands of Aspen Publishers, CCH, Kluwer Law International and Loislaw are aligned within Wolters Kluwer Law & Business to provide comprehensive, in-depth solutions and expert-authored content for the legal, professional and education markets.

CCH was founded in 1913 and has served more than four generations of business professionals and their clients. The CCH products in the Wolters Kluwer Law & Business group are highly regarded electronic and print resources for legal, securities, antitrust and trade regulation, government contracting, banking, pension, payroll, employment and labor, and healthcare reimbursement and compliance professionals.

Aspen Publishers is a leading information provider for attorneys, business professionals and law students. Written by preeminent authorities, Aspen products offer analytical and practical information in a range of specialty practice areas from securities law and intellectual property to mergers and acquisitions and pension/benefits. Aspen's trusted legal education resources provide professors and students with high-quality, up-to-date and effective resources for successful instruction and study in all areas of the law.

Kluwer Law International supplies the global business community with comprehensive English-language international legal information. Legal practitioners, corporate counsel and business executives around the world rely on the Kluwer Law International journals, loose-leafs, books and electronic products for authoritative information in many areas of international legal practice.

Loislaw is a premier provider of digitized legal content to small law firm practitioners of various specializations. Loislaw provides attorneys with the ability to quickly and efficiently find the necessary legal information they need, when and where they need it, by facilitating access to primary law as well as state-specific law, records, forms and treatises.

Wolters Kluwer Law & Business, a unit of Wolters Kluwer, is headquartered in New York and Riverwoods, Illinois. Wolters Kluwer is a leading multinational publisher and information services company.

Check Out These Other Great Titles

BLOND'S LAW GUIDES

Comprehensive, Yet Concise . . . JUST RIGHT!

Each Blond's Law Guide book contains: Black Letter Law Outline · EasyFlow™ Charts · Case Clips · Mnemonics

Available titles in this series include:

Blond's Civil Procedure

Blond's Constitutional Law

Blond's Contracts

Blond's Criminal Law

Blond's Criminal Procedure

Blond's Evidence

Blond's Property

Blond's Torts

ASK FOR THEM AT YOUR LOCAL BOOKSTORE IF UNAVAILABLE, PURCHASE ONLINE AT *http://lawschool.aspenpublishers.com*

Table of Contents

Constitutional Law

Constitutional Law

Questions 1–2 are based upon the following fact situation.

The federal government enacted a $100 tax on all persons running in a marathon sanctioned by a national athletic organization. The law specified that all monies raised by the marathon tax would be used to build a shelter for homeless persons in the state.

Question 1

Which of the following people have the best chance of asserting a successful challenge to the statute?

(A) a running shoe company

(B) the city of New York because, although home of the country's largest homeless population, the city has not received federal money for the homeless

(C) a woman registered for the Honolulu Marathon

(D) the American Heart Association

Question 2

Should the statute be declared constitutional?

(A) Yes, if it is related to the public interest.

(B) Yes, because society has an interest in helping poor persons.

(C) No, because the distribution is not apportioned equally among the states.

(D) No, because the tax is unrelated to its use.

Question 3

The Federal Hazardous Waste Act of 1987 contained the clause "All disposal of Lithium 235 must be preceded by rendering the element inert by combining it with Au isotopes. Li-Au compound may only be shipped by rail in lead-reinforced containers." The federal standard was prohibitively expensive compared to the methods previously used by Lithium Chemical, a company incorporated and doing business in the state. Lithium Chemical developed and patented Lithium 235 and was the only company producing it. In 2008, the state passed a statute that "Lithium 235 may be disposed of only after being rendered inert by combining it with Au or Pb isotopes." The state statute will be found unconstitutional:

(A) because it interferes with powers delegated to the federal government.

(B) because it constitutes state interference with interstate commerce.

(C) because of the Supremacy Clause.

(D) unless the state can prove the added cost of the federal standards are not justified.

Questions 4–5 are based upon the following fact situation.

A girl and a boy were seniors at a city high school. On September 1, 2006, the boy was suspended from school for a period of three days for violating a school rule that provided: "All students must wear shoes at all times except during designated physical education courses. Violators of this rule shall be punished by an automatic three-day suspension."

The boy demanded a formal hearing after explaining to the principal that he walked without shoes for medical reasons. The boy's request for a hearing was denied.

On October 1, 2006, the girl used profane language after her homeroom teacher scolded her for being late. The homeroom teacher reacted with a brief, but obscene, response. Later that day, the girl was suspended from school for one week. Her request for a hearing was denied.

Question 4

Which of the following statements most accurately describes the September 1 suspension?

(A) The boy was unlawfully deprived of property and liberty guaranteed by the Fourteenth Amendment.

(B) The suspension violated the boy's due process rights.

(C) The school rule should be found a violation of the students' due process rights.

(D) The suspension was lawful and proper.

Question 5

Which of the following statements is best?

(A) The girl's suspension violated her rights to due process and free speech.

(B) A formal evidentiary hearing is required before a student may be temporarily suspended from a public school.

(C) A formal evidentiary hearing is not required before a student may be temporarily suspended from a public school.

(D) The girl's suspension did not violate her due process or First Amendment rights.

Question 6

A high school principal instituted a plan that would, according to the principal, "help students reach their ultimate potential." She sectioned off a portion of the auditorium for students to voluntarily pray, and next to each chair was a short prayer that students could recite. A group of seniors protested. One of the student's parents hired a lawyer to enjoin the voluntary prayer. The seniors are most likely to:

(A) succeed, since the plan violated the Equal Protection Clause of the Fourteenth Amendment.

(B) succeed, since the plan violates the Establishment Clause of the First Amendment.

(C) not succeed, since the prayer is voluntary.

(D) not succeed, since the prayer would not take place inside a classroom.

Question 7

In 2009, Congress passed a sweeping new immigration law providing, in part, that all employers must file proof of citizenship for every new employee. A state enacted the following statute providing that "all voters in the state must fill out a new registration form before voting in the 2010 elections. Such form shall be accompanied by proof of United States citizenship and birth place for all persons not born in the United States."

A candidate for mayor of Miami challenged the constitutionality of the statute in federal district court. The candidate depended heavily on votes from the state's immigrants from poorer nations, who would have difficulty obtaining the documents from their native states. Counsel to the state challenged the court's jurisdiction. Should a federal court hear the case?

(A) Yes, the court should hear the case on its merits.

(B) The court should not hear the case until it has been tested in the state courts.

(C) The court should not hear the case, because the case involves a nonjusticiable political question.

(D) The court should not hear the case, because of the Preemption Doctrine.

Question 8

A marine acted as a liaison between the White House, the U.S. Marines, and several foreign governments. It was later revealed that the marine had violated U.S. law by trading arms with hostile powers and diverting the profits to a Pacific island to which aid was prohibited by U.S. law. Despite the fact that the marine had received orders from his superior, a general, the marine was asked to resign his position.

All U.S. armed forces personnel, veterans, and their families have shopping privileges at special stores that sell goods at below market prices. A federal statute provided that the stores be closed to servicemen and officers dismissed from the service. The marine asserted an action in a federal district court challenging the constitutionality of the denial of his shopping rights, alleging, *inter alia*, that he followed orders given by his military superior and hence the military should not violate his employment contract. The government's most persuasive argument in defending its actions would be to assert that:

(A) the marine had prior notice because the armed forces often revoked shopping privileges.

(B) the marine had been awarded due process.

(C) implied in the marine's employment agreement with the U.S. Marines was a condition that he not violate the laws of the United States.

(D) one may not violate the laws of the United States even if ordered to do so by a military superior.

Question 9

On January 15, 2009, Congress passed the "Surplus Federal Property Statute," which ordered the General Services Administration to dispose of excess federal property. The bill provided that half the property be given to charities operating "within the public interest." The General Services Administration decided shortly thereafter to donate a city's Old Customs House to the Nature Society, which was located in the same state as the Old Custom House, to be used as a natural history museum. The General Services Administration reversed its decision on September 1, 2009, deciding to donate the building to the President Society, a group formed to honor former Presidents. A suit was filed alleging, *inter alia*, that the building's use would not be considered "within the public interest" if it were to be donated to the President Society. Which of the following parties would most likely have standing to challenge the General Services Administration?

(A) a taxpayer residing in Big City

(B) the Big City Mayor

(C) a nature enthusiast residing in the state

(D) the Nature Society

Question 10

A devout member of a church lived in the church commune. He spent fourteen hours a day selling CDs for the church. The church maintained a very complex philosophy enumerated on ten holy CDs and six holy bootlegged concert DVDs. The flip side of the fourth CD declares, "It is a sin to thwart the will of God by providing medical treatment. Only God may decide who shall live and who shall die, who shall be sick and who shall be well. Sometimes one must die to atone for his sins; healing such a person will prevent such atonement and condemn that person to hell." The member's six-year-old son was born with a defective heart. Before his fourth birthday, he was hours away from death. A boy with the exact blood type died in a car accident, and his heart was offered to the son, but the member refused to allow the operation. The son's physician, and the Human Heart Institute, asserted an action to compel the operation. Upon which of the following issues will the outcome of the case depend?

(A) whether the religious objections of the parents outweighs the minor's health and safety in this instance

(B) the fact that the five-year survival rate for heart transplant patients is less than fifty percent

(C) whether or not medical treatment of the son will save his life

(D) whether or not the physician's decision to perform the transplant violates the Establishment Clause

Question 11

State W enacted the following statute:

> (a) No milk may be sold within State W unless such milk is pasteurized in a plant regularly inspected by State W's Department of Agriculture; (b) no firm may dispose the wastes from milk pasteurized in a state other than State W within State W; (c) milk may not be sold in State W more than three days after it has been pasteurized; and (d) milk may not be sold in State W unless its fat content is clearly stated on the label.

State W's Department of Agriculture refused to send inspectors father than one hour from Capital City due to budgetary considerations.

State K Milk, a company incorporated in State K with its principal offices and plants in State K, challenged the constitutionality of section (a). State W Toxic, a company who owned a dump in Capital City used by milk producers, asserted an action on constitutional grounds against section (b) of the statute. The most likely outcome will be that:

(A) neither State K Milk nor State W Toxic will prevail, because a state has the right to protect the health, morals, and welfare of its citizens.

(B) only one of the challenges will be successful, and the court will rule in favor of the challenge by relying on the Privileges and Immunities Clause of Article IV, Section II, as the strongest constitutional challenge.

(C) only one of the challenges will be successful, and the court will rule in favor of the challenge by relying on the Equal Protection Clause of the Fourteenth Amendment as the strongest constitutional challenge.

(D) both challenges will succeed and in both cases the court will rule that the Commerce Clause was the most persuasive challenge.

Question 12

A company marketed a patented condom coated with an anti-viral fluid under the trade name NoAIDS. The condoms were thoroughly tested by the Federal Drug Administration and approved as an effective AIDS virus killer. NoAIDS was available only with a prescription from a licensed physician. A No-condom Law, prohibiting the use of contraceptives by married persons, was passed after evangelists convinced many that the availability of NoAIDS would lead to sexual immorality. Which of the following choices is most correct?

(A) The law will be held constitutional as promoting the general welfare.

(B) The law will be held unconstitutional as a violation of privacy if challenged by a NoAIDS user.

(C) The law will be held unconstitutional as a deprivation of property if challenged by the manufacturers of NoAIDS.

(D) The law will be held unconstitutional if a doctor asserts a third-party suit because he cannot prescribe NoAIDS.

Questions 13–14 are based upon the following fact situation.

A city passed the following statute providing that "Aliens may not reside within 500 yards of City Park. Violation of this statute shall be punishable by eviction, imprisonment, and fine." An alien and vice-president of a Mexican oil monopoly purchased an apartment overlooking the park.

Question 13

If prosecuted for violating the statute, the alien's best constitutional challenge will be based upon:

(A) the Privileges and Immunities Clause.

(B) the Commerce Clause.

(C) the Equal Protection Clause.

(D) the Immigration, Naturalization and Citizenship Clause.

Question 14

The statute will be ruled constitutional if:

(A) the state can prove the statute is narrowly tailored to a compelling state interest.

(B) the alien cannot prove the statute is not narrowly tailored to a compelling state interest.

(C) the state can prove the statute is rationally related to an important government interest.

(D) the alien cannot prove that the statute is not rationally related to a legitimate state interest.

Question 15

On July 20, 2007, the flags of several countries were lowered on oil tankers in the Persian Gulf. United States flags were raised on these same vessels. A spokesperson for the U.S. State Department announced that the tankers were being protected by American warships and that any interference with such vessels would constitute an act of war. The spokesperson said that conflict in the Persian Gulf could threaten U.S. national security by disrupting the shipment of oil through the Persian Gulf, and the United States was, therefore, forced into protecting its interests.

On September 1, 2007, a federal grand jury was convened to investigate the Deputy Secretary of State for Near Eastern Affairs. The investigation sought to determine the veracity of press reports that the Deputy Secretary masterminded a plan to convince the President to protect the Persian Gulf after receiving a $7,000,000 bribe from a Persian Oil Company.

The Deputy Secretary testified that he had, indeed, strongly recommended defense of the Gulf and had so convinced the President, who had been leaning against implementing the operation prior to meeting with the Deputy Secretary.

On September 15, the grand jury returned a criminal indictment against the Deputy Secretary and two White House aides for perjury, bribery, and conspiracy. A written request was forwarded to the President for notes taken during meetings with the persons indicted. The President sought to avoid complying with the request and asked his counsel whether he could be forced to comply with the request.

The President's counsel should advise the President that:

(A) the President may avoid complying with the request by asserting executive privilege.

(B) presidential aides share executive immunity and, therefore, the request need not be granted.

(C) the President must grant the request because of the nature of the indictment.

(D) the President should grant the request despite the presumption of privilege because military, diplomatic, and sensitive national secrets are given great deference.

Question 16

Which of the following government practices will NOT survive a constitutional challenge based on the establishment clause?

(A) The federal government provides a tax deduction for charitable contributions, where contributors to churches are eligible.

(B) A state enacts a tuition voucher plan where children who go to parochial or secular schools can receive partial reimbursement of tuition.

(C) The federal government provides a church-related elementary school with $2,000,000 to hire mathematics teachers.

(D) A public university decides to fund non-religion oriented student publications as well as evangelical Christian publications.

Question 17

A condominium development company based in State O, with offices in O and State A, was in the business of developing luxury condominiums in undeveloped areas near large cities. The company had recently purchased 500 acres of land north of the state's largest city. Before the company began construction, State O enacted a statute requiring in part that a certain percentage of the land surrounding its cities must be used as state recreational facilities. The state court ordered possession, after a hearing, of the 500 acres of land, subject to compensation that would be awarded for damages. The company sued to enjoin the sale. The best argument for upholding the court-ordered possession is:

(A) the power of eminent domain does not require that payment be made prior to condemnation of the property.

(B) the power of eminent domain may only be delegated to a private enterprise for a publicly related use or activity.

(C) there has been no violation of substantive due process.

(D) it is in the public interest to have parks surrounding cities.

Question 18

A state would most likely be able to regulate which of the following?

(A) a state official from discriminating against an African American

(B) a private individual from discriminating against a woman

(C) a federal official from discriminating against an elderly person

(D) a federal official from discriminating against a state official

Question 19

A devotee maintains a religious belief that the firstborn daughter of every woman should be sacrificed to God. Her belief is that the baby should be sacrificed by tossing it off a high suspension bridge. May the devotee be successfully prosecuted?

(A) No, if she asserts her constitutional freedom of religion.

(B) Yes, because religious beliefs are not absolutely protected.

(C) No, because the court should balance the burden of an individual's belief against the state's interest.

(D) No, because the rights of the baby are paramount to the rights of the devoutee.

Question 20

A state statute provided, "Any male having had sexual intercourse with a woman below the age of sixteen shall be found guilty of statutory rape, regardless of whether the woman consented." The defendant, a male charged with statutory rape, challenged the constitutionality of the statute. The court should rule the statute:

(A) valid, if the law is substantially related to an important government interest of preventing teenage pregnancy.

(B) valid, if the law accomplishes the compelling state interest of preventing teenage pregnancy.

(C) not valid, because it distinguishes between two classes.

(D) not valid, since consent negates the intent of the defendant.

Question 21

A state statute provided, "No alien may serve as a teacher in the public school system." The statute will survive a constitutional challenge invoking if the state can prove the statute:

(A) is rationally related to a legitimate state interest.

(B) is narrowly tailored to a compelling state interest.

(C) protects the fundamental right of education.

(D) is merely de jure discrimination.

Question 22

Which of the following rights guaranteed by the Bill of Rights MUST also be respected by the states?

(A) the Second Amendment right to bear arms

(B) the Seventh Amendment right to a jury in civil cases

(C) the Sixth Amendment right to a speedy and public trial by an impartial jury

(D) the Grand Jury Clause of the Fifth Amendment

Question 23

A Japanese-American architect moved into an upper-class town with her husband and two kids. After residing in the town for two months, she befriended a designer, who recently joined a golf club with her husband. The architect and her husband went to the golf club one week later to check out the facilities and to ask about membership. When they met the owner, he refused to accept their application and suggested that they join another private golf club on the other side of town. The architect and her husband brought suit against the owner and the club, claiming that denial of membership to Japanese violated their equal protection rights. Which of the following statements is best?

(A) Plaintiffs will win, because discrimination based on national origin violates the Fourteenth Amendment.

(B) Plaintiffs will win, if they can prove that other Japanese have been discriminated against by the club.

(C) The owner and the club will win, because its denial of membership to Japanese lacks the requisite "state action."

(D) The owner and the club will prevail, because the architect lacks standing to assert the rights of discrimination against the Japanese as a group.

Question 24

A state seeks to enact a statute to limit or substantially reduce the number of advertising billboards alongside its highways. In order to survive a challenge based upon the First Amendment, one criterion the statute must satisfy should be that it is:

(A) rationally related to an important government interest.

(B) narrowly tailored to a legitimate government interest.

(C) viewpoint neutral.

(D) narrowly tailored to serve a significant government interest.

Question 25

A couple challenged a state statute whereby the government could take away a newborn if either the mother or the father were currently receiving welfare. The couple had just given birth to a baby and the father is currently on welfare. Will the couple prevail?

(A) Yes, because the rights of the child are paramount to those of the state.

(B) Yes, because the statute infringes on a fundamental right.

(C) No, because both men and women are treated equally.

(D) No, because discouraging the abuse of the welfare system is a compelling government interest.

Question 26

Federal law provides employees of foreign embassies and consulates with diplomatic immunity. Under the law, the employees are immune from prosecution for parking tickets.

A junior diplomat employed by an embassy was arrested and incarcerated, pursuant to a city statute providing that diplomats may be prosecuted for constant disregard of the law. The diplomat was arrested as a traffic scofflaw after accumulating 2,000 traffic summonses. If the diplomat attacks the constitutionality of the city statute, his best argument will be based upon:

(A) the Due Process Clause.
(B) the Equal Protection Clause.
(C) the Privileges and Immunity Clause.
(D) the Supremacy Clause.

Question 27

A state enacted a new voter registration act. The act required a voter to be a resident of the state for one year and a resident of the county where the election would take place for three months prior to voting. The state argued that the time periods encouraged voters to know about the candidates and issues in their counties prior to voting. The statute, if challenged, would be found to:

(A) violate the Commerce Clause.
(B) violate a fundamental right.
(C) violate the Fifteenth Amendment, which governs voter registration.
(D) be valid, because the regulation merely has the effect of burdening the right to vote, instead of preventing the voter to vote at all.

Question 28

A state legislature passed a bill that provided, "An election shall be held on the first Tuesday in March of odd-numbered years. Only persons owning stores within the state may participate in such elections. Persons owning more than one store may cast one ballot for each store owned." A storeowner challenged the constitutionality of the statute because it allowed some storeowners more than one vote. A forensic pathologist challenged the statute on the grounds that persons not owning stores were not permitted to vote. Which of the following choices is most correct?

(A) The storeowner will prevail but the pathologist will not.
(B) The pathologist will prevail but the storeowner will not.
(C) Both the storeowner and the pathologist will prevail.
(D) Neither the storeowner nor the pathologist will prevail.

Question 29

Which of the following plaintiffs will the state have to demonstrate that a regulation is not substantially related to an important government interest?

(A) a resident alien who challenges a state statute that gives preference to U.S. citizens in all government jobs
(B) a man who challenges a state statute that allows only women to retain custody of their children in the event of a divorce

(C) A legal immigrant who challenges a statute that provides, "Citizens must be fluent in English to obtain a driver's license." The immigrant argues that the law discriminates against him on the basis of race.
(D) A teenager who challenges a law allowing only persons over the age of twenty-one may to be a public park ranger.

Question 30

A man was arrested and charged with violating a state statute that provided that "One may neither smoke nor carry a lit cigar or pipe in an elevator." The man challenged the constitutionality of the state statute on the grounds that it violated his right of free exercise of religion. The man was a member of a religion that required its members to smoke in elevators while the elevator was moving upwards as a means of achieving higher levels of consciousness.

Which of the following choices may not be considered by a court in determining the man's challenge to the constitutionality of the statute?

(A) whether the man's beliefs were reasonable
(B) whether the state statute is a valid and neutral law of general applicability
(C) whether the religion actually required smoking in elevators
(D) whether the man is sincere in his beliefs

Question 31

The National Association of Left-Handed Persons asserted an action in federal district court, alleging state discrimination against left-handed persons. The action alleges that desks in public schools were designed for students who write with their right hands and caused discomfort to left-handed persons. The suit further alleges that the handwriting of left-handed persons was adversely affected by the desks, causing lower grades and resulting in lower economic achievement.

If the state moves to dismiss the case:

(A) the motion should be granted, because left-handed persons are not a suspect class.
(B) the motion should be granted, because the plaintiff does not have standing.
(C) the motion should not be granted, because a real and actual injury has been incurred.
(D) the motion should not be granted because left-handed persons have been discriminated against for hundreds of years.

Question 32

Congress enacted the Federal Aid to Education Act, which provided, "Federal transportation funds may be used to transport students to and from public, private, and parochial schools. Gymnasiums and other physical education facilities at public, private, and parochial schools may be built with federal assistance. The federal government will pay one-half of health insurance premiums provided to teachers in public, private, or parochial schools, only if the teacher is not involved in the teaching of religion."

An ordinary citizen challenged the Federal Aid to Education Act. Assuming that the case is decided on its merits, will the citizen prevail in his challenge of the clause providing aid for construction of physical education facilities?

(A) Yes, because the federal government may not provide aid to an organization whose purpose is to teach religion.

(B) Yes, because the clause creates an excessive entanglement between religion and state.

(C) No, because the construction will not aid religion in any way.

(D) No, because aid given satisfies a secular purpose that may only incidentally benefit religion.

Question 33

The University Association is an organization of private citizens formed as an open forum for discussion of social issues. The association is headquartered in a plush downtown building, where it often sponsors speakers and forums. The downtown headquarters include several lounges and a restaurant. Obtaining membership in the University Association is a long and arduous process. Most people feel the effort expended to obtain membership is a small price to pay because the "powerful" gather in the association and many important contacts are made. The association has neither blacks nor women among its members.

Several association members were employees and elected officials of the state, because the state felt that in order to advance the state's interests it was important for state officials to maintain contact with the state's "elite."

An action was asserted in a federal district court, seeking to enjoin the state from payments of dues to the University Association.

Which of the following arguments will best support the plaintiff's suit?

(A) Race and gender are protected classes.

(B) The state is promoting discrimination

(C) The state is protecting a long and arduous process that is unduly burdensome on its members.

(D) The state is not promoting the health, welfare, and morality of its citizens.

Question 34

A state enacted a statute in the summer of 2008 that prohibited movie theatres from the showing of "objectional sexually explicit films that would suggest moral turpitude." A proprietor owned a theatre on Route 10 in the state. The proprietor advertised that his theatre showed adult movies. The proprietor is arrested and convicted for violating the statute. On appeal, the proprietor's conviction most probably will be:

(A) sustained, because the statute is a reasonable police power measure.

(B) sustained, because the adult movies are films that suggest moral turpitude.

(C) overturned, because sexually explicit films are not immoral for the purposes of the First Amendment.

(D) overturned, because the statute violates the First Amendment.

Question 35

In which of the following cases will a defendant fail in arguing that the state has passed an *ex post facto* law?

(A) The defendant is charged with possession of marijuana. Marijuana possession had been legal on the date the defendant was alleged to possess it, but it has since been legislated as a controlled substance.

(B) The maximum sentence for possession of marijuana was increased from 60 days to one year while the defendant awaited trial for the same charge. After being convicted for possession of marijuana, the defendant was sentenced to six months in prison.

(C) While the defendant awaited trial, the state legislature changed the burden required to prove possession with intent to sell from "beyond a reasonable doubt" to "clear and convincing." The defendant is convicted.

(D) While the defendant awaited trial, the statute under which he was charged was struck down as having overly vague procedural aspects. A new, similar statute was enacted. The defendant was convicted under the new statute.

Question 36

A hiker asserted an action in a federal court against a veterinarian who was employed by the National Park System. The hiker alleged that the veterinarian was negligent in sedating a bear. The bear, known to be violent, escaped and mauled the hiker while she was visiting the National Park. The veterinarian motioned to dismiss the case due to improper jurisdiction. The court should rule jurisdiction is:

(A) proper, because the alleged injury and negligence occurred with a wild animal who was known to be violent.

(B) proper, because the veterinarian was an officer of the federal government.

(C) not proper, because no diversity has been shown.

(D) not proper, because the veterinarian has federal immunity.

Question 37

The father of an illegitimate son abandoned the son. The son felt love for his father and tried to befriend him on many occasions, but the father refused to admit that he was his son. The son purchased a life insurance policy on his father's life.

The father died and the insurance company refused to pay the son, citing a state law that provided, "An unacknowledged, illegitimate child is not considered a child for legal purposes." Since the father was not legally related to the son, the son did not have an insurable interest and could not recover.

If the son challenges the state law, his best argument will be that:

(A) the statute is an unconstitutional *ex post facto law.*

(B) the law violates the Obligation of Contracts Clause of insurance companies.

(C) the law violates the Equal Protection Clause.

(D) he has been deprived his property right to the insurance proceeds without due process.

Question 38

An armed services general was subpoenaed to testify before a congressional committee investigating the loss of a military satellite aboard a space shuttle during a tragic explosion. The general refused to answer certain questions. Congress ordered a state district attorney to prosecute the general for contempt. The district attorney refused.

May the district attorney refuse to prosecute the general?

(A) Yes, because a general is not accountable for judgment decisions.

(B) Yes, because the district attorney's duties are executive actions.

(C) No, because the district attorney must act as directed.

(D) No, because the general is granted federal immunity.

Question 39

A pharmaceutical company manufactured a new pill that was supposed to relieve headaches within five minutes. The pill was called "Nohed." The federal Food and Drug Administration, however, announced that the drug caused side effects such as vomiting and foot aches. As a result, Congress enacted legislation prohibiting shipment of Nohed across state lines. The legislation is most likely:

(A) unconstitutional as a violation of due process.

(B) unconstitutional as a deprivation of the company's property right.

(C) constitutional as within the state's police power.

(D) constitutional, because Congress has the power to regulate interstate commerce.

Question 40

A state enacted a statute restricting the sale of magazines showing partially clothed women to persons below the age of eighteen. A fifteen-year-old boy challenged

the statute after he was not allowed to purchase a world culture magazine featuring women in native garb. Which of the following choices is NOT correct?

(A) Regulation of speech must accomplish a compelling government interest.

(B) Material sexually explicit but not obscene may be zoned away from residential areas.

(C) Material considered obscene for children will be considered obscene for adults.

(D) Material deemed to be obscene may be read but not sold.

Question 41

In which of the following choices will the defendant be UNABLE to invoke the Fourteenth Amendment and force the state to honor a federal right?

(A) A man's house was condemned by the state to make room for a new baseball stadium. The man argues that his property was taken without just compensation, in violation of the Fifth Amendment.

(B) A skater was arrested for ice-skating with a pen in his skates. The judge imposed $500,000 bail. The skater argues that his right against excessive bail has been violated.

(C) A man kept a small arsenal of semi-automatic weapons to protect his house filled with chocolate bars. The man challenged a state statute prohibiting citizens from owning any type of firearms.

(D) A man left work for two weeks without permission in order to demonstrate with the Support the Death Penalty Society. The state refused to apply the First Amendment to local law.

Question 42

Congress enacted the "No Marijuana" Law, making it a crime to cultivate marijuana for one's personal medical use. If the constitutionality of this law is challenged, which of the following provisions should be advanced to justify the statute?

(A) the General Welfare Clause

(B) the Due Process Clause

(C) the Commerce Clause

(D) the Equal Protection Clause of the Fourteenth Amendment

Question 43

A federal statute provides that any state not enforcing certain educational standards among public high schools will be denied federal aid for secondary education. One state did not comply with the standards, and federal funding was eliminated. Will a court be likely to rule the federal statute constitutional?

(A) No, because it is an unlawful intrusion of a right reserved to the states.

(B) No, because of the Fourteenth Amendment.

(C) No, because of the Privileges and Immunities Clause.

(D) Yes.

Questions 44–45 are based upon the following fact situation.

A stripper protested in front of the City Church on Sunday morning. The stripper, upset about church support for anti-pornography legislation proposed by the City Council, screamed as loud as she could, "Kill all ministers afraid to look at skin."

A large audience gathered to watch the stripper, who had received much media attention. The stripper was arrested and charged with violating a local statute that provides, "No speechmaking or protesting shall be permitted within seventy-five feet of a church on Sunday mornings."

Question 44

If the stripper challenges the constitutionality of the statute, which of the following choices is best?

(A) The city must prove the statute's enactment was intended to prevent imminent lawless action.

(B) The city must prove the statute is narrowly tailored to serve a compelling government interest and no less restrictive means of satisfying the need were available.

(C) The stripper must prove the statute was not enacted with a rational basis.

(D) The stripper must prove that the statute was enacted to regulate content.

Question 45

Which of the following persons may also challenge the statute?

(A) an owner of a movie theater that shows pornographic movies

(B) the city councilman who led the opposition to the statute

(C) an anti-pornography organizer who wanted to demonstrate on a Sunday morning

(D) a person who owned a home on the same street as the church

Question 46

In November of 1987, a town decided to attract more rich people to the area, so it leased a sizable portion of a lake to a successful company in order to build a yacht house and club, complete with marina, restaurant, and health club. The new private club would be owned by the owners of the company that was granted the lease to build the club. Town residents who could not afford the high membership rates brought an action against the club two months after the club began operating. The residents claimed that the club discriminated against the poor in violation of the Equal Protection Clause. Which of the following statements is most accurate?

(A) The club will prevail, because the deprivation does not trigger the Equal Protection Clause.

(B) The club will win, because it is a private company, and not the town, who is discriminating.

(C) The residents will win, because discrimination against the poor violates the Equal Protection Clause.

(D) The residents will win, because there is state action involved since the town is promoting discrimination.

Questions 47–48 are based upon the following fact situation.

A religious high school limits its enrollment to "white, third-generation Americans." The school is accredited by the state. The state sets accreditation standards and inspects religious, private, and public schools. Free transportation to all accredited schools is provided by the state.

Question 47

Which of the following choices is the best argument in a suit to end free bus service for the students of the high school?

(A) There is no constitutional right to free bus service.

(B) The state is aiding a religion.

(C) Discrimination of any kind is forbidden by the federal constitution.

(D) The state is furthering discrimination on the basis of race by providing bus service to the high school.

Question 48

Which of the following choices is the best argument in favor of the high school in the above suit?

(A) A school's selection process is not subject to review.

(B) Religious education is a constitutional right.

(C) Bus transportation is secular and nonpolitical.

(D) A state may not regulate the philosophy of private schools.

Question 49

A minister had seven wives as he followed a church doctrine that preached that every man must serve God by taking at least six wives. The minister was arrested and charged with polygamy. The minister made a motion to dismiss the case. Should the motion be granted?

(A) Yes, because conviction of the minister would violate his free exercise of religion.

(B) Yes, because the church's beliefs are honest and sincere.

(C) No, because sincere religious beliefs are not a defense to polygamy.

(D) No, because a belief in polygamy is by definition not a religion.

Question 50

A corporation breeds exotic birds. The birds are transported across the United States by trucks that are both company owned and operated. A state government passed legislation prohibiting the use of trucks with more than one trailer on interstate highways elevated more than 4,000 feet above sea level. The corporation operated ten such trucks.

The corporation asserted a constitutional challenge to the statute based on the Fourteenth Amendment clause that provides, "No state shall make or enforce any law which shall abridge the privilege or immunities of citizens of the United States."

Which of the following choices is most correct?

(A) The state will prevail by showing a rational basis for the statute.

(B) The corporation's action will be dismissed before being heard on its merits.

(C) The corporation will prevail, because the state has unlawfully interfered with interstate commerce.

(D) The corporation will prevail, because the state has unlawfully interfered with the right to transport animals across state lines.

Question 51

A city signed an agreement with a general contractor to build a junior high school. The city suffered a slight fiscal deficit before construction began, and the city repealed a statute that formed the basis of the agreement, thereby canceling the agreement, so that it could save money. The contractor asserted an action to enforce the agreement. Should the court rule that the city statute canceling the agreement is valid?

(A) Yes, because a municipality may repeal its own laws.

(B) Yes, because the contract was revoked due to necessity.

(C) No, because it violates the constitutional prohibition against the impairment of contracts.

(D) No, because the state is acting contrary to the general welfare of its citizens in having a junior high school.

Questions 52–53 are based upon the following fact situation.

A state enacted a statute that provided, "All drivers licensed after May 1, 2006, will receive an 'In-State License' valid for driving only within the state. Drivers will be granted an unrestricted driver's license after attending a six-hour class educating them on safety

measures necessary for long trips." The minimum age required for any type of driving license in the state is seventeen.

Question 52

A fourteen-year-old driver, who was a resident of the state, asserted an action in a federal district court challenging the constitutionality of the act. Which of the following choices present the best reason for dismissing the driver's action?

(A) A fourteen-year-old may not challenge the constitutionality of a state statute.

(B) The state is acting validly under its police powers.

(C) The suit presents a nonjusticiable political question.

(D) The suit is not ripe.

Question 53

Assume for this question that the constitutional challenge will be judged on its merits. The burden of persuasion will be on the:

(A) state, because a fundamental right is affected.

(B) state, because the suit involves a question regarding the abuse of a state's police power.

(C) party challenging the statute, because the law provided for the presumption that a state statute is constitutional under its police powers.

(D) party challenging the statute, because the issue involves public safety.

Questions 54–55 are based upon the following fact situation.

Congress enacted a statute that provided, "The federal courts are prohibited from issuing any order with respect to the First Amendment."

Question 54

If the statute is challenged, which of the following arguments will best support the statute's constitutionality?

(A) Regulation of First Amendment does not require the judiciary to preside over such matters.

(B) The First Amendment affects interstate commerce.

(C) Article III provides that Congress may restrict the jurisdiction of federal courts.

(D) Congress has exclusive power over the First Amendment.

Question 55

Which of the following arguments will best support the challenge to the statute's constitutionality?

(A) Congress may not limit the jurisdiction of a federal court.

(B) Congress may not alter the rights of its citizens in this manner.

(C) The statute violates the Privileges and Immunities Clause of the Fourteenth Amendment.

(D) The statute unfairly discriminates against state judicial systems.

Questions 56–57 are based upon the following fact situation.

A state enacted a statute that provided, "Every corporation doing business in the state must first give preference to citizens of the state and then to United States' citizens when hiring employees."

Question 56

Which of the following choices LEAST supports the statute's constitutionality?

(A) The statute will help assure that a stable supply of workers exists in the state.

(B) The statute will help assure that the state will have a quality work force.

(C) The statute will help assure that the workers in the state are dedicated to their employers.

(D) The statute will help assure that citizens of the state can get jobs over non-citizens even if they are not qualified.

Question 57

Assume for this question only that the Supreme Court of the state rules the statute unconstitutional as a violation of the privileges and immunities clause of the Fourteenth Amendment to the United States Constitution and the Equal Protection Clause of the state constitution. If the state attempts to test the statute before the United States Supreme Court:

(A) the statute should be reviewed by *certiorari* only.

(B) the statute should be reviewed by *certiorari* or appeal.

(C) the statute should be reviewed by appeal only.

(D) the statute should not be reviewed.

Question 58

A state statute provided that "whenever the Secretary of Commerce shall determine that commercial mail sent to residents of the state is inappropriate for minors, the Secretary shall have the power to prohibit such mailing." A video store in the state sent brochures of its stock to local residents, and many of its movies were in the adult film category. The video store instituted an action in state court after the Secretary of Commerce attempted to stop the mailing of the video store's brochures containing photos of scenes in the adult films. The state's highest court affirmed the lower courts, holding that the statute was unconstitutional. If the U.S. Supreme Court reviews the case, it will reach that court:

(A) under the doctrine of adequate and independent state grounds.

(B) by appeal.

(C) by *certiorari.*

(D) as a matter of right.

Question 59

A citizen, outraged at the mayor's support of the sale of pretzels on city streets, demonstrated in front of City Hall. The citizen chanted, "Mayor, you liar, I'll set your rear on fire." While being handcuffed and arrested by police, the citizen shouted several offensive obscenities. A state statute provided, "One may not utter obscene or highly offensive language in public." If prosecuted for violating this statute, which of the following choices should the citizen advance?

(A) The statute prohibits certain religious activity, and, therefore, violates the Free Exercise Clause.

(B) The statute is vague and, therefore, violates the Due Process Clause.

(C) The citizen's arrest denied him equal protection guaranteed by the Fourteenth Amendment.

(D) The citizen's arrest denied him freedom of speech guaranteed by the Fourteenth Amendment.

Question 60

The President announced that an army would be sent to a small country in South America for joint training exercises with the country's military forces. One week later, Congress enacted a statute prohibiting the U.S. armed forces from interference with the country's army unless Congress has received notice of such intention to take action at least 90 days prior to the commencement of the training exercises. This statute is most likely:

(A) unconstitutional, because of President's authority to execute the laws of the United States.

(B) unconstitutional, because of President's authority as Commander-in-Chief of the armed forces.

(C) constitutional, because of congressional power under the War Powers Act.

(D) constitutional, because of congressional power to raise and support the armed forces.

Question 61

An annual ceremony is held to inaugurate new members of the State Highway Patrol. All candidates are required to swear or affirm that they will "use every measure at their means to uphold, defend, and enforce the constitutions of the state and federal governments." Candidates must also swear or affirm that they "do not support the overthrow of the United States government by illegal means and will help defend the country from any individual or organization that seeks to do so."

An anarchist was not hired as a State Highway patrolman, because he refused to take the required oath. He filed suit in a federal court, challenging the statute. Which of the following arguments best supports the constitutionality of the statute?

(A) Law enforcement employees are subject to a higher degree of scrutiny than ordinary citizens.
(B) The oath merely affirms a commitment to abide by the law.
(C) The Fourteenth Amendment allows a state to set conditions of employment.
(D) The government has a compelling right to assume the loyalty of its employees.

Question 62

A city passed a law providing for thirty days of incarceration for "vagrancy." The statute defined vagrancy as "rogues, vagabonds, and lewd, wanton, and lascivious persons. A person wandering from place to place or loitering without any meaningful purpose or object is a vagrant." A homeless person was arrested and charged with vagrancy after spending three nights in a city bus depot.

If the homeless person decides to attack the constitutionality of the city vagrancy statute, which of the following arguments will help her case most?

(A) The ordinance is overly broad.
(B) The ordinance is unconstitutional because it violates freedom of movement.
(C) The ordinance violates the Equal Protection Clause.
(D) The ordinance is a prior restraint.

Question 63

A sixteen-year-old asserted an action in a federal court, challenging the state driving statute. The statute provided that, "Any citizen eighteen years of age or older may apply for a driver's license." The teenager alleged that the law discriminated against him based on his age. The teenager further alleged that the law had no rational basis, nor did it achieve any legitimate state interest. The case was finally heard by the district court two years after the teenager filed his complaint. The court should:

(A) rule that the statute is unconstitutional.
(B) rule that the statute is constitutional as a valid exercise of state police action.
(C) rule the statute is constitutional as a valid exercise for the public welfare.
(D) dismiss the case.

Question 64

A federal statute required members of the United States Army holding the rank of captain or higher to retire upon reaching the age of sixty-five. The statute provides further that members of the armed forces holding the rank of lieutenant or lower must retire upon reaching the age of sixty.

A lieutenant, a sixty-year-old officer in the U.S. Army, asserted an action challenging the statute's constitutionality. The lieutenant's best argument is that the law:

(A) deprives him of property.
(B) deprives him of a privilege or immunity.
(C) is an invidious discrimination on the basis of age.
(D) is outside the power of congress.

Question 65

The federal government appointed a major general of the Army's Judge Advocate General Corps to judge disputes between the United States government and citizens of other countries. The foreign citizens submitted claims demanding compensation for damages inflicted by the U.S. Army.

In 2006, the major general's work with the foreign citizens was completed; he was removed from office and reassigned to another branch of the Army. The major general filed suit against the U.S. government, claiming that a federal judge may not be removed from office while exhibiting good behavior. Will the major general prevail?

(A) Yes, if he can show damages.
(B) Yes, because his constitutional rights were violated.
(C) No, because the position was eliminated.
(D) No, because the major general's position was not covered by Article III.

Question 66

A state enacted a statute authorizing school districts to charge a fee for school bus service. A family refused to agree to a busing fee, since their daughter had no alternative but to take the bus or walk four and a half miles each way. The family claimed that the fee violated the Equal Protection Clause by placing an obstacle in the path of their daughter's education. In reviewing the state statute, the United States Supreme Court would:

(A) apply strict scrutiny because education is a fundamental right.
(B) apply the rational basis test and determine that the statute violates the Equal Protection Clause.
(C) apply the rational basis test and determine that the statute does not violate the Equal Protection Clause.
(D) apply strict scrutiny because the statute interferes with interstate commerce.

Question 67

A state suffered economic problems due to a decline in the price of oil. In an effort to stimulate its local economy and balance the state budget, the state legislature enacted a ten dollar tax on every barrel of

American oil produced out of state. The statute will be deemed:

(A) constitutional because it treats all out of state interests the same.
(B) constitutional since the state may tax for the general welfare of its citizens.
(C) unconstitutional as violative of the Commerce Clause.
(D) unconstitutional as violative of the Due Process Clause.

Question 68

A private in the United States Army, went home for a thirty-six-hour leave. While on leave, the soldier burglarized six of his neighbors' homes. When he returned to his base, the soldier was court-martialed. How should a court rule, if soldier asserts a constitutional challenge to the court-martial's jurisdiction?

(A) Dismiss the action, because a court-martial's jurisdiction is limited to military justice.
(B) Dismiss the action, because the crime was not service-connected.
(C) Overrule the challenge, because the soldier was a member of the U.S. armed forces.
(D) Overrule the challenge if the act occurred during a period of war or natural emergency.

Question 69

A state statute provided that "all women must take a leave of absence from their work during the last trimester of pregnancy." A woman, who was a driver for a trucking company, became pregnant and asserted an action in federal court challenging the constitutionality of the state statute. By the time the woman's case came to trial, the woman had already given birth to twin girls. The state moved to dismiss the woman's case. The court should:

(A) hear the case on its merits because pregnancy lasts only nine months and the woman may become pregnant again.
(B) hear the case on its merits, but only if the statute places an undue burden on pregnant women.
(C) dismiss the case as moot.
(D) dismiss the case, because the government has compelling interest in these types of situations.

Question 70

A man was arrested for driving forty miles an hour above the posted speed limit. The man challenged the constitutionality of the state statute establishing speed limits, on the grounds that it violated his right of free exercise of religion. The man belonged to a religious group whose members believed that they should serve God by driving ninety miles per hour on alternate Tuesday mornings. Which of the following choices may NOT be considered

by a court determining the man's challenge to the constitutionality of the state speed regulations?

(A) Whether the man was required by his religion to exceed the speed limit.
(B) Whether the man is sincere in his beliefs.
(C) Whether the man's religious beliefs are reasonable.
(D) Whether the man was considered a member of the religious group.

Question 71

A town passed an ordinance that provided, "One may not address a public gathering with language that stirs the public to anger or invites dispute." Three days after the ordinance was passed, a driver addressed a gathering of several thousand people protesting a citywide crackdown on motorists driving with one headlight in operation. "We should eliminate those who discriminate against owners of one-headlight cars," said the driver, in an impassioned cry. The crowd responded by shouting enthusiatically.

If prosecuted under the town ordinance, which of the following arguments will help the driver's case most?

(A) The First and Fourteenth Amendments' guarantee of the right of association.
(B) The ordinance is a form of prior restraint.
(C) The public's speech may not be regulated.
(D) The ordinance is an overly broad regulation of speech.

Question 72

The federal government enacted legislation that made 6,000,000 acres of federally owned land into forest preserves. Hunting and harvesting timber are prohibited in forest preserves. Will a court find this legislation constitutional?

(A) Yes, because forest preserves are important to the public's welfare.
(B) Yes, because Congress may regulate federally owned property.
(C) No, because the federal government has usurped local authority.
(D) No, because the right to harvest timber does not affect interstate commerce.

Question 73

A state statute provides that all private and public schools accredited by the state may receive textbooks on secular subjects that will be paid for by state funds. An accredited private high school admits only Caucasian students. In a constitutional challenge to the admissions policy of the school, which of the following choices will best support the challenge?

(A) Government funds may not be used to support racism because it is against public policy.

(B) The state is obligated by the Constitution to prevent racism.

(C) The state's involvement in school regulation and support invokes the Constitution.

(D) By accepting state accreditation, a school impliedly warrants it will not discriminate on the basis of race.

Question 74

A mall, a shopping center complex, was privately owned by a developer who leased retail store space to private retailers. A school club called The Animal Savers planned to distribute pamphlets at the mall on a Saturday afternoon. The literature explained how animals are slaughtered and offered alternatives to purchasing products made from animal skins. When the club members began distributing the pamphlets, the mall management insisted that they leave the premises immediately. Subsequently, the students brought suit in federal court seeking an injunction against prohibiting distribution of the material inside the mall. The students will:

(A) prevail, because their activity amounts to free speech that is protected by the First and Fourteenth Amendments.

(B) prevail, because it is in the public interest to learn about the ideas of others.

(C) not prevail, because the Mall is not subject to the requirements of the Constitution under the First and Fourteenth Amendments.

(D) not prevail, because the common law nuisance doctrine will govern the activity.

Question 75

A man challenged the constitutionality of the statute requiring registration for the draft. The man argued that the statute violated the Equal Protection Clause because it required only males to register. The court should rule the statute:

(A) valid, because it is protective in nature.

(B) valid, if it is substantially related to an important government interest.

(C) not valid, because women can serve in support roles.

(D) not valid, because women are just as capable as men.

Question 76

A state statute provided, "Any alien doing business within the state must pay an excise tax of 0.05% of gross revenue." A manufacturer of polo equipment who was a citizen of a foreign country challenged the statute in federal court. The citizen's most persuasive argument will be that:

(A) the Commerce Clause will prevent a state from limiting the rights of aliens.

(B) the statute is unconstitutional because it violates the citizen's right to equal protection.

(C) the statute is unconstitutional because it violates the Obligation of Contracts Clause.

(D) the statute constituted an unlawful "taking."

Question 77

A county passed an ordinance providing that all dairy products sold in the county must be inspected by a licensed local inspector. The local inspectors were unauthorized to inspect dairy products from plants outside of the county. Which of the following would have the best standing to challenge the constitutionality of the ordinance?

(A) a county licensed inspector

(B) a county dairy producer

(C) a resident-consumer of the county

(D) a milk producer from a neighboring county

Questions 78 and 79 are based upon the following fact situation.

A federal statute provides that any state not enforcing certain civil rights standards among public schools will be denied federal aid for education. A state did not comply with the standards, and federal funding was eliminated.

Question 78

Which of the following persons is most likely to obtain a judicial determination if he challenges the constitutionality of the federal statute?

(A) a teacher laid off because of the cuts in federal aid

(B) a student at a State S public high school

(C) a school principal worried about the education of his students

(D) a taxpayer living in the state

Question 79

Will a court likely rule that the federal statute is constitutional?

(A) Yes.

(B) No, because it is an unlawful intrusion of a right reserved for the states.

(C) No, because of the Privileges and Immunities Clause.

(D) No, because of the Fourteenth Amendment.

Question 80

Federal law provides employees of foreign embassies and consulates with "diplomatic immunity." Under the law, employees are immune from prosecution for any offense.

An employee of an embassy was arrested and incarcerated, pursuant to a city statute that provides,

"Diplomats may be prosecuted for constant disregard of the law." The employee was arrested after repeatedly shooting the lights out at local bars. If the employee attacks the constitutionality of the city statute, his best argument will be based upon:

(A) the Due Process Clause.

(B) the Supremacy Clause.

(C) the Privileges and Immunities Clause.

(D) the Equal Protection Clause.

Question 81

A boy was an illegitimate son of a landowner. The landowner died intestate, leaving a substantial estate. A local statute provided, "An unacknowledged, illegitimate child is not considered a child for the purpose of inheritance." If the boy challenges the state law, his best argument will be that:

(A) The law is not rationally related to a legitimate government interest.

(B) He has been deprived of property without due process.

(C) The law is not substantially related to an important government interest.

(D) A biological relationship between father and child mandates that the father constructively acknowledges his child.

Question 82

The federal government enacted a statute requiring that all gasoline sold be listed by grade based on the gasoline's octane level. The best argument to thwart a constitutional challenge to this statute is that:

(A) the health and safety of the public is at stake.

(B) the sale of gasoline affects interstate commerce.

(C) the law supports the country's general welfare.

(D) gasoline is a necessity and regulation of such would be a deprivation of a property right.

Question 83

A congressional staffer was forced to testify before a congressional committee investigating the disappearance of $2,000,000 in government funds. The staffer refused to answer certain questions. Congress ordered a county district attorney to prosecute the staffer for contempt. If the staffer is prosecuted for refusing to answer questions, which of the following choices, if proved, will best help the staffer's case?

(A) The missing funds came from the state and private corporations.

(B) All of the staffer's decisions were ultimately approved by civilian authorities.

(C) The staffer has only limited and trivial knowledge.

(D) The questions were not related to legislative matters.

Questions 84–85 are based upon the following fact situation.

Congress enacted the National Air Pollution Act. The act established an advisory committee to monitor testing and prosecute those who violate standards. The Department of the Interior and Congress were empowered to appoint members to the commission. An owner of a coal-burning plant, was prosecuted by the advisory committee.

Question 84

Which of the following facts will be most persuasive in favor of the owner's defense that the National Air Pollution Act is unconstitutional?

(A) The owner was not involved in interstate commerce and, therefore, was not under the commission's jurisdiction.

(B) The executive branch may not enforce legislation enacted by Congress.

(C) The commission is powerless because members were appointed by other agencies than the Department of the Interior.

(D) The owner was denied equal protection because the commission has discretion on whom to prosecute.

Question 85

What will be the proper ruling regarding the constitutionality of the National Air Pollution Act?

(A) The committee may make recommendations to the legislative branch.

(B) The committee members must be appointed by the Department of the Interior.

(C) The advisory committee may prosecute those deemed to have violated environmental standards.

(D) The advisory committee is null and void.

Question 86

Two members of the executive branch were old political enemies of a member of the U.S. House of Representatives. After the members heard the Representative give a speech on the House floor, to harass him they initiated a criminal suit relating to the legislative action he proposed. The Representative might:

(A) just grin and bear it, since political feuds are as old as politics.

(B) use a writ of *habeas corpus*.

(C) invoke the Establishment Clause.

(D) invoke the Speech and Debate Clause.

Questions 87–88 are based upon the following fact situation.

The federal government fined the director of the State Motor Vehicle Fleet because several cars and trucks did not meet federal standards. The director moved to dismiss the case, claiming that his actions were in the course of state senate business and that, therefore, he may not be prosecuted.

Question 87

Which of the following is the director's best argument?

(A) The states may delegate local governments to determine environmental standards.

(B) The state should be prosecuted, not the director.

(C) Under the federalism doctrine, federal law may not be imposed upon state senators acting within the scope of state business.

(D) The director is entitled to legislative immunity.

Question 88

Which of the following is the federal government's best argument?

(A) Preferential treatment for legislators would be a violation of equal protection to the ordinary citizen.

(B) State senators are liable for willful misconduct.

(C) Enforcing environmental standards is not a significant interference with state government.

(D) Regulation of trucks affects interstate commerce.

Question 89

High school students asked the superintendent whether the minister of a local church could deliver a prayer at their homecoming, to be held in the school auditorium. None of the students, or their guests, would actually be required to pray while the minister spoke. Would the delivery of such a prayer at the homecoming rally be constitutional?

(A) No, because it would be an unconstitutional establishment of religion.

(B) No, because it would deny attendees who are not members of the minister's denomination the right to freely exercise their religion.

(C) Yes, because none of the students or their guests would be required to pray.

(D) Yes, because the idea for the prayer originated with the students and not with school officials.

Question 90

A knickknack manufacturer operates solely out of one state. The manufacturer developed very realistic-looking fake martini, wine, and beer glasses for people to display as décor on bookshelves. Despite being fake, the glasses are of very high quality, and depict what they are supposed to quite accurately. Other knickknack manufacturers outside of the state have been manufacturing similar glasses, but of lesser quality. Since those glasses are cheaper, they have been cutting into the sales of the manufacturer's glasses. So the state

enacted a law "to protect the citizens of the state from cheap drink ware, and to protect the state's knickknack manufacturers from unfair competition." The law forbids any nonresident manufacturer to sell their knickknacks unless it specifies certain criteria. Is this law constitutional?

(A) No, because it abrogates the obligation of the contracts between other knickknack manufacturers and their state outlets who have agreed to sell drink ware knickknacks.

(B) No, because it imposes an undue burden on interstate commerce.

(C) Yes, because it deals only with a local matter, the sale of knickknacks in the state.

(D) Yes, because the state's interest in protecting citizens from shoddy drink ware knickknacks justifies the burden any burden on interstate commerce.

Question 91

In 2006, a university passed a new regulation prohibiting certain kinds of speech on campus. The leaders behind drafting this regulation were two professors. Anyone found to violate this regulation was subjected to various penalties, including fines, suspensions, and loss of employment or expulsion. Clearly, this new regulation was widely unpopular at the university.

In 2007, the state legislature approved a portion of the appropriations bill for the university declaring that none of the university's funds could be used to pay the either of the professors. The university relied heavily on appropriations from the state, and had no other means of paying the professors.

If the professors challenge the provision, is the court likely to uphold it?

(A) No, because it amounts to the imposition of a punishment by the legislature without trial.

(B) No, because it was based on conduct the professors engaged in before it was enacted.

(C) Yes, because the Eleventh Amendment gives the state legislature plenary power to appropriate state funds in the manner that it deems most conducive to the welfare of its people.

(D) Yes, because the full faith and credit clause requires the court to enforce the provision.

Question 92

A federal statute imposes an excise tax of $200 on each car sold in the United States. It also takes the entire tax proceeds and puts them in a special fund, which is used to fund an auto insurance fund, to help offset accidents in which one party is not insured. Is this constitutional?

(A) No, because the federal government may not impose any direct taxes on U.S. citizens.

(B) No, because this statute entangles the government with private insurance companies.

(C) Yes, because it is a reasonable exercise of Congress's power to tax and spend for the general welfare.

(D) Yes, because Congress has the power to regulate interstate commerce.

Question 93

A man really disliked his neighbors, but only because they were Jewish. He decided to frighten his neighbors, in hopes they would move, and spray-painted their house with epithets and threats that they would be lynched, as well as references to the Holocaust. The man was arrested right away, as it was obvious to anyone in the neighborhood who did it, under a state statute providing that "Any person who threatens violence against another person with intent to cause that person to fear for his or her life or safety may be imprisoned for up to five years." In his defense, the man claimed that he did not actually intend to harm his neighbors, only frighten them, so they would move away from his neighborhood, and that he would never really hurt anyone.

Can the man constitutionally be convicted under this law?

(A) No, because he was only expressing his views and had not taken any overt action to harm the neighbors.

(B) Yes, because he was engaged in a trespass when he spray-painted.

(C) Yes, because his expressions were a threat intended to intimidate the neighbors.

(D) Yes, because his communication was racially/religiously motivated and so violated the protections of the Thirteenth Amendment.

Question 94

George Washington's former home is part of a national park located in a city. The National Park Service entered into an agreement with an antique dealer to acquire items owned by residents of the city during the time that Washington lived there. According to the contract, the antique dealer purchases items and then sells them to the Park Service at a price equal to the antique dealer's cost plus a 12 percent commission. These types of purchases of antiques are normally subject to a sales tax in the city. The antique dealer, not wanting to pay taxes, brings suit in state court to enjoin collection of the tax, claiming that the tax is unconstitutional as applied to him. Should the court issue an injunction?

(A) No, because since the antique dealer is the actual purchaser of the antiques, he is liable, not the federal government, for the tax.

(B) No, because the suit is within the exclusive jurisdiction of the federal courts.

(C) Yes, because the federal government is contractually obligated to pay the amount of the sales tax

when it covers the antique dealer's costs of the antiques.

(D) Yes, because under the Supremacy Clause, the federal program to acquire antiques preempts the state sales tax on the purchase of such items.

Question 95

The state enforced a private agreement among neighbors in Green Community, an elite private community, that none of them will sell houses to single women. When a woman wanted to buy a house in the Green Community, she was turned down on the basis of the private agreement. The woman brought suit against Green Community in federal court claiming that her constitutional rights were violated. The court will:

(A) decline to hear the case, because Green Community is made up of private individuals.

(B) decline to hear the case, because Green Community is not performing an essential public function.

(C) hear the case, because the state and Green Community have a mutually beneficial relationship.

(D) hear the case, because there is significant state involvement when the state chose to enforce the private agreement.

Question 96

A state gives a liquor license to a bar that refuses to serve aliens. The state has only a very limited number of liquor licenses, and knows that the bar will not serve aliens. A man who immigrated to the United States ten years ago but had not yet gotten his U.S. Citizenship, challenges the constitutionality of the bar's policy after he was refused alcohol. The court will:

(A) hear the case, because the state acquiesced to the bar's discrimination.

(B) hear the case, because by licensing a private institution that discriminates, the state encourages the bar to discriminate.

(C) decline to hear the case, because there is no state action.

(D) decline to hear the case, because the right to drink liquor is not a right guaranteed in the Constitution.

Question 97

A city decides to conduct interviews for their security guard force in response to a series of break-ins in various city buildings. A guard who worked for a private mall for ten years applied for the job and was denied the position without an interview. If the guard claims that his constitutional rights were violated since he did not get an interview, a hearing, or a statement of why he was denied the position, the court will rule:

(A) for the guard, since he had a property interest in obtaining the job.

(B) for the guard, because he was denied the equal protection of the laws.

(C) for the city, since the guard is not a member of a protected class.

(D) for the city, since it had no obligation to give the guard procedures to ensure he was treated fairly in the job selection process.

Question 98

A man has been receiving welfare for six months. One day when the man went to collect his welfare check, he was informed that his benefits had been terminated. When he asked the desk clerk why, she replied "I don't think there has to be any reason. You should be lucky that you got it in the first place!" If the man asserts a claim based on the Constitution, will he prevail?

(A) Yes, because the man has a property interest in continuing to get welfare benefits, and such benefit cannot be terminated without proper procedures.

(B) Yes, because the man is being denied the equal protection of the laws since he belongs to a protected class.

(C) No, because there is no property interest in receiving welfare.

(D) No, because although a property interest, welfare benefits can be cut off at any time without notice or a hearing.

Question 99

A tenured employee is fired from a government job due to unsatisfactory job performance. The employee received notice of the charges and an opportunity to present evidence, but not a full adversarial evidentiary hearing with right to counsel. If the employee claims that his constitutional rights have been violated, will he prevail?

(A) Yes, because the employee's benefits may not be terminated without awarding him a full evidentiary hearing.

(B) Yes, because the employee has the right to present evidence that he in fact performed in a satisfactory manner.

(C) No, because being a tenured employee is not a right protected by the Constitution.

(D) No, because the government's interest in being able to fire unsatisfactory employees outweighs the employee's right to a full evidentiary hearing.

Question 100

A state passed a statute that before a doctor may perform a second trimester abortion, he must perform a sonogram, show the sonogram images to the woman, and let her know through written material that by getting an abortion, she is going against the state's

profound respect for her unborn child. Is this statute constitutional?

(A) No, because abortion is a fundamental right and restrictions placed on it will be strictly scrutinized.

(B) No, because the state may regulate abortion only if it does not place an undue burden on the woman's right to choose pre-viability abortion.

(C) Yes, because the state can impose procedures that must be followed prior to any abortion, even if the purpose and effect of the procedure is to induce the mother to decide not to abort.

(D) Yes, because the second trimester is no longer considered the early stages of pregnancy.

Question 101

Two parents, frustrated by the poor educational system in the state, decided to form a community-based elementary school in their neighborhood in which students would learn by singing songs, studying nature, and playing games without the constraint of grades, desks, chairs, and time constraints. Other parents who were interested in sending their kids to this school could do so as long as they contributed in some way in helping with the running and continued existence of the school. When state officials found out that the parents had removed their own children from public school and placed them in the new community school, the state brought suit claiming that the parents were in violation of a state statute requiring that children go to public school if not already placed in private school. The parents challenged the constitutionality of the statute. Who will prevail?

(A) The state, since the right to education is not a fundamental right.

(B) The state, because learning in the method taught by the community school is not a acceptable mechanism by which to educate children.

(C) The parents, since it may be against their religion to send their children to public schools, and the state statute would be in violation of the Free Exercise Clause.

(D) The parents, since a parent's right to direct the upbringing and education of their children is fundamental.

Question 102

In order to prevent teenagers from misbehaving in the classroom, a city school board authorized city public high schools to punish, after notice and a hearing, any teenager in violation of the "misbehavior code." The code listed a variety of punishments, including, but not limited to, requiring the offending teenager to sit in a designated "school punishment room" (which was essentially a converted utility closet with no windows that only locks from the outside) during the entire school day and hold one leg in his hand while covering his eyes with the other hand for a period of not less than ten but no more then twenty school days. Is the code constitutional?

(A) Yes, because a school has the right to impose a reasonable punishment on its students for violation of school rules to which they had notice of and were granted a hearing for.

(B) Yes, since "behaving students" versus "misbehaving students" is a permissible classification that would only be reviewed under a rational basis standard.

(C) No, unless the application of the punishment is proportionate to the offense and circumstances surrounding each violation.

(D) No, if the student is under sixteen years of age.

Question 103

The Federal National Obesity Report has shown a drastic increase in the incidence of adult consent diabetes among children. In response, Congress enacted a statute requiring that each state enact a state law making in unlawful for any public elementary, junior high, or high school to cook, possess, sell, or otherwise distribute any foods that contained saturated fats that had previously been transported in interstate commerce. The federal statute is:

(A) unconstitutional, since possession, selling, cooking, or distributing foods with saturated fat that had been previously transported through interstate commerce has a very tenuous nexus to commerce.

(B) unconstitutional, because Congress has no authority to require the state to enact legislation.

(C) constitutional, since foods containing saturated fats subject to the terms of the statutes affects interstate commerce.

(D) constitutional, because protecting children from diabetes and obesity is within Congress' broad power under the general welfare clause.

Constitutional Law

Answer 1

(C) To have standing, one must have a significant stake in the outcome of the controversy. This requirement is met if the litigant has suffered an "injury in fact." Federal taxpayers, such as the woman in (C), have standing if they establish that the tax imposes some injury. Here, as she is a marathon registrant, it does. The other choices are less likely to be successful because each would have difficulty proving injury in fact.

Answer 2

(B) Article I, Section 8, declares that Congress may spend to "provide for the common defense and general welfare." Congress's spending power is for any public purpose. A tax will usually be upheld if it bears some reasonable relationship to revenue production. (B) is a better choice than (A) because (B) is more specific. When two answers look similar, or seem to take a similar stance, pick the answer that is more specific.

Answer 3

(C) The Supremacy Clause invalidates state or local laws that conflict with a federal statute. (A) and (B) may also be correct but, when given the choice on the Multistate Exam, choose a legal theory over an explanation of the facts. For instance, the regulation probably WOULD be in violation of the Dormant Commerce Clause for interfering with interstate commerce, but you want to first go to (B), which addresses the Supremacy Clause BEFORE talking about any potential violation of interstate commerce. It makes logical sense to first address supremacy, and if and only if there is not issue of supremacy, to then move onto an interstate commerce analysis.

Answer 4

(D) The Supreme Court has defined a suspension of ten days or less to be a "short suspension" (*Gross v. Lopez*, 419 U.S. 505 (1975)). The Court held that no formal evidentiary hearing is required for a short suspension; due process is satisfied with notice of charges and opportunity to explain. Note: The Court in *Gross* ruled that there is a property interest in public education when school attendance is required, so a longer suspension or expulsion would require a hearing.

Answer 5

(D) The rule stated in the previous explanation applies. (B) and (C) are not correct, because neither includes reference to the "10-day short suspension" rule set in *Gross v. Lopez*, 419 U.S. 505 (1975).

Answer 6

(B) The voluntary prayer that takes place inside the school building violates the Establishment Clause of the First Amendment. It does not matter that the prayer is voluntary, since the primary effect of the plan advances religion.

Answer 7

(B) Under the Abstention Doctrine, the federal courts will not decide a case based on an untested state law. The doctrine is used (1) to avoid decision of a federal question where the controversy can be based on question of state law; (2) to avoid conflict with a state's administration of its own affairs; (3) to leave to the states the resolution of unsettled questions of state law; (4) to ease congestion in the federal courts. When taking the Multistate Exam, you must carefully note who is asserting the action, in which court, and whether it is based on a state or federal action. In the instant case, an action based on a state statute is apparently raised for the first time in a federal court. (C) is not correct, because the case will not be based on a political question.

Answer 8

(C) Plaintiff challenges the statute as allowing the unconstitutional impairment of the obligation to contract. Since the marine performed his work, he was owed a salary and fringe benefits. The government should argue that the marine violated his contract by violating the law. The Contract Clause cannot be asserted by one who has violated the contract at issue.

Answer 9

(D) Congress has the power to dispose of federal property under Article IV, Section 3, Clause 2. A taxpayer has standing to challenge a federal appropriation that has exceeded a specific limitation of the federal taxing and spending powers. In general, taxpayers have been successful only on challenges based on the Establishment Clause, a ground with little merit in the instant case. (A), (B), and (C) are incorrect because persons have no standing as citizens to challenge the disposal of federal property. (D) is correct because the society will be granted standing since it has a direct interest in the outcome of a decision, making the Nature Society the only group with an actual injury.

Answer 10

(A) While the Free Exercise Clause allows persons to freely exercise their religion without government interference, courts have allowed the state to force medical treatment for minors despite the religious objections of their parents, on the grounds of the minors' health and safety. (B) and (C) are merely evidence toward this test, and (D) is the wrong law since the government is not trying to promote or establish religion.

Answer 11

(D) In this case, sections (a) and (b) of the statute place a severe burden on out-of-state firms, which most likely outweigh the benefit to the state. Therefore, both provisions would most clearly violate the dormant commerce clause. (A) is incorrect because, while a true statement, such regulations may not intentionally discriminate against out-of-staters by claiming they are protecting their state's interest in a manner that unduly burdens interstate commerce. Here, the burdens these regulations place on interstate commerce are substantially greater than the in-state benefits produced by the regulation.

Answer 12

(B) The Supreme Court in *Griswold v. Connecticut*, 381 U.S. 479 (1965), ruled that a statute restricting the use of contraceptives by married persons violated the right to privacy of such persons. (D) is incorrect because the Court ruled in *Tileston v. Ullman*, 318 U.S. 44 (1943), that a medical doctor does not have third-party standing to attack a state anti-contraceptive statute. In addition, it reaches outside the scope of the question, as there is no mention of a doctor asserting any claims. (A) is incorrect because Congress has no such power,

and (C) is incorrect because the statement is simply false.

Answer 13

(C) Congress has the power to limit admission of aliens, but once aliens are admitted, discrimination is suspect and they are entitled to rights under the Equal Protection Clause. This makes all other option choices the incorrect rule of law.

Answer 14

(A) The law regards aliens as a suspect class. The burden of validating a statute that discriminates against a suspect class rests upon the state, which must prove the law is narrowly tailored to a compelling state interest.

Answer 15

(C) The executive privilege will be overruled in criminal proceedings when a need for such information is demonstrated, and (C) refers to the fact that the indictment is a criminal proceeding. Presidential aides do share executive privilege (B), but that fact will not help them in this case. Military, diplomatic, or other sensitive national security secrets (D) are given great deference, but it does not seem that a bribery investigation would fall under this exception.

Answer 16

(C) A grant to parochial schools to be used for teachers' salaries is a violation of the Establishment Clause, which attempts to keep the government from sponsoring religious observances, from preferring one religion over another, or even preferring religious beliefs over non-religious beliefs. (A), (B), and (C) will survive an Establishment Clause challenge because in those examples, the government is treating religious and non-religious activities *equally.*

Answer 17

(B) The Taking Clause of the Fifth Amendment prohibits the taking of private property for private use, even if just compensation is made. In this case, (B) is correct because the power of eminent domain can be delegated to a private corporation or person if the taking is for public use and just compensation is given.

Answer 18

(A) State action must be involved in order for a state to protect one's constitutional rights. (B) is not correct, because a private individual rather than a state is doing the discriminating. (C) and (D) are wrong because the discrimination is at the hands of federal officials rather than by state action.

Answer 19

(A) The Free Exercise Clause prevents the government from unduly burdening a person's religious beliefs. "One has an absolute privilege to maintain any religious beliefs, and hence the devotee will not be successfully prosecuted . . ."

Answer 20

(A) Gender is a quasi-suspect class. In order for a law to survive a constitutional challenge based on equal protection alleging discrimination between sexes, it must be substantially related to an important government interest. The stricter test in (B) is applied when the law affects a suspect class (i.e., race, alienage, citizenship). (C) is incorrect because distinguishing between two classes is not per se unconstitutional. (D) is also incorrect, since the law makes this a strict liability crime, which requires no mental state.

Answer 21

(A) Under equal protection, discrimination against aliens is usually subject to strict scrutiny. One major exception is that strict scrutiny for alienage classification does not apply where the discrimination against aliens relates to a function that goes to the heart of a representative government. A public school teacher is considered one such important government job or official position, and the courts need only use mere rational basis. (C) is not only outside the scope, but also education is not a fundamental right.

Answer 22

(C) The Fourteenth Amendment makes the Bill of Rights' guarantees applicable to the states. The Supreme Court has ruled that only parts of the Bill of Rights are applicable to the states. The parts applicable are the First, Fourth, Sixth, Eighth, and parts of the Fifth Amendment.

Answer 23

(C) The Fourteenth Amendment prevents states from deprivations of equal protection of the law. In the instant case, there is no state action to trigger the Fourteenth Amendment. Over the years, courts have ruled that private racial or sex discrimination can be imputed to states in cases where the private actor is actually an agent of the government or otherwise closely intertwined with it. That is not the case here, however.

Note: The Thirteenth Amendment ("Neither slavery or involuntary servitude . . .") is the only constitutional provision that limits private individual acts on its face. (D) is not applicable to the facts because the plaintiffs are not attempting to bring a claim representing the Japanese as a group.

Answer 24

(D) Time, place, and manner regulations must be content-neutral, leave open alternative channels of communication, and be narrowly tailored to serve a significant government interest. Note that (C) does not indicate content neutrality; in fact, this kind of speech regulation is still considered content based.

Answer 25

(B) The right to privacy and personal autonomy are fundamental rights. This involves child-bearing. The burden of proof is that of strict scrutiny. It is not enough for the state to show that the state is pursuing a compelling government objective (as (D) states), the means that are chosen must be *necessary*. Note, (C) is wrong because while men and women are being treated equally for equal protection purposes, the statute still infringes on a fundamental right.

Answer 26

(D) The Supremacy Clause is the popularized title for Article VI, Section 2, of the U.S. Constitution. The clause provides that acts of the federal government operate as supreme law throughout the union. The states have no power to impede, burden, or in any manner control the operation of the laws enacted by the federal government.

Answer 27

(B) In *Dunn v. Blumstein*, 405 U.S. 330 (1972), the Supreme Court determined that Tennessee's duration requirements for voting interfered with the fundamental right to vote and the right to travel. The requirement that a voter has resided within the state for more than a certain time proper to election day will be strictly scrutinized. (C) is wrong because the Fifteenth Amendment, in relevant part, states that "The right of citizens of the United States to vote shall not be denied or abridged by the United States or by any State on the account of race, color, or previous condition of servitude." It does not cover the situation at hand. (D) is wrong for the reasons that (B) is right.

Answer 28

(C) Both the storeowner and the pathologist have standing to challenge the statute. The statute should be found unconstitutional because it unduly infringes on the storeowner's and the pathologist's rights to vote. A requirement that the voter own property or otherwise have some special interest in order to vote burdens the fundamental right to vote and will be struck down.

Answer 29

(B) is middle-level review, as the regulations affects gender. (A) and (C) require strict scrutiny review, and (D) gets mere rational basis, since age is neither a suspect or semi-suspect class.

Answer 30

(A) Under the Free Exercise Clause, the government is barred from making any law prohibiting the free exercise of religion. The court may not consider whether the belief is reasonable. Even a belief that the reasonable person would consider "unreasonable" is not deprived of protection as long it is sincere.

Answer 31

(B) The NALHP has not in itself suffered harm, and hence does not have standing. An exception to this rule was invoked for a suit by the NAACP, because its members could not file suit without disclosing their identities.

Answer 32

(D) The Establishment Clause prohibits governmental assistance to religion. It does not forbid every action by the government that favors or benefits religion. A statute will not violate the Establishment Clause if it (1) has a secular purpose, (2) has a principal or primary effect that neither advances nor inhibits religion, and (3) does not produce excessive government entanglement with religion. Here, the government satisfies all three prongs above.

Answer 33

(B) The plaintiff should argue that the state and the private actor have a relationship between the two that is mutually beneficial in addition to being financially assisted by the state, and therefore there is "state action" in the promotion of discrimination. Here, the plaintiff can argue that the state is involved enough in the private actor's activities that a symbiotic relationship exists between the two. Since this may be enough to support a claim of state action, the private actor's discrimination is also the state's promotion of discrimination.

Answer 34

(D) The doctrine of overbreadth is important in determining whether a regulation of speech violates the First Amendment. A statute is overbroad if it bans speech that could be constitutionally forbidden in addition to protected speech. While "obscene" speech is not protected by the constitution, the regulation in place here potentially bans speech that is perfectly constitutional.

Answer 35

(D) Neither the state nor the federal government may pass an *ex post facto* law. Laws creating new crimes, an increase in punishment, or a reduction in the evidence required are deemed *ex post facto*. A procedural change that does not affect the substantive elements is not deemed *ex post facto*.

Answer 36

(B) The federal judiciary's jurisdiction extends to cases to which the United States is a party. An action asserted against a federal officer qualifies as a case against the United States if a judgment may result in federal liability. In the instant case, the veterinarian was an agent of the U.S. government which could be liable for his acts under *respondeat superior*.

Answer 37

(C) Children born out of wedlock are awarded protection under the Equal Protection Clause using intermediate scrutiny. Hence, the best argument here is that the Equal Protection Clause has been violated.

Answer 38

(B) Congress may legislate but may not deprive the executive branch of its discretion in executing the laws. Because the district attorney's duties are executive actions, Congress may not, under the doctrine of separation of powers, order the executive branch to carry out its powers according to what congress wants.

Answer 39

(D) Under the "affectation doctrine," Congress has the power to regulate interstate commerce. Regulation of the sale of medicine would fall under this power because courts have extended this rule to cover almost all goods traveling through interstate commerce.

Answer 40

(C) A different definition of obscenity may be adopted for materials sold to minors. This standard may be more restrictive than the standards applied for adults. As for choice (D), the right of privacy encompasses the freedom to read obscene material in one's home.

Answer 41

(C) The Supreme Court has not incorporated the Second Amendment right to bear arms, the Grand Jury Clause of the Fifth Amendment, and the Seventh Amendment right to a jury in civil cases into the Fourteenth Amendment. These rights may be denied by a state.

Answer 42

(C) In *Gonzales v. Raich*, an identical law was considered to be a valid exercise of commerce power. Congress feared that some of the marijuana would be illegally drawn into the interstate market, threatening Congress' overall goal of banning drugs.

Answer 43

(D) The statute should be held valid as an exercise of the federal spending power. While the federal government cannot tell the states what to do, they can condition federal funds even if it is for the purpose of regulating states.

Answer 44

(B) This is a content neutral regulation, and hence the government has the burden of showing that it is narrowly tailored to serve a significant government interest and it must leave open alternative channels of communication. (A) is wrong because the government must not only show that the regulation was intended to prevent imminent lawless action, they must also show that the communication it is trying to prohibit is in fact likely to incite or produce that imminent lawless action. (D) is wrong because speech doesn't have to be content-based to be awarded the standard presented in (B). Content-based speech has a slightly different standard, as the law must be necessary to achieve a compelling government interest.

Answer 45

(C) The issue in this question is standing. Only a person who seeks to demonstrate on a Sunday morning will be affected by the statute and will therefore have standing to sue.

Answer 46

(A) Wealth is not a protected class under the Equal Protection Clause. Do not make up rights that do not exist. The Equal Protection Clause protects a very limited number of classes. There is state action here, as the town's purpose is to attract more rich people and they benefit in their mission by purposefully leasing to the company to effectuate the town's goals, so (B) is incorrect. However, (D) is also incorrect because while it is true that there is "state action," the state has not violated the constitution for the reason described for (A) above.

Answer 47

(D) Classifications based on race are reviewed under strict scrutiny. The government has the burden of proof, and must show that the law/action is necessary to achieve a compelling government purpose. The government rarely wins in such cases. Here, the plaintiffs' best chance of winning is to trigger a strict scrutiny analysis. While (A) is factually correct, that there is no constitutional right to free bus service, this does not mean it is constitutionally prohibited. (B) is not a strong argument because the state provides bussing to all accredited schools, regardless of their religious affiliation, and the bussing law is therefore considered secular in its purpose. (C) is incorrect because the Constitution does not forbid *all* forms of discrimination, only those, by a state actor, that are protected by the Constitution.

Answer 48

(C) A law will hold up to Establishment Clause challenges if it has a secular purpose, its effect neither advances nor inhibits religion, and there is not excessive entanglement with religion. Here, the bus transportation law applies to all accredited schools, regardless of religious affiliation. (A) is incorrect because a school's selection process may be subject to review, for a variety of reasons. (B) is legally incorrect; while the right to a K-12 education is guaranteed, an education of one's choice is not (hence that education need not be religious in nature). (D) is factually correct, but does not provide a strong legal basis in this case.

Answer 49

(C) The First Amendment prohibits laws that infringe upon the free exercise of religion. However, a generally applicable, nondiscriminatory criminal prohibition is enforceable even as against a person whose religious expression is burdened by it, as long as the prohibition directly advances an important government interest. The U.S. Supreme Court [*Reynolds v. United States* (1879)] has ruled that polygamy is not protected. "There has never been a time in any state of the union when polygamy has not been a crime against society." (D) is wrong because even obscure or unorganized religions get the same protection as the major religions. Even if the religion only has one follower, that one follower is entitled to free exercise protection.

Answer 50

(B) Corporations are not citizens of the United States and are not protected by the Privileges and Immunities Clause. (A) is an incorrect statement of the law: In rational basis analysis, the plaintiff has the burden of proof. (C) would be the correct answer for a Commerce Clause challenge, but this is a Privileges and Immunities challenge.

Answer 51

(C) Under the Contracts Clause, no state is allowed to impair the obligations of contacts. Any state or local interference with private contracts must meet intermediate scrutiny: The state must show that the law — or repeal of the law, in this case — is narrowly tailored and promotes an important and legitimate state interest. Here, the fiscal deficit is only slight, and the city's budget probably consists of more than just this one contract. It will be difficult for the city to show that the impairment of the contract with the general contractor is a narrowly tailored way with no less restrictive means to improve the budget.

Answer 52

(D) Article III of the Constitution requires that there be cases and controversies for a federal court to hear a case. Courts will only resolve constitutional issues when a party can show that he has been injured or will immediately be injured. Because the minimum age requirement for *any* license in the state is seventeen, a fourteen-year-old plaintiff has not been injured, and will not face immediate injury. (C) is incorrect because this is a justiciable question, just not for this particular plaintiff. And this would not be considered a political question because it is not an issue that has been committed by the Constitution to another branch of government nor does it lack manageable standards by which a court could resolve the issue. (D) is incorrect because, while the suit may not be ripe, dismissal is guaranteed based on the driver's age.

Answer 53

(A) The Supreme Court has recognized a citizen's fundamental right to interstate travel. Fundamental rights invoke a strict scrutiny analysis: The government must show that the law is necessary to achieve a compelling government purpose.

Answer 54

(C) Article III, Section 2, of the Constitution provides Congress with the power to determine the jurisdiction of the federal courts. (A), (B), and (D) are all incorrect statements of law.

Answer 55

(B) Congress may only repeal or alter provisions of the Constitution through the amendment process, not by a statute. (A) is incorrect because Article III, Section 2, explicitly allows Congress the power to decide the jurisdiction of federal courts. (C) and (D) are incorrect because the state judicial system is not a person for the purposes of Constitutional jurisprudence.

Answer 56

(D) The state must try to show the statute's discrimination was justified because of a compelling state interest. (A), (B), and (C) all advance arguments concerning the benefits of the statute to the state. Under (D), individuals within the state benefit, but no compelling state interest is argued.

Answer 57

(D) The United States Supreme Court does not have jurisdiction to rule on the validity of a state court's invalidation of a state statute which is made on independent and adequate state grounds. Though there is a federal privileges and immunities issue, the U.S. Supreme Court's ruling would not alter the outcome of the case, and it therefore should not review the the state's supreme court ruling.

Answer 58

(C) When a state statute is declared unconstitutional, the route of appeal to the U.S. Supreme Court is by *certiorari*.

Answer 59

(B) In order for a statute that denies a citizen of liberty to be valid under the Due Process Clause, the statute must give notice and opportunity for hearing. Here, the vagueness of the statute's language does not provide adequate notice as to what language is prohibited. A First Amendment argument would most likely be the citizen's strongest argument, but that is not a choice here. (B) is the best of the answers presented. (A) is incorrect because there is no issue of religion in this case. (C) is incorrect because this is not an issue of freedoms being denied based on group classifications. (D) is incorrect because freedom of speech is guaranteed by the First Amendment, not the Fourteenth.

Answer 60

(B) The President, under Article II, Section 2, has the power to command and direct the military and naval forces. (C) is incorrect because the War Powers Act applies when the armed forces are engaged in hostilities, which is not the case here.

Answer 61

(B) The oath does not obligate members of the State Highway Patrol to anything that would not otherwise be required of them to do. (D) may be a correct statement of fact, but the government need not even demonstrate a compelling government interest.

Answer 62

(A) Certain speech and conduct, such as vagrancy, may be prohibited by a proper statute. A statute that is overly broad, however, is one that bans speech or conduct that could be constitutionally forbidden but also bans speech or conduct that is protected by the First Amendment. For instance, wandering without any "meaningful" purpose, may involve protected conduct under the first amendment. (B) is incorrect because the freedom of movement only applies to *interstate* movement. (C) is incorrect because the statute does not regulate a protected class. (D) is incorrect because prior restraint is an issue of published materials.

Answer 63

(D) The Supreme Court's interpretation of Article III's "case and controversy" bars actions that are moot. A decision becomes moot when the controversy is no longer live. When the teenager turned eighteen, and became eligible to be licensed in the state, the suit became moot.

Answer 64

(C) Mandatory retirement ages have been upheld if they pass the "rational basis standard." In order to overturn the statute, the lieutenant will have to show that the law is not rationally related to a legitimate government purpose. Though this will be difficult, (C) is still the best answer. (A) and (B) would be far more difficult to prove, and (D) is just not true.

Answer 65

(D) Lifetime tenure is a right only enjoyed by judges appointed to Article III courts. The major general was appointed to a specific court position, not an Article III court.

Answer 66

(C) In *Kadrmas v. Dickinson Public Schools*, 108 S. Ct. 2481 (1988), a similar fact pattern applied, and the court applied the rational basis test to determine that a state's decision to allow a local school board the option of charging patrons a user fee for bus service is constitutionally permissible. Encouraging local school boards to provide bus service is a legitimate state interest. (A) is wrong because education has never been declared a fundamental right by a majority in the Supreme Court. (D) is incorrect because the fact pattern does not involve interstate commerce.

Answer 67

(C) The Commerce Clause is violated because the statute discriminates between out-of-state and in-state oil producers. A state may not use its tax system to help state business, and any state taxation of interstate business must be fairly apportioned.

Answer 68

(B) The constitutional basis for courts of military justice is Article I. A soldier cannot constitutionally be tried by court-martial unless his crime is service-connected. A crime committed while on leave and far from a military base is not considered service-connected.

Answer 69

(A) The case and controversy requirement bars the court from hearing a case if it becomes moot. A case is moot if it raised a live controversy at the time the complaint was filed, but events occurring after the filing cease to make it a live case or controversy. An exception exists where the case or controversy is "capable of repetition yet evading review." Here, a pregnancy is a short duration and it is likely that this issue will be raised again.

Answer 70

(C) A court may determine the sincerity of a party who is asserting his religion as a defense. The court may also determine the exact beliefs of the religion. The court may not form a judgment as to the reasonableness of the beliefs.

Answer 71

(D) Certain speech and conduct, such as demonstrations and other public meetings, may be prohibited by a proper statute. However, the statute must not be overbroad or vague. Here, the driver's best argument is that the statute is overbroad, as it bans speech that could be constitutionally forbidden but also bans speech that is protected by the First Amendment. (A) does not apply in this case, as the freedom of association pertains to membership in groups. (B) applies only to published materials, and (C) is a misstatement of the law.

Answer 72

(B) Article IV, Section 3, of the Constitution expressly grants Congress the power to regulate property belonging to the United States. (D) is wrong because Congress is not acting pursuant to Commerce Clause.

Answer 73

(C) The plaintiff's best argument would be to show that the state is so involved with the school by the accreditation process and by providing aid that the Fourteenth Amendment is applicable to the school under Equal Protection. (A) is incorrect because discrimination based on race is not merely a public policy issue, it is also a matter of equal protection under the Constitution. (B) is incorrect because the state is not required by the Constitution to *prevent* racism. (D) is not correct because the question is not about what the school warrants, but that of state action.

Answer 74

(C) Since no state action is present, the owner of a private shopping center complex may exclude persons who want to distribute pamphlets. Pamphleteering on private property is not a constitutionally protected activity.

Answer 75

(B) Gender is a semi-suspect class, and receives intermediate scrutiny "with bite." A constitutional challenge based on equal protection, alleging discrimination between sexes, is valid if the government shows that the law is substantially related to an important government interest.

Answer 76

(B) An alien is a "person" within the protection of the Due Process and Equal Protection Clauses of the Fourteenth Amendment. Discrimination based on alienage generally receives strict scrutiny. Therefore, the government must show that the law is necessary to achieve a compelling state interest. This is a difficult test to meet, and therefore would be the citizen's strongest argument.

Answer 77

(D) The out-of-county milk producer would have the best grounds to challenge the constitutionality of a local ordinance such as this one. Because local inspectors are not authorized to inspect out-of-county products, the other milk producers are injured in that they are prohibited from selling their product within the county. Such a regulation discriminates against interstate commerce. See *Dean Milk Co. v. City of Madison*, 340 U.S. 349 (1951).

Answer 78

(A) Among the choices, the teacher is the only one to have standing. He has been directly injured by the statute. (B) and (C) are wrong because there is no information that illustrates an injury suffered by the student or the principal. (D) is wrong because there is generally no tax payer standing, except in certain cases where the government has allocated funds in violation of a particular part of the Constitution. That is not applicable here.

Answer 79

(A) The statute should be held valid as an exercise of the federal spending power. Congress may spend to provide for the common defense and general welfare (Article I, Section 8). This spending may be for any public purpose. While the federal government may not tell the states what to do, they can condition federal funding on certain behavior by the state.

Answer 80

(B) The Supremacy Clause is the popularized title for Article VI, Section 2, of the U.S. Constitution. The clause provides that acts of the federal government are operative as supreme law throughout the union. The states have no power to impede, burden, or in any manner control the operation of the laws enacted by the government or the nation.

Answer 81

(C) Classifications disadvantaging illegitimate children get middle-level review under the Equal Protection Clause. States cannot simply bar unacknowledged illegitimate children from having any chance to inherit. Such children must be given a reasonable opportunity to obtain a judicial declaration of paternity. (D) is just made up law that doesn't exist.

Answer 82

(B) The federal government has power to tax interstate commerce. Courts have extended this rule to cover virtually all goods sold in the country, as the majority of goods cross state lines. Gasoline would, therefore, fall under the Commerce Clause.

Answer 83

(D) A witness testifying before a congressional committee may refuse to answer questions unrelated to congressional powers.

Answer 84

(C) Enforcement and execution of legislation may only be performed by members of the executive branch. Here, the advisory committee members were appointed from both the executive and legislative branches of the government. (A) is incorrect because the National Air Pollution Act is silent on the matter of jurisdiction, and issues of commerce are not implied. (B) is an incorrect statement of law. (D) is incorrect because prosecutorial discretion does not invoke the equal protection clause, as it is not a law or statute.

Answer 85

(A) A commission appointed by the legislative branch may only exercise powers available to the executive branch. Here, so long as the committee is only providing advisory recommendations, it is not encroaching upon the powers of the other branches of the government. Therefore (C) is incorrect.

Answer 86

(D) The Speech and Debate Clause (Article I, Section 6) gives legislators immunity from criminal and grand jury investigations relating to their lawmaking activities. This example of "separation of powers" helps keep political vendettas from interfering with congressional work. (B) is incorrect because *habeas corpus* is used in criminal cases to free prisoners. (C) is incorrect because there is no question of religion in this issue. (A) may be partially true, but is an incorrect answer in light of the Speech and Debate Clause.

Answer 87

(C) Congress cannot unduly burden the operation of essential state services. The work of the state senate is considered an essential function.

Answer 88

(C) Even though the federal government has interfered with local function, the intrusion was arguably not a great burden. (A) is incorrect because the "ordinary citizen" is not a protected class. (B) is true, but is too broad an answer. (D) is true, but the correct answer, (C), is a more specific analysis of this law.

Answer 89

(A) is correct, as the Supreme Court has held that officially sponsored prayers as part of any public high school event, such as a football game, graduation, etc., violate the Establishment Clause of the First Amendment. A homecoming rally could easily be lumped into this kind of category. (B) is incorrect since the question does not implicate the free exercise clause, because nothing here restricts the right to practice a particular religion.

Answer 90

(B) is correct, as the Commerce Clause gives Congress the power to regulate commerce, and thus, by negative implication, restricts the power of the states to negatively impact interstate commerce. This is referred to as the "Dormant Commerce Clause," and for a state statute to survive, any burden on interstate commerce must be outweighed by the benefit to the state. (A) is incorrect because it misstates the reason why the statute is unconstitutional, and (C) is incorrect because local matters CAN be the subject of the Dormant Commerce Clause, and (D) is incorrect because although it accurately states the standard, it is not likely true that an interest in protecting citizens from shoddy drink ware outweighs any interest in protecting interstate commerce.

Answer 91

(A) is correct, as the provision amounts to a bill of attainder in violation of Article I, Section 10, Clause 1, of the Constitution. A bill of attainder is something that provides for the punishment of the particular person without a trial, and this provision does just that. (B) is incorrect because the answer misstates the reason for why the court would strike down the law. (B) refers to "ex post facto" laws, which go back and punish someone for something they have already done. This makes no mention of any specific act. (C) is incorrect because the Eleventh Amendment does not extend sovereign immunity to states, and (D) is incorrect because the Full Faith and Credit Clause applies to actions from state to state, so it doesn't apply here.

Answer 92

(C) is the correct answer, as Congress has the power to tax and spend for the general welfare. Be careful though, this is the ONLY time that "general welfare" attached to anything Congress does is the correct answer. (A) is incorrect, because it is a false statement, (B) is incorrect because it is simply a false statement. (D) is incorrect because although it comes to the correct conclusion, taxes are not covered under Interstate Commerce.

Answer 93

(C) is correct, as the Supreme Court has held that a threat communicated with the intent to intimidate, like in this case, is not protected by the First Amendment. (A) is incorrect for the same reason that (C) IS correct. (B) is incorrect because it misstates the legal conclusion, which has nothing to do with unlawful conduct such as trespassing. It is because of the threat he will be convicted. (D) is incorrect because the Supreme Court has NOT held that such threats have anything to do with the Thirteenth Amendment.

Answer 94

(A) is correct, since the tax is on the antique dealer's purchases of antiques, and the antique dealer is independent of the Park Service, and thus independent of the federal government. (D) would apply if the state were taxing the federal government, but it is not. (B) is an incorrect statement of law.

Answer 95

(D) There is state action when there is state involvement with a private actor. Here, the state and the residents of Green Community are so closely involved that Green's acts become state action. The state is judicially enforcing a private contract. The combination of the enforcement and private discrimination violates the Equal Protection Clause. (C) is wrong because even if a private individual is not performing activities that are traditionally a public function, the private conduct may constitute state action if the state is heavily involved in such activities.

Answer 96

(C) When a state merely gives a license, no matter how few are available for granting, to a private entity that discriminates, there is no state action. Here, the state's act of licensing is not enough to turn the bar's action into state action. (A) is wrong because if the state merely acquiesces in the private party's discrimination, this is not enough state involvement to constitute state action. (B) in wrong for the reasons that (C) is correct. While (D) is factually true, that doesn't help us here.

Answer 97

(D) The state must act with reasonably adequate and fair procedures when it deprives an individual of life, liberty, or property. Here, the city doesn't have to be fair in their procedures, since the guard has no liberty or property interest in obtaining the job. Since the guard is only applying for the job, he doesn't yet have any property interest in it. (B) and (C) are wrong because this is not an equal protection claim because this only applies when the government is making a classification. (A) is wrong for the same reasons that (D) is right.

Answer 98

(A) If a person is already getting welfare benefits, then he has a property interest in continuing to get them. Hence, the government cannot terminate such benefits without giving the person procedural due process. (B) is wrong because this is not an equal protection problem. (C) is wrong because government benefits may or may not constitute a property right, depending on whether the person is simply applying for such benefits (no property interest) or is already receiving them (probably a property interest). (D) is wrong because while a state statute can say that welfare benefits may be cut off at any time and be valid statute where the claimant most likely does not have a property interest, there is no indication in this fact pattern that the state in fact did this.

Answer 99

(D) In the case of a tenured employee being fired from a government job, the employee is awarded fewer procedural safeguards than, say, a person who has been receiving welfare benefits. Since the termination of welfare benefits is likely to lead to extreme hardship, the claimant would be entitled to an evidentiary hearing. However, in situations like the case at hand, the employee has the opportunity to present some evidence, but is not entitled to a full evidentiary hearing with counsel since the government's interest in being able to fire employees who do poor work is balanced against the employee's right to tenured employment.

Answer 100

(C) In the 2007 decision of *Gonzales v. Carhart*, the court ruled that the government can impose procedures that must be followed prior to any abortion, even if the effect and purpose of those procedures was to induce women not to abort. These procedures cannot be an undue burden, but they can create a mechanism by which the "state may express a profound respect for the life of the unborn." (D) is wrong because the procedures may be required even in the early stages of pregnancy. (A) is wrong because abortion is no longer a fundamental right. (B) is wrong because while this is the correct standard, the procedures in place in this case would not constitute an undue burden on the woman's right to choose a second-trimester abortion.

Answer 101

(D) A parent's right to upbringing and education of her children is fundamental. As established in *Pierce v. Society of Sisters*, the state may not require parents to send their children to public schools. (A) is wrong because, though it is a correct statement of law, it is inapplicable to the facts at hand. The question is not whether education is a fundamental right, it's rather whether a parent's right to choose the type of education for her children is fundamental. (B) is wrong for the same reason (D) is right. (C) is inapplicable to the facts at hand because it rests on the condition that sending the parent's children to public schools "might" be against their religion. First, we don't know this, and we must not assume facts. Second, we don't need to address the Free Exercise Clause issue since it is already established that a parent's right to direct the upbringing and education of her children is fundamental in and of itself.

Answer 102

(C) A person has a substantive due process right not to be subjected to a punishment that consists of restraints on her physical movement out of all proportion to the severity of the offense. (A) is a correct statement of law, but the school could still be in violation of a student's substantive due process rights if such punishment is grossly disproportionate to the offense. (B) is wrong because while it is true that such a classification under Equal Protection gets mere rational basis review, the issue is about substantive due process, which requires strict scrutiny. (D) is not a rule with any legal significance.

Answer 103

(B) Congress's attempt to force states to enact a particular legislation is in violation of the Tenth Amendment. The federal government cannot tell the states what to do, though they may condition federal funds on whether or not states pass the statute. (A) is wrong because the movement of items in interstate commerce does have a sufficient nexus with Congress. (C) is wrong because of the Tenth Amendment issue. (D) is wrong because there is no independent power of Congress to act for "the general welfare."

Criminal Law and Procedure

1. Fifth Amendment
2. Homicide
3. Homicide
4. Aggravated Assault
5. Fifth Amendment
6. Theft Crimes
7. Accomplice Liability
8. Accomplice Liability
9. Theft Crimes
10. Homicide
11. Involuntary Manslaughter
12. Larceny
13. Theft Crimes
14. Voluntary Intoxication
15. Embezzlement
16. Theft Crimes
17. Intoxication
18. Defense of Intoxication
19. Defense of Intoxication
20. Robbery
21. Homicide
22. Statutory Rape
23. Robbery
24. Conspiracy
25. Conspiracy
26. Conspiracy
27. Conspiracy
28. Larceny
29. Burglary
30. Homicide
31. Accomplice
32. Assault
33. Arson
34. Defense of Intoxication
35. Fourth Amendment
36. Felony Murder
37. Battery
38. Battery
39. Photo Identification
40. Accessory Liability
41. Fourth Amendment

42. Fourth Amendment
43. Homicide
44. Burglary
45. Larceny
46. Homicide
47. Fifth Amendment
48. Homicide
49. Homicide
50. Murder
51. Force — Privileged for Arrest
52. Force — Privileged for Arrest
53. Homicide
54. *Mens Rea*
55. Battery
56. *Mens Rea*
57. Fourth Amendment
58. Larceny
59. Homicide
60. Fourth Amendment
61. Conspiracy
62. Larceny
63. Homicide
64. Insanity
65. Homicide
66. Conspiracy
67. *Mens Rea*
68. Embezzlement
69. Legal Impossibility
70. Fourth Amendment
71. Fifth Amendment
72. Legal Impossibility
73. *Mens Rea*
74. Fourth Amendment
75. Homicide
76. Larceny
77. Murder
78. Fourth Amendment
79. Murder
80. Insanity
81. Defense of Intoxication
82. Accomplice

83. Fourth Amendment
84. Accomplice Liability
85. Self Defense
86. Theft Crimes
87. Theft Crimes
88. Murder
89. Homicide
90. Fourth Amendment
91. Theft Crimes
92. Theft Crimes
93. Murder

94. Theft Crimes
95. Factual Impossibility
96. Homicide
97. Homicide
98. Homicide
99. Fourth Amendment
100. Fourth Amendment
101. Intent
102. Intent
103. Aborted Rescue Attempt
104. Fourth Amendment

Criminal Law and Procedure

Question 1

A daughter was given a new sports car for her college graduation. On one occasion she had sought to impress her friends by driving the car in third gear at ninety miles per hour down a small side street. The daughter swerved the car to avoid a squirrel running across her path. She hit the squirrel and her tires locked, causing her to lose control of the car. The car skidded onto the sidewalk, killing a poodle and its owner.

The police arrived several moments later and questioned the daughter. Still in a severe daze, she said, "It's all my fault. I was driving at triple the speed limit. I must have been out of my mind."

If charged with manslaughter, should the daughter's statement be admitted to evidence?

(A) Yes, because the daughter volunteered the statement.

(B) Yes, because the questions were for an investigation in a non-custodial setting.

(C) No, because the daughter did not receive Miranda warnings.

(D) No, because at the time of questioning, the daughter was not in the proper mental state to make an admission.

Question 2

A husband loved his wife despite her infidelity. The wife had been having an affair with her lover for the past two years. Blood tests confirmed that the lover was the father of the wife's soon-to-be-born baby. The husband tried everything he could think of to win back his wife's love and attention, but she continued her affair with her lover. Finally, out of desperation, and with the hope of shocking his wife, the husband filed for divorce. The wife wanted to remain married to her husband and said she would contest the divorce, but still continued to see her lover. While the divorce action was pending the husband and the wife continued to share the same house. The husband took their eight-year-old twin sons to their Little League game on a beautiful Sunday afternoon. The opposing team didn't show up, and the game was canceled. The husband and the boys returned to the house to find the wife and her lover together in the brand new Jacuzzi the husband had built for the wife's last birthday. The husband, usually quiet and relaxed, became enraged, grabbed one of the boy's bats, and slammed his wife in the abdomen with tremendous force. Two months later, in the middle of her seventh month of pregnancy, the wife's child was stillborn. Based on testimony by several physicians, the jury concluded that the stillbirth was due to subdural hemorrhaging and other complications arising from a skull fracture caused by the impact of the husband's bat. The testimony also revealed that the premature birth was unrelated to the husband's beating. An epidemiologist testified that a baby born in the seventh month has a 98 percent chance of surviving.

The husband should be found guilty of:

(A) murder.

(B) first-degree murder.

(C) manslaughter.

(D) none of the above.

Question 3

A single mother worked at a fast food restaurant in order to pay her bills and medical costs for her and her baby. She lived in relative poverty with a coworker. They shared expenses and housework and took turns caring for the baby. As the mother and the coworker were only friends, the mother wanted companionship and a father for her child. She met a young upwardly mobile professional who loved children at a singles bar. The professional became instantly infatuated with the mother and asked her to spend a month at his ski lodge. The mother left her infant with her coworker, who she claimed had agreed to watch the child as long as she continued to pay her share of the rent. The coworker denies the rent was ever discussed.

Both the mother and the coworker agree that the mother told the coworker, "Don't feed the kid too much. He's getting fat." The coworker ignored the baby while he was in his care. The mother and the professional returned two months later as husband and wife and discovered that the baby had died of malnutrition. The coworker is charged with involuntary manslaughter. Which of the following choices is most accurate?

(A) To be convicted, the jury must find beyond a reasonable doubt that the coworker was under a legal duty to supply food and necessities to the infant.

(B) The coworker's omission was insufficient to satisfy the requirements of involuntary manslaughter.

(C) The prosecution's best argument is that failure to act breached the coworker's legal duty in a manner sufficient to satisfy involuntary manslaughter because he stood in a special relationship to the child.

(D) The general rule that one is under no legal duty to rescue a stranger may be superseded by showing an obligation by the preponderance of the evidence.

Question 4

A man answered his front door. It was a door-to-door saleswoman. The man, who was drunk at the time, invited the woman inside, pretending he wanted to buy some cosmetics for his wife. While they sat on the couch, the man first forcibly hugged the woman, then pinned her down, forcing her to have sexual intercourse with him while she loudly voiced her objections.

The neighbor testified that he heard the saleswoman resisting in the beginning when the man told her, "I am going to rape you." The neighbor said he later heard the saleswoman say, "Your caress is so nice. Let's get undressed." If the jury believes the neighbor's testimony, of the following offenses, the most serious crime of which the man can be found guilty is:

(A) aggravated assault.

(B) assault.

(C) rape.

(D) kidnapping.

Question 5

Pursuant to a valid warrant, the police broke into the suspect's house in the middle of the night. One officer stood at the foot of the suspect's bed watching him sleep, while several other officers searched the premises. After the police found twelve pounds of cocaine behind a false wall, they woke the suspect to ask him several questions. The police did not give the suspect his Miranda warnings. The suspect answered the questions and made several incriminating statements. He was then handcuffed, brought to the police station, booked, and put in a holding cell. A police officer told the suspect he was being charged with possession of cocaine with the intent to sell. He did not give the suspect his Miranda warnings, nor did

he inform the suspect that he was also being investigated for the murder of a cocaine importer. When asked about the cocaine importer the suspect made several more incriminating statements.

The suspect was given his Miranda warnings during his second day in custody, but was not told about the cocaine importer murder investigation. The suspect then made even more incriminating statements in reference to the murder. The suspect's Miranda warnings were repeated to him on the third day he was incarcerated. "I will make an oral statement, but I refuse to make a written statement without my lawyer," the suspect said and then made some incriminating statements about the cocaine found in his apartment as well as statements indicating that he might not be the cocaine importer's murderer. The suspect was indicted and brought to trial on cocaine and murder charges. Which of the following arguments advanced by the suspect's counsel will be LEAST persuasive?

(A) The suspect was under custody while he was being questioned in bed because he did not have the ability to leave, and, therefore, the Miranda rule applies to those statements.

(B) The suspect's statements regarding the cocaine importer made at the police station during his first day in custody should be excluded because the Miranda custody requirement was fulfilled despite the fact that the suspect was being held on cocaine, and not murder charges.

(C) The incriminating statements made on the second day should not be admitted, because the failure to inform the suspect about the murder investigation invalidated his Miranda warnings.

(D) The suspect's Miranda warning on the third day was insufficient because the suspect demanded counsel and was not told that Miranda applies to both inculpatory statements and exculpatory statements.

Question 6

A man broke into a local dealership at midnight and took three personal computers. As he was leaving, he realized that he had left his fingerprints all over the showroom. The man took out his lighter and set fire to a life-size cardboard figure. The fire spread, consuming the entire showroom.

Using Common Law, the man could be convicted of which of the following crimes?

(A) burglary

(B) arson

(C) larceny

(D) burglary and arson, but not larceny

Question 7

A man met his friend while walking down the street. "Give me a boost. I want to rob that house," the friend said. The man bent over, and the friend climbed onto the man's shoulders to scale the wall surrounding the house. The friend entered the house through an open window. He then walked through the house and into the living room, where he went to grab the large television. Just then the homeowner came through the front door and saw the friend, who promptly shot him, and then left the house with a television. "I had to kill a witness," said the friend. The friend's success convinced the man that crime does pay. He walked over to his boss's car, which was parked in the road. The man saw his boss sleeping in the front seat. The man then spilled a gallon of gasoline on the car's roof and tossed a lit match onto it. His boss woke up just as the car had caught fire, and escaped unharmed.

The most serious crime the man should be charged with is:

(A) attempted murder.

(B) murder.

(C) arson.

(D) malicious mischief.

Question 8

A woman felt betrayed by her former lover. She waited outside his office until he appeared and then stuck a gun up his nose and demanded his diamond-studded watch. The woman took the watch, valued at several thousand dollars, to her friend. After bragging to the friend about how she obtained the watch, the woman sold it to her for $20

Several hours later, the friend looked out her front window to see several police officers and members of the press. "Open up, we know you possess a stolen watch," said the police. Both the police and press were unaware that there was a back door, and the friend escaped through it. She took a taxi to the house of her boyfriend. "You must help me," said the friend. "The cops are after me because I have this stolen watch."

"Don't worry, I'll hide you," said the boyfriend. The boyfriend was arrested in his own home, along with the friend, pursuant to a valid warrant. The trial court should rule that the boyfriend was a(n):

(A) principal in the first degree.

(B) principal in the second degree.

(C) accessory after the fact.

(D) none of the above.

Question 9

A woman planned to hijack a plane and then demand that the press print her political motives for the hijacking. She filled her carry-on luggage with plastic explosives undetectable by X-rays. A man was a professional luggage snatcher who searched airports for prime suitcases to snatch. He spied the woman struggling with her heavy luggage and offered to help her carry it. As soon as the woman gave the man the bag loaded with explosives, he ran off and disappeared into the crowd. As he walked through another terminal, the luggage ripped open and the contents spilled out onto the floor. An undercover security officer noticed the explosives and arrested him.

The man should be found guilty of:

(A) both larceny and carrying explosives.

(B) embezzlement.

(C) larceny.

(D) larceny by trick.

Question 10

A man stopped on his way to a college football game and purchased a new revolver. The game was very exciting and the man had an excellent seat, but all he could think about was his new gun. The score was tied at the beginning of the fourth quarter. The man left his seat to stand in the tunnel connecting the spectator stands with the area housing the concession stands and the exits. The tunnel seemed deserted because people were glued to their seats in this close game. The man decided that this would be a nice opportunity to test his new revolver and fired a shot into the darkness. A concessionaire was killed by the man's bullet after it ricocheted off a wall. The most serious offense of which the man might be properly convicted is:

(A) battery.

(B) voluntary manslaughter.

(C) involuntary manslaughter.

(D) murder.

Question 11

A defendant will most likely be convicted of involuntary manslaughter in which of the following cases?

(A) The defendant, an attorney, worked six days a week from 8:00 A.M. until midnight. This particular evening there was a power failure in his office, so the defendant took his work home with him at 7:00 P.M. when it began to get dark. Arriving home, the defendant opened the front door to find his wife and another man, both naked. The living room was lit up with bright spotlights. Three clothed men stood behind a video camera. The defendant reached over to the mantle above the fireplace where he had a ceremonial machete on display and killed the naked man with it.

(B) On his lunch hour the defendant went up to the observation deck of a skyscraper, where he purchased a canned beverage. Before opening the can, the defendant decided he wasn't thirsty and threw the can off the ledge of the building. The can smashed through the roof of a bus killing a passenger.

(C) The defendant was a passenger on a long car trip. Despite the beautiful scenery along the interstate, the defendant became extremely bored on the ride. He took out and polished his new gun to keep himself busy. The defendant had recently shoplifted the gun and did not own the statutorily required permit. "Do you think I could hit the writing on that truck?" the defendant asked his traveling companion as he aimed at the trailer of a truck driving alongside them. The defendant did hit the writing and he also hit a stowaway sleeping in the back of the truck. The stowaway died two days later.

(D) The defendant had a very sensitive stomach. He was suffering from severe stomach distress during his commute to work one morning and needed to arrive at the office as quickly as he possibly could. As the defendant drove down the main street leading into the downtown area, an accident ahead of him caused the traffic to come to a halt. The defendant drove onto the sidewalk to bypass the traffic, whereupon he struck and killed a pedestrian.

Question 12

A husband, a native of Texas, decided to take his wife to New York on the occasion of their twentieth wedding anniversary. The husband became disappointed when his order for two baseball tickets to see the New York team play the Texas team could not be filled because the game was already sold out. The husband, a professional typesetter, decided to print himself two tickets to the game.

Just before they left for New York, the husband read an article in the local paper describing a Civil War army poster that had recently been purchased for $5,000. The husband printed a similar poster in his shop and took it to New York with him. He sold the poster for $4,000 in New York, bragging to the collector who purchased it, "This is the finest nineteenth-century poster to be found."

The husband and wife successfully entered the baseball stadium using the tickets he printed and sat down in two empty box seats behind the visitor's dugout to watch the game. A man sat down next to the husband. Star baseball player hit a home run for the New York team in the third inning and the man, like most others in the stadium, had fallen off the edge of his seat in his excitement. The husband slipped some papers out of the man's sport coat without the man noticing. The papers contained the deed to the man's casino in New Jersey.

After the game, the husband and his wife took a taxi from the baseball stadium to the theater district, a distance of about fifteen miles. When the driver requested payment of the seventeen dollar fare, the husband screamed, "You are trying to cheat me because you can tell I am a tourist." The driver did not speak English very well and did not respond. The husband and his wife ran out of the cab without paying and got lost in the crowd.

Assume for this question only, the state of New York follows the common law.

(A) The husband should be found guilty of larceny for wrongfully obtaining entrance to the baseball stadium.

(B) The husband should be found guilty of larceny for wrongfully obtaining the deed to the man's casino.

(C) The husband should be found guilty of forgery for printing and selling the poster.

(D) The husband's failure to pay the cab fare will not result in liability for a crime unless New York has enacted a statute specifically designating theft of a service a crime.

Question 13

Beach Towers is a complex of 350 residential units in Florida. The complex, built before World War II as a rental property, was vacated in 1995 and renovated. The apartments were sold as condominiums to be occupied on December 1, 1999. On Thanksgiving Eve, 1999, a plumber employed by the city broke into the complex, and took three marble bathtubs. Under the common law, the most serious offense for which the plumber should be convicted is:

(A) larceny.
(B) robbery.
(C) burglary.
(D) common law burglary.

Question 14

A son received a call at work from his mother. "Congratulations, son, you passed the bar exam," she said.

The son was ecstatic. He ran through his firm's office shouting the news to everyone, pounding his hand on every desk he passed. An hour later, the son calmed down and sat down at his desk to enjoy the view of the air shaft outside his window. Then he thought of his best friend, roommate for three years, and study partner. The son called his friend and found out that his friend had passed the exam too. The son and his friend decided to leave work that instant and meet at a nearby tavern, where they cavorted with other inebriated celebrating lawyers. Seven hours later, the son and his friend, both extremely drunk, said good-bye to each other and walked in opposite directions toward their homes. The friend walked into a clothing store to try on the leather jacket he had admired in the window display. When the salesperson went to answer a phone call, the friend walked out wearing the coat. Still severely intoxicated, the friend continued his walk home when he happened to see his seventh-grade teacher walking her dog. The friend had never forgiven the teacher for the failing grade she gave him in spelling. It had kept him out of the college of his choice, and he was ready for revenge. Before she saw him coming, the friend punched the teacher in the side of her head, and she fell to the sidewalk, suffering a serious concussion.

Meanwhile, the son, despite his own extreme intoxication, was still thirsty. He saw a passerby walking down the street carrying a bottle of wine and a dozen roses. It was the son's favorite wine. He was in such a stupor that he thought the wine was his own. "Give me my wine or I'll punch your lights out," the son told the man. The passerby knew he could defeat the drunk son in a brawl, but he gave the son the wine because he was afraid he would soil his clothing. Several moments later, the son saw his ex-wife. Threatening her with the empty wine bottle he had just drunk from, the son led her to a dark and deserted alley and forced himself on her.

The friend and son should be found guilty of which of the following offenses?

(A) The friend should be found guilty of battery and robbery, and the son should be found guilty of rape and robbery.

(B) The friend should be found guilty of battery and larceny, and the son should be found guilty of rape.

(C) The friend should be found guilty of aggravated battery, and the son should be found guilty of rape.

(D) The friend should be found guilty of battery, the son of nothing.

Questions 15–16 are based upon the following fact situation.

A football player played for a university football team. After the team played their last game of the season the player took home his football helmet, thinking it was his to keep. In reality, the helmet belonged to the school. The coach had twice announced that all equipment was to be returned. The player skipped a practice to study for a pre-med course and did not hear the first announcement. He was present for the second announcement but was not listening when the coach spoke.

On the way home, the player was stuck in terrible traffic due to construction on the expressway. A driver who was driving in a car alongside the player's, saw the helmet and asked, "Can I try on your helmet? I always wanted to wear a real football helmet." The player handed the helmet to the driver who took it and quickly exited the expressway without even signaling. Before the player realized what had happened, the driver was gone.

Question 15

If charged with embezzlement, should the player be found guilty?

(A) Yes, if it was unreasonable for the player to assume the helmet was his to keep.

(B) Yes, because the player took the helmet in a violation of trust.

(C) No, because embezzlement is a specific intent crime.

(D) No, only if the player's mistake was reasonable.

Question 16

The driver should be found guilty of:

(A) false pretenses.

(B) larceny.

(C) larceny by trick.

(D) none of the above.

Question 17

A student attended the largest party in the history of the state. Thousands of people celebrated in the streets for six days in honor of the university's football championship. The student drank ten beers in less than an hour and became enraged when he misplaced his favorite drinking mug. He searched throughout the sorority house he had been invited into and entered a room where cheerleaders were practicing their leg splits. The student was extremely aroused and forced himself on one cheerleader as the other girl looked on in horror. When he had finished with the first cheerleader, the student began to disrobe the second cheerleader, but the quarterback heard her screaming, ran into the room, and beat the student severely before calling the police. In response to the charges of rape and attempted rape against him, the student testified that he was so drunk that he honestly thought the cheerleaders' leg splits were meant to convey their consent to his advances. If the student did indeed honestly believe the cheerleaders had consented, he should be found:

(A) guilty, if his intoxication was voluntary.

(B) not guilty, because he lacked the required intent.

(C) guilty, if a reasonable person would not have interpreted the cheerleaders' action as provocative.

(D) guilty of rape, but not guilty of attempted rape due to his lack of intent.

Questions 18–19 are based upon the following fact situation.

A girl was intoxicated. She went into a clothing store, tried on a coat, and then walked out of the store wearing the coat. She sat down on some steps in front of a house and lit a cigarette, throwing the match into a nearby garbage pail. The garbage caught fire, and the fire spread to the house next door, burning it to the ground. A statute in the jurisdiction provides that "arson is the malicious burning of a dwelling."

Question 18

If the girl asserts her intoxication as a defense to larceny, the girl's assertion:

(A) will not help her case if she ingested the substances voluntarily.

(B) will help her case only if she decided to take the coat after she was high.

(C) may negate the element of intent and, therefore, allow the girl to defeat the charges.

(D) will allow the girl to defeat the larceny charges, if "but for" her intoxication, she would not have taken the coat.

Question 19

Which of the following would serve as the girl's best defense if charged with arson?

(A) She was so intoxicated, her acts were not voluntary.

(B) She was so intoxicated, she could not have formed intent.

(C) She was so intoxicated, her actions could not have been malicious.

(D) The person that provided the girl with the drugs should be held liable.

Question 20

Two men decided to rob a store. One man volunteered to be the lookout and stand outside to warn the other man, who would be inside the store, if he saw a police officer coming. The inside man went inside and the lookout stood outside for a brief moment and then ran away. He had become too frightened to take part in the robbery. The inside man told the storekeeper, "Give me your money or I'll break your neck." The storekeeper laughed, then assumed a stern expression as he pulled out a shotgun from underneath the counter and pointed it within an inch of the inside man's face.

If both men are charged with robbery, the lookout's best defense is that:

(A) he withdrew before any crime was committed, thwarting the inside man's attempt.

(B) the inside man performed the illegal act.

(C) he never intended to take anything.

(D) the storekeeper was not intimidated by the inside man and nothing was actually taken.

Question 21

A plumber came to repair a husband and wife's leaky sink. The husband was away on a business trip and the wife was home alone. The wife let the plumber in the house, answering the door dressed in a sexy negligee. She offered the plumber a glass of champagne, which he accepted. The husband arrived home unexpectedly and accused the plumber of having an affair with his wife. The husband's charges enraged the plumber. The plumber smashed the bottom off the champagne bottle on the kitchen counter, and rushed toward the husband with the jagged glass. The husband pulled out a gun and shot the plumber in the chest, killing him instantly.

If the husband is charged with murder, should he be found guilty?

(A) Yes, because his accusations prompted an understandable response from the plumber.

(B) Yes, because his actions resulted in the plumber's death.

(C) No, because a broken bottle is a deadly weapon.

(D) No, because the plumber invited the husband's reaction by allowing the circumstances.

Question 22

A fourteen-year-old girl lied about her age in order to join the Marines. She looked older and told everyone, including her best friends, that she was twenty-one. The girl dated a sergeant, who also thought she was twenty-one. One night, the girl suggested that they park the jeep alongside a lake. The girl started kissing the sergeant, but then became frightened and cried out, "Don't touch me. I'm only fourteen." The sergeant was charged with rape and statutory rape. The sergeant is likely to be convicted of:

(A) statutory rape if his knowledge of the girl's true age is proved.

(B) statutory rape if he did not stop his advances after the girl told him her age.

(C) both charges if the girl resisted and the sergeant used force to accomplish intercourse.

(D) both charges if he was inebriated while with the girl.

Question 23

In which of the following cases is the defendant least likely to be convicted of robbery?

(A) By opening an unlocked door, the defendant entered an automobile that was stopped at a traffic light. "Get out of the car right now," the defendant told the driver. The driver left the car, and the defendant drove the car away.

(B) The defendant kicked a man's hand, causing the man to drop a briefcase that he was carrying. The defendant grabbed the briefcase and ran away.

(C) On a crowded bus, the defendant took a man's wallet out of his coat pocket. The man did not notice that his wallet was missing until after he left the bus.

(D) The defendant grabbed a man's dog while the man was walking the dog outside the house. "Give me your money or I'll kill the dog," the defendant told the man. The man gave the defendant all of his money.

Question 24

A man's friend told him that she would love to have a new DVD player, but could not afford one. "How would you like to buy one for $100?" the man asked his friend. "Sure," she replied. The man went out and stole a DVD player in order to sell it to his friend. The man and his friend were arrested and charged with several offenses, including conspiracy to commit larceny.

Should the friend be found guilty of conspiracy to commit larceny?

(A) Yes, because the man was solicited to take the DVD player by his friend's offer.

(B) Yes, because she should have known the goods were stolen.

(C) No, because the man acted without her knowledge or assent.

(D) No, because the man was the primary actor.

Questions 25–26 are based upon the following fact situation.

A woman and four other people formed a gang. They called themselves the "Fast Food Gang." They would go into local fast food restaurants, place large and complicated orders, and when the clerk totaled their bill, they would pull out handguns and demand to be given the contents of the cash register. The gang committed twelve robberies in twelve months. As they ended a meeting finalizing the plans for another robbery, the woman announced to all the members, "I quit this gang and I quit my life of crime!" The gang completed the thirteenth robbery, as planned.

Question 25

If the woman is charged with conspiracy, in connection with the thirteenth fast food robbery, she will be found:

(A) not guilty, because she did not assist the robbery in any way.

(B) not guilty, because all the conspirators saw the woman quit.

(C) guilty, because her withdrawal did not erase her participation in the conspiracy.

(D) guilty, because the conspiracy could not have functioned without her assistance in its planning.

Question 26

If the woman is charged with armed robbery of the thirteenth restaurant, she should be found:

(A) not guilty, because she did not assist the robbery in any way.

(B) not guilty, because all the conspirators saw the woman quit.

(C) guilty, because her withdrawal did not erase her participation in the conspiracy.

(D) guilty, because the robbery was completed.

Question 27

A woman wrote a letter to a friend containing the details of her plans to rob a candy store. The letter stated that the friend was to rob the store and the woman was to wait in a getaway car. The Post Office erroneously delivered the letter to a neighbor instead of the friend.

The neighbor read the letter and at first was horrified. She considered calling the police, but then thought twice. The plan seemed flawless. The neighbor decided to participate in the robbery, by replacing the friend in the scheme. The neighbor wrote back to the woman saying, "Will be there, (signed) Friend."

The woman was involved in a car accident the morning of the planned robbery and never arrived at the scene of the crime. The neighbor robbed the store and escaped on foot, when she didn't see the woman waiting outside.

The woman's best defense, if charged with conspiracy to rob, is that:

(A) the letter was merely a suggestion.

(B) her accident prevented her from participating in the robbery.

(C) there was no agreement between her and the friend or her and the neighbor.

(D) the plan was too vague to be a conspiracy.

Question 28

Two classmates were upset because their textbooks for the fall semester cost a lot more money than they had spent the previous semester. They hadn't budgeted for this added cost. To make ends meet they decided to steal some of the books they needed from the college bookstore. According to the plan, one girl would enter the bookstore while the other would be the driver and wait outside in her new car. The first girl entered the bookstore as planned and walked over to the anthropology section. She placed a textbook under her jacket and walked down the aisle. The girl then noticed the sales clerk, staring at her, so instead of leaving the store with the book, she placed it back on the shelf.

If the girl is subsequently prosecuted, she should be found guilty of:

(A) conspiracy to commit larceny only.

(B) attempted larceny.

(C) conspiracy to commit larceny and attempted larceny.

(D) conspiracy to commit larceny and actual larceny.

Question 29

A man pretended to be a health inspector, employed by the county. One night, he gained admission to a house by showing false identification. When the homeowner was not looking, the man took the homeowner's wallet off a table and put it in his pocket. Is the man guilty of burglary?

(A) Yes, if he intended to steal the wallet all along.

(B) Yes, because he entered under false pretenses.

(C) No, because there was no breaking.

(D) No, if he truly intended to take one of the homeowner's pets.

Question 30

A father came home and found a girl threatening his son with a butcher knife. The father had no idea that the girl and his son were rehearsing for a school play. The father grabbed a baseball bat and lunged toward the girl. The girl stabbed the father with the very real and sharp knife she had taken from the kitchen drawer to use as a prop. The father later died from the knife wound.

If the girl is charged with murder, should she be found guilty?

(A) Yes, because her actions prompted an understandable response from the father.

(B) Yes, because her actions resulted in the father's death.

(C) No, because a baseball bat is a deadly weapon.

(D) No, because the father's behavior invited the girl's reaction.

Question 31

A trader was placed on probation after her conviction for stock fraud. The terms of her probation provided that she was not to be permitted to purchase stock on the American or the New York Stock Exchanges. A broker, who did not know of the trader's past, called her and, after a lengthy conversation and much cajoling, talked the trader into opening a portfolio, which he would manage for her. The broker bought the trader stock on both exchanges. In the jurisdiction, violating terms of probation is a felony.

If the broker is charged with being an accessory to a violation of probation terms, he should be found:

(A) not guilty, because he did not force the trader to buy stock.

(B) not guilty, because he lacked the requisite *mens rea*.

(C) guilty, because he encouraged the trader to buy stock.

(D) guilty, because he was present when the crime was committed.

Question 32

A businessman was walking home from work when he saw a man attempting to rape a woman. The businessman pressed the point of his umbrella against the man's neck and said, "Watch out. I am about to make a hole in your neck!"

If the state charges the businessman with assault, the businessman most likely will:

(A) not prevail, because the man's fear of immediate harm was real and reasonable.

(B) not prevail, because the businessman threatened the man with deadly force.

(C) prevail, because the man was the aggressor.

(D) prevail, if a reasonable person would think the man was about to commit a battery.

Questions 33–34 are based upon the following fact situation.

After drinking two six-packs of beer, a man decided he wanted some pretzels. He drove to the nearest 24-hour convenience store, grabbed a carton of pretzels, and ran outside. Feeling real drunk and real good, the man decided to burn down a neighbor's house. He lit a match, and the house, unoccupied at the time, burned to the ground.

The applicable statutes provide:

"Larceny is the taking of property from possession of another, without consent, with intent to steal."

"Arson is the malicious burning of a dwelling."

The man was charged with larceny and arson.

Question 33

Which of the following would serve as the man's best defense to the arson charge?

(A) The man was so intoxicated, his acts were not voluntary.

(B) The man was so intoxicated, he could not have formed intent.

(C) The man was so intoxicated, his actions could not have been malicious.

(D) The person who sold the man the beer should be held liable.

Question 34

The prosecution's best argument to counter the defense set forth in the previous question is that:

(A) voluntary intoxication cannot be a defense to a general intent crime.

(B) voluntary intoxication is a defense to a specific intent crime.

(C) "malicious" refers to the man's course of conduct from the time he took his first drink and knew he could become dangerous.

(D) "malicious" could be imputed to the seller of the beer.

Question 35

The local police heard a rumor that a smoker had converted her basement into a marijuana farm. The police walked behind her house and saw empty bags of fertilizer and old fluorescent bulbs often used to provide light for indoor growth. The policemen knocked on the smoker's door and asked if they could come in. The smoker assented. One of the policemen looked through the smoker's open basement door, turned on a light in the stairwell leading down to the basement, and saw a sea of green plants. The smoker was arrested, and the house was searched. The police discovered several hundred marijuana plants.

Over proper objection, should evidence of the marijuana be admitted into evidence?

(A) Yes, if the fact finder decides that the smoker voluntarily opened the door.

(B) Yes, because the search was incident to a valid arrest.

(C) No, if the defendant can prove that fertilizer and light bulbs are not used exclusively to grow marijuana.

(D) No, because the smoker's reasonable expectation of privacy was violated.

Question 36

A father did not like the woman that his son was dating. The woman was a lawyer and the father preferred that his son go out with physical education teachers. One night, when the father knew that the son and the woman were at the local movies, the father drove up to the woman's house, poured gasoline all around the outside, and lit a match. The woman's house was engulfed in flames. A firefighter who responded to the scene with the local fire department was fatally injured when he fell through the roof into the burning inferno of the house. The father would most likely be convicted of:

(A) endangering the life of another.

(B) criminal negligence.

(C) felony murder.

(D) voluntary manslaughter.

Question 37

The defendant punched the victim in his nose. The state prosecutor charged the defendant with assault and battery. Under which of the following conditions is the defendant least likely to be convicted?

(A) The defendant was severely inebriated and was, therefore, unaware of his actions.

(B) The defendant thought the victim had stolen his watch.

(C) The defendant was only joking and did not intend serious harm.

(D) The defendant had just received an electrical shock, which caused involuntary motion.

Question 38

The local jurisdiction enacted the criminal offense of "attempted criminal battery," defined as "an attempt to perpetrate a criminal battery." "Criminal battery" was defined as "an unlawful application of force, resulting in a harmful or offensive touching." A skier was skiing for the very first time. He inadvertently took an expert trail marked with a black diamond. He pointed his ski tips downhill, began to gain speed, and lost all control. He closed his eyes and crouched down in order to cushion his eventual fall. He then began flying down the mountain, shooting off moguls and into the air. A snowboarder looked up and saw the skier coming straight toward her. She jumped out of the way, and as the skier passed, she pushed him from the side, hoping he would fall and no longer be a menace to himself and others.

If charged with criminal battery, should the snowboarder be found guilty?

(A) Yes, because she intentionally applied offensive contact.

(B) Yes, because she touched the skier.

(C) No, because the touch was not offensive.

(D) No, because the snowboarder was justified in touching the skier.

Question 39

A witness was an eyewitness to a murder. She spent several hours at a police station, answering questions about the murder. The police gave her a book containing the photographs of several thousand people. When she came across the defendant's photograph, the witness identified her as the murderer.

If the defendant objects to testimony concerning the identification, the judge should rule the identification:

(A) admissible.

(B) inadmissible, if the photo is not recent.

(C) inadmissible, if the identification was done before the defendant retained counsel.

(D) inadmissible, unless the witness had a perfectly clear view of the murder.

Question 40

A husband hired a hit man to kill his estranged wife. Late one night, the hit man climbed through an open window into the wife's living room. The wife was watching television, and the hit man snuck up from behind her and shot the wife five times in the head. The wife lived alone, but her boyfriend happened to be visiting. When he heard the gunshot, the boyfriend screamed. The hit man shot and killed the boyfriend. If the husband is charged with the murder of the boyfriend, he will be found:

(A) not guilty because the hit man was only hired to kill the wife.

(B) not guilty, if the boyfriend's murder was probable or foreseeable.

(C) guilty, because the boyfriend's murder would not have occurred but for the wife's murder.

(D) guilty, if the boyfriend's murder was a probable or foreseeable result of the wife's murder.

Question 41

The defendant left his keys with his neighbor before flying to his parents' home for the holidays. The neighbor had asked for permission to use the apartment on Christmas Day, when members of his own family planned to visit. On New Year's Day, a police officer happened to pass the defendant's apartment with his drug-sniffing dog on his way to another call. The dog barked very loudly as they passed the defendant's front door.

Just then, the neighbor was in the hallway and volunteered to open the door. The police officer found cocaine and a letter requesting a shipment of marijuana.

The neighbor's unlocking of the door was:

(A) a waiving of the defendant's rights against search and seizure, because the neighbor was consenting to the policeman's entry to the apartment.

(B) a waiving of the defendant's right against search and seizure, because of the probable cause that existed.

(C) not a waiving of the defendant's rights against search and seizure, because the police officer lacked probable cause for a search.

(D) not a waiving of the defendant's rights against search and seizure, because the neighbor did not have a right to permit entry.

Question 42

A driver was arrested for driving without a license. The driver, who was a licensed driver but had left her wallet at home, was taken to a police station, where she was booked. The driver was searched by the police, who found two ounces of cocaine on her person.

Over proper objection, will the cocaine be admitted into evidence?

(A) Yes, because the policeman may rely upon a reasonable suspicion.

(B) Yes, because the search was incident to a valid arrest.

(C) No, because the officer had no reason to be in fear or to suspect that the driver was carrying drugs.

(D) No, because failure to carry a license is a minor offense.

Question 43

A grandson could not stand to watch his grandmother suffer from terminal cancer, so he decided to kill her to relieve her pain. The grandson carried his grandmother out of the hospital cancer ward and drove her to the nearest beach, eight hours away. While the grandson and the grandmother were driving, a flash fire killed all the patients in the hospital cancer ward. The grandson rented a sailboat, went out to sea, and threw the grandmother overboard. She quickly drowned.

If charged with criminal homicide, should the grandson be found guilty?

(A) Yes.

(B) No, because the grandson actually prolonged the grandmother's life.

(C) No, because the grandson acted out of compassion and love.

(D) No, because the grandmother could have survived had she known how to swim, and the grandson was not under an obligation to rescue her.

Question 44

A man and a woman happened to sit together at a night baseball game. "I am so hungry," said the man. "So am I," the woman replied. Neither one of them had money to purchase food. The woman told the man that she had left a shopping bag full of food at her mother's house, which was nearby, but her mother was out of town. The woman also told the man that her mother was very absent-minded and often left the back door unlocked.

The man agreed to go into the woman's mother's house, but made a mistake and went into the wrong house. The owner woke up and called the police. The woman and the man were arrested.

The man's best defense against burglary charges is that:

(A) the door was not locked.

(B) he reasonably thought he had lawful permission to enter the house.

(C) only the woman should be held responsible.

(D) a mistake of law was the proximate cause of entry.

Question 45

In which of the following situations will the defendant most likely be convicted of larceny?

(A) The defendant took a stranger's car for a drive, intending to return the car before the gas ran out. The defendant was involved in a serious accident, which destroyed the car.

(B) The defendant drove a stranger's car home, thinking that it was his own car.

(C) The defendant walked past a convertible. The top was down, and the keys were in the ignition. Under the assumption that he was not committing larceny, the defendant drove the car away and gave it to his grandson as a graduation present.

(D) The defendant took his friend's car, because the friend had damaged the defendant's car and had refused to pay for it. The defendant's car was much more valuable than the friend's.

Question 46

A homeowner's boiler was leaking gas, but the homeowner decided to ignore the leak. He was having seventy-five people over and he could not waste time messing with the boiler. A gas explosion in the middle of the party caused the death of sixteen persons. The homeowner has committed:

(A) no form of criminal homicide.

(B) voluntary manslaughter.

(C) involuntary manslaughter.

(D) murder.

Question 47

The defendant was arrested and charged with armed robbery. The arresting officer gave the defendant his Miranda warnings. The defendant asked for counsel and was told he would receive counsel. The defendant then proceeded to make several incriminating statements. Over proper objections, these statements should be ruled:

(A) admissible, because the period after receiving the Miranda warnings is not a critical element of the prosecution that would require counsel.

(B) admissible, because the statements were voluntary and not the result of improper questioning.

(C) not admissible, because the defendant had requested but not received counsel.

(D) not admissible, because the right to counsel had not vested at the time the statement was made.

Question 48

Two teenagers decided to play a game. The sixteen-year-old took a machete off the wall above her father's bed and stood the seventeen-year-old next to a tree. The sixteen-year-old threw the machete toward the seventeen-year-old. The object of the game was for the sixteen-year-old to throw the machete as close as possible to the seventeen-year-old, without striking her. The seventeen-year-old knew the sixteen-year-old had never tried throwing a machete before. The sixteen-year-old threw the machete four times. She narrowly missed the seventeen-year-old the first three times. On the fourth throw, the machete struck the seventeen-year-old in the throat, killing her. In the jurisdiction, one is legally accountable as an adult for committing a crime at the age of sixteen.

If the sixteen-year-old is prosecuted, she will be found:

(A) guilty of murder.
(B) guilty of manslaughter.
(C) not guilty, because she was merely negligent.
(D) not guilty, because the seventeen-year-old consented.

Question 49

The defendant, a police officer, had valid legal grounds on which to arrest the deceased. The defendant, driving a squad car, pursued the deceased, who was riding a motorcycle. Realizing that he could not keep up with the motorcycle, the defendant forced the motorcycle off the road. The deceased lost control of the bike, fell down a ravine, and died.

The defendant will be found guilty of murder:

(A) unless the court determines that he was using non-deadly force, because, if he was using deadly force, he will be guilty.

(B) unless the court determines that he was using deadly force to effectuate a felony or misdemeanor arrest.

(C) unless the court determines that he was privileged to use deadly force in effectuating a felony arrest.

(D) because he was not privileged to use non-deadly or deadly force.

Question 50

First-degree murder is defined by a state statute as "murder with premeditation and deliberation."

In which of the following situations is it most likely that the defendant will be convicted of first-degree murder?

(A) The defendant tried to injure the victim by punching him in the nose. The victim died from the injuries he sustained.

(B) The victim insulted the defendant's mother. The defendant flew into a rage and killed the victim.

(C) Severely inebriated, the defendant drove ninety miles per hour in the wrong direction on a one-way street, striking and killing a pedestrian.

(D) The victim cheated against the defendant in a card game. The defendant ran to a local sporting good store and bought a shotgun with which he shot and killed the victim.

Questions 51–52 are based upon the following fact situation.

An Olympic sprinter was walking down the street, window-shopping. He saw a police officer chasing a woman. The woman was running faster than the police officer, and the sprinter joined the chase.

Question 51

Is the police officer privileged to use force to effectuate an arrest of the woman?

(A) He may not use force.
(B) He may use non-deadly force only.
(C) He may use deadly force.
(D) He may use deadly force only to effectuate an arrest for a felony.

Question 52

Is the sprinter privileged to use force to effectuate an arrest of the woman?

(A) He may not use force.
(B) He may use non-deadly force only.
(C) He may use deadly force.
(D) He may use deadly force only to effectuate an arrest for a felony if the woman is guilty.

Question 53

A driver knew his car's brakes were not in proper order and were about to fail. The driver continued to drive the car anyway, because he had to get to work and did not have time to take care of repairs. The driver was driving a coworker home from work when the brakes ultimately failed. When they approached a red light at the bottom of a hill, the driver crashed into the car in front of him. The coworker was killed in the accident. The driver has committed:

(A) no form of criminal homicide.

(B) voluntary manslaughter.

(C) involuntary manslaughter.

(D) murder.

Question 54

A local ordinance provides that one who "knowingly sells a grade of gasoline differing from the grade advertised is guilty of aggravated larceny." The defendant owned a franchised gas station. Unbeknownst to the defendant, the gas company filled his 91-octane tank with 89-octane fuel. An inspector discovered the octane difference, and the defendant was charged with aggravated larceny. If a jury believes the defendant's testimony, will he be found guilty of aggravated larceny?

(A) Yes, because the defendant is admitting that he has not complied with the statute.

(B) Yes, because ignorance is no excuse.

(C) No, because the defendant was not aware of the octane difference.

(D) No, because the gas station used the parent company's name in relating with the public.

Question 55

The defendant kicked the victim, causing severe injuries. The state brought charges against the defendant for assault and battery. In which of the following situations is the defendant LEAST likely to be convicted?

(A) The defendant was severely inebriated and was, therefore, unaware of his actions.

(B) The defendant believed that the victim had stolen his girlfriend.

(C) The defendant was only joking and did not intend serious harm.

(D) The defendant accidentally touched a live wire, and the resulting shock caused an involuntary kick.

Question 56

Bigamy was defined by a local statute as "having a husband or wife and marrying another person" or "marrying another person who has a husband or wife." Another statute provided that "one who has been absent for more than seven years without notice is presumed dead." A wife and husband were married in 2001, when the husband disappeared without notice. The wife married another man in 2007 without telling him that she had been married before.

If charged with bigamy:

(A) both the wife and the man should be held guilty.

(B) only the wife should be held guilty.

(C) only the man should be held guilty.

(D) neither the man nor the wife should be held guilty.

Question 57

Acting on a "gut" feeling, a police officer knocked on a tenant's door and demanded that he be allowed to search the apartment for narcotics. The tenant refused, and the police officer told him, "If you let me use your bathroom, I won't arrest you." The tenant assented and told the officer that the bathroom was the second door on the right. The police officer turned left and found a room full of sprouting marijuana plants. The tenant was arrested. At trial for possession of drugs with intent to sell, the tenant moved to exclude the evidence. The evidence should be ruled:

(A) admissible, if the trier of fact determines that the police officer's turn to the left was an honest mistake.

(B) admissible, because the police officer entered the apartment with tenant's permission.

(C) inadmissible, because the police officer was not privileged to do a search.

(D) inadmissible, if the police officer did not, in fact, really need to use the bathroom.

Question 58

In which of the following fact situations is the defendant most likely to be held guilty of the crime charged?

(A) The defendant saw $5,000 on his boss's desk. The defendant took the money, intending to return it, which he in fact did three hours later. The defendant is charged with larceny.

(B) The defendant borrowed $5,000, using his brother's driver's license as identification. He returned the money in a timely manner. The defendant is charged with obtaining property under false pretenses.

(C) The defendant begged his boss for a $5,000 advance against future wages. The defendant knew he was not going to return to the job or repay the money. The defendant is charged with larceny by trick.

(D) The defendant borrowed $5,000 from his boss, intending to return the money when due. On the due date, The defendant decided not to return the money. The defendant is charged with obtaining property under false pretenses.

Question 59

The defendant, an Olympic skier, wanted to neutralize his opponent. The defendant altered the opponent's ski bindings so that they would not release upon impact. Ski bindings are adjusted to release the skier's boots in a bad fall in order to mitigate any injury. The defendant hoped his alteration would cause the opponent severe leg injuries and keep the opponent from competing. The opponent fell during a practice run and broke both his legs when his skis didn't come off. The pain was so severe that the opponent went into shock and died. Of the following offenses, which is the most serious crime of which the defendant could be convicted?

(A) involuntary manslaughter
(B) voluntary manslaughter
(C) murder
(D) none of the above

Question 60

A police officer testified that he had ordered a driver to pull to the side of a road and produce identification because "this is a wealthy area and our orders are to pull over cars that look like they don't belong here." When asked why the driver's car looked like it did not belong, the police said, "It was old, dented, and had a hippie bumper sticker."

The officer found a packet of illegally obtained Quaaludes on the floor by the driver's passenger seat. If the driver makes a motion to suppress this evidence, the motion should be:

(A) sustained, because the officer was not privileged to look around the car.
(B) sustained, because the car was not lawfully stopped.
(C) denied, because the policeman was acting pursuant to an established plan.
(D) denied, because the policeman had a reasonable suspicion for which to stop the car.

Question 61

Two roommates wanted to rent a movie. One roommate talked the other into driving to the nearby video store to rent the movie. "Take my car," said the roommate. "It's the blue car in front. The keys are in the ignition." The other roommate went outside and drove off in the wrong car. The owner of the car called the police, who arrested both of the roommates.

The roommate's best defense against conspiracy charges is that:

(A) neither intended to commit larceny.
(B) there was no meeting of the minds.
(C) the car was returned.
(D) both acted under a mistake of law.

Question 62

A passenger walked out of an airline terminal with a suitcase that belonged to someone else. When charged with larceny, the passenger claimed he had made an honest mistake—he thought the suitcase was his own. The passenger should be found:

(A) guilty, for taking and carrying away property from the possession of another person.
(B) guilty, because he was criminally negligent in not inspecting the suitcase.
(C) not guilty, if the passenger had left a suitcase in the airport with a similar appearance.
(D) not guilty, if the jury determines that the passenger honestly believed that the luggage was his own.

Question 63

The defendant killed her business partner, after learning that her partner had made them lose their biggest client. The defendant asserts that the murder charge should be reduced to manslaughter because the killing was not premeditated. It was perpetrated in the heat of passion since she was so distraught upon learning of this huge loss of business. The jury should be instructed that:

(A) the state must prove beyond a reasonable doubt, and by a preponderance of the evidence, that the killing was not provoked by the heat of passion.
(B) the state must prove beyond a reasonable doubt both the killing and the absence of heat of passion.
(C) the state must prove the killing beyond a reasonable doubt. Once the killing is proved, it is presumed to be murder.
(D) the state must prove the killing beyond a reasonable doubt. Once the killing is proved, the defendant has the burden of showing, by a fair preponderance of the evidence, that the killing was committed in the heat of passion.

Questions 64–65 are based upon the following fact situation.

A man believed he was a prophet. He spent hours practicing long rituals, whereby he claimed to communicate with God. The man, who was diagnosed by a licensed physician as a severe schizophrenic, toured the country preaching to anyone who would listen, and to some who would not listen, that they should refrain from sinning. The man decided that the government was the enemy of God. Knowing he was to be punished by the government, the man shot a receptionist at the state capitol because, he said, God ordered him to do so. The receptionist died two days later. The man is charged with murder and asserts the insanity defense.

Question 64

The man's best defense, in a jurisdiction that has adopted the M'Naghten test, is that:

(A) he did not know that he was killing someone.

(B) he did not know that killing was wrong.

(C) his mental illness was the cause of the killing.

(D) he could not stop himself from killing.

Question 65

In which of the following situations is the man LEAST likely to be found the legal cause of the receptionist's death?

(A) The receptionist would have survived but for the fact that she was a hemophiliac and she bled to death.

(B) The receptionist was recovering from an operation and would not have died from the man's shots had she not been in a weakened condition.

(C) The receptionist was killed by a fire that engulfed the hospital, where she was successfully recuperating from wounds inflicted by the man.

(D) The man's brother decided to shoot the receptionist too. She would not have died if just the man or just his brother had shot her.

Question 66

A gunman and a driver planned and committed the armed robbery of an ice cream parlor. The gunman threatened a waitress with a gun, while the driver emptied the store's cash register. The gunman fired a few shots at the store's lights and said, "Anyone that follows us gets it." The driver drove the getaway car and when it appeared that they were safe, they both relaxed. The gunman turned a corner and saw a man walking down the street. "Boy do I hate that jerk," said the gunman. The driver took his gun and shot a man, who died three weeks later.

If the gunman is charged with murder, he will most likely be found:

(A) guilty, because the killing took place during a conspiracy.

(B) guilty, because he provoked the shooting.

(C) not guilty, because the gunman and the driver did not plan on killing the man.

(D) not guilty, because the killing was not in furtherance of the conspiracy.

Question 67

A local bigamy statute provided, "Any person who has a husband or wife and marries another person, or one who marries a person he or she knows has a husband or wife, is guilty of bigamy." A man and a woman were engaged to be married. The man never told the woman that he was already married. One day the man and the woman shared two bottles of Scotch. The man was feeling very

guilty and told the woman he was already married. The woman was so drunk that his words did not register in her mind. The next morning, relieved that the woman did not remember the conversation, the man decided never to tell her of his previous marriage. The woman and the man married. If prosecuted for bigamy under the above listed statutes, the woman should be found:

(A) not guilty, if she was voluntarily intoxicated.

(B) not guilty, if she was involuntarily intoxicated.

(C) not guilty, regardless of how she became intoxicated.

(D) guilty.

Question 68

A clerk sold the tickets at a movie theater. On a busy weekend he often sold $5,000 worth of tickets. The clerk was heavily in debt from his recent purchase of a new house. Late one Sunday night the clerk was the only employee on duty. He hid the day's receipts in the lining of his coat, called the police, and told them that he had been robbed at gunpoint.

The clerk has committed the crime of:

(A) larceny.

(B) embezzlement.

(C) larceny by trick.

(D) false pretenses.

Question 69

A captain and first mate together hid sixteen cases of rum in their boat when they sailed from the Virgin Islands to Florida. The captain had consulted an attorney before the excursion, who advised her it would be unlawful to import rum from the Virgin Islands to Florida without paying a duty on it. The first mate had also consulted an attorney, who told her of the United States Virgin Rum Exclusion Act of 1985 excluding duty collection on rum imported from the Virgin Islands.

If charged with attempting the crime of Virgin Island Rum import-duty evasion:

(A) neither the captain nor the first mate should be found guilty if the Act of 1985 is valid.

(B) only the captain should be found guilty if the Act of 1985 is valid.

(C) only the first mate should be found guilty if the Act of 1985 is not valid.

(D) both the captain and the first mate should be found guilty.

Question 70

A bookie ran an illegal gambling operation. Every day he traveled a specific route and accepted bets on games that would be played the following weekend. He confirmed the bets with printed forms that said across the top, "Bookie Wishes You Luck."

A gambler was stopped by police because his brake lights had malfunctioned. The police searched the gambler's car and found several betting forms with the bookie's name.

The bookie, charged with illegal gambling, seeks to prevent introduction of the forms into evidence. Should the forms be admitted?

(A) Yes, because the search was proper.

(B) Yes, because the bookie does not have standing to challenge the search.

(C) No, because the search was improper.

(D) No, because an officer may stop a car for an immediate threat, such as a broken headlight, but not for a brake light.

Question 71

A defendant was arrested and charged with murder. She was handcuffed, given her Miranda warnings, and placed in the back seat of a police car. The defendant demanded to speak with a lawyer and was told she would be provided with counsel shortly. "He better be a good one because I am guilty as hell," she muttered. Over proper objection, the defendant's confession should be ruled:

(A) admissible, because riding to the police station is not a critical element of the prosecution requiring counsel.

(B) admissible, because the statements were volunteered and not the result of improper questioning.

(C) not admissible, because the defendant had requested counsel and had not received it.

(D) not admissible, because the right to counsel had not vested at the time the statement was made.

Question 72

In which of the following situations is the defendant most likely to be found NOT GUILTY as charged?

(A) The defendant took a picnic table from his neighbor's yard. Unknown to the defendant, his neighbor had tired of the table and was planning to give it to the defendant. The defendant is charged with attempted larceny.

(B) Believing that federal law considers it a crime to melt down U.S. coins, the defendant melted down $2,000 face value of pre-1965 silver coins. The law that prohibited the melting down of coins had been repealed years earlier, but the defendant did not know about the law's repeal. The defendant is charged with melting down coins.

(C) The defendant hired a hit man to murder his mother-in-law. Unknown to the hit man and the defendant, the defendant's mother-in-law had died hours earlier. The defendant is charged with attempted murder.

(D) The defendant tried to sell a car that was not his as a trade-in for a new car. The car dealer was not fooled and refused to sell a car to the defendant. The defendant is charged with attempt to obtain property under false pretenses.

Question 73

A state statute provides that "members of the state legislature must not accept gifts valued at more than $500." The state was considering repealing the windfall profits tax on crude oil. For her birthday, a state senator received a diamond necklace from the vice president of a large oil company. The necklace had a fair market value of $25,000.

If the vice president is charged with violating the statute, his best argument is that:

(A) he was not an accessory to the senator's crime.

(B) the accessory may only be tried after the principal is convicted.

(C) he did not intend to influence the senator with the gift.

(D) the legislature did not intend to punish one who gave gifts.

Question 74

A professional football player was identified as a cocaine user from the results of a mandatory drug test he had taken. The player was granted immunity from prosecution in exchange for cooperating with authorities. He became an extremely reliable informant and was responsible for more than forty drug-related convictions.

The player told investigators that he had purchased cocaine two years earlier from an assistant coach. A search warrant for the coach's home was issued based on the player's statements. The coach's house was subsequently raided by the narcotics squad, and 200 pounds of cocaine were found. Should the coach's motion to suppress the evidence be granted?

(A) Yes, because testimony of a drug abuser is not sufficient grounds on which to issue a search warrant.

(B) Yes, because two years had passed since the player purchased drugs from the coach.

(C) No, because the player was an extremely reliable witness.

(D) No, because testimony of a witness is sufficient to satisfy the requirements of granting a search warrant.

Question 75

In which of the following situations is the defendant most likely to be found guilty of murder?

(A) Disturbed by the noises made when his garbage cans over turned, the defendant put some cake laced with poison in his garbage, hoping to kill the animals that frequent the area. A homeless person ate the cake and died.

(B) The defendant was threatened by a man holding a toy gun. Believing his life to be in danger, the defendant killed the man.

(C) While in the process of robbing a barber shop, the defendant threw a rock at the mirror to scare the barber out of the shop. A shard of broken glass cut the barber's jugular vein, causing his death.

(D) The defendant's boiler did not meet the efficiency standards mandated in a local ordinance. The boiler caught fire, killing three persons.

Question 76

The defendant was caught climbing the fence surrounding a new car dealer's lot. The defendant was carrying tools that are commonly used for removing radios from cars. If the defendant is charged with attempted larceny, he should be found:

(A) guilty, because he was committed to completing the crime.

(B) guilty, if he had the necessary mental state, because he was in close proximity to the cars.

(C) not guilty, because one may not be punished for an act not yet committed.

(D) not guilty, if the cars did not have radios.

Question 77

The defendant is most likely to be convicted of common law murder in which of the following situations?

(A) The defendant came home and found his wife in bed with another woman. The defendant grabbed a gun, then shot and killed both women.

(B) The defendant, driving while intoxicated, lost control of his car and killed a pedestrian on the sidewalk.

(C) The defendant shot a spitball into a classmate's eye. The eye became infected, the infection spread, and the classmate died.

(D) The defendant threw a full beer can from his seat in a baseball stadium. He intended to seriously injure a player from the visiting team. Instead, he killed a member of the home team.

Question 78

The local police set up a roadblock to check the driver of every fifth car that passed for obvious signs of intoxication. While checking a driver, a police officer spotted marijuana on the back seat of his car. The driver was ordered from the car and searched. Eight grams of cocaine were found in his pants pocket.

The driver was charged with the illegal possession of narcotics. If the driver makes a motion to suppress the admission of the cocaine into evidence, should he be successful?

(A) Yes, because he was improperly searched.

(B) Yes, because the car was stopped without cause.

(C) No, because the driver was stopped pursuant to a valid plan.

(D) No, because an officer of the law may act on a "hunch."

Question 79

A caregiver operated a small home for mentally handicapped adults. The caregiver despised one of the home's residents because he was a slob, and the caregiver was in love with the resident's sister. The caregiver struck the resident's head as hard as he could with his fists several times a day. On the last occasion the resident died just moments after being hit by the caregiver. A pathologist performed an autopsy on the resident. "The resident died of pancreatic cancer, although, continued blows to the resident's head would have resulted in his death within two weeks," the pathologist testified.

If prosecuted for murder, the caregiver should be held:

(A) not guilty, because he had the authority to discipline the resident.

(B) not guilty, because his actions did not cause the resident's death.

(C) guilty, because the resident would have died from the blows had he not died of cancer first.

(D) guilty, if the caregiver did not know that the resident was ill.

Question 80

The defendant firmly believed he was the savior of the universe. He also believed that people with freckles were polluting the world's gene pool. The defendant would stand on chairs in airports and preach his philosophy. Most people remained apathetic when the defendant made his speeches. The defendant decided it was his obligation to take definitive action. He obtained a gun through legal channels and shot three freckled people dead on a crowded street. In a jurisdiction that has adopted the M'Naghten test of insanity, the defendant's best argument is that he had a disease of the mind and:

(A) did not know the nature of the act he performed.

(B) did not know the quality of the act he performed.

(C) did not know the killings were wrong.

(D) his acts would not have occurred if not for his mental disease.

Question 81

In which of the following situations will the defendant be LEAST likely to be found guilty by asserting in his defense that he was intoxicated?

(A) The defendant, charged with murder, claimed he was so drunk that he thought he was carving a turkey.

(B) The defendant, charged with incest, claimed he was so drunk that he thought his partner was his wife.

(C) The defendant, charged with armed robbery, claimed he was so drunk that he thought that he was carrying a watergun.

(D) The defendant, charged with intent to commit embezzlement, claimed he was so drunk that he did not realize he was walking away with company property.

Question 82

A woman was released from prison on probation after serving ten years of a sixteen-year sentence. The woman was required to meet with her probation officer every two weeks. She was not permitted to leave the country.

The woman kept to her probation terms and got a good job. She met and fell in love with a man, but never told him of her past life of crime. One day the man told the woman, "Surprise! I purchased tickets for us to fly to the Caribbean for the weekend." "But I don't have a passport," the woman replied. "U.S. citizens don't need a passport to travel to the Caribbean." The woman and the man flew to the Caribbean. A violation of the terms of probation is a felony in the jurisdiction.

If the man is charged with being an accessory to violating probation terms, he should be found:

(A) not guilty, because he did not force the woman to leave the country.

(B) not guilty, because he lacked the *mens rea* required for aiding and abetting a criminal.

(C) guilty, because he encouraged the woman to violate the law.

(D) guilty, because he was present when the crime was committed.

Question 83

The defendant checked into a quiet hotel situated off an interstate highway exit. After a week the manager became very suspicious of the defendant who wore clothing stereotypical of someone in the mafia. The defendant also carried several violin cases back and forth from his car to his room. The manager and the owner of the hotel arranged with the local racketeering squad to have the defendant's room bugged. Using the tapes, a search warrant was obtained. A stockpile of automatic weapons was discovered. At trial, the defendant objected to the admission of the guns as evidence.

The trial judge should rule the evidence obtained pursuant to the search warrant:

(A) admissible, because the warrant was validly issued with probable cause shown.

(B) admissible, because the hotel may allow surveillance of its own premises.

(C) not admissible, because a violin case and one's taste in clothing are not inherently suspicious.

(D) not admissible, because the defendant's privacy was improperly invaded.

Question 84

Seven members of a mafia family were indicted for the murder of a victim who had been working with the FBI as an informant. The father of the family pleaded guilty. At the trial of the others, state evidence showed that the father had announced a party to celebrate his daughter's engagement, and had planned to announce the victim as a member of the wedding party. However, at that point the father already knew that the victim was an informant, and had invited the other members of the family to the party so they could see how he made an example of the victim. He had told no one of this plan. At the party, after announcing the engagement of his daughter, and after all present had consumed a large amount of wine, the father took the others into the basement and announced that the victim was a rat and shot him point blank, in front of the rest. The others watched and did nothing to help the victim, as they all feared the father. The jury found the other family members guilty of murder and they appealed.

Should the appellate court uphold the conviction?

(A) No, because mere presence at the scene of the crime is not sufficient to make one an accomplice.

(B) No, because murder is a specific intent crime, and there is insufficient evidence to show that the others had intent.

(C) Yes, because the family members made no effort to save the victim.

(D) Yes, because voluntary intoxication does not negate criminal responsibility.

Question 85

A defendant was charged with assault and battery in a jurisdiction that followed the "Retreat" doctrine, and he pleaded self-defense. At his trial, it was established that a husband and wife were enjoying dinner and drinks at a local restaurant. The defendant entered the restaurant and stood near the door. The wife whispered to the husband that the defendant was the man who had insulted her earlier, so the husband, being the "macho man" that he was, approached the defendant and said, "Get out of here, or I'll break your nose!" The defendant replied, "Don't come any closer, or I'll hurt you." When the husband raised his fists ready to punch the defendant, the defendant pulled a can of mace from his pocket and sprayed it in the husband's face. The husband promptly fell on the floor, crying in pain.

Should the defendant be convicted?

(A) No, because he had no obligation to retreat before resorting to non-deadly force.

(B) No, because there is no obligation to retreat when one is an occupied structure.

(C) Yes, because he failed to retreat even though there was an opportunity available.

(D) Yes, because the husband did not threaten to use deadly force against him.

Question 86

A thief, on his day off, went to a high-end jewelry store, and started talking to the store clerk. The thief lied to the clerk, stating that he was the son of the mayor. He asked the clerk if he could try on a watch, and walk around the store in it, to see how it felt. He then asked if he could see what it looked like in the natural light, outside. The clerk naively agreed, stating, "I know I can trust you!" The thief walked out of the store with the watch, never to return.

What is the most serious crime of which the thief may be convicted?

(A) robbery
(B) larceny
(C) false pretenses
(D) embezzlement

Question 87

The defendant drove up to a fast food restaurant, and when she reached the window she stated, "There is a man on the roof next door, he can see everything and if you don't do what I say, he will shoot you. Put all the money from the register in the sack, as well as two cheese-burgers and fries." The clerk did not see anyone, but was still frightened, so put the money and food in the bag. The defendant drove off with the money, and was subsequently arrested, and admitted that she lied about the man with the rifle, and actually acted alone.

What crime or crimes may she be convicted of?

(A) embezzlement
(B) obtaining property by false pretenses
(C) robbery and larceny
(D) robbery or larceny

Question 88

The mistress was a tough dominatrix. One evening, a client came to her dungeon to request her services. He asked to be bound and gagged, and requested that the mistress whip him as hard as she could. Know-ing that some people like this sort of thing, and hey, it is all part her job, the mistress agreed. She led client to the center of the dungeon, put him in handcuffs and a ball gag, and started whipping him with a cat-o'-nine-tails. Unfortunately, the mistress got a bit overzealous with her beatings and soon noticed that client had died.

What is the most serious crime that the mistress may be convicted of?

(A) None, because client clearly consented to the beat-ings.
(B) Murder, since the mistress had intent to kill the client.
(C) Murder, since the mistress had intent to cause client serious harm.
(D) Involuntary manslaughter, since the mistress had no intent, and was merely criminally negligent.

Question 89

A state statute provides that "murder in the first degree is knowingly causing the death of another person after deliberation upon the matter." Second-degree murder is defined as "knowingly causing the death of another person." Manslaughter is defined the same way it is at common law. A worker was very distraught over losing his job, and contemplated suicide. He took his gun, and went to the bar, thinking he was going to drink to build up some courage to commit suicide. He became very intoxicated. A customer on the next stool was telling the bartender how it was necessary for companies to downsize. This enraged the worker, and he told the customer to shut up. The customer responded by telling him that he could say what he wanted, and shook his finger at the worker. This enraged the worker even more, and he took his gun and shot the customer.

What crime did the worker commit?

(A) Manslaughter, because there was a reasonable explanation for his anger.
(B) Murder in the first degree, because deliberation can take place in an instant.
(C) Murder in the first degree, because he contem-plated taking a human life before becoming intoxi-cated.
(D) Murder in the second degree, because he knowingly caused the customer's death without deliberation.

Question 90

State troopers stopped a driver for speeding. When the troopers ran her information, it turned out there was a warrant for driver's arrest due to unpaid parking tickets. The troopers then arrested the driver, and after doing so, searched her car. They found bags of heroin and cocaine in a shopping bag on the back seat of the car. However, before trial it was learned that the driver had indeed paid all of her parking tickets and the warrant had thus been quashed, before she was pulled over. However, the clerk failed to update the computer system. Driver was charged with unlawful possession of drugs. Her attorney filed a motion to suppress the use as evidence of the heroin and cocaine found in the car.

Should the motion be granted?

(A) No, because the troopers could reasonably rely on the computer report and the search was incident to arrest.
(B) No, because troopers may lawfully search the pas-senger compartment of a car incident to a valid traffic stop.
(C) Yes, because there was no arrest for the traffic vio-lation and no lawful arrest could be made on the basis of the nonexistent warrant.
(D) Yes, because there was no probable cause or rea-sonable suspicion to believe drugs were in the car.

Questions 91–92 are based upon the following fact situation.

An engineer and a teacher were neighbors and on good terms. One day the teacher decided he needed to borrow some of the engineer's tools. The engineer had previously given the teacher permission to use his tools, so the teacher did not think that the engineer would mind. The teacher walked in, unannounced, to the teacher's apartment, and found no one home. He went downstairs looking for the tools, but along the way he saw tickets to an upcoming concert, and decided to take those instead.

Question 91

What is the most serious crime that the teacher can be charged with?

(A) embezzlement
(B) larceny
(C) burglary
(D) robbery

Question 92

If the teacher honestly believed that the concert tickets were his, because he thought the engineer had purchased them for him, what may he be charged with?

(A) embezzlement
(B) larceny
(C) burglary
(D) no crime, since the teacher thought the tickets belonged to him

Question 93

In which scenario would a defendant most likely be guilty of murder?

(A) The defendant, thinking it would be a funny practical joke, throws a small firecracker into a fairly crowded movie theatre. The victim, an elderly lady with a weak heart, hears the firecracker and assumes someone is firing a gun. She becomes frightened and suffers a heart attacking, dying shortly thereafter.

(B) The defendant likes to keep a loaded gun around his house just for protection. One morning, running late for work, the defendant leaves the gun on the table, rather than in its usual gun drawer. Later that day, a robber breaks into the defendant's home and steals the gun, and then uses it to rob a convenience store and kill the proprietor with the defendant's gun.

(C) The defendant and his friend go to a party together and both become extremely drunk. The friend asks the defendant to borrow his car to go get more liquor, and although the defendant is perfectly aware of how drunk his friend is, the defendant

allows his friend to take the car. While on his way to the liquor store, the friend dives through a red light and collides with the victim's car, killing her.

(D) The defendant learns that her husband is having an affair with her best friend, so becomes quite angry and hurt. She knows that her husband owes a large amount of money to a debtor, and her husband refuses to pay. One night, the defendant looks out the window and sees the debtor hiding outside with a gun, right before her husband is about to leave. The defendant decides not to warn husband, who then walks outside and is shot and killed by the debtor.

Question 94

A woman was walking her dog one day, when the dog escaped from his collar and ran away. Later that same day, a pedestrian saw the dog wandering around, looking lost. The pedestrian took the dog home and placed an ad in the newspaper, describing the dog. When the woman saw the ad, she called the pedestrian and arranged to pick up her beloved dog, and agreed to pay the award described in the paper.

When the woman went to pay the pedestrian, she realized she left her wallet at home, so she asked the pedestrian to hold on to the dog for a few more minutes while she went to retrieve the wallet.

However, the pedestrian, deciding he really liked the dog and wanted one of his own, decided to keep the dog. He then went home, taking the dog with him.

The pedestrian is guilty of:

(A) false pretenses.
(B) embezzlement.
(C) larceny.
(D) larceny by trick.

Question 95

A woman knew that a man hated a victim. The woman gave the man a gun and said "hey, why don't you go kill the victim? I know you hate him!" The woman knew the gun was not loaded. The man then pointed the gun at the victim, stating "I hate your guts, prepare to die!" and pulled the trigger. Nothing happened since the gun was unloaded.

Which is the most accurate statement regarding the man and the woman's criminal liability?

(A) Neither of them are guilty of attempted murder of the victim.

(B) The woman and the man are both guilty of attempted murder of the victim.

(C) The man is guilty of attempted murder of the victim, and the woman is guilty of solicitation.

(D) The man is guilty of attempted murder and the woman is not guilty of anything.

Question 96

A man and his friend liked to go out west and practice shooting their guns. They would usually use proper targets, but as the friend was setting up new targets, the man decided to draw his pistol and quickly fired several shots at his friend's feet, aiming to miss each time. However, one bullet struck the ground and ricocheted striking the friend and killing him.

As an assistant district attorney, you must charge the man with the most serious crime that these facts will support:

(A) no crime, because the killing was accidental.
(B) involuntary manslaughter, because man did not intent to kill or injure friend.
(C) voluntary manslaughter, because man did not intend to kill or injure friend.
(D) murder, because man acted with reckless disregard for human life.

Question 97

A father was watching his son's little league game, but became quite angry at some of the umpire's calls. When the game was over, the father decided to confront the umpire over what he thought were incorrect calls. The father and the umpire had a heated argument and the father got a baseball bat from the side of the field. The father then beat the umpire to death with the baseball bat.

The father is put on trial for homicide of the umpire, and testified that during the argument, the umpire seized him by the throat, and this caused him to fear he was going to be choked to death, and that's why he used the bat on umpire.

In the following scenarios, if the jury makes the stated finding, what is the LEAST likely outcome?

(A) Conviction of no crime, but only if the jury finds that the father's life was in danger.
(B) Conviction of no crime, if the jury believes the father's testimony and finds that the father's beliefs were reasonable.
(C) Conviction for premeditated and deliberate first-degree murder, if the jury believes the father's testimony.
(D) Conviction of voluntary manslaughter, if the jury believes the father's testimony.

Question 98

A professor was attending the state fair with his daughter and her family, and was quite bored. He started wandering around the fair, and came across a psychic, who was claiming to be able to bend things with his mind.

The professor kept debunking the psychic's "tricks" and so the psychic became enraged and threatened to kill the professor with his psychic powers, by bursting his blood vessels in his brain. The professor shot and hilled the psychic.

At the professor's trial for the criminal homicide of the psychic, the professor testified that he shot the psychic because he believed it was necessary to prevent the psychic from killing him. The professor should be convicted of:

(A) Involuntary manslaughter, if the jury believes the professor's testimony and also finds that the professor's belief was reasonable.
(B) Voluntary manslaughter, if the jury believes the professor's testimony and also finds that the professor's belief was reasonable.
(C) Voluntary manslaughter, if the jury believes the professor's testimony.
(D) Murder, because no one could honestly believe that the psychic had the power to burst his blood vessels.

Question 99

A man and wife are having marital discord, and thus, file for a divorce. The wife starts the process of moving out, when she sees a police officer approaching the house. The wife knows that the man has been growing marijuana in their basement, in fact, it is one of many things leading to the divorce.

The police officer suspects the man of dealing marijuana out of his house, but does not have a warrant to search the home. He sees the wife walking out of the house with a box, and politely asks if he can search the house. She says "sure" and gets in her car with the box, and drives away.

A police officer enters the home and finds marijuana in the basement. At the man's trial for drug possession, he seeks to suppress the marijuana, arguing that the search was illegal. Will he succeed?

(A) Yes, because the officer had no warrant.
(B) Yes, if the wife no longer had authority to consent to the search.
(C) No, because the wife consented to the search.
(D) No, because man had a reasonable expectation of privacy in his home.

Question 100

An officer is on routine patrol when he sees a boat docked and leaking oil. He pulls over and docks, and boards the boat. He immediately enters the engine room, and sees large quantities of cocaine.

The owner of the boat is on trial for possession of cocaine, and seeks to suppress the cocaine. Will he be successful?

(A) Yes, because the officer had no warrant.
(B) Yes, because the officer entered the engine room.
(C) No, because officer had reason to be on the boat due to the leak.
(D) No, because there is no expectation of privacy in a boat.

Question 101

A woman decides that she has had it up to here with financial woes and bank fees, and in order to pay next month's rent, she hatches a scheme to rob a bank. She asks a friend to drive her to the bank, and her friend agrees. The friend drives the woman to bank, and parks the car and waits. The woman goes in, pulls a gun on the teller, and demands all the money in the till. The teller turns over the money to the woman, and the woman runs back to the parking lot and gets in her friend's car. The friend is quite alarmed to see the woman carrying bags with money signs on them.

What can the friend be charged with?

(A) attempted robbery
(B) robbery
(C) conspiracy to commit robbery
(D) nothing

Question 102

A man is recklessly swerving his car in and out of lanes on a windy road when he sideswipes a woman's car. As the road is windy and on a hillside, the woman's car falls down the side of the hill, into an embankment, severely injuring her. Luckily, the woman survives. At trial, the man testifies that he did not intend to harm anyone, he was merely trying out what his new and fast car could do on such a road.

The man can be convicted of:

(A) attempted murder
(B) attempted involuntary manslaughter
(C) voluntary manslaughter
(D) battery

Question 103

A pedestrian is casually walking down the street, when he sees the victim, intoxicated, stumbling around in a well-lit paddock where a farmer keeps his prized bull. The pedestrian watches the victim make a few unsuccessful attempts at climbing over the fence, and out of the paddock, when he decides to help out victim. The pedestrian climbs into the paddock, and tries to lead the victim towards the gate he entered. The victim becomes belligerent, shouting that he doesn't need any stinking help. The pedestrian, angered at the lack of gratitude, leaves, exiting the paddock by the gate and closing it after him. The bull, enraged after the commotion, gores the victim to death.

If the pedestrian is prosecuted for the homicide of the victim, the jury should find him:

(A) guilty, because he violated the general duty to come to the aid of another person in peril.
(B) guilty, because his aborted rescue attempt left victim in a worse position than before he acted.
(C) not guilty, because he had no legal duty to aid victim.
(D) not guilty, because he had no intent to harm victim.

Question 104

A candidate was running for the office of mayor. After receiving a reliable tip, the city attorney began investigations into the candidate's campaign contributions. During the investigation, the city attorney demanded and received the candidate's bank records and telephone records, both from the bank and telephone company, respectively. The investigation eventually led to the candidate being prosecuted for failing to comply with state laws requiring public disclosure of all campaign contributions.

The candidate is now seeking suppression of the bank and telephone records. Will he succeed?

(A) Yes, because a search warrant should have been secured prior to the seizure of the bank and telephone records.
(B) Yes, because the seizure of the records constituted a violation of candidate's reasonable expectation of privacy.
(C) No, because the relative ease with which the records could be destroyed created an exigent circumstance.
(D) No, because both the bank and telephone records were records belonging to the business in which candidate had no reasonable expectation of privacy.

Criminal Law and Procedure

Answer 1

(B) Miranda warnings are only necessary when an admission is made during custodial questioning. Whether questioning is custodial is determined by whether the person reasonably believes they are able to leave. The daughter was not in custody, hence, the admission did not need to be preceded by Miranda warnings, making (C) incorrect. (A) is factually correct, since the daughter did volunteer the statement. However, custody needs to be established first. (D) is incorrect because the daughter was not in any way coerced into giving a statement.

Answer 2

(D) Since the baby was in the wife's womb when the husband harmed it, the baby is not legally considered a "human being"; therefore, the husband should not be found guilty of any of the listed offenses. The majority view is that a fetus becomes a human being when it is born and establishes "independent circulation." Some states (i.e., California) have enacted statutes to make the killing of a fetus murder, but this is not the rule on the MBE. If a fetus was considered a human being, the husband would have to have intent for (A) or (B) to be correct. At the most, it may be inferred that his actions were reckless, without regard to human life, which would be (A) not (B). If his actions were merely criminally negligent, the answer would be (C). In addition, if the jury considers this a heat of passion crime, it will be mitigated from murder to manslaughter. However, since all homicide requires a death of a human, none of those are correct answers. Your personal beliefs might not coincide with this answer, and that is ok. However, sometimes on the MBE, when questions or issues are a bit controversial, you must put those personal feelings aside and remember what the law is under common law.

Answer 3

(A) The failure to act may constitute a breach of legal duty. A defendant will be found criminally liable if he was under a duty imposed by (1) statute, (2) a special relationship, (3) a voluntary obligation of responsibility, or (4) contract. The obligation must be proved beyond a reasonable doubt. In this case, the co-worker voluntarily undertook the responsibility to care for the baby. The question stem asks what is most accurate, and this is an exact statement of law. (C) is what the prosecution must prove; it is not the best argument. Although one is not generally under a duty to rescue a stranger (Choice D), the infant was not a stranger to the coworker. Because the facts do not match the answer, i.e., the infant is not a stranger, it is a bad answer, and should be eliminated right away. (B) is incorrect because whether the co-worker's actions met the requirements for involuntary manslaughter (criminal negligence) can be a matter of debate, therefore it would not be the best answer since the question asks what is most accurate. In addition, if the coworker does have a legal duty, it would likely be murder, not manslaughter, he would be charged with.

Answer 4

(A) Assault is the intentional creation of a reasonable fear in a victim that she is in danger of imminent bodily harm. While the man might be guilty of assault, every state also has an aggravated assault statute, which is a more serious crime. Aggravated assault includes assault with a deadly weapon and assault with the intent to rape or murder. The neighbor's testimony states that the man intended to rape the saleswoman, thus fulfilling the elements of aggravated assault, thus (B) plain assault, is incorrect. Since the testimony that the saleswoman manifested assent to the sexual act was accepted by the jury, the man cannot be convicted of rape (C) because rape requires penetration without consent.

If the jury believes the neighbor's testimony that the saleswoman consented, this negates the requisite element of rape. In addition, the elements of a kidnapping were not present. Kidnapping requires movement or concealment of the victim (D).

Answer 5

(C) Under the Miranda rule, a person must be informed of his rights to remain silent, to presence of counsel, and to the appointment of counsel at public expense, and told that his statements may be used against him. This rule applies only when the interrogation takes place in custody. (C) is the correct answer (least persuasive) because the Supreme Court has held (*Colorado v. Spring*, 1987) that the defendant need not be told the subject the authorities intend to question him about even if charges are not related. Justice Powell noted that the Miranda warnings inform a suspect that "anything" he says may be used against him. (A) is not correct because one may be considered "in custody" although in his own home. In *Orozco v. Texas* (1969), the court held that a person questioned in his bedroom at 4:00 A.M. was deprived of his freedom of action and, therefore, was in custody for Miranda purposes. (B) is incorrect because when a person is confined to jail for any reason, regardless of its relationship to the subject matter of the questioning, that person is in custody and Miranda will apply (*Mathis v. United States* (1968)). Although (D) is not a persuasive argument, it is more persuasive than (C) because it is true that Miranda applies to both inculpatory and exculpatory statements. An inculpatory statement is one tending to establish guilt, while an exculpatory statement tends to exonerate guilt. The Court in *Connecticut v. Barrett* (1987) ruled that police may question a suspect after he says he is willing to make an oral statement but not a written statement. Please keep in mind that when you get questions like this that ask for the least persuasive, you are not being asked to pick a right or wrong answer, but rather, out of the options, which is going to help you the LEAST. It's very important to pay attention to answering what the question is asking.

Answer 6

(C) Common law larceny consists of a taking and carrying away of personal property of another by trespass with intent to deprive. The man's actions constituted common law larceny; therefore, (D) is not correct. (A) and (B) are not correct because at common law both burglary and arson involve the dwelling of another. The man did not commit common law burglary or arson because the dealership is a business establishment and not a "dwelling."

Answer 7

(B) The man can be charged as an accomplice of the murder of the witness inside the house. The friend is liable for murder under the felony murder rule, because he killed a witness in the commission of the felony of larceny. An accomplice is liable for any probable or foreseeable result of a crime that he has assisted. The murder of a witness is a foreseeable result of such a crime and, as a result, the man can be charged with the same offense as the friend. (A) is legally correct but not the best answer. The man will be liable for the attempt on his boss's life, but murder is a more serious offense than attempted murder, and that is what the question is asking for; the most serious offense, not any offense!

Answer 8

(D) Since receiving stolen property is a misdemeanor, the boyfriend could not be an accessory after the fact for helping to hide the friend. The Multistate people like to trick you with fine-line distinctions. They want you to choose (C). There are three basic elements necessary to render a person an accessory after the fact: (1) a complete felony must have been committed, (2) the aider must have knowledge of the crime, and (3) the aid must be given with the purpose of impeding law enforcement. Though the woman is guilty of robbery, a felony, the friend is guilty only of receiving stolen property, a misdemeanor defined by the Model Penal Code Section 223.6 as: purposely receiving, retaining, or disposing of movable property of another knowing that it has been stolen, or believing that it probably has been stolen, unless the property is held with the intention of restoring it to the true owner. Because the friend's crime was a misdemeanor, and the boyfriend aided in that crime, he cannot be charged as an accessory after the fact. (A) and (B) are both incorrect because the boyfriend did not act as a principal.

Answer 9

(C) is the correct answer. In order to be guilty of an offense, a person must have knowledge that he has committed the prohibited act. People will generally not be held strictly liable for acts they did not know they were committing. Since the man was unaware that he was carrying explosives, he cannot be prosecuted for possessing them, thus (A) is an incorrect answer. Larceny is defined as a trespass by the taking and carrying away of the property of another with intent to deprive the owner of that property. For larceny to have occurred, the offender must have interfered with the victim's "possession" of the property as distinguished from the "custody" of it. When the man took the bag from the woman, he obtained custody of it, and she retained possession; he then carried it away with the intent to steal it, making him guilty of larceny. Larceny by trick has occurred where the true owner willingly surrenders possession of the property under false pretenses. The man never obtained possession of the luggage from the woman, he only had custody; therefore he has not committed larceny by trick, which makes answer (D) incorrect. (B) is incorrect because embezzlement is the fraudulent conversion of misappropriation of the property of another by one who is already in lawful possession, such as an employee or a bailee. Here, the man never had legal possession of the suitcase.

Answer 10

(D) This question presents a fine-line distinction between depraved-heart murder and involuntary manslaughter. Both offenses involve (1) an unintentional killing (2) caused by a negligent act. The difference between the two is the degree of negligence. Under depraved-heart murder, the defendant should have known his actions created a very high degree of danger and risk. Involuntary manslaughter is satisfied by lesser degree of negligence than depraved-heart murder. In this question, a reasonable person would realize that another person was likely to enter the tunnel; therefore, the man can be convicted of murder. Had the man shot the pistol in the same place at 3:00 A.M., when the stadium was deserted, and killed a homeless person sleeping in the tunnel, he would probably be guilty of the lesser charge of involuntary manslaughter. In addition, the question is asking for the most serious offense, so even if there is a debate between depraved-heart and involuntary manslaughter, depraved-heart will always win, IF there is a chance that the act could rise to the level of recklessness needed for depraved-heart murder.

Answer 11

(B) For this question, students should be able to distinguish between murder, voluntary manslaughter, and involuntary manslaughter. Murder is the unlawful killing of a human being with malice aforethought. Under the depraved-heart murder rule, extremely negligent conduct resulting in death that a reasonable person would know creates a high risk of death is murder. The defendants should be charged with murder in (B) and (D) under this rule because their actions were so reckless that a death was likely to result. Though the facts may make the situation in (C) seem negligent to the point of a depraved heart, it would not have been reasonable for the defendant to be aware of the stowaway in the back of the truck. Also, it is much less reckless than the other two options. Lastly, voluntary manslaughter is an intentional killing prompted by an adequate provocation. Most courts have only recognized two types of

provocation: (1) exposure to deadly force and (2) discovery of a spouse in bed with a stranger. Therefore choice (A) would be voluntary manslaughter, not involuntary. That leaves (B) as the correct choice since involuntary manslaughter involves criminal negligence or an unlawful act causing death. Involuntary manslaughter is an appropriate charge when a reasonable person would not have assumed the action might result in death, which is applicable here where the defendant was negligent in shooting the truck, but not so negligent to rise to the level of depraved heart.

Answer 12

(D) Larceny, at common law, is defined as a trespass by the taking and carrying away of the tangible personal property of another with intent to deprive the person of that property. At common law, intangibles could not give rise to larceny; therefore, entering the baseball stadium did not constitute larceny. Written instruments that represent property rights are not considered tangible under the common law. By taking the deed, the husband did not obtain title to the man's casino; therefore, he did not commit larceny. Forgery is the making or altering of a false writing with intent to defraud. A subject of forgery must have a legal significance, such as a deed or contract. Writings that derive their value by the fact of their existence, such as writings of historical or artistic value, cannot be the subject of forgery. The husband's poster is valued for its historic value; therefore, it could not be the subject of forgery. He may be liable if charged with misrepresentation, depending on what he said at the time of the sale. (D) is correct because theft of services is not larceny under common law. Many states have made it a crime by statute.

Answer 13

(A) Larceny is a trespass by the taking and removing of property from the possession of another without consent and with the intent to steal that property. The plumber's actions satisfied all the requisite elements of larceny. Larceny is the only one of the listed offenses that the plumber could be convicted of and therefore is also the most serious offense of which he should be convicted. (B) is inapplicable because robbery is a taking of the personal property of another directly from that person by force or intimidation. Here, there is no force, so robbery would not be applicable. (C) and (D) are not applicable, because burglary is defined, at common law, as a breaking and entry into the dwelling of another at night with the intent to commit a felony. A structure is a dwelling if used regularly for sleeping, even if those sleeping in the dwelling are temporarily absent. A building is not considered a dwelling if unoccupied by residents. In this question, Boca

Towers would not be considered a dwelling, and the plumber could not be found guilty of burglary.

Answer 14

(C) Battery is an unlawful use of force against another, resulting in bodily injury or an offensive contact. Many statutes distinguish between battery, a misdemeanor, and aggravated battery, a felony. Battery becomes aggravated if a deadly weapon is used or serious bodily injury is caused, or if the victim is a child, police officer, or woman. When he hit his teacher, this constituted a battery. Intent is not an element of the criminal charge of battery; therefore, the friend should be found guilty of aggravated battery. In addition, the son should be found guilty of rape, as he intentionally forced himself on his ex-wife. This may be obvious, and in fact, is the answer choice in all but (D). The only question left for you to decide is what the friend should be found guilty of. (B) is incorrect because larceny is defined as the taking and transporting of property from another by trespass with the intent to permanently deprive that person of the property. The key to this question is intent. The friend's intoxication was voluntary, and voluntary intoxication may be a defense to a crime that requires intent if the intoxication made the perpetrator incapable of forming such intent. Although the friend took the jacket, he was so intoxicated that he might not have intended to effectuate a deprivation. Though it is possible that a jury could convict the friend of larceny, because they might find he was able to form the intent, it is not as certain as battery, making (C) the better answer.

Answer 15

(C) The intent required to prove embezzlement may be negated by a claim of right or by an intent to restore the exact property. Here, the player thought that the helmet had been given to him. In general, (C) ignorance or a mistake of fact may excuse an action otherwise a crime by negating the state of mind required. For a crime requiring a general intent the mistake must be reasonable. For a specific intent crime any mistake of fact will excuse the action whether reasonable or not. Embezzlement is a specific intent crime. The elements of embezzlement are a (1) fraudulent (2) conversion of (3) the property (4) of another (5) by one who has been entrusted with the item. The player had been a bailee, i.e., he had been entrusted with the item, of the helmet while he was using it. While the player did convert the property of another, by giving the helmet away, the player believed that the helmet had been given to him (his mistake of fact) so he did not act fraudulently. Therefore, he did not commit embezzlement.

Answer 16

(C) Larceny by trick is the (1) taking and transporting of (2) another's personal property (3) when possession of that property was obtained by fraud (4) with intent to steal. For the Multistate exam, students are required to make the fine-line distinctions between larceny by trick, false pretenses, and embezzlement. To satisfy the requirements of larceny by trick, defendant must only obtain possession. False pretenses applies when defendant fraudulently obtains *title*. Defendant must have been given possession under a trust for embezzlement to apply.

Answer 17

(D) Voluntary intoxication is only a defense to a crime when it negates an element of the crime. The elements that it may negate are usually specific intent or knowledge. Rape is an offense that requires only a general intent, and not a specific one. A general intent will be present if the offender intended to perform the "bad act." Student will most likely be found guilty of rape because he intended to have intercourse with the cheerleader and because his mistaken belief that she consented was unreasonable. Specific intent requires that the offender intended to do even more than the "bad act" actually committed. An honest mistake of fact, no matter how unreasonable, will serve to negate a specific intent. All "attempt" crimes require the specific intent of the offender to commit the entire crime he is charged with attempting. For the student to be convicted of attempted rape he must have had the specific intent to rape the cheerleader. Such intent may be negated by his intoxication and the honest belief that she consented to acquit him of the charge.

Answer 18

(C) Voluntary intoxication is a defense to a crime when it negates the existence of an element of the crime. Thus (A) is wrong. If the girl was so inebriated that she was unable to form the intent required for larceny, intoxication may by a successful defense. (B) is incorrect because in this case she would still have had the intent to take the coat. (D) is an incorrect statement of the law.

Answer 19

(C) In this question the statute requires that the burning be done maliciously. This makes maliciousness an element of the crime. If the girl didn't act maliciously she will not be guilty of arson under this statute.

Answer 20

(D) The elements of robbery are (1) a taking (2) of personal property of another (3) from the other's person or presence (4) by force or intimidation

(5) with intent of permanent deprivation. The inside man was not successful in using fear or in effectuating a deprivation; thus, the elements of robbery have not been fulfilled, and neither of the men had committed robbery. Please be aware that withdrawal (A) is only a defense where the accomplice not only renounces the crime but also takes sufficient steps to neutralize any assistance or material he has provided before the commission of the crime can no longer be prevented. Once the inside man was inside the store, the lookout's withdrawal was ineffective.

Answer 21

(C) A person may use deadly force in self-defense if she is without fault in creating the situation, confronted with unlawful force, and threatened with imminent death or great bodily harm. (A) and (D) are not good answers and are factually spurious; The plumber's response was irrational. (B) is incorrect since the elements required for man to be guilty of murder are missing.

Answer 22

(C) Statutory rape is the carnal knowledge of a female under the age of consent. The age of consent generally varies from sixteen to eighteen years old. This is a strict liability crime, in which the defendant's intent is irrelevant. A mistake as to the woman's age, no matter how reasonable, is not a defense. Rape is the unlawful carnal knowledge of a woman by a man who is not her husband. As there are no defenses mentioned in this fact pattern, the sergeant is likely to be convicted of rape as well. Also of note is that the answer choice says IF he completed intercourse. If he did not actually have intercourse with the girl, there would be no rape, and since statutory rape is a strict liability crime, he could not be charged with "attempted" statutory rape.

Answer 23

(C) The elements of robbery are (1) a taking (2) of personal property of another (3) from another's presence (4) by force or intimidation (5) with intent to permanently deprive him of it. The element of "force or intimidation" is missing in (C). The prosecution should charge the defendant with larceny in such a fact pattern. It is important to note that the question is asking in which case is the defendant LEAST likely to be convicted of robbery, which means you have to change your mindset and look for the three options that would satisfy robbery, and then pick the answer that doesn't satisfy robbery.

Answer 24

(C) Conspiracy is an agreement between two or more persons formed with the objective to commit an unlawful act. The man and his friend never entered into an agreement to steal a DVD player, thus there can be no conspiracy. (A) is incorrect because the friend did not ask the man to STEAL a DVD player, but rather mentioned he would like one. (B) might be correct if the question was asking about whether the friend could be found guilty of receiving stolen property, but not conspiracy. (D) is incorrect because HAD the man and his friend entered into an agreement to steal a DVD player, it would not matter that the man, and not the friend, was the primary actor; they would both be guilty of conspiracy to commit larceny.

Answer 25

(C) Under the common law, withdrawal is not recognized as a valid defense to conspiracy because the conspiracy is complete as soon as the parties agree to commit the crime.

Answer 26

(B) A person may limit her liability for subsequent acts of the other members of a conspiracy if she withdraws. In order to withdraw, she must perform an affirmative act that notifies all members of the conspiracy and gives them an opportunity to abandon their plans. It is not necessary that she thwart the objective of the conspiracy. Because she announced her intent to quit, she effectively withdrew.

Answer 27

(C) Conspiracy is defined as an agreement between two or more persons with the specific intent to commit an unlawful act. If there is no agreement, there is no conspiracy. This requires a close reading of the call of the question: Though you may think that the woman entered into an agreement with the neighbor, it is still her best defense to argue that no agreement was made. Remember, the question is not asking if plotter will prevail, but what is the BEST defense. It's easy to get frustrated when you do not think an answer is 100 percent correct, but sometimes it does not have to be. When the question is asking for the "best" or "least likely," pay careful attention.

Answer 28

(C) The girl would be found guilty of conspiracy to commit larceny because she entered into an agreement with the driver to carry out their criminal objective. The girl would also be found guilty of attempt. Attempt requires the specific intent to bring about a criminal result and a significant overt act in furtherance of that intent. The girl removed the book from the shelf—a significant overt act—with the intent to take it from the store, thereby committing attempted larceny. (A) is incorrect because the girl did not ONLY conspire, but also had the requisite intent AND took necessary steps towards larceny, as stated above. (B) is incorrect for the same reason. She also committed conspiracy, not JUST attempted larceny. (D) is incorrect because they did not actually commit larceny.

Answer 29

(A) Burglary is the breaking and entering into the dwelling place of another, with an intent to commit a felony therein. Entry obtained by fraud will satisfy the "breaking" requirement of burglary. The man must have also intended to commit a crime inside; in this case that crime is the theft of the homeowner's wallet. (D) is incorrect because if he entered with the intent to take a pet, that could still be a felony, as it could still be larceny. (C) is incorrect for the reasons stated above; constructive breaking, which is what happened when he showed false identification

Answer 30

(C) A person may justifiably use deadly force in self-defense if he has a reasonable belief that it is necessary to prevent his own unlawful death or serious bodily harm. However, an initial aggressor, who instigated the attack, is not entitled to self-defense. The amount of force allowed in self-defense must also be in proportion to the threat. The right to use deadly force will generally not be justified against an unarmed aggressor. The girl reasonably believed that her life was threatened when the father lunged toward her with a bat, and she was not the initial aggressor, despite the father's belief. You also have to make a bit of a leap in this question, and realize that (C) says "because a baseball bat is a deadly weapon" is the right answer because, since the father was using a deadly weapon, self defense is an appropriate defense. (A) is incorrect for the reasons stated above. (B) is incorrect because it does not go far enough; actions resulting in someone's death can constitute murder, but that is not enough. Remember that for an answer to be correct, it has to be completely correct.

Answer 31

(B) An accessory before the fact is one who aids, abets, counsels, or otherwise encourages the commission of a felony, but is not present at the scene. Under the common law, the accomplice must have had the intent to help to encourage the principal to commit the crime charged. Since the broker did not know of the trader's criminal history, he lacked the mental state (*mens rea*) to assist in a crime.

Answer 32

(D) A defendant is justified in defending another person with reasonable force only if he reasonably believes the victim had a right to use such force. The businessman was trying to rescue the woman and, therefore, assumes her privilege of self-defense. (A) is incorrect because that is a correct statement of law in regards to assault. If the man's fear was immediate and reasonable, the businessman can be guilty of assault, so the answer does not make sense. It also does not take into account the issue of self-defense. (B) is incorrect for two reasons (1) it is doubtful that an umbrella is deadly force, in which case, the answer is not factually correct and (2) even if it is deadly force, if the businessman was justified because he thought the woman's life was in danger.

Answer 33

(C) Voluntary intoxication cannot negate a crime but can negate an element of that crime. In this question the element is "maliciousness." Read the statute in the fact pattern carefully. A quick reading could lead to selecting (B), but "intent" is not mentioned in the statute. It is important to note that intent and maliciousness are not always the same thing. (D) is incorrect because even if the person selling the beer was held liable, that would not serve as a defense for the drinker.

Answer 34

(C) This is the most logical argument. (A) and (B) cannot be correct because intent is not an element of arson in the statute. (D)—even if true—would not relieve the drinker's culpability.

Answer 35

(A) The Constitution requires that all searches and seizures be conducted pursuant to a valid search warrant unless some exception exists. If the smoker allowed the police to enter the smoker's home, that is consent, which is an exception to the warrant requirement. That consent must be a voluntary and intelligent decision made without coercion. Though consent may be revoked, the facts in this case do not support that. The smoker opened the door and assented to the policemen's entrance. (B) is incorrect because it is not factually correct, as the search was done before the arrest. (C) and (D) are irrelevant if the smoker consented to the search.

Answer 36

(C) The father would be found guilty of felony murder since the fireman's death resulted as a natural consequence of his felonious conduct. Felony murder is an unintentional killing proximately caused during the commission or attempted commission of a serious or inherently dangerous felony. The father would be held accountable since it was foreseeable that firefighters would come to the house and could be endangered. (D) is incorrect. Voluntary manslaughter consists of an intentional homicide committed under extenuating circumstances

Answer 37

(D) An act must be voluntary, or the result of extremely gross negligence behavior, to be considered criminal. If he defendant received an electrical shock, then the punch was beyond his control, and thus neither voluntary nor extremely gross negligence.

Answer 38

(D) This question tests you on the defenses to battery. Don't jump to answer choices that just test your knowledge of the elements of battery, make sure you look for any defenses that may apply. Justification is a valid defense for battery. The snowboarder was justified in touching the skier to prevent more serious injury.

Answer 39

(A) The accused does not have a right to counsel during photo identifications, therefore the identification is admissible.

Answer 40

(D) An accessory before the fact is responsible for the crimes he did or counseled and for any crimes committed in the course of committing the crime contemplated, so long as the other crimes were probable or foreseeable. Here, since he hired a hit man to kill the wife, it was foreseeable that someone else, such as a boyfriend, could also be killed. (B) is incorrect, because although it talks about forseeability, which is the ultimate issue, it comes to the incorrect conclusion.

Answer 41

(D) The neighbor did not have authority to use the apartment on New Year's Day, nor did he have the authority to permit a search. It would have been different if it was reasonable for the police to believe that the neighbor had authority to use the apartment during that time, but there is nothing in the facts to suggest that this is the case. Especially since the facts tell us that the neighbor was in the hallway, which would not give the police any reason to believe he owned or lived in the apartment. Had he been in the apartment, and let them in, the police might have the argument that they had every reason to believe he had authority to consent, but that is not the case here. (B) and (C) are incorrect because even if the police had probable cause, they would still need to obtain a warrant, or find an exception to the warrant requirement.

Answer 42

(B) Police may conduct a full search of a person as incident to a lawful arrest, with or without probable cause. Note that students may be tempted to pick (D), but remember, as long as the arrest is valid (no matter how "minor" the offense), so is the search. It may also be tempting to think that one cannot be arrested for minor things like speeding, but if the fact pattern says it is a valid arrest, believe that it is. (A) is legally incorrect. You need more than reasonable suspicion, you would need probable cause for a warrant, and for most warrant exceptions (except stop and frisk) the police officers would need probable cause as well. (C) is incorrect because the search incident to a lawful arrest has nothing to do with drugs, so there is no need for the officer to be in suspicion of drugs. Searches incident to a lawful arrest are done to search for weapons, and if while searching for weapons, drugs are found, they are admissible.

Answer 43

(A) The grandson is guilty of criminal homicide, although the examiners are not asking you to pick what kind of homicide, since here it could be either murder or voluntary manslaughter. In jurisdictions that find that this kind of "suffering sympathy" of a loved one constitutes adequate provocation, the grandson could be guilty of voluntary manslaughter. In those jurisdictions that view this as a premeditated intentional killing, the grandson would be guilty of murder. Also note that (C) is irrelevant, since the question is asking about homicide, and as stated above, even if the charges are mitigated because he acted out of compassion and love, voluntary manslaughter is still homicide. (D) is incorrect because the grandson had a duty to rescue the grandma if he put her in such peril. (B) is incorrect, and probably the wrong answer that most students pick. It does not matter that he actually prolonged her life, since he still caused her death. It also does not matter that she would have died had he left her there, since he still caused her death.

Answer 44

(B) The elements of burglary are (1) breaking (2) and entry (3) into the dwelling, (4) of another (5) at night (6) with intent to commit a felony. The man should assert the defense that he did not intend to commit a felony, since he thought he had permission to enter the home.

Answer 45

(C) Larceny is the taking and asportation (carrying away) of property from the possession of another person without consent and with intent to steal. The "intent to steal" element was satisfied in this choice. The defendant took a car that he knew belonged to another. A mistake of law, a person's honest belief that his actions do not constitute a crime, is generally not a defense. In choice (A), the defendant intended to return the car, so all necessary elements are not meant, since there was not intent to steal. In addition, in (B) the defendant thinks the car is his, and that is an applicable defense to larceny. Lastly, (D) is not larceny since the defendant believes that he is "owed" the car.

Answer 46

(C) Death caused by criminal negligence is involuntary manslaughter. The standard for criminal negligence is higher than that for civil negligence. Here, the element of "intent" is missing to invoke voluntary manslaughter or murder, (making (B) and (D) incorrect answers) since the homeowner did not intend to kill anyone. However, his actions were grossly negligent, and thus involuntary manslaughter will be the appropriate charge (also making (A) an incorrect choice).

Answer 47

(B) Statements are not admissible if made under custodial interrogation without Miranda warnings. However, a defendant may voluntarily make statements without counsel present if constitutional requirements are met. Here, the defendant asked for an attorney so all questioning must cease. However, the defendant's statements were voluntary since he proceeded to make unsolicited incriminating statements subsequent to a valid Miranda warning. By volunteering his statements, the defendant waived his right to counsel for that period of time. Read the question carefully, it said the defendant then proceeded to make many incriminating statements, and said nothing about being questioned. Be careful not to read into the facts and assume questioning was taking place. (A) is incorrect, and mixes the rules of the Fifth Amendment with the rules of the Sixth Amendment. (C) would be correct if the defendant was questioned, but he was not. (D) is legally incorrect because there was a right to counsel while being questioned, but the defendant had not been questioned.

Answer 48

(A) Murder is the unlawful killing of a human being with malice aforethought. Awareness of an unjustifiably high risk to human life will satisfy the malice aforethought element, often referred to as "depraved-heart" murder. Here, throwing a machete close to someone's head presents an unjustifiably high risk to human life. (D) is incorrect because consent is not a defense to murder.

Answer 49

(C) Deadly force may be used if the officer reasonably believes it is necessary to effectuate the arrest of a person that he reasonably believes has committed a felony. (A) and (D) are incorrect because a police officer is privileged to use deadly force under certain circumstances. (B) is incorrect because deadly force is not allowed in misdemeanor cases.

Answer 50

(D) This is the only choice where premeditation and intent are shown. In (A), the defendant had intent to injure but not murder. (B) involved the heat of passion and not premeditation. (C) was a case of involuntary murder.

Answer 51

(D) Deadly force may be used if it appears reasonably necessary in order for the officer to effectuate an arrest of a person he reasonably believes committed a felony.

Answer 52

(D) A private person has the same right to use force to make an arrest as a police officer except that the private person has a valid defense *only* if the person being harmed is actually guilty of the offense for which the arrest is being made.

Answer 53

(C) Death caused by criminal negligence is involuntary manslaughter. The negligence must be more grievous than the "reasonable man" standard required for civil liability. Since the driver did not intend to kill the coworker, the element of "intent" is missing; therefore, he cannot be charged with voluntary manslaughter or murder ((B) and (D)). Also, since there was criminal negligence, (A) is incorrect as well.

Answer 54

(C) The statute specifically provides that the offense must be perpetrated "knowingly." Therefore, knowledge must be an element of the crime. Since the jury believed the defendant's story, they must acquit him of the crime. This is an example of a specific intent crime.

Answer 55

(D) An act must be voluntary, or the result of extremely gross behavior, to be criminal. The defendant's kick was beyond his control. The question asks in which scenario would the defendant LEAST likely be convicted. Here, since the kick was beyond the defendant's control, he cannot be convicted. In the other answer choices, conviction is at least possible.

Answer 56

(B) Bigamy is not a strict liability offense. Only the wife could have had the requisite intent to commit bigamy since she knew she was already legally betrothed. The man has a valid defense of mistake of fact because he had no idea that the wife was legally married. He will not be held guilty.

Answer 57

(C) The evidence was the fruit of an unlawful search because a warrant was not obtained. Without a warrant, there needs to be a warrant exception. It might be tempting to think that consent was given here, but the tenant only consented to let the officer use the bathroom. (B) is incorrect because even though tenant consented to let officer use the restroom, that does not mean the officer can then search the entire apartment. It is also for this reason (A) is incorrect, as well as (D).

Answer 58

(C) Larceny by trick is the taking of property from possession of another, with consent obtained by fraud and with intent to steal. (C) is the only choice satisfying all the elements of the crime charged. (A) is incorrect because larceny requires an intent to steal, but defendant did not intend to steal the money. The elements of false pretenses (Choices (B) and (D)) are (1) a lie concerning a material fact, (2) intending to defraud the true owner, and (3) causing the owner to transfer title. In (B), the victim did not transfer title, and the loan was repaid. In (D), the defendant originally intended to return the money; therefore, the defendant did not make a misrepresentation.

Answer 59

(C) Since the defendant intended to seriously injure the opponent, he is liable for his act resulting in death. Remember that intent to cause serious bodily injury is one way you can be charged with murder. Also, this question asks for the MOST serious offense, so when you encounter a question like this, remember to start with the most serious crime, see if the facts would support a conviction of that crime, and work your way down.

Answer 60

(B) A car may not be stopped merely because it is old and has a bumper sticker the police dislike. The police need to have reasonable suspicion to pull over a vehicle. Thus, the search was not valid. (A) is incorrect because had the car been lawfully stopped, the police officer MIGHT have had reason to look around. (C) is incorrect because it does not state the correct facts; there was no plan, as "cars that don't belong here" is not a valid plan. A border stop or DUI stop, where the cars are not stopped at random, is acceptable, but stopping cars that "don't belong" is not. (D) is incorrect because, again, the police did NOT have reasonable suspicion based on a hippie bumper sticker.

Answer 61

(A) Intent to commit a crime is an element of conspiracy. Conspiracy requires an agreement, the object of which is to commit a crime, or requires that a crime be committed. The roommate's taking of the wrong car was a mistake of fact, which is a defense for larceny, no matter how unreasonable. Since they did not intend to commit any crime, there can be no conspiracy. A mistake of law (D) occurs when an offender has misinterpreted the law or was ignorant of the law. Mistake of law will usually not be a valid defense. (C) is incorrect because it would not matter.

Answer 62

(D) Larceny is the taking and asportation (carrying away) of property from the possession of another person without consent, or with consent obtained by fraud with intent to steal. If the passenger honestly believed that the suitcase was his, the element of "intent to steal" would be absent and he would not be guilty of larceny. The fact that the two pieces of luggage resembled each other and that the passenger left one behind (C) may help in proving the honest mistake theory, but a person might mistakenly take luggage not resembling his own or intentionally take luggage resembling his own. Remember, the standard is the same here as for the intent to conspire. If you honestly believe the item is yours, it cannot be larceny. Also, note that all that is required is an honest belief, not necessarily a reasonable one.

Answer 63

(B) The prosecution has the burden of proving all elements of a crime beyond a reasonable doubt to obtain a conviction. A killing is not presumed to be murder (C).

Answer 64

(B) Under the M'Naghten rule, a defendant is entitled to acquittal if he proved that he possessed a disease of the mind that caused a defect of reason, causing the defendant to either (1) not know the wrongfulness of his actions or (2) not understand the nature and quality of his actions.

Answer 65

(C) The man will be guilty of murder in any of the other situations. In regard to (A), (B), and (D), a wrongdoer is responsible for any unusual conditions that make the victim susceptible to suffer worse consequences. This is similar to torts in that you take the plaintiff as you find him, so if the receptionist was particular vulnerable due to a disease or a recent operation, that does not negate causation. In (C) the death was independently caused by the fire. The man would still have been guilty of murder if the receptionist was at death's door at the time of the fire, but not if she was recovering and the FIRE, not the bullet, caused her death. Also, bear in mind that the man would still be guilty of attempted murder in this situation.

Answer 66

(D) One is liable for the crimes of other conspirators provided the crimes were committed in furtherance of the conspiracy's objectives and the crimes were a natural and probable outcome of the conspiracy. The man's killing was not related to the conspiracy even though it occurred while the conspiracy was still viable (A). (B) is false. (C) is incorrect because if the killing had been related to the conspiracy the gunman would be liable despite the fact that the killing was unplanned.

Answer 67

(C) The statute demands "knowledge." The woman did not obtain that knowledge, and therefore, cannot be guilty under the statute. The reasons for her intoxication are not relevant since the intoxication prevented her from having the requisite mental state.

Answer 68

(B) Embezzlement is the conversion of property held pursuant to a trust agreement, using the property in a way inconsistent with the terms of that trust, and with intent to defraud. Larceny is defined as the taking and carrying away of corporal personal property of another by trespass with intent to deprive that person of the property. False pretenses involves the taking of property fraudulently. Here, he had the property in trust, and used it for his own purposes, thus satisfying the elements of embezzlement. This is not false pretenses because he had the property pursuant to a trust agreement. For the same reason, it is not larceny.

Answer 69

(A) If the Act of 1985 was valid, there was no law requiring that an import duty be paid on Virgin Island Rum. Individuals cannot be charged with the attempt to violate a law that does not exist. This is the doctrine of legal impossibility. Although the captain believed she was committing a crime, people may not be prosecuted for "bad" thoughts alone. There must be an accompanying "bad act."

Answer 70

(B) The bookie does not have standing to challenge the search despite the fact that the evidence is being used against him. The search, not the stopping of the car, was improper (C) because the officer had no reason to suspect that the gambler had violated the law. However, only the gambler may prevent the evidence from being used, making (B) the better answer. As stated above, the search was not proper, therefore (A) is incorrect, and while (D) is a good reason for stopping a car, it is not a reason to conduct a search.

Answer 71

(B) Statements are admissible if made under custodial interrogation after Miranda warnings. The defendant's statements were voluntary and subsequent to a valid Miranda warning. By speaking without counsel present she waived her objection. Remember that despite the fact that she was, indeed, in custody, she was never interrogated. Both prongs are necessary for the Fifth Amendment to trigger.

Answer 72

(B) Repeal of an offense negates any action for attempt of the repealed offense regardless of the defendant's intent. This is called legal impossibility. You cannot be convicted of a law that does not exist. Each of the other choices is a bungled attempt at violating a law that is in effect.

Answer 73

(D) There was no conspiracy between the senator and the vice president to violate the statute. The language of the statute clearly places all obligations on the senator. The legislature would need to have intended to hold criminally liable the givers of the gifts for the vice president to be prosecuted.

Answer 74

(B) The remoteness in time of the player-coach drug deal would make the player's testimony insufficient grounds upon which to issue a search warrant. Since the warrant was not valid, the evidence is not admissible. Under average circumstances, (D) will be correct. How else would prosecutors prove their cases? (C) is incorrect because the jury (or other trier of fact) determines a witness's reliability.

Answer 75

(C) The defendant is liable for the unforeseen consequences of his illegal act. Intent is lacking under (A) since the defendant only intended to kill animals. The defendant may assert self-defense in (B). In (D), the statute was not enacted to prevent death and no "bad" intent or gross negligence was shown.

This leaves only (C) and, despite the fact that the defendant only intended to scare, throwing a rock at a mirror could potentially be reckless enough to trigger depraved-heart. Also note that the question asks, out of the options, what is the MOST LIKELY option to result in a murder conviction. (A), (B), and (D) will not result in a murder conviction for the reasons stated above, and (C) MIGHT, making it the best answer.

Answer 76

(B) The defendant began performing the crime when he started climbing the fence into the dealership. He also had the intent necessary to be guilty of attempt. Thus, the close proximity of the cars would indicate he was taking necessary steps toward the act itself, therefore satisfying all necessary elements of the crime. (D) is irrelevant, why would whether the cars have radios matter to the theft of the car itself? (A) merely proves that the defendant had the necessary mental state, which is part of being charged for attempt and (C) is incorrect because it is not legally true; one MAY be punished for committed attempted crimes.

Answer 77

(D) Common law murder is the unlawful killing of a human being with malice aforethought. Malice aforethought is an intent to kill or inflict great bodily injury, awareness of an unjustifiably high risk to human life, or an intent to commit a felony. The level below murder is voluntary manslaughter, an intentional killing caused by adequate provocation. (A) involves voluntary manslaughter. (B) and (C) involve either involuntary manslaughter or extremely negligent conduct. When asked questions like this, you want to consider the necessary elements for the crime being asked about, here murder, and eliminate all answer choices that will not satisfy all elements. Here, there is an argument that (D) might NOT be murder, but the other three can NOT be murder, leaving (D) the only right choice.

Answer 78

(C) A search conducted in accordance with a plan, whereby some cars are systematically stopped, is valid. Since the marijuana was seen pursuant to a valid search, the police were then empowered to arrest the driver and further search him.

Answer 79

(B) The caregiver's actions were nasty, but not the cause of the resident's death. The fact that the resident would have died from more blows but for the cancer will not impose liability for murder on the caregiver. The caregiver had not delivered those additional blows that would have killed the resident.

Answer 80

(C) The M'Naghten Insanity Test provides that a defendant is entitled to assert the defense of insanity if the proof establishes that the defendant had a disease of the mind causing a defect of reason such that the defendant lacked the ability, at the time of his actions, to either know the wrongfulness of his actions (C) or understand the nature (A) and the quality (B) of his actions. (A) and (B) are both partially correct, but a failure to understand the nature of the action will not satisfy the test without a failure to understand the quality of the action and vice versa.

Answer 81

(D) Intoxication is not a valid defense; however, if a defendant is not capable of forming the "intent" necessary for a crime his intoxication will prevent liability. Here, the defendant was too intoxicated to form the intent to commit larceny, and since there can be no attempt crime without intent, intoxication will be a defense.

Answer 82

(B) Since the man did not know of the woman's history, he lacked the mental state (*mens rea*) to assist in a crime.

Answer 83

(D) Electronic surveillance is a "search and seizure" requiring a warrant. The hotel did not possess any rights capable of defeating the defendant's expectations of privacy, and there was nothing to gain probable cause for a warrant. (C) is incorrect because it would be irrelevant to any probable cause. (A) is incorrect because the question rests on the electronic surveillance, and if that was a violation, then any fruits of that search would also be suppressed. (B) is incorrect, if such surveillance violates any right to privacy.

Answer 84

(A) is correct, the rest of the members of the family should not be found guilty. Just because they took no affirmative action to stop the crime does not make them accomplices, so (C) is incorrect. There is no legal duty to act to save someone, and just witnessing a crime does not make you an accomplice. (D) is incorrect because it speaks of a defense, and you need to make sure that the elements of a crime can be met before you discuss defenses.

Answer 85

(A) is correct. There is no obligation to retreat unless the defender intends to use deadly force. This was a tricky question because it was tempting to choose (C) since the question tells you we are in a "Retreat" jurisdiction. However, remember that the doctrine only applies to DEADLY force. (B) is incorrect because it misstates the legal doctrine, the fact that there was an occupied structure doesn't apply here. (D) is incorrect because in order to use self defense, a threat of deadly force is not necessary. Remember that if you use DEADLY force, a threat of deadly force must precede the use, but you can always use self defense so long as the force is equal to what is threatened.

Answer 86

(B) is the correct answer, as the thief carried away the possession of another. (A) is incorrect because there was no force, or threat of force; (C) is incorrect because there were no false pretenses. He only obtained possession of, not title to, the watch. Remember that in false pretenses you must obtain TITLE, not merely possession. (D) is incorrect because the thief was not in lawful possession of the watch at any time, which is a requirement of embezzlement.

Answer 87

(D) is correct. (A) is incorrect because the defendant never had lawful possession of the money and burgers, which are elements necessary for embezzlement. (B) is incorrect because the defendant never obtained title to the money or burgers, a requirement of false pretenses. (C) is incorrect because while all elements of both larceny and robbery are met, robbery and larceny are greater and lesser included offenses, meaning a defendant cannot be convicted of both, leaving (D) the correct answer.

Answer 88

(C) is the correct answer, as the mistress had intent to cause client serious bodily harm, which is one way to form the requisite intent for murder. (D) may be tempting, and the mistress's defense attorney would certainly try to argue that she should only be charged with involuntary manslaughter, but the question asks the MOST serious crime the mistress may be charged with. (A) is incorrect because a victim may not consent to homicide, and (B) is incorrect because it misstates a fact, the mistress never formed intent.

Answer 89

(D) is correct, per the statute. (A) is incorrect because a mere explanation for anger is not enough to mitigate murder to manslaughter. (B) is incorrect because the defendant's intoxicated anger prevented any deliberation, and (C) is incorrect because it is factually incorrect. He did not contemplate taking a life of another before becoming intoxicated. Pay careful attention to facts, and do not let tempting answers mislead you; ensure that they are factually, as well as legally, correct.

Answer 90

(A) is correct, because evidence will not be suppressed where the police reasonably rely in good faith that their actions are authorized by a valid warrant or a valid exception to that warrant Here, even though the parking tickets were paid, the officer had reason to believe that the arrest warrant was valid, and thus, there was cause to arrest and subsequently conduct a search incident to lawful arrest. (B) is incorrect because a car may only be searched pursuant to a valid arrest, or if there is sufficient probable cause for an automobile search. (C) is incorrect for the same reason (A) is correct; the officers had no reason to know that the arrest was not lawful. (D) is incorrect because, if there is a valid arrest, you do not need probable cause to do the search; the valid arrest is a sufficient basis.

Answer 91

(B) is correct since the teacher carried away the tickets. (A) is incorrect because the teacher never had lawful possession of the tickets, a necessary element for embezzlement. (C) is incorrect because the teacher did not enter with intent to commit a felony, a necessary element of burglary, and (D) is incorrect because there was no threat of force.

Answer 92

(D) is correct, because in order to commit larceny, you need the necessary intent, and mistake of fact, as long as it's honest, will negate the necessary elements. (A) is incorrect because for embezzlement to be the correct answer, the teacher would have had to have been in lawful possession of the concert tickets, and then misappropriate them. The facts do not state that this happened. (B) is incorrect, because there is no larceny since, as stated above, if the teacher honestly believed the concert tickets were for him, he did not have the necessary intent to commit larceny. (C) is incorrect because to commit burglary, one must break and enter with the intent to commit a felony and the teacher did not have that intent.

Answer 93

(D) is the correct answer. First, remember the question asks you in which scenario the defendant is MOST LIKELY to have committed murder. Murder is the intentional killing of a human with malice aforethought. One can satisfy the "malice" element with (1) intent (premeditation and deliberation), (2) felony murder, (3) reckless indifference to human life, or (4) intent to commit serious bodily harm. The best thing to do in these types of questions is to take each answer choice one at a time. In (A), the defendant's throwing of the firecracker has no malice. Some of you may be thinking that it is reckless indifference to human life, but generally, people are not killed by "small" firecrackers, so the likelihood of death is small, making depraved-heart murder, or reckless indifference to human life, unlikely. With (B) we have mere negligence, and maybe not even that. The defendant left his gun, in his own home, on a table. It is unforeseeable that a robber would steal it, and then use it to kill someone. Even if it IS foreseeable, that is only negligence, and not one of the four ways to achieve malice mentioned above. (C) is incorrect for very similar reasons; the defendant was perhaps negligent, and maybe even grossly negligent, which would make him guilty of involuntary manslaughter, but he has done nothing to satisfy the malice requirement. This leaves only (D), in which the defendant has special relationship with the husband, that is, he is her spouse. This creates a duty to act, and when she fails to act, knowing the husband will likely be killed, that creates the malice necessary to satisfy murder.

Answer 94

(B) The pedestrian is guilty of embezzlement. Embezzlement is the fraudulent conversion of the property of another by one who is already in lawful possession of it. Here, the pedestrian is in lawful possession of the dog since the woman gave it to him. But he has converted the dog (taking it home with him) by fraud. It is important to note that a dog is property for purposes of the MBE, no matter what little Fido might think. In addition, it IS possible to embezzle a dog since it is property. (A) is incorrect because in false pretenses, one must obtain title, and here, the pedestrian has not obtained title to the dog. In addition, neither (C) nor (D) is correct because there is no larceny, it has already been established that the pedestrian was in lawful possession of the dog, and therefore, there is no taking away.

Answer 95

(D) is the correct answer. The woman is not guilty of anything because she knew the gun was not loaded, and thus, knew that any killing was impossible. However, the man is guilty of attempted murder because he was NOT aware that the gun was not loaded, and thus, had the requisite intent, and the necessary step (pointing the gun and pulling the trigger) for attempted murder. (A) is incorrect because, as just stated, man IS guilty of attempted murder, and (B) is incorrect for the reasons just stated above; the woman did not have the requisite intent to be guilty. (C) is the answer most people pick as a wrong choice; but remember, someone cannot solicit for something they know is not a crime.

Answer 96

(D) is the correct answer. First, pay attention to the fact that the question is asking for the MOST serious crime that man can be charged with. It can be argued shooting at someone's feet, even without intending to kill or injure, is dangerous enough to constitute reckless disregard for human life, which constitutes the malice needed for murder. It can probably be argued that there is not enough recklessness, merely gross negligence to constitute involuntary manslaughter (B), but the question asks for the most SERIOUS, which here would be murder.

Answer 97

(A) is correct because the jury could find that the father's life was not actually in danger, but that the father reasonably and honestly believed his life was in danger, so he would still be able to use self-defense. Remember the question asks for the LEAST likely outcome. (B) is incorrect because if the jury believes the father, and finds his belief reasonable, the father will be permitted to use reasonable force (the baseball bat) and thus, argue self-defense. That would mean he would not be convicted of any crime, and thus, this is a possible outcome. (C) is incorrect because if the jury believes the father's testimony, but finds it unreasonable, they could convict him of murder. (D) is incorrect for the same reasons, it is a completely probable outcome. (A) is the only outcome that is NOT likely.

Answer 98

(C) is the correct answer because if the jury believes the professor's testimony, but does not find it reasonable, the professor may be convicted of voluntary manslaughter due to the fact that the professor can argue he was adequately provoked. (A) and (B) are incorrect because if the jury both believes the testimony, AND finds it reasonable, that would be valid self-defense, and therefore, the professor would be convicted of no crime. (D) is incorrect because it is not factually correct; some people might believe that the psychic did indeed have the appropriate powers.

Answer 99

(B) is the correct answer. If the wife no longer had authority to consent, the search was invalid. There was no warrant, and the only possible warrant exception would be consent. Consent can be given by anyone who has authority over the premises; essentially, one that lives there. The facts tell us that the wife was in the process of moving out, and therefore, she may no longer have consent. (A) is incorrect because, even though the office has no warrant, if the wife has authority to consent, that would be a valid exception to the warrant requirement. (C) is incorrect because it is not just that she consented, we have to analyze whether she has authority. Note that both (A) and (C) are PART of the answer; there is an issue with the wife consenting and the lack of the warrant, but (B) is the best answer because it addresses all required elements. (D) is incorrect because it is simply not correct; an expectation of privacy in his home would HELP the man, not hurt him.

Answer 100

(C) is the correct answer. The leak on the boat created a public emergency, and thus, an exception to the warrant requirement. (A) is incorrect because even though there was no warrant, as stated above, the leak created an exigent circumstance. (B) is incorrect because, given the circumstances, it was reasonable for the officer to enter the engine room. (D) is incorrect because there may be a reasonable expectation of privacy on a boat.

Answer 101

(D) is the correct answer. The friend can be charged with nothing, as she never formed the requisite intent to commit any crime. Had she known about the woman's intent, and agreed to help her rob the bank, she would be guilty of both conspiracy to commit robbery and robbery. However, as the friend is completely unaware of the woman's plan, she lacks any requisite *mens rea*.

Answer 102

(D) is the correct answer. (A) is incorrect because if we believe the man (and you do, if the facts tell you to!) he has no intent to kill or harm, and therefore lacks the requisite *mens rea* for attempted murder. (B) should have been a choice that is quite easy to eliminate because you can not attempt to do something that is involuntary. Likewise, if you pay close attention to the facts (C) should be easily eliminated since you can not have a homicide crime without a death. Here, the woman survived, and thus, there can be only attempted homicide, and as stated above, the man did not have the required intent. (D) is correct because, at most, he can be convicted of battery even though he did not have intent. It can be argued that his actions were so reckless, they were sure to bring about the result of someone being injured.

Answer 103

(B) is the right answer. (A) is incorrect because it is simply not true; there is not general duty to aid another in peril. (C) is incorrect because, although it is legally correct that there IS no duty to come to the aid of another, once you start a rescue, you cannot leave the person in a worse position than they were when you began the rescue. This is why (B) is the correct answer; the pedestrian had no duty to aid the victim, but he started to rescue him, and left him in a worse position, with an enraged bull and closed gate. (D) is incorrect because even without intent, one can be guilty of homicide.

Answer 104

(D) is the correct answer. This is difficult for most students to hear, but there is no expectation of privacy when another company holds your records, such as the telephone company or a bank. Therefore, as there was no expectation of privacy, there is no Fourth Amendment issue.

Contracts

85. Damages
86. Formation
87. Damages
88. Damages
89. Delegation
90. Specific Performance

91. Parole Evidence
92. Mailbox Rule
93. Anticipatory Repudiation
94. Modification
95. Modification

Contracts

Question 1

A yacht owner had become dissatisfied with it. Instead, he became infatuated with the magnificent yacht owned by his neighbor, who rented an adjacent slip at the dock. The yacht owner let the neighbor know that if and when the neighbor decided to sell his yacht, he would be interested in purchasing it. Several months later, the neighbor called the yacht owner and told him, "Good news, I'm buying a real boat. You can have my scrap heap for $650,000." "You have a deal," said the excited yacht owner. The neighbor immediately sent a letter confirming transfer of ownership of his yacht in three weeks for a price of $650,000 and signed it "Sincerely, your neighbor."

The neighbor's yacht was only one year old and conforming models were still in limited distribution by its manufacturer. Several days later, the neighbor's wife confessed that she had been having an affair with the yacht owner. The neighbor immediately called the yacht owner and said, "Our deal is off. You can have my wife, but never my boat. Not at any price." An identical boat was listed for sale at one million dollars. The yacht owner asserted an action demanding specific performance.

Is the yacht owner likely to prevail?

(A) No, because the agreement did not satisfy the relevant Statute of Frauds.

(B) Yes, because there was an offer and acceptance.

(C) No, because there is an adequate remedy at law.

(D) Yes, because the neighbor's letter satisfied the requirement of a writing.

Question 2

On October 19, 1987, a day that became known as "Black Monday," stock markets across the world plunged. The Dow Jones Industrial Average, which gauges the value of thirty Stock Exchange "Blue Chip" issues, declined more than 500 points. This represents 20 percent of its value. At 2 P.M., an investor decided to sell his entire portfolio. He dialed his broker but the line was busy. For the next half-hour, the investor kept redialing his broker's number but could not get through. At 2:30 P.M., the investor heard a report that many people could not reach their swamped brokers. Those who did reach their brokers still could not sell their stocks because buyers were nowhere to be found.

"My God, my stocks are worthless! I better pull my money out of the bank before the banks go, too," the investor thought. The investor ran to his bank, withdrew $100,000, stuffed the cash in his attaché case, and ran home. When he arrived home, he heard a report that the dollar had fallen to postwar lows against the Japanese yen, Swiss franc, and German mark. On that basis, the investor decided to trade in his cash for gold.

"I'd better buy some gold before this green is worthless," the investor thought. He was too exhausted to run around any more so he made his building's doorman a proposition. "I need your help. I have to invest in gold. I'll pay you $5,000 if you take this money downtown and buy as many one-ounce Canadian gold coins as they'll give you. Don't worry about the door, I'll open it for whoever comes by," the investor said. The doorman agreed to the deal, hailed a cab, and went to find that the supply of Canadian coins had already been depleted. He could not contact the investor because the apartment house's lobby did not have a phone. The doorman decided to buy one-ounce South African Krugerrands instead. The Krugerrands were composed of the same percentage of gold as the Canadian coins. When the doorman returned with the coins, the investor told him, "I can't believe you did this. I refuse to lend my support to apartheid. Forget about the money I promised you."

In an action asserted by the doorman against the investor, the trial judge should rule that the doorman's purchase of Krugerrands:

(A) failed to satisfy a condition precedent.

(B) effected a rescission.

(C) was a justifiable modification.

(D) was conditional on satisfaction.

Question 3

A buyer signed a contract with a local car dealer, on January 1. The price of the car was $42,000, including options, license fees, taxes, and dealer preparation. The buyer gave a certified check for $4,000 to the car dealer as a deposit and was told by a salesman, "Delivery time varies, but it should take no longer than three months." Later that day, as was its custom, the car dealer contracted to pay a car manufacturing company $32,000 to procure the car it had promised to the buyer. The car manufacturer promised delivery on February 28.

On January 15, the president of the car manufacturing company, who was afraid to fly, died in a train crash en route to a race in Monaco. A public concern that the manufacturing company's cars in production might decrease in quality due to the president's death caused the demand for the cars to plummet. The buyer notified the car dealership that he wanted to cancel his order. The car dealership notified the car manufacturing company that it could not accept delivery of the car the buyer had ordered because of the buyer's actions. The manufacturing company asserted an action against the buyer based on the buyer's failure to honor his contract with the car dealership.

Which of the following assertions would most aid the buyer's defense?

(A) The order was subject to the buyer's satisfaction.

(B) The car manufacturing company was not an intended beneficiary of the contract.

(C) The buyer contracted for a car built under the president's supervision, and his death rendered the contract's performance impossible.

(D) The proper suit is between the car manufacturing company and the car dealership because the car dealership was the original party to the agreement.

Question 4

A window installer was hired by a contractor to install windows in the new mayor's mansion, which was under construction. The mansion was on a cliff overlooking a beach. The agreement between the window installer and the contractor incorporated the architects' plans and specified, "The window installer agrees to purchase and install all windows, as illustrated in the attached plans, within sixty days of construction of the house's frame for the sum of $78,000, to be paid within ten days of completion of installation."

An earthquake struck the beach forty-eight days after the frame was constructed. The window installer had completed 90 percent of his work and incurred substantial expenses. The cliff on which the house rested collapsed and fell into the sea.

The window installer's best chance to recover compensation for his work will be to base his action on

(A) equitable restitution.

(B) impossibility.

(C) quasi-contract.

(D) commercial impracticability.

Question 5

After several weeks of negotiations, two friends agreed over the phone that one would buy the other's art collection. "Let me review our agreement," the buyer said to the seller. "I will purchase all seventy-four of the oils listed in your letter of last week, including their frames, for $874,000 to be paid in twenty-four monthly installments, after a down payment of $374,000."

"Exactly," said the seller. "Just apprise your lawyer of the terms and let him prepare a contract."

The buyer's lawyer prepared the contract, which provided, "The buyer agrees to purchase from the seller, and the seller agrees to sell to the buyer, the seventy-four oil paintings named below. The buyer agrees to compensate the seller $374,000 at this signing, followed by twenty-four monthly payments of $20,833.33 to be paid on the thirteenth of each month."

The buyer made the down payment, and the seller delivered the paintings without their frames. The buyer asserted an action against the seller to recover the frames. Which of the following statements is most accurate?

(A) If the contract between the buyer and the seller is ruled a total integration, evidence of their phone call agreement will be accepted.

(B) If the contract between the buyer and the seller is ruled a total integration, evidence of their phone call agreement will be accepted only if it does not contradict the writing.

(C) The question of whether a written agreement is an integration is a question of fact to be decided by the judge.

(D) The question of whether a written agreement is an integration is a question of fact to be decided by the jury.

Question 6

An owner of a chain of bookstores occupied a store in a mall. The bookstore owner's lease for this store from the landlord, the owners of the mall, provided him with 5,000 square feet of space. When the lease was about to expire, the bookstore owner devoted significant time and effort to find a suitable new site for his store. After months of negotiation, the bookstore was about to sign a lease on the new location he had found, when he received a phone call from the landlord. The landlord's representative convinced the bookstore owner to stay on by stating, "We'll give you a two-month option to renew your five-year lease." The bookstore owner subsequently paid an architect $9,000 to redesign the store and included the mall's address when preparing a $24,000 direct-mail campaign. With more than a week remaining on the option, the bookstore owner was notified by the landlord that they were revoking the option because the mall was to be demolished. The bookstore owner brought an action to compel the landlord to honor its option and the lease. Of the following arguments, which will be most persuasive in the landlord's favor?

(A) A business context will not negate a donative intent.

(B) Consideration must be given to render an option irrevocable.

(C) Plans to do remodeling in the future do not constitute a detriment.

(D) An offeror may revoke an offer at any time before acceptance.

Question 7

Of the following arguments, which would be most persuasive in the bookstore owner's favor?

(A) Promissory estoppel.

(B) An option may not be revoked if supported by consideration.

(C) The option was part of a bargained-for agreement.

(D) The bookstore owner's expenses before and after the agreement constitute consideration.

Question 8

After many months of intense bargaining, a seller sent the following letter to a buyer on January 1, 2007.

"The seller hereby offers the buyer's 10,000 dolls at $120 per dozen, shipped freight collect UPS. Terms are 50 percent down payment with acceptance, balance 2/10, net/30. This offer is not revocable and will be held open until April 30, 2007."

On April 12, the seller cabled the buyer, "The dolls offer withdrawn."

On April 15, the buyer responded to the seller with the following letter: "Accept your January 1 offer, but want dolls shipped parcel post. Will prepay."

The seller called the buyer upon receipt of the acceptance letter and said, "We are sorry. The price has doubled for the dolls, and we cannot deliver. Don't worry about this one; we'll give you a good deal on racing cars instead."

In an action brought by the buyer, the court should rule in favor of:

(A) the seller, because the buyer's counteroffer was a rejection of the seller's offer.

(B) the seller, because an offeree can demand performance only if it had extended consideration for the offer.

(C) the seller, because it could revoke the offer.

(D) the buyer, because a merchant may not withdraw an offer to sell goods when he has stated that the offer will be irrevocable.

Question 9

A movie studio mailed the following letter to a large video retailer on January 15: "Due to an oversupply, we can offer you 29,000 videos of our $50,000,000 Movie 1 for $27.50 per unit. We will also sell any quantity of Movie 2 at $59.00 per unit. Delivery for both movies in March. This offer will expire on February 15." The movie studio sent a cable to the video retailer on February 10 that

stated, "Offer regarding Movie 1 and Movie 2 is hereby revoked."

On February 15, the video retailer nonetheless cabled the movie studio: "We accept your offer, send 20,000 of Movie 1 in March, balance by April 15; 50,000 copies of Movie 2 in March." What is the legal relationship between the parties on February 16?

(A) The movie studio's February 10 cable was an effective revocation because consideration was not given for the offer.

(B) The video retailer's modification constituted a counteroffer that invalidated the original offer.

(C) The movie studio is obligated to ship Movie 2, but not Movie 1.

(D) The video retailer's February 15 cable constituted a valid acceptance.

Question 10

On March 1, a southern realtor sent a letter to a northern realtor via U.S. Postal Service Express Overnight mail stating: "We hereby offer Blackacre and all of its fixtures for $2,000,000 cash." The offer did not reach the northern realtor until March 3, and the southern realtor received a $10.75 refund from the Postal Service. On March 5, the northern realtor sent a letter via Express Mail to the southern realtor responding: "Thank you for your offer; it sounds agreeable, but would you be willing to accept $500,000 cash, monthly installments of $100,000 plus interest of 8 percent on unpaid principal?" The southern realtor sent a letter back the same day it received the northern realtor's missive: "Forget about it. Money talks; everything else walks." On March 10, the northern realtor mailed a certified check for $2,000,000 and a letter advising that the southern realtor's original offer had been accepted. The northern realtor had not yet received the southern realtor's response to its March 5 letter.

Was there a valid contract between the northern realtor and the southern realtor?

(A) Yes, as soon as the northern realtor mailed the acceptance.

(B) Yes, as soon as the southern realtor received the acceptance.

(C) No, because the northern realtor's March 5 counteroffer terminated the offer.

(D) No, because there is no evidence that a "meeting of the minds" occurred.

Question 11

A clam bar restaurant was the only restaurant of its kind in the town. The restaurant's owner, who had tired after forty years of clam baking, decided to sell the restaurant. She contacted a broker who brought the restaurant to his client's attention. When the restaurant's owner met the client and saw that the client was serious about buying the restaurant, the restaurant owner made the following offer on October 25: "I hereby offer the clam bar restaurant to the client for $1,000,000 to be received on December 15." On November 15, the client wired $1,000,000 to the restaurant owner's account and mailed a certified letter stating her acceptance of the restaurant owner's offer. On December 13, the restaurant owner told the client, "Forget our deal. There's no way I can give up the restaurant."

The restaurant owner's statement:

(A) was an anticipatory repudiation.

(B) will void any agreement.

(C) must be written to be effective.

(D) is not effective.

Question 12

A landlord owned residential property in a city. The maintenance for some of his properties became economically burdensome during the oil crisis. In 1974, the landlord decided to abandon an oceanfront apartment building when he could not find a buyer. The building rapidly deteriorated and was vandalized considerably. When the state legalized gambling, the value of the landlord's building skyrocketed. The landlord turned down several multimillion dollar offers for his abandoned building. He assumed the value would continue to rise. He had good information that the new casino was to be built to the east of his property and that another casino was to be built to the west. However, both casinos were concerned that the landlord's building would be an eyesore, and offered to pay for the building's demolition. Finally, in 2007, the landlord signed a contract to sell the land to a corporation, represented by a married couple, who planned to build a theme park and a casino on the landlord's property. "The Lord should receive money from blackjack and craps, not only from bingo," said the husband at a press conference. The landlord was to receive 3 percent of the casino's profits in exchange for his land.

The married couple was forced to resign from their corporation several months later when the corporation experienced severe financial difficulties. As part of their economic retrenchment, the corporation announced that they would not begin any new projects. The landlord's building was in worse condition than ever before. Now, it was filled with nasty graffiti criticizing the wife's makeup.

If the casino asserts an action against the corporation to compel performance of the contract with landlord, should the action succeed?

(A) Yes, because the casino suffered actual pecuniary damage and was a third-party beneficiary.

(B) No, because privity of contract is absent between a party to a contract and one who is not a party but receives a benefit from the contract.

(C) No, because the casino was an incidental beneficiary to the contract.

(D) No, because the damages to the casino were abstract and difficult to substantiate.

Question 13

A first-year student at a law school worked nights as a stripper to support herself. When her grandfather found out how the student supported herself, he became furious and called her up.

"Why didn't you tell me you needed money? Quit your job and I'll send you signed notes guaranteeing you support for the next three years. You can even use these notes for collateral if you need a loan," he said.

The student received C's in all her first-year courses. She was elated and celebrated by buying herself a brand new car. A car dealership extended her a loan to finance the car with her grandfather's notes as security. The student's grandfather died before the car had been driven 1,000 miles. The executor of the estate refused to honor the notes. The car dealership brought an action against the estate after the student defaulted on her loan and they couldn't find any other assets to seize.

Is the estate likely to prevail?

(A) Yes, because there was no bargained-for exchange between the student and her grandfather.

(B) Yes, because the validity of the notes is in issue between the estate and the student, not the car dealership.

(C) No, because the student's grandfather authorized her to use the notes as collateral.

(D) No, because the student relied on the notes, which were intended to benefit the student's creditors.

Question 14

A shipping company incorporated in a state owned six supertankers and was engaged in shipping crude and refined oil between the Persian Gulf and Europe, and Asia and North America. The shipping company signed a ten-year contract with an oil company, agreeing to ship 100,000,000 barrels of oil per year from Kuwait to New Orleans at a price of $2.05 per barrel. Cost accountants at the shipping company estimated a gross profit of nine cents per barrel on the transaction. In 1985, Persian Gulf hostilities between Iran and Iraq caused the shipping company's insurance premiums to quintuple. The shipping company continued to ship the oil company's oil despite the reality that it could not earn a profit at the $2.05 per barrel price. The oil company earned a substantial windfall when crude prices rose to $6.00 per barrel in response to the Gulf hostilities.

In 1987, the Gulf became closed to shipping. The oil company notified the shipping company that it expected the shipping company to honor its shipping agreements. The most economical means to ship the oil was to truck it 1,200 miles over land to the Saudi Arabian Ru-Ba-Khali pipeline and then on to Oman, where tankers could be filled in the safe waters of the Arabian Sea. The total shipping cost to the shipping company was approximately $8.00 a barrel.

The shipping company's best chance to suspend its agreement with the oil company is by pleading the doctrine of:

(A) mutual mistake.

(B) unilateral mistake.

(C) impossibility.

(D) impracticability.

Question 15

A fashion designer was embarrassed that his friend dressed like a slob and a pauper. The fashion designer constantly nagged his friend about his appearance. "What can I do?" his friend replied. "I am a law student. I can't afford nice clothing."

"Come on. Your father is loaded, and he gives you plenty of cash," The fashion designer replied.

"Yeah, but my girlfriend won't eat in a restaurant that charges less than $100 for dinner. I also buy lots of lottery tickets in the hope that I might be able to drop out of law school," answered his friend.

The fashion designer went to a local clothing store and ordered $400 worth of clothing for his friend. The clothing store delivered the clothing on the basis of the fashion designer's statement that, "My friend is honest, he'll pay. If he doesn't, I will."

His friend wore the clothing but could not and did not pay the bill. The clothing store brought an action against the fashion designer for $400.

Is the clothing store likely to prevail?

(A) No, because a promise to pay the debt of another must be in writing to be enforceable.

(B) No, because a suretyship agreement is within the Statute of Frauds.

(C) Yes, because the fashion designer's promise to pay for the clothing is enforceable.

(D) Yes, but only if the clothing store has exhausted its recourse against the friend.

Question 16

A rookie fullback for the a football team was excited that, after years of hard work at a high school and a state university, he finally achieved his lifetime dream of playing for a professional team. The football player purchased a condominium and a new car shortly after he signed a three-year $1,500,000 contract. On September 1, 2007, the football association decided to call a strike. The football player was called into the management office of the football team.

"We need you for our next game. This is your chance to get off the bench and become a star," the general manager said.

The football player replied, "I know, but I can't be a scab."

Management replied, "You don't want to lose your new car and condo because you can't pay your bills, do you?" The football player responded, "That's true, I don't, but I'm afraid those guys are going kill me. After the strike is resolved, every time I get tackled I'll be afraid for my life." The football player watched the next three games on TV, knowing he could have been the hero of those games.

On September 18, the football player received an envelope from the football team that said, "Inside, an offer you can't refuse." Inside the envelope a letter stated, "In exchange for five dollars which we have received from you, we hereby guarantee to give you a three-day option to accept a contract for the balance of the season at $40,000 per game."

The strike was settled on September 19. Hours after the settlement, the football player conveyed his acceptance of the September 18 offer. "The offer has been revoked. You are going to collect splinters on the bench at your regular salary," the football team told the football player. The football player then brought an action to recover $40,000 per game.

Which of the following statements is the best answer?

(A) The football player's action will succeed if he can prove he gave five dollars for the three-day option.

(B) The football player's action will succeed regardless of whether he tendered five dollars because a signed, written offer may not be revoked if it has a clause that guarantees it will stay open.

(C) The football player will not succeed because the end of the strike reinstated his previous contract and made the option impossible to perform.

(D) The football player will succeed because he made a proper acceptance of a valid offer.

Question 17

An attorney invested his life savings in a new company that manufactured tests for AIDS. The contract stipulated that the attorney was to receive 49 percent of the company's profit and provided, "This contract may not be assigned." After producing the capital for the new company, the attorney had completed his performance, and he assigned all of his rights in the company to his grandmother.

A mechanic formed a partnership with a car designer. The contract provided that the mechanic would receive 49 percent of all winnings in exchange for providing the car designer with a customized racing car. The contract between the mechanic and the car designer provided, "Rights under this contract may not be assigned." Two weeks after delivering the car and one day before its first race, the mechanic assigned all his rights in the car's profits to his grandmother.

A runner ran ten miles every morning before he went to school. One day, he wrote the following: "I am going to be an Olympic marathon champion. I hereby assign to my grandmother all proceeds from any running shoe endorsement I might receive." The runner gave this writing to her grandmother.

Which of the following grandmothers will be able to successfully enforce their assignment?

(A) the attorney's grandmother
(B) the mechanic's grandmother
(C) the runner's grandmother's
(D) none of the above

Question 18

A professor hired a research assistant to search an ancient burial site for artifacts. The professor told the research assistant, "I will pay you one hundred dollars for every day you spend digging, regardless of how many artifacts you find, so long as you spend ten hours a day digging."

The professor can terminate his offer:

(A) only after lapse of a reasonable amount of time.
(B) only by effective revocation.
(C) by either effective revocation or by lapse of a reasonable amount of time.
(D) only after giving the research assistant sufficient notice.

Question 19

A university contracted with a general contractor to build an academic building. The contract stated that all work should be completed by August 1, and contained a clause stating that "both parties are aware that classes begin the Wednesday after September 1." The building was not completed until the middle of October and the university withheld all payment. The court's decision on whether the university will be liable for the contractual price of the construction will most likely be determined by whether:

(A) the clause stating the date the school began classes is construed to make time of the essence.
(B) each party acted in good faith.
(C) the university can prove undue hardship.
(D) the contractor acted in good faith.

Question 20

A repairman spent two hours inside a homeowner's house checking all of the windows in expectation of doing repair work on them. On April 1, the homeowner wrote the repairman a letter that said, "If you strip and seal all of my windows, I will pay you $750. I promise to keep this offer open for thirty days." The repairman wrote back on April 5, "I cannot do the work for one penny less than $1,000." On April 10 the repairman wrote again, "I'll do it for $750; your silence will constitute an acceptance." The homeowner received the repairman's second letter on April 13 and chose not to

respond. The repairman performed the work on April 30. The homeowner was out of town at the time.

A contract between the repairman and the homeowner was formed on:

(A) April 10, the date the repairman mailed his letter.
(B) April 13, the date the homeowner received the repairman's offer.
(C) April 30, the date the repairman performed the work.
(D) The homeowner and the repairman did not form a contract.

Question 21

A producer signed a written agreement to purchase 100 cases of film from a film distributor. The parties had orally agreed that the contract would be voided if the producer could not obtain financing for the movie for which he needed the film. Will the producer's failure to obtain financing act as a defense to a breach of contract action brought by the film distributor when the producer refuses to purchase the film?

(A) Yes, because the financing clause need not be a written modification of a contract not within the Statute of Frauds.
(B) Yes, because obtaining the financing was a condition precedent to the formation of the contract.
(C) No, because of the parol evidence rule.
(D) No, because he producer will be estopped from denying his agreement with the film distributor.

Question 22

Two car owners agreed to trade title to their cars. One car owner drove his red car to the other car owner's house, where he had his blue car parked.

Which of the following statements is LEAST accurate?

(A) The red car owner's conveyance of his car to the blue car owner is a concurrent condition to the blue car owner's duty to convey his car to the red car owner.
(B) The red car owner's conveyance of his car to the blue car owner is a condition precedent to the blue car owner's duty to convey his car to the red car owner.
(C) The blue car owner's conveyance of his car to the red car owner is a condition precedent to the red car owner's duty to convey his car to the blue owner.
(D) The red car owner's conveyance of his car to the blue owner is a condition subsequent to the blue owner's duty to convey his car to the red car owner.

Questions 23–24 are based upon the following fact situation.

An interior designer claimed that she could increase the sales volume of any store by remodeling it in a scientific manner. The interior designer orally agreed with a store owner to remodel her shoe store within ninety days. Both parties later signed an agreement whereby the store owner was to pay a $75,000 remodeling fee in ten equal payments of $7,500. Payment in full was due within ten days of the completion of construction, provided that the store owner's retail sales increased by 25 percent. The agreement further provided that it could be modified only by a writing signed by both parties.

Two weeks after construction began, the interior designer demanded payment of $7,500, which was the amount of the first installment. She showed the store owner bills for materials she used totaling $8,200. The store owner denied any obligation to pay until the job was completed, but, reluctantly, she orally agreed to pay half of the designer's out-of-pocket expenses while the job progressed to show her goodwill.

When the renovation was complete, the store owner's sales increased by $200,000, 24 percent above the previous year. The designer said the store owner could further increase her sales (at least another 1 percent) if she changed her advertisements. The store owner refused to pay the remaining balance on the remodeling expenses and demanded that the designer return the money he had advanced.

Question 23

If the designer claims that the store owner orally agreed to change her advertisements as part of the plan to increase sales by 25 percent, the store owner will most likely be able to exclude the agreement by arguing:

(A) that the original written agreement was completely integrated.
(B) that under the Parol Evidence Rule, a contract may not be interpreted by subsequent evidence.
(C) that the original written agreement was partially integrated.
(D) promissory estoppel.

Question 24

Was the agreement to pay half the expenses as construction proceeded a valid modification?

(A) Yes, because the contract was a partially integrated agreement.
(B) Yes, if the agreement was a compromise by both parties reached after an honest dispute.
(C) No, because it was not in writing.
(D) No, because of an absence of valid consideration.

Question 25

A roller bearing company agreed in writing to supply a motor company with 1,000,000 roller bearings for $7,000,000 on March 1. On March 1, the roller bearing company had in its inventory only 970,000 roller bearings, and they delivered that number to the motor

company. The motor company refused delivery and payment and asserted an action against the roller bearing company for breach of contract. Should the motor company prevail?

(A) Yes, because the roller bearing company has not fulfilled its contractual obligations.
(B) Yes, if the roller bearing company does not deliver 30,000 additional roller bearings in a reasonable amount of time.
(C) No, because the roller bearing company has substantially performed the contract.
(D) No, the roller bearing company will be excused under the doctrine of impossibility.

Questions 26–27 are based upon the following fact situation.

A mechanic rebuilt the engine in a car owner's car, pursuant to a written contract, at an agreed price of $1,400. The car owner called the mechanic and told him in good faith that the car was still not operating properly and he refused to tender payment.

The mechanic sent the car owner a letter reminding him that payment was overdue. On January 1, the car owner responded with a letter agreeing to pay $1,200 if the mechanic agreed to rebuild the car again within ten days. The mechanic did not answer the letter. The car owner mailed a check for $1,200 and wrote, "Payment in full in accordance with terms of letter sent January 1." The mechanic cashed the check but did not rebuild the car within ten days. The car owner sent letters and called to demand performance, but the mechanic has not responded.

Question 26

When the mechanic first rebuilt the car, the car owner refused to tender payment. If the car owner's actions did not constitute a breach it was because:

(A) the mechanic had substantially or properly rebuilt the engine.
(B) the mechanic acted in bad faith.
(C) the engine was improperly repaired.
(D) the mechanic refused to re-check the engine.

Question 27

If the mechanic asserts an action against the car owner for $200 (i.e., the difference between the price agreed upon in the original contract and the amount actually tendered), the mechanic will most likely:

(A) prevail, because he never assented to the new terms.
(B) prevail, if he can prove he properly rebuilt the car.
(C) not prevail, if the original price was excessive.
(D) not prevail, because the check was cashed without objection.

Questions 28–29 are based upon the following fact situation.

An owner of a supermarket chain and an owner of a department store chain agreed on a cooperative advertising program whereby both parties would share the costs of the campaign based on their respective average retail sales. They appointed an independent auditor to monitor their sales and bill them for their respective shares. The supermarket owner paid several bills without complaint, but then he said he had discovered an accounting error made by the auditor that had led him to pay a disproportionate amount. The supermarket owner asked the department store owner to refund the amount the auditor had caused him to overpay. The department store owner refused to give the supermarket owner a refund. The department store owner found it hard to believe that the auditor had erred.

The supermarket owner proposed a settlement to their dispute. The supermarket owner offered not to pursue his claim for the refund in exchange for the department store owner's promise to pay the supermarket owner's maintenance costs for the common areas of their shopping center for a two-year period. The department store owner said, "Okay, I'll agree because you're stubborn, but I still think that you're wrong."

Six months after the advertising agreement was signed, the department store in the mall experienced a sharp decline in sales. The department store owner closed the store to cut her losses. She managed to sublease the store to a tenant, who agreed in the sublease to maintain the common areas as per the supermarket-department store agreement. Shortly after the tenant subleased the department store owner' store, he realized his sales were very low and moved the store to another shopping center. The supermarket store owner was forced to pay for maintaining the common areas.

Question 28

Was the department store owner's promise to maintain the common areas supported by consideration if the accountant did not in fact err?

(A) Yes.
(B) No, if the department store owner never believed the supermarket store owner had a valid claim.
(C) No, because the supermarket store owner would have lost any claim asserted against the department store owner.
(D) No, because the department store's settlement was vague.

Question 29

If the court rules that the department-supermarket store maintenance agreement was an enforceable contract, will the supermarket owner be able to bring an action against the department store owner for the tenant's refusal to maintain the common areas?

(A) Yes, because the supermarket owner is a third-party beneficiary.
(B) Yes, because the department store remains liable to fulfill the maintenance agreement.
(C) No, because the supermarket owner may assert an action against the tenant.
(D) No, because the department store owner-tenant contract ended the obligation between the supermarket store owner and the department store owner.

Questions 30–31 are based upon the following fact situation.

A mayor placed full-page advertisements in the city's three daily newspapers offering a $100,000 reward to anyone who supplied information leading to the arrest and conviction of the murderer of the mayor's predecessor.

Question 30

The mayor's offer could be accepted by:

(A) arresting and convicting the murderer.
(B) apprehending the murderer.
(C) agreeing to make every possible effort to bring about the arrest and conviction of the murderer.
(D) supplying the information necessary to identify the murderer and have him arrested and convicted.

Question 31

The mayor can effectively revoke the offer:

(A) only by placing full-page ads in the city's three dailies.
(B) by placing small advertisements in the newspapers.
(C) by notifying any person actively pursuing the murderer.
(D) by placing a full-page advertisement in the city's dailies, or by a comparable medium and frequency of publicity.

Questions 32–33 are based upon the following fact situation.

A buyer and a seller orally agreed that the seller would sell his office building to the buyer for $2 million. The seller agreed to send a check for $1 million to a creditor to satisfy a debt owed to her by the seller. The buyer and the seller agreed that the title would pass immediately even though the agreement was not yet in writing.

The seller had the agreement typed a week later. He failed to include a clause in reference to the debt he had agreed to pay the creditor. There was a typographical error in the printing of the contract that erroneously stated the sale price to be $1.5 million. Neither party noticed the error, nor questioned the omission of the payment to the creditor. Both the buyer and the seller signed the contract.

Question 32

The creditor's action against the seller will be most significantly affected by whether:

(A) the seller was negligent by not exercising care in reading the agreement.

(B) the buyer was negligent by not exercising care in reading the agreement.

(C) the buyer's agreement with the seller was fully integrated.

(D) the Statute of Frauds will be at issue.

Question 33

Which of the following will be the seller's best argument in his defense?

(A) The buyer and the seller agreed not to pay any part of the purchase price to the debtor before she found out about the original agreement.

(B) The seller's original agreement to pay $1 million of the purchase price to the debtor will fail due to lack of consideration.

(C) The debtor was obligated to notify both parties in writing of the acceptance of the contract.

(D) The action will fail due to the Statute of Limitations.

Questions 34–35 are based upon the following fact situation.

A driver operated a tractor for a constructor. Without informing the constructor, the driver drove the tractor home after work to use in the landscaping of his neighbor's yard. The neighbor was so thankful that he gave the driver a six-pack of beer that the driver drank while driving the tractor back to the construction site.

The driver negligently lost control of the tractor, ramming into a crowd of pedestrians and a puppy on the sidewalk. One of the pedestrians was seriously injured requiring six months of physical therapy for a fractured hip. The constructor mistakenly believed that he was liable for the damages in the accident. He visited the pedestrian in the hospital and told the very distraught man, "Don't worry about anything. I am going to pay for everything." The constructor then told the pedestrian's physical therapist, "Take care of the pedestrian, and I'll take care of you."

An owner of the puppy who died a slow painful death from wounds received in the accident threatened to sue the driver, who had no assets. The constructor contacted the puppy owner and told her, "If you agree not to sue the driver, I will compensate you for all of your damages."

Question 34

If the pedestrian brings an action against the constructor for pain and suffering, the constructor should assert in his defense:

(A) mistake of fact.

(B) the Statute of Frauds.

(C) lack of consideration.

(D) indefiniteness.

Question 35

If the therapist decided not to treat the pedestrian anymore and the pedestrian asserted a claim based on breach of contract, is the therapist likely to prevail?

(A) Yes, because the therapist contracted with the constructor, not the pedestrian.

(B) Yes, because the pedestrian did not provide any consideration.

(C) No, because the pedestrian was a third-party beneficiary.

(D) Yes, because the therapist never promised to treat the pedestrian.

Questions 36–37 are based upon the following fact situation.

A buyer signed a written agreement to purchase 100 gross plush toys at $288 per gross from a seller. The contract provided that the buyer would not be bound if the stuffed animals were not delivered by June 1 or if they did not meet certain specifications. If the buyer accepted the delivery, he then had ninety days in which to pay the seller. The seller delivered ninety-two gross on June 1 and promised that the remaining stuffed animals would be delivered on June 4. "Don't bother," said the buyer, "keep all of them." The stuffed animals that were delivered had met the buyer's specifications.

Question 36

If the seller asserts an action against the buyer for breach of contract, which of the following will be the buyer's best defense?

(A) The market value had steadily increased from the date the parties contracted until delivery date.

(B) The market value had steadily decreased from the date the parties contracted until delivery date.

(C) The seller had not performed by the agreed date, thus constituting a breach of contract.

(D) A stuffing shortage caused the delay.

Question 37

Which of the following choices, if true, would best support the seller's position?

(A) The stuffed animals were custom-made.

(B) The buyer had cash-flow problems.

(C) The stuffing factory had burned down.

(D) On April 15, the buyer had told the seller, "Don't worry about the delivery date, just do a good job."

Question 38

A computer manufacturer contracted to buy 300 cathode ray screens at $100 each, F.O.B. buyer, from a seller. The contract provided that thirty screens would be delivered on the first of each month; payment was to be due ten days thereafter. A computer manufacturer purchased the cathode ray screens with the expectation that her computers would become 10 percent faster once the new screens were installed. The contract specified that the screens were purchased to increase efficiency.

The computer manufacturer mailed the seller a check for payment of the first installment within ten days after the first delivery. She performed tests on the screens to measure their speed, taking sixteen days and costing $2,000. These tests showed that the new screens were actually slower than the ones she was replacing. The computer manufacturer installed five of the new screens in her computers and, as expected, the computers slowed down. The computer manufacturer notified the seller that she was returning the screens that had been delivered and repudiating the rest of the contract because the screens did not meet contractual specifications.

Which of the following statements is the most accurate?

(A) The computer manufacturer had a right to inspect the cathode ray screens only before she paid for them.

(B) The computer manufacturer had a right to inspect the screens.

(C) The computer manufacturer's right to inspect the screens terminated when she signed the contract.

(D) The computer manufacturer had a right to inspect the screens only if the rights were expressly set forth in the contract.

Questions 39–40 are based upon the following fact situation.

A twenty-one-year-old college senior loved cars. He worked long hours after school to make the payments on his car. A bank had extended him a two-year loan with no pre-payment penalty. The student fell behind in his payments, prompting the bank to write him a letter stating, "If payments are not resumed by January 15, we will be forced to repossess your car." The student dropped out of school to work longer hours at the local fast food restaurant so that he would be able to resume his payments.

On January 6, the student's uncle, a fifty-five-year-old real estate tycoon and bachelor, discovered the student's plans to pay his debt. He called the student on the telephone and said, "I can't let my favorite nephew mess up his life. If you stay in school and quit your part-time job, I will assume all payments on your car and provide you with $200 spending money every month until next May."

The student agreed to quit his job and stay in school.

The uncle called the bank and left a message with the receptionist stating, "I will pay you all the money the student owes and assume all his future payments if you guarantee not to repossess his car. If the bank does not return my call, I will assume it has accepted the offer." The bank did not respond to the uncle's call, did not repossess the car, and cashed the uncle's checks over the next six months.

The student drove off the side of a winding mountain road four months before his graduation from college. The student died in the crash and the car was reduced to ashes. The bank sued the uncle for the remaining payments due on the car. The student's estate brought suit against the uncle for six remaining monthly payments of $200 spending money promised to the student.

Question 39

If the uncle argues that the bank's original agreement to give the student a two-year loan to buy the car was void because it was oral, will the court rule in the uncle's favor on this issue?

(A) Yes, because the contract could not have been performed in less than a year.

(B) Yes, because the contract was for the sale of goods in excess of $500.

(C) No, because the contract could have been satisfied in less than a year.

(D) Yes, because in some jurisdictions the student would have been considered a minor at the time of the contract.

Question 40

Did the uncle and the student enter into an enforceable contract on January 6?

(A) Yes, because the uncle sought to induce the student to refrain from working and stay in school.

(B) Yes, because the uncle received pecuniary benefit from the agreement.

(C) No, because the uncle did not receive any consideration.

(D) No, because the promise of a gift is not enforceable.

Question 41

A university hired a professor under a one-year contract as an adjunct professor of music. The professor taught two classes every Monday and Wednesday. The professor missed the second week of classes because of injuries he had sustained in a car accident. When he returned to class on the third week, the professor discovered he had been replaced by an adjunct professor. The university refused to reinstate the professor or allow him to teach. The professor brought a claim for breach of contract against the university.

Which of the following arguments will help the professor's case most?

(A) The professor's one-week absence was not a material breach.

(B) The professor had relied on the contract with the university when he refused other offers.

(C) The contract may be divided into a series of agreements, one for each week of teaching.

(D) The professor was excused from his obligation due to physical impossibility.

Questions 42–43 are based upon the following fact situation.

A store owner owned a fishing supply store. In the course of business, he purchased 10,000 yards of 12-pound test fishing line from a fish supply corporation. The contract provided that the store owner would remit payment immediately upon receiving the merchandise. The store owner received delivery, mailed a check for payment in full, and then inspected the fishing line. It was only 10-pound test. The store owner tried to return the line, but the fish supply corporation refused to take it back, claiming that 10-pound line was as good as 12-pound line.

Question 42

In general, a contract clause providing for payment before inspection of goods:

(A) is void as against public policy.

(B) does not preclude a buyer from inspecting the goods and pursuing remedies for non-conformance.

(C) will preclude the buyer from seeking redress for non-conformance.

(D) will preclude the buyer from recovering the incidental damages associated with the inspection of non-conforming goods.

Question 43

The store owner should try to:

(A) return the goods and demand the fish supply corporation supply him with 10,000 yards of 12-pound test fishing line.

(B) return the goods and recover damages based on the difference in the value of 10,000 yards of 12-pound and 10-pound test lines.

(C) return the goods and recover the contract price and damages based on the difference between the

contract price and the cost of procuring substitute goods.

(D) keep the goods and not recover damages because he waived his remedies by agreeing to the payment before inspection clause.

Question 44

A seller orally agreed to sell his mercantile shop to a buyer. The buyer remodeled the store for $15,000 and spent $3,000 in moving expenses and supplies. The seller repudiated the contract, relying on the Statute of Frauds. Which of the following facts will the judge rely on in reaching a decision that the contract is enforceable?

(A) the contractual price of the store.

(B) whether the seller was aware of the repairs.

(C) the doctrine of part performance.

(D) the local real estate market.

Questions 45–46 are based upon the following fact situation.

An oil company had the following contract with a refinery:

"The oil company agrees to purchase all of its refined heating oil for the next six months from the refinery. The price will be determined by the heating oil price on the Mercantile Exchange on the day of delivery. The oil company reserves the right to purchase all or part of the refinery's output. The refinery agrees to produce a minimum of 10,000 barrels of heating oil per day." The contract was written and properly authenticated.

After three months, the refinery asked the oil company if they would agree to lower the minimum to 5,000 barrels per day. The oil company agreed, but only if the refinery agreed to accept payment after twenty days rather than after ten days as they had previously agreed. The refinery and the oil company shook hands on this new arrangement.

Four months into the contract, a tremendous explosion destroyed the refinery's primary refinery. The refinery stopped delivering oil to the oil company.

Question 45

Was the original agreement between the oil refinery and the oil company enforceable?

(A) Yes.

(B) No, because of lack of consideration.

(C) No, because the contract was replaced.

(D) No, because the price, an essential term, was missing.

Question 46

Assume for this question only that the contract and modification were valid. For what reason would the oil company not be able to win an action for breach after the explosion?

(A) Because the oil company assumed the risk of explosion under the contract.

(B) Because the explosion excused the refinery from fulfilling the contract.

(C) Because the refinery had not violated the contract by not supplying the daily quota.

(D) Because the explosion was due to the refinery's negligence.

Question 47

A seller contracted to sell a farm to a buyer. The written signed contract contained the exact boundaries and description of the land selling price, terms of payment, and effective date of contract. The contract contained all essential information except for the quality of title to be conveyed. Which of the following statements is most accurate?

(A) The contract is voidable by either party.

(B) The seller is obligated to convey whatever interest he owned in the farm on the contractual date.

(C) The seller will be required to convey a marketable title.

(D) The seller will be required to convey the title he owned on the date of contractual closing.

Questions 48–49 are based upon the following fact situation.

A seller sold a sixty-foot boat to a buyer pursuant to a signed contract. The contract provided that the buyer make sixty monthly payments of $20,000 starting January 1. On January 15 of the following year, reasonably fearing the buyer would lose his job and leave the country, the seller conveyed his rights under the contract to his neighbor for a lump sum. Neither party notified the buyer, who made six payments to the seller before learning that the neighbor had obtained the right to payment.

Question 48

If the neighbor asserts an action against the buyer for $120,000 to recover the six payments the buyer erroneously paid to the seller, should the neighbor prevail?

(A) Yes, because the neighbor was legally entitled to the payments.

(B) Yes, if the conveyance was properly reported to the appropriate government officials.

(C) No, because the buyer did not receive notice of the conveyance.

(D) No, only if the buyer can prove the parties intended to deceive him.

Question 49

The buyer subsequently sold the boat to a new buyer, who assumed the buyer's payments on his contract but failed to keep up with them. The neighbor asserted an action against the new buyer for payments of $20,000 per month. The neighbor will most likely be successful:

(A) because there is privity of contract between the neighbor and the new buyer.

(B) because justice demands payment for services.

(C) if the buyer defaulted on his obligations.

(D) until the new buyer gives notice of default.

Questions 50–51 are based upon the following fact situation.

A rare coin dealer cabled an investor on April 1, "We will sell you up to fifty 1885 gold U.S. twenty-dollar pieces at $500 each. Specifics have been sent by U.S. Mail." The letter, containing the legal details including postage, insurance, grantees, and a clause stating that "the offer will be held open for 100 days" was received by the investor on April 4. On April 3, the investor sent a cable to the coin dealer that said, "I accept your offer for five gold coins." Three hours after the investor sent the cable, a riot set off a panic that caused the price of gold to immediately double.

Question 50

Assume that on April 4 the coin dealer sent a cable to the investor, "Confirm your order of five coins, must retract offer for other coins." The investor responded, "Pursuant to the offer you promised to keep open, I purchase the remaining 45 coins at $500 each." The coin dealer refused to send the coins. If the investor asserts an action based on breach of contract against the coin dealer, should the investor succeed?

(A) Yes, because the coin dealer expressly promised to keep the offer open for 100 days.

(B) Yes, because the attempted revocation was ineffective.

(C) No, because the contract's material terms were changed by the riots.

(D) No, because the revocation was effective.

Question 51

Assume for this question only that before the coin dealer was able to revoke his offer, the investor sent a second cable requesting delivery of all fifty coins. Shortly after receiving the second cable, the coin dealer discovered that the coins had been stolen. The coin dealer's best defense to an action brought by the investor for breach of contract is:

(A) unilateral mistake.

(B) impossibility of performance.

(C) the offer had been terminated by the investor's prior actions.

(D) an absence of condition precedent.

Questions 52–53 are based upon the following fact situation.

On May 1, a homeowner told a painter, "If you paint my house, I will give you $5,000. This offer will not be revoked or altered until September 1."

Question 52

What is the legal effect of the clause "This offer will not be revoked or changed until September 1"?

(A) It provides the painter with a binding non-negotiable option.

(B) It provides the painter with a binding negotiable option.

(C) It does not affect the homeowner's power of revocation.

(D) It prevents the homeowner from revoking the offer any time before September 1.

Question 53

On May 15, the painter started painting the homeowner's house. On June 1, the homeowner told the painter, "I retract my offer of May 1." The painter had painted one-third of the house. Which of the following choices is most accurate?

(A) The painter may complete painting the house and recover in full because the homeowner could not revoke the offer before September 1.

(B) The painter could complete the painting and recover in full because he started painting before the homeowner revoked the offer.

(C) The painter must stop painting on June 1, but will recover for his work between May 15 and June 1.

(D) The painter must stop painting. He will not recover for his work.

Questions 54–55 are based upon the following fact situation.

A planter contracted with a homeowner to plant grass, trees, and bushes on the plot where the homeowner was constructing a new house. The homeowner was afraid that the job would not be completed before the first frost, so the parties agreed that "all work will be completed by November 1." The planter also agreed to extend a warranty of "the homeowner's 100 percent satisfaction." The contract provided that the homeowner would be obligated to pay in full within fifteen days of the work's completion.

The planter's work was delayed because the homeowner was delinquent in paying the general contractor building the house. The general contractor suspended work for two months. The planter could not begin the landscaping until the house was completed and all building-related refuse was carted away. The planter completed landscaping on November 7. The homeowner was dissatisfied with the results. When the planter

asked what he specifically did not care for, the homeowner shrugged his shoulders and said, "I don't know, I just don't like it."

Question 54

Which of the following statements is most accurate?

(A) The homeowner's duty to pay was a condition precedent to the planter's duty to landscape.

(B) The planter's duty to landscape was a condition precedent to the homeowner's duty to pay.

(C) The homeowner's duty to pay was a condition subsequent to the planter's duty to landscape.

(D) The planter's duty to landscape was a condition subsequent to the homeowner's duty to pay.

Question 55

Which of the following choices is LEAST accurate?

(A) The homeowner's dispute with the general contractor excused the planter from the November 1 deadline.

(B) The homeowner was obligated to give prompt notice to the planter when the house was ready to be landscaped.

(C) By allowing the planter to proceed with the job, the homeowner waived the November 1 deadline.

(D) The November 1 deadline was not affected by developments subsequent to the signing of the contract.

Question 56

A company engaged in hauling boulders contracted to provide its services, charging $2.00 per pound hauled, to a construction company engaged in clearing timber. The agreement provided that the boulder company would remove boulders from all the construction company's construction sites for the next four years. The agreement further provided that payments would be made to a creditor of the boulder company. The construction company shut down its operations. The creditor asserted an action against the construction company for breach of contract. The construction company should assert which of the following defenses?

(A) The boulder company's rights were not assignable.

(B) The construction company's contract with the boulder company was not enforceable, due to a lack of consideration.

(C) The construction company, in good faith, did not have any need for the boulder company's services.

(D) The construction company's rights were personal.

Question 57

The owner of a shopping mall entered into a contract with a buyer to sell a store located in the shopping mall. The buyer tendered a $1,000 down payment, as required by the contract, to buy "the mall's northernmost store and a small amount of land surrounding the store." The purchase price was set at $200,000, and both parties signed a written agreement. The buyer seeks to repudiate the contract. Should the trial court allow it?

(A) Yes, because contracts for the sale of real property are not final until "closed."

(B) Yes, because the agreement is too vague to be enforced.

(C) No, because the agreement satisfies the Statute of Frauds.

(D) No, because $1,000 is more than sufficient consideration.

Questions 58–59 are based upon the following fact situation.

A landlord signed a thirty-year lease with a tenant for a wire-hanger factory. The lease provided that the tenant pay $100,000 rent per year plus all taxes due on the factory. The tenant had an option in the lease to purchase the premises at any time for $1 million in cash. The landlord conveyed the factory to a buyer soon thereafter. The tenant assigned the lease to a sublessee without mentioning the clause specifying payment of taxes.

Question 58

Must the sublessee pay taxes?

(A) Yes.

(B) No, because the agreement to pay taxes does not touch or concern the land.

(C) No, because the agreement to pay taxes is collateral and does not run with the land.

(D) No, because the sublessee never agreed to pay the taxes.

Question 59

Assume for this question only that the sublessee fulfilled all of her contractual obligations. She notified the buyer that she had decided to exercise her option to purchase the factory. The buyer refused to sell it. The sublessee brought an action for specific performance. Is the sublessee likely to prevail?

(A) Yes.

(B) No, because the option did not run with the land.

(C) No, because the option did not touch or concern the land.

(D) No, because the sublessee merely had priority over other purchasers.

Questions 60–61 are based upon the following fact situation.

A painter and a model entered into a written contract providing, "The painter is to paint a portrait of the model at the model's house. The painter guarantees the subject's satisfaction. If satisfied, she must pay the painter $1,000 within thirty days of completion of the painting." Although the model's husband was thrilled with the painting, the model did not like it and refused to make payment. The painter asserted an action based on breach of contract.

Question 60

Of the following arguments, which is LEAST helpful to the painter?

(A) The model's dissatisfaction with the portrait was not genuine.

(B) The model never looked at the portrait.

(C) The model refused to accept the portrait because a personality conflict arose between artist and subject during the long hours the model spend modeling for the painter.

(D) The painter's portrait was an accurate reproduction of the model's appearance.

Question 61

Assume for this question only that the model refused to make herself available to model for the painter. Which of the following statements would be LEAST accurate?

(A) The model's cooperation with the painter was an implied condition of the contract.

(B) The painter assumed the risk of the model not cooperating.

(C) The painter was under an implied obligation to cooperate with the model's schedule.

(D) If the model refused to cooperate, the painter would be excused from performance and could maintain an action for breach of contract.

Questions 62–63 are based upon the following fact situation.

A buyer and a seller had known each other for twenty years. The buyer heard through his neighbor that the seller was thinking of selling his lawnmower. The warranty on the buyer's mower had recently expired, and the mower had expired as well. Since the buyer was in need of a mower he wrote a signed letter to the seller, dated March 1, that said: "If you deliver your lawnmower in working condition to my house by 6:00 P.M. on March 15, I will pay you $400. This offer is not subject to change or revocation." The seller wrote to the buyer on March 3 and told him, "I accept your offer, and will deliver the lawn mower before March 15." The letter was properly addressed and posted on March 3, but did not arrive until March 14, two days after the buyer purchased a mower from a home goods store for $450.

The home goods store owner was also the seller's friend. The home goods store owner bragged to the seller on March 13 that he had sold his used mower to the buyer at a very high price.

The seller brought the mower to the buyer's house at 5:30 P.M. on March 15. The buyer was out, but the seller waited until the buyer arrived at 7:00 P.M. The buyer refused to pay for the mower.

Question 62

What is the legal effect of the clause "this offer is not subject to change or revocation" in the buyer's letter of March 1?

(A) It prevented the buyer from revoking the offer any time before March 15.
(B) It created a binding non-negotiable option for the seller.
(C) It created a binding negotiable option for the seller.
(D) It did not affect the seller's power of revocation.

Question 63

If the seller asserts an action based on breach of contract against the buyer, the court should rule that the seller's March 3 letter:

(A) did not affect the seller's rights to revoke his offer.
(B) bound both parties to a unilateral contract.
(C) bound both parties to a bilateral contract.
(D) is an effective acceptance.

Question 64

An owner personally owns a large company that manufactures commercial airplanes. A neighbor told the owner, "I convinced a friend of mine to buy three of your airplanes for his company." The planes were indeed sold by the owner to the friend. The neighbor demanded a 1 percent commission, as is customarily given to airplane salesmen. Which of the following arguments would support the owner's refusal to pay the commission?

(A) The owner never promised to pay a commission.
(B) Even if the owner had promised to pay a commission, the promise would not have been supported by consideration.
(C) The contractual elements of offer and acceptance were absent.
(D) A and C.

Questions 65–66 are based upon the following fact situation.

A helicopter company purchased its steel from a steel company. The companies signed a two-year agreement that contained a clause prohibiting either party from assigning its rights under the contract. The contract further provided that the helicopter company tender its payment directly to a creditor of the steel company.

The steel company subsequently assigned its rights to a bank as collateral for a loan. The steel company

billed the helicopter company upon completion of the contract. The helicopter company tendered payment of the full contract price to the steel company ten days later.

Question 65

The clause in the original agreement prohibiting either party from assigning its rights will:

(A) be enforceable only against the helicopter company.
(B) not be enforceable by any party.
(C) invalidate any rights the bank may have had.
(D) make the steel company's assignment to the bank a breach of contract although the assignment will be enforceable.

Question 66

If the court rules that the steel company's assignment to the bank was valid, and the helicopter company, unaware of the assignment, paid its debt to the steel company:

(A) the bank will not be able to recover from either the steel company or the helicopter company.
(B) the bank will recover from the steel company only.
(C) the bank will recover from both the steel company and the helicopter company.
(D) the bank will recover from the helicopter company only.

Questions 67–68 are based upon the following fact situation.

A grandson told his paternal grandfather that he was thinking of trying to quit smoking. The paternal grandfather decided to encourage the grandson, so he signed a written agreement promising to give the grandson $10,000 if the grandson completely refrained from smoking for the next year. The grandson's maternal grandfather found out about his paternal grandfather's promise and told the grandson, "I will also give you $10,000." The grandson did not smoke for a year, and he asked his paternal grandfather for the money. His paternal grandfather replied, "I was just kidding. I never intended to give you ten grand, but I really did you a favor, since you quit smoking." The grandson then contacted his maternal grandfather who also refused to pay.

Question 67

The grandson asserted an action against his paternal grandfather, who raised the argument of lack of consideration as his only defense. Is the grandson likely to prevail?

(A) Yes, if he asserts the theory of promissory estoppel.
(B) Yes, if he asserts there was a bargained-for exchange.

(C) No, because the grandson was thinking about quitting.

(D) No, because the grandson received the benefit of no longer being a smoker.

Question 68

Assume for this question only that the grandson is unable to recover against the grandfather. If the grandson asserts a claim against his maternal grandfather, which of the following arguments will best support the maternal grandfather's position?

(A) The grandson was going to stop smoking anyway.

(B) The grandson has not provided any consideration.

(C) The agreement between the two parties was oral.

(D) There was no intent by the maternal grandfather to form a contract.

Question 69

On March 1, a buyer looked at a seller's boat. The seller said, "You can have the boat for $20,000. I promise to keep this offer open for thirty days." On March 15, the seller called the buyer and told her, "the boat was destroyed in a fire." On March 22, the buyer found out the seller had lied, the boat was actually in good condition, and she told the seller that she wanted to buy the boat. The seller refused. If the buyer brings an action against the seller for breach of contract, the buyer will most likely:

(A) prevail, because the seller promised to keep the offer open.

(B) prevail, because the boat had not been destroyed.

(C) not succeed, because of the March 15 phone call.

(D) not succeed, because the offer of March 1 was not valid.

Question 70

A buyer wanted to purchase a car, but he didn't have any free time to go to the dealers. He authorized an agent to buy him a new car from a car dealership. The agent signed the contract, "Buyer by Agent, his agent." When the car arrived at the showroom three weeks later, the buyer refused to accept or pay for it. The car dealership asserted an action against the buyer based on breach of contract.

Which of the following choices is LEAST accurate?

(A) The car dealership will prevail if the agent's authority was in writing.

(B) The car dealership will prevail if the car was custom-made and is not suitable for use by others.

(C) The buyer will prevail despite written authority for the agent.

(D) The buyer will prevail because a contract for the sale of goods valued at more than $500 must satisfy the Statute of Frauds.

Question 71

A homeowner hired a roofer to build the roof on his new house. The homeowner agreed to pay $14,000 to the roofer upon completion of the work. After the roofer had completed approximately half the roof, he sent a signed writing to the homeowner asking him to send the $14,000 that would be coming due to him to his creditor. The roofer completed the work. The creditor brought an action against the homeowner for refusing to pay the $14,000. The homeowner's best defense will be:

(A) the creditor could not have completed the roofing project.

(B) the roofer had previously agreed not to assign the contract.

(C) the roof leaks.

(D) the creditor was not an intended beneficiary of the original contract.

Questions 72–73 are based on the following fact situation.

A fifteen-year-old computer designer owned a computer software company that he had started at the age of ten. In 2005, the company had sales of $41,000,000. One of the software company's clients gave the computer designer a 6-month note for $10,000 to settle an insurance claim between them. The computer designer sold the note to his neighbor for $9,000, and then told his client that the note had been ruined when he left it in the pocket of a pair of jeans that his mother washed. The client gave the computer designer a note identical to the first. The computer designer sold the second note to his bank for $9,500. His client had still not paid the note thirty days after it was due.

Question 72

Will the computer designer be able to assert an action against the client for failure to pay on the note?

(A) Yes, because the computer designer still owned the right to collect $10,000 from the client.

(B) No, because a minor cannot collect the value of a note.

(C) No, because the computer designer assigned the note to a third party.

(D) No, because the note is no longer physically possessed by the computer designer.

Question 73

Assume the neighbor and the friend bring actions against the client for payment on the notes. Assume further that the client argues, *inter alia*, the computer designer was a minor. The trial court will rule:

(A) one of the banks may recover, based on priority.

(B) neither may recover, because the computer designer's minor status voided the note.

(C) neither may recover if the client knew that the computer designer was a minor.

(D) neither may recover, because a holder in due course can never receive more than his predecessor.

Question 74

In February, a counselor contracted with a cooking camp for kids to serve as its head counselor at a salary of $10,000 for ten weeks of service from the June 1 to the middle of August. In March, the camp notified the counselor that it had hired another counselor instead, and that his services would no longer be needed. In April, the first counselor spent $200 traveling to interview at various other cooking camps with equal pay and prestige, but was not offered any positions. Finally, the first counselor took a job teaching at a local craft camp for only $6,000 for the same period.

In a breach of contract action against the camp, what can the first counselor recover?

(A) $4,000
(B) $4,200
(C) $10,000
(D) $10,200

Question 75

A tomato supplier agreed to sell and a spaghetti sauce manufacturer agreed to buy all of the tomatoes that the manufacturer required over a two-year period. The sales contract provided that payment was due sixty days after delivery, but that a 3 percent discount would be allowed if the manufacturer paid within ten days of delivery. During the first year of the contract, the manufacturer regularly paid within the ten-day period and received the discount. However, fifteen days after the supplier made the most recent tomato delivery, the supplier had still not received payment. At this time, the supplier became aware of rumors from a credible source that the manufacturer's financial condition was not exactly stable. The supplier wrote to the manufacturer, demanding assurances regarding the manufacturer's financial status and ability to pay. The manufacturer immediately mailed its latest audited financial statements to the supplier, as well as a satisfactory credit report prepared by the manufacturer's banker. Despite the credible source, the rumors proved false. Even so, the supplier refused to resume deliveries, and the manufacturer sued the supplier for breach.

Will the manufacturer prevail?

(A) No, because the contract was unenforceable since the manufacturer had not committed to purchase a definite quantity of tomatoes.

(B) No, because the supplier had reasonable grounds for insecurity and was therefore entitled to cancel the contract and refuse to make any future deliveries.

(C) Yes, because the credit report and audited financial statements provided adequate assurances of the due performance under the contract.

(D) Yes, because the supplier was not entitled to condition resumption of deliveries on the receipt of financial status information.

Question 76

A buyer decided to purchase a used car, and when she settled on one she liked, she asked the dealer whether the car had ever been in an accident. The dealer replied "Well, that is a fine car you are looking at, and has been inspected, and also comes with a certificate of assured quality. Feel free to have the car inspected by your own mechanic." In reality, the car had been in an accident and the dealer had known about it since he had done the repairs himself, carefully concealing any evidence of an accident. The buyer declined to have the car inspected, relying on the dealer's obvious charms, and at no time did the dealer disclose that the car had been in an accident. Both parties signed the contract of sale and, after the car was delivered and paid for, the buyer learned about the major accident.

If the buyer sues the dealer to rescind the contract, is she likely to succeed?

(A) No, because the buyer had the opportunity to have the car inspected by her own mechanic and declined.

(B) No, because the dealer did not assert that the car had not been in an accident.

(C) Yes, because the contract was unconscionable.

(D) Yes, because the dealer's statement was intentionally misleading and the dealer concealed evidence of the accident.

Question 77

On January 5, a brother lent $1,000 to his sister. The two agreed that the sister would repay the loan at the rate of $100 per month, payable on the first day of each month. On February 1, at the sister's request, the brother agreed to permit payment on the 5th. On March 1, the sister again requested additional time, and the brother responded, "Don't keep bugging me, just change the date of payment to the 5th, but if you do, make the payments by cashier's check." The sister said OK, and continued to make payments on the 5th of each month until April 6th, when the brother sold the loan to a bank. However, the brother, being forgetful, neglected to tell the bank about the agreement permitting payment on the 5th. On April 6th, the bank wrote to the sister, "Your debt to your brother has been assigned to us. We hereby inform you that all payments must be made on the first day of the month."

Can the sister insist that the payment date for the rest of the installments is the 5th, instead of the 1st?

(A) No, because a contract modification is not binding on an assignee who had no knowledge of the modification.

(B) No, because although the brother waived the condition of payment on the first of the month, the bank reinstated it.

(C) Yes, because although the brother waived the condition of payment on the first of the month, he could not assign to the bank his right to reinstate the condition.

(D) Yes, because the brother could assign to the bank only those rights he had in the contract at the time of the assignment.

Question 78

A buyer entered into a written agreement with a seller to purchase 1,000 sets of specially manufactured hand buzzers of a nonstandard dimension for a price of $10 per set. The seller calculated that it would cost $8 to make each set, and delivery was scheduled for sixty days later. Fifty-five days later, after the seller had completed production, the buyer repudiated the contract with the seller because he decided to quit childish pranks. After he notified the buyer of his intention to sell, the seller resold the hand buzzers to a salvage company for $2 per set. The seller then sued the buyer for damages.

What damages should be awarded to the seller?

(A) $2 per set, representing the difference between the cost of production and the price the buyer agreed to pay.

(B) $6 per set, representing the difference between the cost of manufacture and the salvage price.

(C) $8 per set, representing the lost profits plus the unrecovered cost of production.

(D) Nominal damages, as the seller failed to resell the goods by public auction.

Question 79

A debtor owed a creditor $1,500, but the Statute of Limitations barred recovery. The debtor wrote to the creditor, "I promise to pay you $500 if you will extinguish the debt." The creditor, being kindhearted, agreed.

Is the debtor's promise to pay the creditor enforceable?

(A) No, because the debtor made no promise not to plead the statute of limitations as defense.

(B) No, because there was no consideration for the debtor's promise.

(C) Yes, because the debtor's promise provided a benefit to the creditor.

(D) Yes, because the debtor's promise to pay part of the barred debt is enforceable.

Question 80

A computer company sent a purchase order to a wholesaler for keyboards, stating, "Please ship 100,000 keyboards at the posted price." Two days after receipt of the purchase order, the wholesaler shipped the keyboards and the computer company accepted. A week after delivery, the computer company received the wholesaler's acknowledgement form, and it included a provision disclaiming any consequential damages. However, as luck would have it, after using the keyboards for two months, the computer company discovered a defect. This meant that the computer company had to recall 10,000 computers that had already been shipped, incurring a loss in profits of $40,000.

Assuming all appropriate defenses are raised, will the computer company succeed in recovering $40,000 in consequential damages?

(A) No, because buyers are generally not entitled to recover consequential damages.

(B) No, because the computer company's acceptance of the goods also constituted an acceptance of the terms included in the wholesaler's acknowledgement.

(C) Yes, because the disclaimer of consequential damages is unconscionable.

(D) Yes, because the wholesaler's acknowledgement did not alter the terms of an existing contract between the parties.

Question 81

A buyer and a seller have dealt with each other many times in separate contracts for the sale of skis over the last five years. Every time a contract was performed, the seller delivered the skis to the buyer, and upon delivery the buyer would sign an invoice that showed an agreed upon price for that particular delivery. Each invoice was silent in regard to any discounts for prompt payment, even though the custom of the ski trade was to allow a 2 percent discount from the invoice price for payment within ten days of delivery. In all their prior transactions, and without objection from the seller, the buyer would take fifteen days to pay and deduct 5 percent from the invoice price.

The buyer and the seller's present contract calls for a single delivery of 3,000 skis at a price of $300,000. The seller delivered the skis and the buyer signed the invoice. On the fourth day after delivery, the buyer received the following note from the seller: "Paying in full in accordance with signed invoice is due immediately, no discounts permitted. S/Seller."

Which of the following statements is the most accurate?

(A) The custom and trade controls, and the buyer is entitled to take a 2 percent discount if he pays within ten days.

(B) The parties' course of dealing controls, and the buyer is entitled to take a 5 percent discount if he pays within fifteen days.

(C) The seller's retraction of his prior waiver controls, and the seller is entitled to no discount.

(D) The written contract controls, and the seller is entitled to no discount because of the Parol Evidence Rule.

Question 82

A mother had an adult daughter who had recently graduated law school. The mother contracted with a tutor to give the daughter a bar exam preparation course. The mother explained to the tutor that the daughter had been promised a job with a prestigious law firm that would pay $155,000 per year if the daughter passed the bar. The tutor agreed to be the daughter's tutor for $5,000 even though her going rate was $6,000. Before the tutoring was to begin, the tutor decided to fly to Spain and repudiate the contract. Even though the mother could have easily found another qualified instructor, or the daughter herself could have found an instructor, neither looked for one. The daughter failed the bar exam and her dreams of working for the infamous law firm dwindled away when they refused to hire her. It can be shown that if the daughter had received instruction she would have passed.

If the mother and the daughter join as parties and sue the tutor for breach of contract, how much, if anything, are they entitled to recover?

(A) $1,000 because all other damages could have been avoided by employing another equally qualified instructor.

(B) $155,000, because damages of that amount were within the contemplation of the parties at the time they contracted.

(C) Nominal damages only, because the mother was not injured by the breach and the tutor made no promises to the daughter.

(D) Nothing, because neither the mother nor the daughter took steps to avoid the consequences of the tutor's breach.

Question 83

On May 1, the uncle mailed a letter to his nephew that stated "I'm thinking of selling my yacht, which I know you enjoy. I would consider taking $20,000 for it." On May 3, the nephew mailed a response that said "You know I love that yacht, I will buy it for $20,000 cash." The uncle received the letter on May 5, and then on May 6 mailed the nephew a note that stated, "You have a deal!" On May 7, before the nephew received the May 6 letter, he phoned his uncle and reported that, unfortunately he was no longer allowed on the high seas due to a rather unfortunate incident, so could not buy the yacht.

Which of the following is accurate?

(A) There is a contract as of May 3.

(B) There is a contract as of May 5.

(C) There is a contract as of May 6.

(D) There is no contract.

Question 84

A seller and a buyer entered into a contract in which the seller would sell Blackacre to the buyer for $100,000. The contract provided that the buyer's obligation to purchase Blackacre was expressly conditioned upon the buyer obtaining a loan at an interest rate no higher than 10 percent. The buyer was unable to do so, but did obtain an interest rate of 10.5 percent and tendered the purchase price to the seller. However, because the value of the land had increased since the signing of the contract, the seller refused to tender title.

The buyer sued the seller, will the buyer prevail?

(A) No, because an express condition will only be excused to avoid forfeiture.

(B) No, because the contract called for a loan at an interest rate not to exceed 10 percent and it could not be modified without the consent of the seller.

(C) Yes, because the buyer detrimentally changed position in reliance on the seller's promise to convey.

(D) Yes, because the buyer's obtaining a new loan at an interest rate no higher than 10 percent was not a condition to the seller's duty to perform.

Question 85

A contractor was hired by a homeowner to remodel the homeowner's home for $10,000 to be paid on the completion of the work. On May 29, relying on the fact that he planned to finish the work by June 1, and thus have the homeowner's payment in hand, the contractor agreed to buy a car. The agreement stated that the contractor would buy the car "for $10,000 if payment is made on June 1, and if payment is made after, the price will be $12,000." The contractor completed the work, adhering to all specifications on June 1 and demanded payment from the homeowner. The homeowner refused to pay, and this caused the contractor to be very excited, suffering a minor heart attack, and as a result, incurred medical expenses of $1,000. The reasonable value of the contractor's services in remodeling the homeowner's home was $13,000.

In an action by the contractor against the homeowner, which of the following should be the contractor's recovery?

(A) $10,000, the contract price.

(B) $11,000, the contract price plus $1,000 for the medical expenses incurred because the homeowner refused to pay.

(C) $12,000, the contract price plus $2,000, the bargain that was lost because the contractor could not pay cash for the car on June 1.

(D) $13,000, the amount the homeowner was enriched by the contractor's services.

Questions 86–87 are based upon the following fact situation.

A student graduates the top of her law school class and is immediately offered a job with a prestigious law firm making $100,000 per year. The student studies hard for the bar exam and passes. A week before she is to begin at the law firm, which would have been September 1, she receives notice that, due to budget cuts, they will no longer be needing her. The student looks for work but by this point most attorney positions are filled. All she can find is work as a paralegal for $50,000 a year, and she chooses to turn that down. The student finally finds work six months later, making $90,000 per year. The student sues the original law firm for breach of contract.

Question 86

What is the best defense that the law firm can assert?

(A) When the student failed to take the paralegal job, she did not mitigate her damages, and therefore is not entitled to recover damages.

(B) There was never any contract for employment, merely an offer.

(C) The budget cuts, due to a poor economy, were an unforeseeable event that made the contract commercially impracticable.

(D) There was no consideration.

Question 87

Assuming that there is an enforceable contract, what are the student's damages?

(A) nothing, as she failed to mitigate by taking the paralegal job

(B) $40,000

(C) $60,000

(D) $10,000

Question 88

A buyer agrees to buy from a seller a brand new cell phone for $400. The phone is due to come out next week, so the contract calls for buyer to make a deposit of $50, and pick up the phone in one week. The phone costs seller $300, and seller routinely sells these types of phones. The buyer breaches the contract by refusing to pick up the phone and pay the remaining balance. The seller resells the phone at $400. If the seller sues for breach of contract, what will his damages be?

(A) $100

(B) $400

(C) $50

(D) Nothing

Questions 89–90 are based upon the following fact pattern.

A homeowner hires a particularly skilled painter to create a mural for her foyer. She chose the painter based on previous murals he had created, and because his artwork was particular to her taste. Without the homeowner's knowledge or consent, the painter delegates the mural to his apprentice, who is not nearly as skilled.

Question 89

If the homeowner sues for breach of contract based on the delegation, will she prevail?

(A) Yes, because the painting was a duty too personal to be delegated.

(B) Yes, if the contract prohibited delegation.

(C) No, unless the apprentice painted an objectively poor mural.

(D) No, because duties can almost always be delegated.

Question 90

Assume for this question that the painter did not delegate his duties, but instead, merely breached the contract. If the homeowner asks the court to compel the painter to continue to paint the mural, will she prevail?

(A) Yes, since money damages are not adequate in this scenario.

(B) Yes, since no one else but this particular painter could give the homeowner the mural she desired.

(C) No, because courts never award specific performance for service contracts.

(D) No, because someone else can adequately paint the mural.

Question 91

A dancer contracted with a contractor to construct a dance studio addition for her in her home. The dancer and the contractor orally agreed that the contractor would only build the dance studio if the dancer was able to obtain a zoning variance to put an addition on to her house, since adding square footage to one's house was currently against a zoning law in her neighborhood. Subsequent to their oral agreement, the dancer and the contractor signed a written agreement with respect to the construction of the dance studio that appeared to be complete but made no mention of the oral agreement regarding the zoning variance. The dancer, after diligent effort, was not granted the variance. The dancer wants to submit evidence of the prior oral agreement, but the contractor claims that any evidence of the oral agreement should be barred.

On the issue of whether or not the prior oral agreement will come in, who will prevail?

(A) The contractor will prevail, because any evidence of the prior oral agreement may not come in to contradict a writing that is intended to be complete.

(B) The contractor, because the dancer lost the ability to benefit from the non-occurrence of the oral condition and hence she will be found to have constructively waived such condition.

(C) The dancer, becuase evidence of the prior oral agreement is only coming in to supplement the written agreement.

(D) The dancer, because proof of the oral agreement to determine the enforceability of the written contract should be allowed to demonstrate that no valid contract exists unless the dancer was permitted the zoning variance.

Question 92

On April 2, a seller offers sell 300 widgets to a buyer at $1 each. The seller states that she must get the buyer's acceptance by April 5. On April 3, the buyer mails his acceptance to the seller. On April 4, the seller mails her revocation of the offer to the buyer, which is then received by the buyer on April 5. The buyer receives the seller's acceptance in the mail on April 6. Has a valid contract been formed?

(A) Yes, because when the buyer mailed his acceptance on April 3, the contract was deemed to have been formed on that date.

(B) Yes, because the seller's revocation was not received by the buyer until after the buyer mailed his acceptance.

(C) No, because the buyer received the seller's acceptance on April 6.

(D) No, because the contract is void for indefiniteness.

Question 93

A seller agrees to sell to a buyer 100 widgets for $5 each, payment to be made May 1, and delivery to be made June 1. On April 30, the buyer sends a check for $500 to the seller, which the seller receives on May 1. On May 3, the seller calls the buyer and says "I am out of widgets, there is no way I'll make the delivery."

The statement that the seller would not be delivering the widgets had what kind of legal effect?

(A) It acted as an anticipatory repudiation, allowing the buyer to bring suit for breach of contract on May 4.

(B) It acted as an anticipatory repudiation, allowing the buyer to bring suit on June 1.

(C) It had no operative legal effect.

(D) The seller did not breach, because of unanticipated circumstances.

Question 94

A homeowner contracts with a contractor to build him a home, three stories high, for $900,000. The contract states that in addition to the three stories, the home will have a one-car garage. The homeowner decides that he wants a two-car garage, and asks the contractor if this is possible. The contractor says, "Sure, why not? I really have nothing better to do!"

The contractor completes the entire three stories, but only builds a one-car garage. The homeowner refuses to pay the $900,000 to the contractor.

If the contractor brings a claim for payment, who will prevail?

(A) The homeowner will prevail, because the contract was effectively modified to include the bigger garage.

(B) The homeowner will prevail, because he did not get what he bargained for.

(C) The contractor will prevail, because the homeowner had a preexisting duty to pay $900,000 for a three-story home with a one-car garage.

(D) The contractor will prevail, because he fulfilled his contractual obligations.

Question 95

A homeowner hired a painter to restore her old house. The house was over a century old and hadn't been kept up very well. The painter came to the house and assessed the work, and quoted the homeowner a price of $50,000 for a full restoration.

About a week into work, the painter noticed that upon removing one layer of paint, the paint underneath was lead, which would require quite a substantial change in the removal process. This was not something that either the painter or homeowner knew when they negotiated the original contract. It would cost the painter an extra $10,000 to complete the job, not to mention the time and labor. The painter explained this to the homeowner who said, "Well, I really want the job done right, so go ahead and I'll pay $60,000."

Is the modification enforceable?

(A) No, because there painter had a preexisting duty to paint the house for 50,000.

(B) No, because the painter should have foreseen the lead paint.

(C) Yes, because even though the painter had a preexisting duty, the surprise of lead paint was enough to enforce the modification.

(D) Yes, because the homeowner agreed.

Contracts

Answer 1

(C) In a contract for the sale of goods, a buyer may demand specific performance when the goods are sufficiently unique (UCC 2-716). The contract was valid because there was an offer and acceptance, and the letter satisfied the Statute of Frauds' requirement of a writing. However, the existence of a valid contract will not automatically justify the remedy of specific performance. A mass-produced boat will not be considered sufficiently unique. The yacht owner should sue at law (for money damages) for the difference between his contract price with the neighbor and the cost of a comparable boat. These are his expectation damages and "an adequate remedy." If this had been a custom-made yacht, the yacht owner would have had a better probability of obtaining specific performance. (D) might have been a tempting answer since it correctly states why the transaction satisfied the Statute of Frauds. However, pay close attention to the question stem, which is asking will the yacht owner prevail in his request for SPECIFIC PERFOMANCE. It is not asking whether he can enforce the contract, or if he can get damages. Remember also that specific performance is only adequate if the goods are sufficiently unique.

Answer 2

(A) The oral agreement between the doorman and the investor was a unilateral contract therefore there was no obligation on the investor's part until the doorman bought Canadian coins. When the doorman bought Krugerrands, he failed to fulfill the contract's condition for payment. The investor specifically stated that he would pay the doorman if the doorman bought Canadian coins for him. The doorman's performance, specifically purchasing Canadian coins, and no other, was a condition precedent to the investor's obligation to compensate him. (D) is incorrect because personal satisfaction must be contracted for. The doorman's purchase was neither a rescission nor a modification (B and C) because no contract existed until the doorman

bought the proper coins, therefore there can be no modification or rescission.

Answer 3

(B) Only an intended beneficiary may sue, i.e., the car dealer, and the buyer must have intended, by the contract, to confer a benefit on the car manufacturing company. According to these facts, the car manufacturing company is not a creditor beneficiary or a donee beneficiary. The car manufacturing company merely "happens to gain" by virtue of the agreement. This makes the company an incidental beneficiary who will not be entitled to sue on the contract. See Restatement (Second) of Contracts §302 illus. 17. (A) is incorrect because a condition of personal satisfaction must be expressly provided for in the contract. (C) assumes too many facts not in the question. (D) is true, but will not aid the buyer in his defense because the car manufacturer could still bring suit against the buyer if the buyer were in fact a third-party beneficiary.

Answer 4

(C) The window installer cannot recover "on the contract" because the contract's conditions have not been fulfilled. However, a court will attempt to rectify the inequity of forcing the window installer to bear all of his expenses by allowing him an action in quasi-contract. Quasi-contract is a legal fiction used to prevent unjust enrichment of one party to the detriment of another when there was no contract or the contract is unenforceable. The party who suffered a detriment is awarded restitution for expenses and labor or damages to the extent of his reasonable reliance. In this fact pattern, the window installer should recover for the work he completed despite his inability to contractually bind the contractor for the entire $78,000. (D) is not applicable. Commercial impracticability arises when the terms of a contract have become economically onerous and neither party assumed such a risk. Impossibility (B), though applicable, only serves to discharge all of the parties' duties, and would not help the window installer recover any money. (A) is incorrect because it is not a real theory. What one would recover under a quasi-contract theory would be restitution, but there is no such thing as "equitable restitution."

Answer 5

(C) If parties to a written agreement intend the written agreement to be an expression of their oral understandings, the written agreement is said to be an *integration.* An integration is either (1) partial, i.e., not containing all details of the agreement or (2) total, i.e., containing *all* relevant details of the agreement. Evidence of prior oral understandings that contradict an integration may not be admitted in court under the Parol Evidence Rule. Such evidence supplementing but not contradicting an integration may be admitted in the case of a partial integration but not a total integration. In our case, it must be decided whether the written agreement between the seller and the buyer was a partial or total integration because the integration (written contract) was silent concerning the frames. If the contract is ruled to be a partial integration, evidence of the frames will be admissible because it supplements but does not contradict the written agreement. If the contract is ruled a total integration, no evidence of prior or contemporaneous agreements may be admitted. Under the majority view, the question whether a written agreement is an integration, partial or total, is a question of law that is decided by a judge, not a jury. (A) and (B) are both incorrect because if it is ruled a total integration, NO parol evidence will be allowed in.

Answer 6

(B) The promise of a gift is as unenforceable in a business context as it is in a personal matter (A), but the promise to extend the bookstore's time period in which he could enter a new lease was represented as an option. Therefore, the principal issue is whether this "option" will be enforceable. To be binding, an option must be supported by consideration. Since there was no consideration given by the bookstore owner, the landlord's statement amounted to an offer that may be revoked at any point prior to acceptance unless there is partial performance by the offeree (D). The bookstore owner suffered a detriment by expending money in reliance on the offer, but the question is, "What is the landlord's BEST argument?" While there may be reliance, it works in the bookstore owner's favor, thus (C) is incorrect.

Answer 7

(A) Since the bookstore owner did act in reliance on the promise, this will be his best argument. The main issue will be whether this reliance was reasonable.

Since no consideration was given, and the landlord did not bargain for the bookstore owner's reliance, (B) and (C) are incorrect. (D) will not qualify as consideration; it is evidence of reliance.

Answer 8

(C) Under UCC 2-205, "An offer by a merchant to buy or sell goods in a signed writing which by its terms gives assurance that it will be held open is not revocable, for lack of consideration during the time stated or if no time is stated for a reasonable time, but in no event may such period of irrevocability exceed three months." The offer exceeded three months, and therefore it will not be enforceable under this UCC provision. Under common law (but not under the UCC), the buyer's attempt at acceptance would have been considered a counteroffer (A) since it changed the terms of the original offer. A counteroffer rejects an original offer and ends the buyer's power of acceptance. However, the counteroffer is irrelevant because the seller had already revoked its offer on April 12, before it was sent the counteroffer. In addition, UCC is applied here, not common law. (D) is incorrect because of the three-month time limit, which was discussed above.

Answer 9

(D) Since the correspondence between the video retailer and the movie studio is between merchants, it is within the scope of UCC Article 2. UCC 2-205 provides that "an offer by a merchant to buy or sell goods in a signed writing by its terms that gives assurance that it will be held open is not revocable, for lack of consideration during this time stated." The movie studio was prevented by this section from revoking its offer (that makes (A) incorrect). According to UCC 2-207, "A definite and seasonable acceptance or a written confirmation which is sent within a reasonable time operates as an acceptance even though it states terms additional to or different from those offered or agreed upon, unless acceptance is expressly made conditional on assent to the addition of different terms." (B) simply describes the common law method of interpreting acceptances, which does not apply here because we are dealing in the sale of goods, and (C) is incorrect because the video retailer's additional terms do not invalidate the Movie 1 deal.

Answer 10

(A) The common law Mailbox Rule provides that an acceptance is valid upon its mailing, not upon its receipt (B). A revocation or a rejection, on the other hand, is effective upon receipt. Since the northern realtor's acceptance was mailed before it received the southern realtor's revocation, a valid contract was formed. (C) is incorrect because the northern realtor's March 5 response was not a counteroffer. It was merely an inquiry as to whether the southern realtor was willing to change the terms. An inquiry will not terminate an original offer. The Multistate examiners like to test the fine-line distinction between a counteroffer and an inquiry. (D) is false—the facts of the question provide sufficient evidence that there was a meeting of the minds on the original offer.

Answer 11

(D) The statement is not effective because the contract was already formed and could not be revoked by either party. (A) does not apply because there cannot be an anticipatory breach when one party to a unilateral or bilateral contract has already fully performed (in our case, the client).

Answer 12

(C) One who is not a party to a contract but stands to receive a benefit is called a *third-party beneficiary*. The Restatement (Second) of Contracts §302 distinguishes between an intended third-party beneficiary, who has standing to sue a party for a breach of the contract, and an incidental beneficiary, who may not sue. The casino was not a creditor or a donee beneficiary, but merely "happened to gain" from the agreement. This makes the casino an incidental beneficiary without standing to sue on the contract.

Answer 13

(D) This question addresses two issues: consideration and third-party beneficiaries. The promise to the student was a bargained-for exchange since the student quit her job at her grandfather's request. Since she had no legal obligation to quit her job, it was a bargained-for legal detriment. Compare this with a situation where the grandfather asks the student to quit her job as a prostitute, which is illegal. In that situation, there would be no bargained-for legal detriment since the student is not legally entitled to be a prostitute, yet she is legally entitled to be a stripper. One who is a beneficiary but not a party to an agreement is called a third-party beneficiary. The Restatement (Second) of Contracts §302 has done away with the distinction between creditor and donee beneficiaries and instead divides beneficiaries into intended, who may enforce a contract, and incidental, who may not. Since the student's grandfather clearly expected the notes to be used as collateral, he can be considered to have intended to be her surety, and creditors such as the car dealership may enforce the agreement between the student and her grandfather. Although (C) is true, (D) is the better answer because it addresses both issues.

Answer 14

(D) Under the traditional view, performance would not be excused unless it was utterly impossible to perform. Many modern courts, the Restatement (Second) of Contracts ch. 11, and the UCC (2-615(a)) allow a promisor's performance to be excused if changed circumstances make performance commercially infeasible. But if the party assumed the risk of such an occurrence, the party may not be excused. This view equates extreme impracticability with impossibility. The elements necessary for impossibility (C) are much more strict. Impossibility requires that it be objectively impossible to perform the contract through no fault of either party. The contract will then be discharged. Mistake, (A) and (B), is irrelevant to this fact pattern.

Answer 15

(C) is correct because there was never an enforceable promise to pay. A promise to pay the debts of another falls within the Statute of Frauds and must be in writing to be enforceable. Such an agreement is called a suretyship. (A) and (B) are correct statements of law, but do not answer the question. In our case, the fashion designer was not a surety for his friend because the fashion designer incurred the debt; his friend did not. His friend never ordered the clothing and, therefore, was never liable to pay for it. The fashion designer owed the clothing store the money. Whether the clothing store has exhausted its recourse against the friend is irrelevant (D). The fashion designer might be able to recover the $400 from his friend since his friend kept the clothing and wore it.

Answer 16

(D) A promise to keep an offer open is valid only if supported by consideration. The five dollars given in exchange for the option is that consideration. A court will generally not inquire into the adequacy of the consideration (A). Since the offer recites consideration, the court will most likely take it at face value. Because the offer had not been revoked before he accepted it, the football player's acceptance will be valid whether he had an option for three days or not. If not supported by consideration, an offer will be open for a reasonable time or until it is expressly revoked. (B) is the law (UCC 2-205) regarding the sale of goods; it is not applicable to an employment contract. (C) is incorrect because the offer did not mention that it was conditional upon the status of the strike.

Answer 17

(A) An anti-assignment clause barring assignment of a contract will be interpreted to allow assignment of rights only and not duties. An example of a right is to collect payment, while a duty would be to render a performance. Thus, the attorney's grandmother's assignment was valid and enforceable. The mechanic's grandmother will not be able to enforce her assignment because the mechanic's contract stipulated, "Rights under the contract may not be assigned." Compare the clauses in the agreements. An assignment of the future rights to a future contract is not enforceable. The runner's assignment to his grandmother will not be enforceable because the runner assigned rights to a contract that was not yet in existence. To make a contract completely unassignable, the clause should provide that any assignment shall be void.

Answer 18

(C) A unilateral contract offer is automatically revoked by the passage of a reasonable amount of time. The offeror may also revoke the offer prior to acceptance where there has not been partial performance, or reliance.

Answer 19

(A) The court must consider the intent of both parties. In real estate contracts, courts are reluctant to impose a completion date as a condition precedent to payment on the contract, but there are exceptions, as when the contract stipulates, as it does here, that time is of the essence. The university will be bound to pay some compensation for the building because it has kept it and will be enjoying the benefit of it, but may be able to subtract damages for the time it expected to have use of the building, but did not. In situations such as these, the best device is to insert a liquidated damages clause in the contract that sets specific money damages for late performance. (B) and (D) are incorrect because the state of mind of the breaching party is generally not considered. Undue hardship (C) is also not generally considered grounds for discharge.

Answer 20

(D) The homeowner's letter of April 1 was an offer. The promise to keep the offer open was unenforceable because no consideration was given for it and it was not for the sale of goods (i.e., not under the UCC, in which case, no consideration is required). The repairman's letter of April 5 was a counteroffer and a rejection of the homeowner's offer. Therefore, the repairman had relinquished his power of acceptance. The repairman's letter of April 13 was not an acceptance; it was a new offer extended to the homeowner. Under the common law, silence will never be considered an acceptance. The Restatement (Second) of Contracts §69(1) has attempted to change this rule. It states, "Where the offeror has given the offeree reason to understand that silence

or inaction of the offeree will constitute acceptance, the silence or inaction of the offeree will operate as an acceptance if he subjectively intends to be bound." The facts of the question do not show that the repairman intended to be bound by the homeowner's offer. Other exceptions exist to the "silence is not acceptance" rule. Where the offeree silently accepts the benefit of the offeror's services or past dealings of the parties indicate that silence might be an acceptance, the offeree may be held to a contract. Since the repairman was unaware of the homeowner's work and they had no past dealings, the repairman cannot claim that a contract had been formed.

Answer 21

(B) Students may be tempted to think that this is an issue of parol evidence, and if the oral evidence of the condition was in fact parol evidence, it would be barred. However, the evidence of a condition subsequent does not constitute parol evidence. A condition subsequent relates to contract formation, and therefore is not barred by the Parol Evidence Rule. The Parol Evidence Rule only applies to the attempt to prove terms of already existing contracts. Remember that you can always bring in evidence to prove that contract was not formed, or that it should not be enforced.

Answer 22

(D) A condition precedent is one that must occur before an absolute duty of immediate performance arises in the other party. A concurrent condition is when two conditions are supposed to occur simultaneously. A condition subsequent differs significantly from the previous two types. The occurrence of a condition subsequent cuts off an already existing duty. Each party in this question was obligated to convey his car upon the other's performance (condition precedent) or to convey simultaneously (concurrent condition).

Answer 23

(A) A final and complete written integration of a contract may not be contradicted or supplemented by extrinsic evidence, per the Parol Evidence Rule. A partially integrated agreement cannot be contradicted, but may be supplemented with proof of consistent additional terms (C). The statements regarding advertising would be consistent additional terms that are admissible if the writing were a partial integration, but not a complete integration. If the store owner successfully proves that the original agreement was completely integrated, the court may not allow any evidence of supplemental agreements. (B) is false; subsequent statements are never barred by the Parol Evidence Rule. Promissory estoppel (D) is inapplicable since it is a theory that the designer would rely upon.

Answer 24

(B) A compromise settling an honest dispute may always be a valid contract unless the Statute of Frauds has been violated. Both parties' concessions will serve as consideration for each other. This compromise did not violate the Statute of Frauds because the agreement could be performed within one year. (D) is incorrect because the consideration element is satisfied since both parties have an honest dispute. The bargained-for legal determent is giving up legal rights to sue on the contract, if they honestly believe they have a claim. (C) is incorrect because there is nothing here that makes the contract fall under the Statute of Frauds. "No because it's not in writing" is always a tempting answer, but be careful. The contract actually HAS to be in writing before you choose that an answer.

Answer 25

(A) This question deals with the Perfect Tender Rule. If a party tenders an imperfect performance, that party is in breach of contract. This rule is codified in UCC 2-601, which provides, "unless otherwise agreed . . . if the goods or tender of delivery fail in any respect to conform to the contract, the buyer may (a) reject the whole; or (b) accept the whole; or (c) accept any commercial unit or units and reject the rest." The Perfect Tender Rule will not apply to installment contracts; those are covered in UCC 2-612. Courts will also make exceptions if they find the breach insubstantial.

Answer 26

(C) The car owner and the mechanic had a contract for repairs. In such an instance, the performance of the repair (rebuilding of the engine) is a condition precedent to the obligation to pay. The car owner had no obligations and could not be in breach until the mechanic had completely repaired the car. Bad faith (B) might help prove a breach but (C) is still a stronger answer since it describes the fact that the mechanic failed to fulfill his contractual duties. (D) is incorrect because we do not know if rechecking the engine was part of what was agreed to in the contract, so again, (C) is the better answer. (A) is incorrect because if the mechanic had substantially performed, then the car owner might be in breach.

Answer 27

(D) When terms are written on the back of a check above the place of endorsement, cashing the check constitutes a valid accord and satisfaction of those terms, unless words such as "under protest" or the like are written under the signature. Since the mechanic accepted the car owner's check, he also accepted the car owner's terms of payment. The words "payment in full" release the mechanic's claim to another $200 regardless of whether he had properly fixed the car.

Answer 28

(A) A promise to forego an action brought in good faith is sufficient consideration to complete a contract even if the action would have failed (C). Remember that any agreement to settle, when one person thinks they have reason to be sued or reason to bring claim, is valid consideration. (B) is incorrect because Phillips subjective belief is irrelevant. In addition, there is no evidence in the question that the settlement was vague (D).

Answer 29

(B) Despite the fact that the department store owner had obtained an agreement from the tenant to pay the supermarket owner's maintenance costs, the department store owner will still be liable on her contract with the supermarket owner. The department store owner did not delegate her duties in the maintenance agreement to the tenant, but entered another agreement with the tenant that called for satisfaction of the maintenance agreement. As a third-party creditor beneficiary to the department store owner's contract with the tenant, the supermarket owner has the choice to sue either the department store owner (on the basis of their agreement) or the tenant (on the basis of the sublease). (A) is the reason that the supermarket owner may sue the tenant, but not the reason that the department store owner remains liable to the supermarket owner. (C) assumes that the supermarket owner may have standing to sue only one person for breach of contract, and that is incorrect.

Answer 30

(D) Rewards are usually unilateral contracts that may be accepted only by performance. The answer to this question is contained within the facts. The offer was not for an arrest of the murderer (A) or apprehending the murderer (B), but for information leading to the arrest and conviction.

Answer 31

(D) An offer may be revoked through reasonable attempts at substantially similar publicity informing of its revocation. Since the original offer was extended through a full-page ad in the daily newspapers, the revocation must be through a substantially similar medium.

Answer 32

(C) This is a parol evidence issue. If the court decides that the written contract was a complete and final integration, the creditor will not be allowed to submit evidence that payment was to be made to her. Therefore, she will not be able to show that she was a third-party beneficiary to the agreement with standing to sue. (D) is incorrect because the Statute of Frauds is not at issue. Remember not EVERY contract has to be in writing, only those things that fall within the Statute of Frauds. (A) and (B) are incorrect because the negligent reading of the contract, by either party, will not have any bearing on whether prior statements can come in.

Answer 33

(A) The creditor's rights would have vested if she were aware of the agreement, preventing the seller and the buyer from revoking the benefits conferred upon the creditor in the contract. The seller and the buyer were free to rescind their agreement until it vested. (C) is incorrect; such formal notice is not required to vest third-party rights.

Answer 34

(C) The constructor's promise to pay for the pedestrian's damages is not enforceable because the constructor did not receive consideration in exchange for the promise. The constructor has no legal obligation to the pedestrian; therefore, the pedestrian did not give up any valid legal claims against him. This is the most important issue in the question since gratuitous promises are not enforceable. (B) is incorrect because the contract would not fall within the Statute of Frauds since the elements of a surety relationship are missing. Be very wary of answers that lead you to suretyship since, although sometimes correct, they are rarely correct. (D) is incorrect because although the contract was vague, it could have been enforceable if supported by consideration, because the court might reasonably interpret what the constructor meant by "everything." (A) is incorrect because this is not a situation that would fall under the doctrine of mistake. Restatement (Second) of Contracts §152 defines a mutual mistake as where both parties have been in error concerning a basic factual assumption that materially affects the exchange, and the party seeking relief has not born the risk. Restatement (Second) of Contracts §153 addresses a unilateral mistake. It occurs when only one of the parties was in error, and requires that all of the elements of mutual mistake exist plus either the non-mistaking party knew of the error or enforcement of the contract would be unconscionable.

Answer 35

(D) The arrangement between the constructor and the therapist was a unilateral contract. No enforceable contract was formed until the act requested was performed. Each time the therapist treated the pedestrian, the constructor was bound to pay for it. However, the therapist was never bound to treat the pedestrian. The therapist may stop treating the pedestrian at any time without being in breach. The pedestrian is clearly the intended (donee) beneficiary of the constructor-therapist contract (D), but this will not prevent the therapist from winning the suit. The therapist cannot raise any claims that the pedestrian and the constructor may have against each other, and the pedestrian cannot sue the constructor. The proper suit is against the therapist (making (A) and (C) incorrect). (B) is simply false since there was indeed consideration.

Answer 36

(C) This question deals with the Perfect Tender Rule. If a party tenders an imperfect performance, that party is in breach of contract. This rule is codified in UCC 2-601 which provides, "unless otherwise agreed . . . if the goods or tender of delivery fail in any respect to conform to the contract, the buyer may (a) reject the whole; or (b) accept the whole; or (c) accept any commercial unit or units and reject the rest." The Perfect Tender Rule will not apply to installment contracts; those are covered in UCC 2-612. Courts will also make exceptions if they find the breach very insubstantial. This defense will help prove that the seller's failure to deliver the entire contractual amount on time was a material breach. (A) and (B) are incorrect because the market value is irrelevant to whether buyer can reject the goods. In addition (D) is incorrect because it would be a defense that seller could use, not buyer.

Answer 37

(D) The Perfect Tender Rule makes "time of the essence" an implied condition precedent in contracts for the sale of goods. This means that a late tender will constitute a material breach of contract, giving the buyer a right to reject the goods. This contract made "time of the essence" an express condition by relieving the buyer's liability if there was a late delivery. (A) and (C) would not be the best answers. The fact that the animals were custom-made does not relieve the "time of the essence" provision, although it may aid in proving liability for the delivered animals. At first glance, (C) sounds like an impossibility or impracticability defense; however, the seller could have searched for additional stuffing sources. (D) is the best answer since it provides evidence of a subsequent modification (that does not fall within the Parol Evidence Rule) waiving the timeliness provision.

Answer 38

(B) A computer manufacturer had a right at any time to inspect the goods to determine if contractual specifications were met. (A) is incorrect; under many contracts, goods are paid for prior to their receipt. The computer manufacturer still has a reasonable time to inspect the screens after she receives them. (C) and (D) were fabricated. The opposite of (D) is true; a right to inspection must be expressly waived.

Answer 39

(C) is correct. The pre-payment clause made the agreement performable within one year. This is also why (A) is incorrect. (B) is incorrect and deceptive. Although the UCC requires a writing with a contract for the sale of goods over $500, an oral contract will be enforceable when the goods have already been accepted by the buyer. Since the goods have been accepted, that is considered performance. (D) is incorrect; contracts made by minors are not automatically void, but voidable at the minor's discretion if not for the purchase of a necessity. So, even if he was a minor at the time of making the contract, continuing to make payments after reaching the age of majority would make the contract enforceable. In addition, that would have no bearing on whether the contract is oral, which is what the uncle is asserting. Pay close attention to what the question is asking.

Answer 40

(A) When one party acts to his detriment in exchange for a benefit conferred in the contract, there will be sufficient consideration to support the contract. A legal detriment will result if the promisee performs an act he is not otherwise legally obliged to perform or refrains from an action permissible to him. Since the student gave up his legal right to have a part-time job or quit school, there was consideration for the uncle's promise to pay for the car and provide spending money. A contract is formed despite the absence of a monetary loss to the promisee (B) or monetary gain to the promisor. A promise to confer a gift without the intent to induce reliance is not enforceable. In this question, the promise reasonably induced acts by the promisee. (C) is incorrect because peace of mind may be sufficient consideration in some instances (see *Hamer v. Sidway*).

Answer 41

(A) The professor must argue that perfect attendance was not an implied condition of the job. If he can prove that a short absence for legitimate reasons does not impair the quality of his teaching services, it would follow that the absence will not amount to a breach. In fact, the university would be in breach for replacing the professor. The estoppel argument (B), only gives the professor relief to the extent that justice requires and will be harder to prove than the immateriality of the professor's absence. (C) is an inappropriate argument because it would permit the university to fire the professor for a material breach of any one segment of the contract. (D) is also inappropriate because impossibility discharges all parties from performance. The professor is not in a strong position because most contracts for employment are "at will," meaning that the employer may fire the employee at will.

Answer 42

(B) The store owner still has a right to inspect the goods and has maintained his remedies (UCC 2-513). Public policy will not prevent a seller from demanding payment before this point.

Answer 43

(C) A buyer of goods is entitled to "cover" in the event of a breach by the seller. This is the best course of action and will make the store owner "whole" because he will have obtained the goods he wanted at the price he bargained for. "Cover" allows one to buy substitute goods and recover the difference between the price of the substitute goods and the contractual price (UCC 2-712, 2-725). If the substitute goods are bought below the original contract price, there is no additional recovery. In no event will the breaching party be permitted to benefit from the breach.

Answer 44

(C) This contract would ordinarily be void under the Statute of Frauds as an oral contract for the sale of land; however, the buyer may be able to enforce the contract under the quasi-contract theory because of the substantial improvements he made to the store in expectation of ownership. However, for part performance to apply to the sale of land, you need two of the following three; (1) some sort of indicia of ownership, (2) improvements, and/or (3) payment. Here, there are only improvements. The other choices would not be considered.

Answer 45

(A) The original agreement was fully enforceable. Both parties supplied consideration. The oil refinery was guaranteed a buyer for its oil, and the oil company was guaranteed a seller at the market price in exchange for their concessions, making (B) wrong. Although there was not a consistent price each month, the method of determining the price was definite, so (D) is incorrect. All essential elements were present for a contract. The subsequent agreement entered into by the parties modified, but did not replace or invalidate, the original contract. (C) is incorrect because there was a contract modification, not a replacement.

Answer 46

(B) The refinery will be excused from performance under the doctrine of impossibility. This doctrine states that a contract is discharged when, through no fault of the parties, the subject matter essential to the performance of the contract is destroyed. (D) would help the oil company win an action for breach. Neither party assumed the risk of explosion (A). If the refinery had assumed the risk, it would still be held liable to perform the contract. (C) may be true, but impossibility excuses it.

Answer 47

(C) A contract for the sale of land will not be defeated due to a failure to specify the kind of title to be conveyed. The seller will be required to supply a marketable title. The contract is not voidable for indefiniteness since the court has the power to supply the omitted term (A).

Answer 48

(C) If an obligor renders performance before he has notice of an assignment, the assignee takes title subject to the obligor's defense of ignorance. The seller is the proper party for the neighbor to sue since he was unjustly enriched by accepting payment.

Answer 49

(A) The neighbor may enforce the contract against the new buyer because an assignment puts assignees in privity of contract. (B) is an incorrect answer because, while it might be true, it does not apply to this fact pattern. (C) is incorrect because it does not answer the question being asked, which is if there is an obligation that runs from the new buyer to the neighbor. (D) is incorrect because not paying on time acts as notice of default; no "official notice" is needed to breach.

Answer 50

(A) is correct because under the UCC, if a merchant (which the coin dealer is, in this case) offers to keep an option open, and that offer is in writing, no consideration will be needed. Therefore, the coin dealer could not revoke his offer. It should be noted that this will only keep the offer open for 90 days under the UCC, not 100, but 90 days had not passed. (B) is incorrect because (A) is a better answer due to the fact that it states WHY the

revocation was ineffective. (C) is incorrect because the riots had no effect on the contract.

Answer 51

(C) Once the investor accepted the offer by ordering five coins, a contract had been formed and the investor terminated any future power of acceptance on that offer. Although the coin dealer might also have a good argument for impossibility (B), that defense is much more difficult to prove. The coin dealer's performance would not be objectively impossible unless there were no other source of these coins. He most likely would be held responsible for insuring against theft and replacing the coins, even at a loss. (A) is incorrect because there is no mistake on the part of either party.

Answer 52

(C) Offers not supported by consideration or reasonably relied upon may be revoked at will by the offeror, despite promises not to modify or revoke the contract. This question does not fall under the UCC exception allowing a firm offer spanning less than three months to remain irrevocable without consideration, because the contract is for personal services and not the sale of goods

Answer 53

(B) The homeowner's offer was for a unilateral contract because the homeowner was bargaining for performance, not a promise to perform. Under the Restatement, an offer to form a unilateral contract becomes irrevocable once performance has begun, even though the contract is not considered accepted (and hence formed). The reasoning behind this is that once the offeree begins to perform, it is unfair to revoke the offer and the offeree should be given a reasonable time to complete performance. This rule was established to prevent capricious acts of the offeror's from damaging the offeree in a unilateral contract.

Answer 54

(B) Since the homeowner was not obligated to pay until the planter had fulfilled his obligations, the planter's duty to perform was a condition precedent to the homeowner's duty to pay. (C) and (D) are incorrect because a condition subsequent is an event discharging a previous duty to perform. Such conditions are rarely used in contracts and are not involved here.

Answer 55

(D) Since the delay was caused by the homeowner, the planter will be excused from the deadline. A court will estop the homeowner from enforcing the deadline. All of the other choices are irrelevant.

Answer 56

(C) The creditor was a third-party beneficiary to an output contract between the boulder company and the construction company. UCC 2-306 provides that parties must make good-faith efforts under such contracts, which they did. The contracts will not fail due to lack of consideration (B) because both parties had obligated themselves. The construction company agreed to use the boulder company as its services were needed, and the boulder company agreed on a set price. (A) is irrelevant because there was no assignment of a contract. (D) is also irrelevant since it does not matter whether rights were "personal" or not.

Answer 57

(B) A court will not enforce this contract because it lacks the specifics of the transfer. A contract for the sale of land needs to detail the amount of land. (C) is wrong because, although this agreement is in writing and satisfies the Statute of Frauds, (A) is simply not true.

Answer 58

(A) As an assignee of the lease, the sublessee assumed all terms and liabilities in the lease regardless of her actual awareness. Hence, (B) through (D) are false.

Answer 59

(A) Both the burdens and benefits of the landlord-tenant agreement were conveyed to the sublessee and the buyer. The buyer will be bound to allow the sublessee to exercise the option. (B) is incorrect because for the buyer to be bound, the option does not need to run with the land or (C) touch and concern the land.

Answer 60

(D) The model was required to act in good faith. If (A), (B), or (C) is correct, she did not. (D) will not help the painter's case because the model may, in good faith, dislike an accurate portrait of herself.

Answer 61

(B) Both parties were obligated to cooperate. Failure of either party to do so would constitute a breach, and the usual remedies for breach would be available. This makes (B) least accurate since he did NOT assume that particular risk.

Answer 62

(D) Offers not supported by consideration or detrimental reliance can be revoked at will by the offeror, even if he has promised not to do so for a certain period of time. The UCC carves out an exception for a firm offer between merchants to last for less than three months. However, the parties are not merchants, so that rule does not apply here.

Answer 63

(A) The buyer was not asking for a promise of performance, but only the performance itself. He had the right to revoke his offer until the seller began performance. The offer was automatically revoked when the time for performance passed. The "Mailbox Rule" provides that acceptance by mail of a bilateral contract creates a contract at the moment of posting, so long as the acceptance is properly addressed and stamped.

However, this rule will not apply to a unilateral contract since acceptance can occur by performance only, and not posting the acceptance in the mail. (B) is incorrect since the buyer is not effectively bound until the seller commences performance. However, note that most contracts are NOT unilateral, so be careful that when you think a contract is unilateral, that it actually is asking for performance, not a return promise, in return.

Answer 64

(D) A contract is formed only after a "meeting of the minds," offer, acceptance, and consideration. Offer and acceptance were absent. If any of those things were absent, there would have been no contract. (B) is incorrect because the consideration would have been convincing the individual to buy planes.

Answer 65

(D) An agreement not to assign is not a condition of the obligor's promise to pay; therefore, breach of the promise does not excuse the obligor, but does provide an action for damages. (A) is incorrect since the steel company may also be liable. Assignment of rights may be prohibited by an express clause (B). The most effective way to prevent assignment of a contract is to write that "any assignment will be void."

Answer 66

(B) Since the helicopter company did not know of the assignment, it will not be liable to the bank. The steel company is liable to the bank because it was the assignor of the rights. (A) is incorrect because there is no reason why the bank would not recover from the steel company, since they created the original contract and there is no evidence of a novation. (C) is incorrect because of the reasons stated above; the helicopter did not know of the assignment. Had the steel company notified the helicopter company of the assignment to the bank, the helicopter company would be liable to the bank, but that did not happen in this fact pattern. For the same reason, (D) is incorrect as well.

Answer 67

(B) Abstaining from smoking is sufficient consideration in a bargained-for exchange. The grandson was not legally obligated to abstain from smoking, and so gave up a right he did not have to. Hence, this will be considered consideration. Although promissory estoppel may help the grandson to prevail, proving bargained-for exchange is a safer avenue to pursue; the student should always choose the path of least resistance (consideration) rather than promissory estoppel (which we use only when promissory consideration is not available).

Answer 68

(B) The maternal grandfather should argue that since the grandson had already promised the paternal grandfather to quit smoking, the maternal grandfather received no binding consideration for his promise. (C) implies that this case presents a Statute of Frauds problem, but the contract was to be performed within one year, and therefore did not fall under the Statute of Frauds and (D) is incorrect since subjective intent is not an element of contract formation. A valid offer and acceptance depends upon the objective manifestation of the exchange, not upon whether an offer or an acceptance was intended.

Answer 69

(C) An offer may be revoked despite a promise not to do so, unless the promise to hold the offer open was made in exchange for valid consideration. Between merchants, a firm offer will be held open for up to three months without consideration. The seller and the buyer are a casual buyer and seller; they will not qualify as merchants. Hence, in order for the offer to remain irrevocable, and hence an option contract, consideration needed to be provided. The March 15 phone call was an effective revocation because it gave the buyer information inconsistent with the offer. (D) is incorrect — the March 1 offer was valid at the time.

Answer 70

(C) Under the Statute of Frauds, a contract for the sale of goods over $500 must be in writing (UCC 2-201(1)) and signed by the party to be charged. Even though the contract was signed by the agent and not the buyer, the agent was acting as an agent for the buyer. If an agent seeks to enter into a contract that ordinarily must be in writing, the agent's authority must be in writing. (C) is the least accurate choice because if the agent's authority was written, the car dealership will most likely prevail.

Answer 71

(C) An assignee takes his rights subject to the defenses of the obligor. The homeowner could only owe the creditor what he owed the roofer. If the homeowner did not owe the roofer money on the contract because the work was not satisfactorily completed, then he would not be liable to pay the creditor. (B) is incorrect because contractual rights may be assigned despite a clause to the contrary. Violation of the clause may be a breach of the contract, but will not be a breach material enough to excuse payment. (A) is incorrect. Since there was no delegation, whether the creditor could have completed the project is irrelevant. (D) is incorrect because creditor can still have rights in the contract as an assignee; he need not be an intended beneficiary.

Answer 72

(C) When one sells a note, he assigns all benefits and loses standing to bring an action on the note. The fact that the computer designer is a minor is irrelevant because minors can enforce contracts, even if contracts can not be enforced against them, so (B) is incorrect. (A) is incorrect because it's not factually true; he sold his right to collect on the note.

Answer 73

(A) The person, either neighbor or friend, with priority will have an action for the money due on the note. One of the notes will be fully enforceable. An infant may choose to avoid a contract he has entered into with certain exceptions. The client may not choose to avoid the computer designer's contract for him. (B) and (C) are irrelevant, because, as discussed above, his minor status makes the contract voidable, at the minor's discretion, but does not make the contract void.

Answer 74

(B) is the correct answer. The first counselor is entitled to be put in the position he would have been in if the contract had been performed, and when you apply this, you take the difference in the contract salary he would have earned, $10,000, and the amount he actually earned at the lesser camp, which was $6,000, plus the reasonable expenses incurred in seeking to mitigate the breach, which was $200. (A) is incorrect because it doesn't provide for the reasonable expenses in mitigating, and (C) is a wrong answer because it would overcompensate the first counselor, when the goal is to only put him the position he would have been in had the contract been fulfilled.

Answer 75

(C) is the correct answer, as a party to a contract with reasonable grounds to worry that the other party might not be able to perform can request adequate assurances of performance, according to UCC 2-609. In this case, that is what happened, but the information provided by the manufacturer should have been sufficient to satisfy the request for assurance making the supplier in breach of contract. (A) is incorrect because a quantity expressed in terms of requirements is enforceable, and (B) is incorrect, since under the UCC 2-609, a party to a contract who has reasonable grounds for insecurity is entitled to assurance, as discussed above. (D) is incorrect because although it arrives at the correct part, it comes to the wrong reason.

Answer 76

(D) is correct since when a seller induces a buyer's consent by means of a material misrepresentation, which the dealer did by concealing the fact that the car had been in an accident, the resulting contract is voidable at the election of the buyer. Since the buyer asked a direct question about whether the car had been in an accident, coupled with the fact that he concealed the accident with repairs, this amounts to material fraud. (A) is incorrect because although there is an element of "buyer beware" to be had, and most times a buyer does have a duty to inspect, here the buyer did "inspect" when she asked about the accident, and the dealer concealed the relevant information. In addition, since he had carefully concealed evidence of an accident, an inspection would not have changed things.

Answer 77

(D) is correct, as an assignee succeeds to a contract as the contract stands at the time of assignment. Since the brother and the sister had effectively modified the contract before it was assigned, it was assigned with modifications. (A) is incorrect because the answer implied the existence of a rule which would make a contract modification ineffective when an assignee had no notice of it, but such a rule doesn't exist. (B) is incorrect because, while it is true that if a third party waives a condition, that party may reinstate the condition with respect to future acts of performance, but that is not applicable here. (C) is incorrect because it is true that the debtor in this case can insist that the payments be due on the 5th of each month, but misstates the reason why.

Answer 78

(C) is correct, the UCC controls, and the seller is entitled to be put in the position he would have been in if the contract had been performed. (A) is incorrect because $2 fails to accomplish the goal of putting the non-breaching party back in the position they would have been in had the contract not been breached, (B) is incorrect because again, $6 fails to accomplish the above goal, and (D) is incorrect because there is no statutory requirement that goods be resold at a public auction.

Answer 79

(D) is correct since a promise to pay a debt after the running of the Statute of Limitations, like the promise in this case, is enforceable without consideration. (A) is incorrect because it is not responsive to the question. A promise to pay a debt after the Statute of Limitations tolls is enforceable without consideration, (B) is incorrect because yet again, a promise to pay a barred debt is enforceable. (C) is incorrect because promises are not enforceable just because their performance would benefit the promise.

Answer 80

(D) is correct since under the UCC2-206, an offer to buy goods for prompt shipment is accepted when the seller ships the goods. Here, the contract was created when the keyboard wholesaler shipped the keyboards. The contract did not include the subsequent acknowledgement form since it was an effort at modification that was not accepted. (A) is incorrect because the answer mistakes the rule concerning consequential damages, as buyers generally are entitled to recover. (B) is incorrect because the terms of a contract for the sale of goods are established upon acceptance of an offer, which was when the keyboard wholesaler shipped the contracts. This means that the contract was formed without the proposed modifications. (C) is incorrect because, though it correctly concludes the correct party, it misstates the reason.

Answer 81

(B) is correct. Under UCC 2-202, a final written agreement, while it may not be contradicted by a prior agreement, it may be explained or supplemented "by course of dealing or usage of trade or by course of performance." First you look to a course of dealing, and therefore, the agreement would be interpreted to include the 5 percent discount if payment was made within fifteen days. (A) is incorrect because as stated above, the course of dealing controls over trade or custom. (C) is incorrect because the question doesn't raise an issue of waiver or retraction of one. Be careful that when you choose an answer, you are actually choosing something that deals with the fact pattern and call of the question.

Answer 82

(D) is correct because there was no mitigation. We do not know what the damages would have been. (A) is incorrect because we do not know that $1,000 would have been the cost difference in finding a new tutor. (B) is incorrect because the amount of the daughter's future salary is consequential damages, and while sometimes recoverable, would not be here since the daughter did not take steps to mitigate her damages. (C) is incorrect because we would not give nominal damages in contracts to "punish" since the courts only award damages where there is actual injury.

Answer 83

(C) is correct. The uncle's original letter was not an offer, but merely a statement indicating a possible interest in selling the yacht, while the nephew's letter mailed on May 3, was the offer. The uncle's May 6 note was an acceptance, and was effective when it was mailed, so a contract went into effect on May 6.

Answer 84

(D) is correct. If it is clear that the condition clearly benefits one party, as it is clear here, the other party's duty is not subject to the condition. (B) is incorrect for the same reason.

Answer 85

(A) is correct since the contractor is entitled to the contract price for the work done. However, the contractor may not recover for the other items, as they were not foreseeable at the time the contract was made.

Answer 86

(B) would be the firm's best defense. The fact pattern tells you that she received an offer, but never tells you whether a contract was actually formed. If the offer was merely an offer, and never created an enforceable contract, that would be the firm's best defense. (A) is incorrect because even though she did have a duty to mitigate, that would only reduce, not bar, her damages. (C) is incorrect. While the firm might be able to assert that as a defense, it is not as good a defense as (B) since a lack of formation is always the best defense. In addition, it would be unlikely that this situation would meet the requirements of commercial impracticability, which are an unforeseen event that neither party agreed to bear the risk of, and a devastating loss, more than mere lost profits. Budget cuts, even due to a poor economy, would most likely not fit into the category of unforeseen events. (D) is incorrect because there was consideration; she would practice law for the firm, they would pay her, each party bargained for a legal detriment.

Answer 87

(C) is correct, as it correctly takes into account the difference between her expected job ($100,000) and the job she received ($90,000) plus what she should have been making during the six months she was out of work. (A) and (B) are incorrect because they factor in a duty to mitigate. While the student did have a duty to mitigate, that does not include taking a "lesser" job position since she was qualified to be an attorney.

Answer 88

(C) is the correct answer because the seller is a volume seller and is therefore entitled to lost profits. The profit would have been $100, and the seller already had a down payment of $50. The fact pattern does not tell you that the down payment was returned, so do not assume. The remaining balance is therefore $50. (D) is incorrect because although the seller resold the phone for the same amount, he is a volume seller, so is entitled to profits since he presumably could have sold one more phone.

Answer 89

(A) is the correct answer because when services are very personal in nature, that is, call for a specific skill such as painting, they may not be delegated. The fact pattern tells you that the homeowner hired the painter for his particular skill, as well as her taste in his art. That means the duty to paint the mural can not be delegated. This makes (C) incorrect because even if the mural the apprentice created was objectively good, it might not have been to homeowner's taste. (B) is incorrect because, even if the contract did prohibit delegation, there are some instances where the delegation would not rise to breach if the duty did not require a particular skill. (D) is incorrect because that is not legally true, as discussed above.

Answer 90

(C) is the correct answer. Specific performance is ONLY awarded for the sale of land, or very unique goods, and never service contracts, as that would be the same as compelling involuntary servitude. (A) is incorrect because, while it states the correct standard for specific performance — applicable in instances where money damages would not be sufficient — that does not override the policy that we do not compel people to perform services. (B) is incorrect for the same reason, as even if it is true, we still do not compel people to work against their will. (D) is incorrect because that is not true, as explained in the above question.

Answer 91

(D) When parties orally agree on a condition to the enforceability of the contract, but the condition is not then included in the writing, courts generally always allow proof of this condition despite the

Parol Evidence Rule. The Parol Evidence Rule never prevents the introduction of evidence that would show that no valid contract exists or that the contract is voidable. (A) is wrong because while this is a correct statement of law, even oral conditions may be admitted to contradict an otherwise complete writing to demonstrate that the contract is not enforceable without the occurrence of the condition. (B) is wrong because the non-occurrence of a condition does not mean that a party waived that condition. Furthermore, as explained in (D), the dancer is most likely able to bring in the fact that the non-occurrence of the condition voids the contract. (C) is wrong because it implies that usually, evidence to supplement an integration is allowable, which is not correct. In this situation, however, it is inapplicable because even though supplementing the agreement is not ordinarily allowed, the condition will come in for the reasons stated in (D).

Answer 92

(C) The Mailbox Rule mandates that acceptance is valid upon proper dispatch. However, the Mailbox Rule does not apply if the offer provides otherwise. Here the seller, the offeror, specified that she must receive the acceptance by April 5. She did not receive it until April 6, and hence there is no enforceable contract. Since the offeror is the "master of her offer," she may prescribe the method and timing of the acceptance. (A) is wrong because that is the traditional Mailbox Rule where the offeror does not specify the method or timing of her offer. (B) is wrong because even though this is the rule in a traditional Mailbox Rule setting (i.e. the revocation is effective upon receipt, but must be received before acceptance is posted), it doesn't apply when the offeror specified the method or timing for acceptance.

Answer 93

(C) The statement had no operative legal effect since the seller could not breach until performance was due. Many students will assume that (A) is the correct answer, but since one party already performed, the seller remitting payment, there can be no anticipatory repudiation. (B) is incorrect because of the same reason and, in addition, if there WAS anticipatory repudiation, the nonbreaching party would have a right to bring suit as soon as the repudiation occurred. (D) is incorrect because there is nothing to indicate that the breach was excused.

Answer 94

(C) is the correct answer. The contract was never effectively modified since under common law one needs consideration to modify a contract. Here, there was none since the homeowner had a preexisting duty to pay $900,000 for the house originally contracted for. This is also the reason why (A) is incorrect. (D) might be factually true, but it does not solve the problem of whether the contract was effectively modified.

Answer 95

(C) is the correct answer because the finding of lead paint was enough of a circumstance to modify the contract. While under common law one does need consideration to modify a contract, the exception is if there is a "surprise" that changes the duty of one party. (A) is incorrect because of the reason stated above. This would normally be the answer, but for the finding of unforeseen lead paint. (B) is incorrect because the fact pattern stated that neither party knew it was there. (D) is incorrect because, while true, it does not give us a reason to make the contract enforceable absent consideration.

Evidence

Evidence

Question 1

A computer designer was in need of an extremely sophisticated computer chip for a computer mainframe he was designing. He contacted a broker who bought and sold computer components to see if the broker could obtain the chip. "I may be able to find the chip," the broker told the designer, "but it won't be cheap. It will cost $20,000 plus my fee." The broker successfully delivered the chip and demanded $22,000. The designer offered $21,000 for both the chip and commission. In a suit brought by the broker to recover $22,000, the broker seeks to introduce copies of prior receipts of transactions with the designer and others that show the broker charges a 10 percent commission for finding similar computer components. The designer seeks to admit the testimony of six other brokers who specialize in the sale of computer components. They plan to testify that they charge 5 percent commission on rare computer components.

Which of the following statements is most accurate?

(A) The broker's copies should be admitted as a past recollection recorded.

(B) The broker's copies should not be admitted because of the Best Evidence Rule.

(C) The testimony of the six brokers should be admitted to determine the customary business practice in the community.

(D) The broker's statement should not be admitted because it is hearsay, not within any exception.

Question 2

A driver was severely injured when the flux capacitor of his sports car exploded as he was driving through a shopping center. The driver asserted an action against the manufacturer of the automobile, the owner of the mall, and the owner of a truck unlawfully parked near the scene of the accident. The driver is seeking damages for his pain and suffering due to the flux capacitor burning his hand.

Over timely objection, should the court permit a witness to testify that the driver jumped out of his car while screaming, "My hand hurts like it was struck by lightning"?

(A) Yes, as a declaration of a past bodily condition.

(B) Yes, as a declaration of a then existing bodily condition.

(C) Yes, as a declaration of a then existing bodily condition, but only if the witness was a licensed physician.

(D) Yes, as an exception to the Hearsay Rule, but only if the witness was a licensed physician and the statements were made pertinent to diagnosis and treatment.

Questions 3–4 are based upon the following fact situation.

Six residents of a state brought suit against the state to rescind a new regulation permitting the operation of tandem trucks on the state's freeway system. The plaintiffs are a group of farmers with land adjacent to the freeway, and they allege that their crops were damaged by increased vibrations, noise, and exhaust from the passing tandems. The plaintiffs' counsel called as a witness a state highway engineer who had supervised a report concerning the vehicular traffic on the disputed highway. The plaintiffs' counsel asked the witness, "Could you please tell us, according to the report you supervised, what percentage of the state's freeway traffic the tandems represent?" The state objected to the question despite their admission that the witness was a bona fide expert. The plaintiffs' counsel then called another witness, who was one of the plaintiffs, to the stand. While being questioned, the plaintiff witness coughed in a seemingly uncontrollable manner and said, "I am sorry. Ever since the tandems have been allowed to pass, I can hardly breathe." On cross-examination, the plaintiff witness was asked, "Is it not true that you told your neighbor that you did not even notice a difference in your breathing when the law changed?" The plaintiffs' counsel objected to the question.

Question 3

The trial judge should rule the plaintiffs' counsel question of the engineer:

(A) admissible under the business records exception to the Hearsay Rule.

(B) admissible, since the witness had personal knowledge of the matter.

(C) inadmissible, because the reports are the best evidence.

(D) inadmissible as extrinsic evidence of a collateral matter.

Question 4

Which of the following statements is most accurate?

(A) The witness's statement about her breathing problem should be ruled inadmissible as a self-serving declaration.

(B) The witness's statement about her breathing problem should be ruled unfairly prejudicial.

(C) The question asked of the witness on cross-examination should be ruled improper because it cannot be used for impeachment purposes.

(D) The witness's statement about her breathing problem has no relevance to the issue at hand.

Question 5

A speaker delivered the keynote speech at an annual international convention held at club resort. Five thousand club resort members heard the speech live, and hundreds of thousands of others heard the speech over short-wave radios and by official tape recordings. The speaker said, "It is indeed an honor to be allowed to address such a distinguished audience. Please allow me to comment on the previous administration of the President. Although sincere in its actions, much more could have been accomplished during his administration's tenure. We have an obligation to our society, and we must address this obligation in the best way possible. This organization can and will accomplish more in the future than it has in the past." The president of the club resort asserted an action against the speaker for slander. The president's counsel called a witness to relate to the court the contents of the speech. The speaker objected to the witness's testimony.

The court should:

(A) sustain the objection because the witness's recollection amounted to hearsay.

(B) sustain the objection because tape recordings of the speech were available.

(C) overrule the objection if the speaker's speech was identical to the script from which he read.

(D) overrule the objection because a defamatory statement is not hearsay.

Question 6

A boss closed his office door and told his secretary, "I am going out to lunch. Please record all my phone calls in the company log." The company policy provided a standard log book to record messages when an employee was not present to receive the call. The boss was gone from his office less than five minutes when a friend of the boss called. The secretary recorded the following entry in her log book: "Your friend called and said that her husband landed safely at the airport and he was going to take a cab to the estates." A taxi driver was found murdered in his cab. The taxi was parked in a town between the airport and the estates. The friend's husband was charged with first-degree murder. The prosecution moved to admit both the secretary's phone log entry, made when the friend called, as well as the taxi driver's own fare log stating his destination as the town.

Which of the following statements is most accurate?

(A) Both entries will be admitted under the business record exception to the Hearsay Rule.

(B) The secretary's entry will be admitted as a record of regularly conducted activity.

(C) The secretary's entry will be admitted, even though it is double hearsay.

(D) The secretary's entry will not be admitted.

Question 7

Two owners owned a small incorporated charter airline that operated charter flights between the different countries. One plane of the airline had a pilot and a co-pilot flying from one country to another. The plane landed at a different location for refueling. Shortly after take-off, en route to the destination country, the plane exploded, and both the pilot and co-pilot were killed. The pilot's estate asserted an action against the charter airlines company. At trial, the charter airline company called a witness who was a surviving member of the ill-fated plane's crew, to testify. The witness invoked the protection of the Fifth Amendment and refused to testify. The charter airline company then offered properly authenticated transcripts of testimony given by the witness in his criminal trial for freebasing cocaine on board the airline's flight and testimony in a suit asserted by the co-pilot's estate against the charter airline company. The transcripts contained testimony that the witness, the pilot, and the co-pilot were freebasing cocaine on board the plane. The fire used in the free-basing process caused the plane to explode. The charter airline company offered the court stenographer to attest to the transcripts' accuracy. The pilot's estate objected to the admission of the transcripts.

The court should rule:

(A) the transcript of the criminal trial admissible, but the transcript of the civil trial inadmissible.

(B) the transcripts inadmissible because of the constitutional right to cross-examine a witness.

(C) the transcripts inadmissible because they are hearsay and not within any exception.

(D) the transcripts of both trials admissible.

Question 8

A witness testified that she saw the defendant holding a gun and demanding cash from a woman near an automatic cash machine. On cross-examination, the witness admitted she had once told her husband, "It was snowing so heavily that night, I really can't be sure who tried to rob the woman." The witness's testimony about what she had told her husband is:

(A) inadmissible, because it is hearsay not within any exception.

(B) admissible for impeachment only.

(C) admissible to impeach and for substance.

(D) admissible as past recollection recorded.

Question 9

Two soldiers were veterans of an army. They wanted nothing more in life than to see those regimes they believed to be dominated by communists fall. Frustrated at what they perceived as the failure of their government to take concrete action against another country, the soldiers decided to form an army of their own to obliterate this country. The soldiers formed a corporation with the intent of arranging an army. One soldier was named president and the other soldier was named vice president for purchasing. Both soldiers were arrested after a lawful search of the vice president soldier's apartment yielded 200 M-16 rifles. The prosecution seeks to admit a statement made by the president soldier to an arms merchant, in which the president soldier said, "There ain't no way I'm gonna need any guns from you; my man is Vice President for Purchasing." The soldier's counsel objects to admission of the statement.

The court will sustain the president soldier's objection if:

(A) the statement was made during the course and in furtherance of the conspiracy.

(B) the statement was not made during the course and in furtherance of the conspiracy.

(C) the arms merchant was not a party opponent.

(D) the president solider had been legally obligated to perform separate duties under the corporate charter.

Question 10

A passenger was killed in an airplane crash. His estate asserted a wrongful death action based on res ipsa loquitur. The passenger's mother testified, "My son called from the airport and told me he was wearing a yellow shirt."

The testimony is objectionable primarily because it is:

(A) hearsay.

(B) not relevant.

(C) admissible as res gestae.

(D) admissible because the mother is familiar with her son's voice and therefore could testify to what he said.

Question 11

An owner owned a small company in the business of building, installing, and maintaining a machine used in the purification of steel. The company did not sell the machine invented and designed by the owner. It would only lease it accompanied with a service contract. On May 15, the owner inspected a machine leased to a steel company, as required by the service contract. Two days later, an explosion on the steel company's premises caused severe damage and injured a carrier service employee in the process of making a delivery. The owner inspected the premises after the accident and told his friend, "The explosion was caused by my machine. I should have opened it up when I had last inspected it, but I was running late." The employee asserted an action against the steel company. The owner was not available to testify at the trial because he had subsequently died from injuries he sustained when another one of his boilers exploded.

Should the owner's friend be allowed to recount the owner's statements about the cause of the steel company's accident?

(A) Yes, as an admission.

(B) Yes, under the "declaration against interest" hearsay exception.

(C) No, the owner's statement to the owner's friend was hearsay since he did not witness the accident.

(D) No, because the owner's friend's testimony is hearsay not within any exception.

Question 12

In which of the following situations should the defense's objection be sustained?

(A) A witness testified at the trial of a defendant, "The victim knew he was as good as dead. He had been given his last rites and could barely talk, but said, 'I saw the defendant cut my throat.' He died within moments." The defense sought to exclude the testimony on the grounds it was hearsay.

(B) A mother asserted an action to recover custody of her natural child. The case became complicated when the adoption referee fled the country with his mistress and all the relevant case files. A witness testified that the mother's sister had told the referee the baby's natural father was a notorious alcoholic. This statement was used to impeach the mother's sister because she had subsequently stated under oath that the father was a different individual. The mother's sister, who fled the country in the middle of the trial, had given key testimony because she was present when the mother and the adoptive parents signed their agreement that was now lost. The counsel for the adopting parents, defendants in the action, objected to the witness's testimony as hearsay.

(C) In a breach of contract action, a plaintiff sought to introduce the testimony of a witness from a previous action between the same parties. This witness had stated that he was present at the making of an oral agreement between the parties. The witness had since been diagnosed as having a rare disease that is spread by eating infected human brains. As a result the witness was not asked to testify in this action. The defendant objected to the admissibility of the previous testimony.

(D) A plaintiff sought to establish that a victim died on October 13, 1987, by showing that the date was inscribed on her tombstone. The defendant objected to the evidence, claiming it was hearsay and the plaintiff had not subpoenaed the person who carved the inscription, even though he lived less than two miles from the courthouse.

Question 13

An author of a best-selling dictionary died intestate. Several persons claimed entitlement to his estate. A woman asserted a claim based on her allegation that she was the author's biological daughter. The woman called upon a postal worker who had delivered mail to her home for twenty years to testify. The postal worker testified, "The author often spent weeks at a time at the woman's place. The woman's mother's mail was often received addressed in the author's last name. The author once picked the woman up into his arms and asked me if I thought his 'daughter' was cute."

Should all of the postal worker's testimony be admitted?

(A) No, because of the Best Evidence Rule.
(B) No, because of the Hearsay Rule.
(C) Yes, because of personal knowledge.
(D) Yes, because none of the statements are hearsay.

Question 14

An employee was accused by her employer of embezzlement. The employee had, by her own admission, taken 200 computer software programs home and resold them to a discount retailer. The employee used the proceeds from this sale to refurnish her apartment. The prosecution presented the employee's employment contract as evidence. The contract contained a standard clause providing, "The employee understands that all supplies and equipment used by employee, including

but not limited to, writing instruments, paper, stationery, reference books, computer hardware and software, and duplicating equipment, remains the property of employer, and may not be removed by employee from employer's premises without express written permission." On direct examination, the employee testified, "During my contractual negotiations, I complained about the low salary I had been offered. The vice-president said, 'You can make lots of extra money by taking the obsolete software programs we no longer use. They aren't worth enough for the company to bother with, but you can substantially increase your income.'"

A timely objection to the employee's testimony should be:

(A) sustained, because of the Best Evidence Rule.
(B) sustained, as hearsay not within any exception.
(C) sustained, because of the Parol Evidence Rule.
(D) overruled, because the testimony may be used to show the absence of criminal intent.

Questions 15–16 are based upon the following fact situation.

One morning, a farmer looked out his window and to his horror saw that the white picket fence surrounding his house had been overturned. The yard was covered with unusual tire tracks. The farmer decided that the tracks could only have been made by a neighbor's truck. The neighbor was an alcoholic, and the farmer assumed that the neighbor had driven onto his lawn, destroying the fence in the process. The farmer brought suit against the neighbor.

Question 15

The farmer testified that a man had called him. The man never identified himself, but the farmer and the neighbor knew each other well and the farmer was sure that the man who called him was the neighbor. The farmer said that the neighbor told him, "I'm sorry about the fence; send me a bill and I'll take care of it."

This testimony should be ruled:

(A) admissible, because the farmer recognized the neighbor's voice.
(B) admissible, because of the accuracy of the phone system.
(C) inadmissible, as hearsay not within any exception.
(D) inadmissible, because the neighbor did not identify himself.

Question 16

Later that day, the farmer called the neighbor's company that he owned. An employee answered identifying himself and the name of the company. After the farmer identified himself the man said, "I was driving the truck that drove onto your lawn this morning. I hope you'll forgive me." The farmer knew the employee, but could not recognize his voice during the phone call. "I guess it was a bad connection," the farmer explained on cross-examination.

The farmer's testimony of his phone conversation with the employee should be ruled:

(A) admissible, because of the accuracy of the phone system.

(B) admissible, because of the accuracy of the phone system, and because the speaker identified the company and acted as if he worked there.

(C) inadmissible, as hearsay not within any exception.

(D) inadmissible, because the farmer did not recognize the voice as the employee's.

Question 17

A trucker agreed to transport oranges for a produce company, at his cost plus ten cents per mile. In a breach of contract suit, a witness, the trucker's assistant, recounted under oath the expenses she could remember that the trucker incurred. The produce company objected to the witness's testimony because the trucker had kept a written record of all his expenses.

The produce company's objection should be:

(A) sustained, because of the Best Evidence Rule.

(B) sustained, because the records were not so voluminous that they required a summary.

(C) overruled, since it is a record of regularly conducted activity.

(D) overruled, since it is a testimony of firsthand knowledge.

Question 18

Two suspects were arrested and brought to police head-quarters. The officer interrogating them said, "I am going to ask you one more time, what do you know about the computer scheme?" the first suspect said, "I admit it. My family needed the money, so I figured out a way to tap into the bank's code. I needed a connection in the bank, so I approached the second suspect and offered him $10,000." The second suspect remained silent during the confession.

The fact that the second suspect remained silent while being implicated by the first suspect should be ruled:

(A) admissible, as an implied admission.

(B) admissible, because the first suspect's confession was an admission against interest for the co-defendants.

(C) inadmissible, because the first suspect's statements were not relevant to the second suspect's guilt.

(D) inadmissible, if a reasonable person in the second suspect's situation would not have felt obligated to answer.

Question 19

A woman testified that she saw a man hit a second man, who then shot the first man in self-defense. On cross-examination, the woman was asked, "Isn't it true that during the pre-trial hearing you said that the second man had shot the first man without provocation?"

The trial judge should rule the question:

(A) proper, as substantive evidence only.

(B) proper, for impeachment purposes only.

(C) proper, for substantive evidence and impeachment purposes.

(D) improper, since it is hearsay not within any exception.

Question 20

An employee who works in an automobile shop was arrested for auto theft. A new assistant district attorney who had only recently been admitted to practice in the state was assigned to prosecute the case. At trial, the district attorney asked a five-year-old witness, who claimed she saw the employee driving a car that night, "Was the car that you saw on driving red?"

An objection to the district attorney's question would be:

(A) overruled, because the question is relevant.

(B) sustained, because the question is leading.

(C) overruled, even though the question is leading.

(D) sustained, because it is extrinsic evidence offered to prove a collateral matter.

Questions 21–22 are based upon the following fact situation.

A defendant is being tried for his kidnapping of a victim after forcing the victim to rob a bank. The defendant denies all charges.

Question 21

The defendant calls a witness to testify that the victim is paranoid and schizophrenic. The trial judge should rule this testimony inadmissible:

(A) because the witness is not the defendant.

(B) because the issue must be raised by the defendant.

(C) if the witness is not an expert.

(D) because a victim's psychosis cannot justify the crime.

Question 22

Another witness testified for the defendant. The prosecution chose not to cross-examine the defendant. The defense then called a second witness, who testified that the first witness had a reputation as a very honest and truthful man.

Over proper objection, the second witness's testimony should be ruled:

(A) admissible, assuming the second witness knew the first witness well enough.

(B) admissible, as relevant to the first witness's veracity.

(C) inadmissible, as hearsay not within any exception.

(D) inadmissible, because witness's veracity was not brought into issue.

Questions 23–24 are based upon the following fact situation.

A defendant is on trial for murdering his mother. The defendant claims he was in another city on the night in question. He says his mother committed suicide.

Question 23

The defendant called his neighbor as a witness, who testified that the defendant had a reputation in the community as a law-abiding and nonviolent citizen. The trial judge should rule this testimony:

(A) inadmissible, because only the prosecution may raise the issue of reputation.

(B) inadmissible, because actions in a particular instance may not be proved by reputation.

(C) admissible, only to prove the defendant's veracity.

(D) admissible, because a criminal defendant may introduce evidence of his character as substantive evidence of his innocence.

Question 24

The defendant testified that he was in another city at the time of his mother's death and, therefore, could not have committed the murder. The prosecutor asked the defendant, on cross-examination, "Were you convicted of perjury last year?" The defendant answered, "I have never been convicted of perjury." The prosecutor seeks to submit evidence of the defendant's conviction.

The trial judge should rule this evidence:

(A) inadmissible, because the prosecutor may not impeach the defendant.

(B) inadmissible, because specific instances of conduct are not relevant to the issue of whether the defendant murdered his mother.

(C) admissible, because of the nature of the crime of perjury.

(D) admissible, because the crime of perjury is relevant to the issue of whether the defendant murdered his mother.

Question 25

Two men signed a contract in which the first man agreed to lease a hotel to the second man, who agreed to maintain the premises. The second man brought an action for loss of profits. The first man denied that the signature on the contract was his. The second man called as a witness a woman who had taught the first man in high school. The woman testified that she remembered the first man's signature and that the signature on the contract was his. The first man is thirty-two years old. The court should rule the woman's testimony:

(A) admissible.

(B) inadmissible, because she is not an expert.

(C) inadmissible, because genuineness is a question for the jury and not for a witness.

(D) inadmissible, because the first man has not been a high school student for many years.

Question 26

After an accident, a plaintiff produced a photocopy of the defendant's car registration to prove the defendant's ownership. The defendant objected to the photocopy, but did not deny that he owned the car. The trial judge should rule that the copy is:

(A) admissible, only if the original is shown to be unavailable.

(B) admissible, regardless of the availability of the original.

(C) inadmissible, because of the Best Evidence Rule.

(D) inadmissible, unless the car is owned by a business and the photocopy was a business record.

Question 27

A married couple who happened to be returning from the grocery store witnessed an accident between the plaintiff and the defendant. The wife testified, "Just before the accident my husband screamed that the defendant was driving on the wrong side of the street."

The trial judge should rule the wife's testimony:

(A) admissible, only if the husband is shown to be unavailable.

(B) admissible, regardless of the wife's availability.

(C) inadmissible, as hearsay not within any exception.

(D) inadmissible, because of the Best Evidence Rule.

Question 28

The plaintiff called a doctor to testify that the defendant came to his office minutes after an accident. When the doctor saw the bruises and asked, "What happened?" the defendant answered, "I cracked up my car because I was driving on the wrong side of the street."

The doctor's testimony should be ruled:

(A) admissible, as an admission.

(B) inadmissible, if the defendant objects.

(C) inadmissible, as hearsay not within any exception.

(D) admissible, as a declaration against interest.

Questions 29–30 are based on the following fact situation.

A plaintiff sued a defendant for injuries suffered in an automobile accident caused by a driver, who had rented the defendant's car. The plaintiff claims the defendant knew that the young man was under the legal driving age.

Question 29

The defendant called the driver to testify. The defendant expected the driver to say that he was eighteen years old. However, on direct examination, the driver testified that he was fifteen. The defendant then tried to confront the driver with a statement he had made in his deposition claiming that he was eighteen.

Which of the following is true in regard to the driver's statement at trial?

(A) It is inadmissible, because the defendant cannot impeach his own witness.
(B) It is inadmissible, because it is hearsay not within any exception.
(C) It may be used to refresh the driver's memory.
(D) It is admissible for impeachment and as substantive evidence that the driver is above the legal age.

Question 30

The plaintiff offered evidence that after the accident the defendant visited her in the hospital and offered a $10,000 settlement, saying, "I am sorry I rented my car to a fifteen-year-old kid."

The statement "fifteen-year-old kid" is:

(A) inadmissible, as hearsay not within any exception.
(B) admissible, as a factual admission made in connection with an offer of compromise.
(C) inadmissible, as a statement made in connection with an offer to pay medical expenses.
(D) admissible, as an admission by the defendant that the driver was below the legal driving age.

Questions 31–32 are based upon the following fact situation.

A defendant was charged with the crime of assaulting a victim. The defendant admitted to slamming a coconut into the victim's face, thereby causing him to lose seven teeth, but he claimed that he was acting in self-defense because the victim, while heavily intoxicated, had blocked the road with his car and threatened to harm the defendant.

Question 31

The prosecutor, in her case in chief, introduced testimony that the defendant has a reputation in his community as one who likes to settle arguments in a violent manner. The court should rule this testimony:

(A) admissible, to show the possibility of conformity in this instance.
(B) admissible, because the probative value of the evidence outweighs its possible prejudice.
(C) inadmissible, because the defendant's character has not been placed at issue.
(D) inadmissible, as irrelevant.

Question 32

A doctor who is the president of the hospital where the defendant was employed as a physician testified, "I have known the defendant since he was a young boy and he is a hard-working, law-abiding, and peace-loving man." The doctor's testimony should be ruled:

(A) admissible, because it is relevant to the issue of whether the defendant was the aggressor.
(B) admissible, because it is relevant to decide an appropriate punishment if convicted.
(C) inadmissible, because conduct in specific instances may not be proved by character references.
(D) inadmissible, as hearsay not within any exception.

Question 33

A driver sued a second driver for damages arising out of an auto accident in which the second driver had plowed into the first driver's car. The accident took place on October 3, 1997. The first driver filed his lawsuit on September 2, 2000. After the parties could not reach a settlement agreement, the matter was scheduled for trial on December 1, 2001. One day prior to trial, the first driver went to the corner where the accident took place and took four photos with his expensive camera. At trial, the photographs are:

(A) admissible, as a then-existing physical condition.
(B) admissible, but only if the first driver testifies that he took the photos.
(C) inadmissible upon objection by the second driver, because the photos were taken more than four years after the accident.
(D) admissible, if the photos accurately and correctly portray the scene of the accident.

Questions 34–35 are based upon the following fact situation.

A pedestrian, while crossing the street, was hit by a car. There were two passengers in the driver's car. Another pedestrian witnessed the accident and called the police, who sent an officer to investigate.

Question 34

The plaintiff called the first passenger as a witness, who testified that just before the accident the second passenger had screamed, "You're going too fast. You'll never be able to stop for that pedestrian."

The first passenger's testimony should be ruled:

(A) admissible, as an excited utterance.

(B) admissible, as a declaration against interest.

(C) inadmissible, because speed must be determined by an expert.

(D) inadmissible, because it violates the Best Evidence Rule.

Question 35

A neighbor testified that the driver had a reputation in the community as a safe and careful driver. The neighbor and the driver lived on the same block for more than thirty years. The trial judge should rule the neighbor's testimony:

(A) admissible, as tending to prove that the driver was driving safely prior to the accident.

(B) admissible, only if the plaintiff asks for punitive damages.

(C) inadmissible, unless the plaintiff has raised the character issue.

(D) inadmissible, because general reputation cannot be used to prove lack of negligence on a particular occasion.

Questions 36–37 are based upon the following fact situation.

A woman and her friend were driving to a ski resort in late December when the woman's car was hit head-on by a pickup truck driven by driver. No one was injured, but the woman's car was badly wrecked and the woman's friend began to have nightmares about the accident. The woman alleges that the driver was driving without windshield wipers and that that was the cause of the accident.

Question 36

A passenger in the driver's car said to a pedestrian, who happened to be walking his dog at the scene of the accident, "We couldn't see a thing; the wipers weren't working."

The pedestrian's testimony concerning the passenger's statement should be ruled:

(A) admissible, as a declaration against interest.

(B) admissible, as an admission of party opponent.

(C) inadmissible, because of possible bias.

(D) inadmissible, because it is hearsay not within any exception.

Question 37

The pedestrian also seeks to testify that, just before the cars crashed, a man next to him screamed, "That driver can't possibly see where he's going without windshield wipers!" The testimony should be ruled:

(A) admissible, only if the man who screamed is not available to testify.

(B) admissible, even if the man who screamed is available to testify.

(C) inadmissible, as hearsay not within any exception.

(D) inadmissible, because no recording was made.

Question 38

The defense called a witness to testify on behalf of the defendant in a burglary trial. On cross-examination, the prosecutor may properly ask the witness:

(A) about his past felony convictions, but the prosecutor is bound by the witness's answer.

(B) about his past misdemeanor convictions, but the prosecutor is bound by the witness's answer.

(C) about the witness's arrest record.

(D) about the witness's thirty-day suspended sentence for embezzlement.

Question 39

The victim was assaulted, robbed, and raped. Her injuries required four weeks of hospitalization. As she was leaving the hospital she screamed, "That's the man who did it." Her husband grabbed the man she was pointing at. The husband's testimony of the victim's statement should be ruled:

(A) admissible, only if the victim is shown to be unavailable.

(B) admissible, regardless of the victim's availability.

(C) inadmissible, as hearsay not within any exception.

(D) inadmissible, because of the husband-wife privilege.

Questions 40–41 are based upon the following fact situation.

A man stopped by an all-night store to pick up some cat food. As he left the store, he saw his good friend pull up to the store. The man and his friend started talking. A few minutes later, a robber pulled up in his new car and ran into the store. Shots were fired inside and the robber came running out, but he collapsed as he tried to get into his car. The cashier came running out of the store screaming, "No one robs my store and gets away with it." Suddenly, the robber took out a gun and shot the man in the chest, killing him instantly. The robber then aimed at the man's friend and took a shot at him. When the police arrived, the officer ran over to the friend, who was bleeding profusely and said, "I don't think you're gonna make it, kid." The man's friend then said, "That man shot and killed my good friend." Within moments, the friend died.

Question 40

At the robber's trial for double murder and robbery, the prosecutor sought to admit the officer's testimony as to the friend's statement about the man who killed the man. The defense objected.

This testimony should most likely be:

(A) admissible, under the "dying declaration" exception.
(B) admissible, as a then-existing mental condition.
(C) inadmissible, because the office is a police sergeant.
(D) inadmissible, because the declaration was made by the friend.

Question 41

A witness for the defense testified that he was watching television with the robber at the time of the incident. When asked on cross-examination, the witness denied that he had loaned the robber money to pay for the television they had been watching. The prosecution called a salesman who sold the television to the robber to testify that he saw the witness loan the robber the money for a television. The trial judge should rule the salesman's testimony:

(A) admissible, to impeach the witness.
(B) admissible, to show the robber was in debt and had a motive to rob the store.
(C) inadmissible, because not relevant.
(D) inadmissible, because prejudicial.

Questions 42–43 are based upon the following fact situation.

A man walked into a house that he thought belonged to his girlfriend but it was really the house next door to his girlfriend's. The owner of the house had just finished exercising in his basement and was walking upstairs, wearing a black sweat suit, just as the man walked in through the front door, which had been left open. The man attacked the owner, causing grave injuries. The man was charged with assault, battery, and attempted burglary. He claimed that he had thought the house was his girlfriend's, that the owner was a burglar, and that he had used force in self-defense.

Question 42

The man's long-time neighbor testified that the man had a reputation in the community as a hard-working and peaceful man. The trial judge should rule this testimony:

(A) admissible, to assess damages in a possible civil suit.
(B) admissible, to show the unlikelihood that the man had criminal intent.
(C) inadmissible, because reputation cannot be used to prove behavior in a specific instance.
(D) inadmissible, as hearsay not within any exception.

Question 43

A man's neighbor was asked, on cross-examination, whether he knew that the man had been prosecuted for assault and attempted burglary on two prior occasions. The trial judge should rule this question:

(A) proper, to determine the man's neighbor's familiarity with the man.
(B) proper, because it is relevant to prove the man acted in a criminal manner in this instance.
(C) not proper, because the probative value is outweighed by possible prejudice.
(D) not proper, because the incidents are not related.

Question 44

A driver was involved in a collision with a second driver on a street. While they were exchanging phone numbers, the first driver said to the second driver: "Oh my gosh! My insurance company is reliable. They'll pay for your broken nose!" The second driver sued the first driver for personal injuries and plans to testify as to what the first driver said to her. The second driver's testimony will be:

(A) admissible, as an excited utterance.
(B) admissible, but only to prove ownership or control of the vehicle.
(C) admissible, to prove negligence.
(D) inadmissible, as hearsay not within any exception.

Questions 45–46 are based upon the following fact situation.

A pilot owned a private plane, which he used for recreational purposes. One clear afternoon, the pilot experienced mechanical difficulties and was forced to eject himself from the plane. The pilot parachuted safely to the ground, but the plane crashed into a barn, causing substantial damage to the structure. The pilot was rescued by two policemen, who noticed that the pilot was acting strangely. The pilot was brought to a hospital where he was found to be heavily intoxicated.

Question 45

The owner of the barn filed suit against the pilot, alleging that the damages to his barn were a direct result of the pilot's intoxication. The owner of the barn offers the properly authenticated records of the pilot's criminal conviction for flying while intoxicated. The conviction should be ruled:

(A) admissible, only to prove intoxication.
(B) admissible, only to prove character.
(C) inadmissible, because the pilot pleaded guilty only for criminal purposes.
(D) inadmissible, because it is hearsay not within any exception.

Question 46

The owner of the barn joined the airport in his suit, alleging that the airport was negligent for allowing the pilot to fly while obviously inebriated. The owner of the barn seeks to introduce evidence that shortly after the pilot's accident, the airport instituted a new screening procedure in which an airport employee monitors pilots to be sure that they are fit to fly. The trial judge should rule this evidence:

(A) admissible, to show the airport could have prevented the accident.
(B) admissible, to show the pilot was intoxicated.
(C) inadmissible, because not relevant to the airport's negligence.
(D) inadmissible, because the policy of the court is to encourage remedial measures.

Question 47

Three days after having been shot point-blank in the face, the victim knew he was about to die. He said to a nurse, "I only have a couple hours to live. I want you to know the defendant shot me." The victim died less than an hour later. The defendant's counsel called a witness to testify. The witness said that she had visited the victim three days before he died and "he said he could not tell who shot him."

The witness's testimony should be ruled:

(A) admissible, to impeach the victim.
(B) admissible, as a statement under belief at impending death.
(C) inadmissible, because not relevant.
(D) inadmissible, because the last implication is deemed controlling.

Questions 48–49 are based upon the following fact situation.

A burglar was caught trying to burglarize a jewelry store. The police obtained a search warrant for the burglar's apartment and found a handwritten map of the jewelry store, marked with possible escape routes.

Question 48

A witness testified that he had shared a cell with the burglar in the state penitentiary seven years earlier and had seen the burglar write letters. The witness further testified that the map was written by burglar. The trial judge should rule the witness's testimony:

(A) admissible, because the witness is qualified to form an opinion on the handwriting.
(B) admissible, only if corroborated by collateral evidence such as fingerprints.
(C) inadmissible, because the witness is not an expert.
(D) inadmissible, because witness's character is inherently flawed due to his imprisonment.

Question 49

The burglar was found guilty of all charges. At the sentencing hearing, the prosecution introduced evidence of eleven previous felony convictions. The trial judge should rule the prior convictions:

(A) admissible.
(B) inadmissible, because prior convictions not admitted at trial are not admissible at sentencing hearings.
(C) inadmissible, because highly prejudicial.
(D) inadmissible, if the previous convictions were for crimes unrelated to burglary.

Questions 50–51 are based upon the following fact situation.

A witness was familiar with the defendant's voice. The witness testified, during the defendant's suit for negligence, "I received a call and recognized the defendant's voice. After I asked her what was new, she told me she had 'just been driving drunk and hit an old lady.'"

Question 50

The defendant's counsel objected to the witness's identification of the defendant's voice. The trial judge should rule that the phone call was:

(A) properly authenticated, only if a recording was made and examined by an expert.
(B) properly authenticated, because the witness was familiar with the defendant's voice.
(C) not properly authenticated, because the defendant never identified herself.
(D) not properly authenticated, because the witness was the one who received the call.

Question 51

Even if the phone call was ruled authenticated, the defendant's counsel will still object to the contents of the conversation. The trial judge should rule the contents:

(A) admissible, as a then-existing mental condition.
(B) admissible, as an admission.
(C) inadmissible, as hearsay not within any exception.
(D) inadmissible, because no blood alcohol level was taken.

Question 52

A plaintiff brought suit against the defendant for injuries the plaintiff said he had suffered when the defendant stepped on his toe in a clam bar. The defendant claimed he had never been to the bar, nor had he stepped on the plaintiff's toe.

A witness who knew the defendant testified that since the defendant was so religious, his diet was restricted and he did not eat shellfish under any circumstances. The trial judge should rule this testimony:

(A) admissible, to prove the defendant would never lie.

(B) admissible, as tending to prove the defendant would not be found in a clam bar.

(C) inadmissible, because not relevant.

(D) inadmissible, because religious beliefs may not be used as evidence.

Question 53

A woman sued a health spa, alleging that while jogging on the spa's track she slipped on a wet spot left negligently by an employee who had just cleaned and dried the track. She alleges that she suffered a broken hip due to the health spa's negligence. Another employee at the spa testified that he saw the woman trip over her own shoelace as she left the locker room. After assisting her and calling an ambulance, he immediately filled out an accident report, pursuant to spa policy. The health spa seeks to admit this report into evidence.

The trial judge should rule the report:

(A) inadmissible, because both employees are available to testify.

(B) inadmissible, because it is hearsay not within any exception.

(C) admissible, as a recorded recollection.

(D) admissible, as a business record.

Question 54

A suspect pleaded guilty to armed robbery and told the judge, "I did it because my girlfriend is pregnant and I needed the money." The suspect was later allowed to withdraw his guilty plea. During his trial, the prosecutor seeks to introduce evidence of the suspect's plea of guilty and accompanying admission.

The trial judge should rule:

(A) the guilty plea admissible, the admission inadmissible.

(B) the admission admissible, the guilty plea inadmissible.

(C) both the admission and the guilty plea admissible.

(D) neither the admission nor the guilty plea admissible.

Questions 55–56 are based upon the following fact situation.

A pedestrian sued a driver for injuries he claimed to have suffered as a result of the driver's hitting him with his pickup truck while he crossed the street. Two passengers were riding with the driver. A witness was taking his dog on a midnight walk.

Question 55

The witness testified that the driver offered him $10,000 to falsely testify that the accident was due to a pedestrian's negligence. The trial judge should rule this evidence:

(A) inadmissible, as hearsay not within any exception.

(B) inadmissible, because probative value is outweighed by possible prejudice.

(C) admissible, as an admission by conduct.

(D) admissible, as a declaration against interest.

Question 56

On the evening of the accident, the witness wrote in his diary a conversation he had with the driver's passenger in which the passenger told him that the driver was driving thirty miles above the speed limit. At the trial, he cannot remember details of the accident, and the pedestrian requests to allow the witness to look at his diary.

The trial judge should rule this request:

(A) not proper, because of the amount of time that elapsed since the notes were taken.

(B) not proper, because the notes are hearsay not within any exception.

(C) proper, as a past recollection recorded.

(D) proper, as a present recollection refreshed.

Questions 57–58 are based upon the following fact situation.

On a clear day in May, a bank was robbed of $400,050.00. As the robber ran out of the bank with the money bags, he shot and killed a depositor. A teller at the bank pushed the alarm button under the counter as soon as the robber ran out to the street. The next day, the teller identified a suspect in a lineup as the robber.

Question 57

The defense called an owner of a coffee shop, who testified that the suspect is an "honest and peace-loving man." The owner's testimony is:

(A) inadmissible, because the suspect has not testified.

(B) inadmissible, because character may not be proved by reputation.

(C) admissible, to prove the suspect's innocence.

(D) admissible, to prove the suspect is believable.

Question 58

At the suspect's trial the prosecutor asked the suspect, on cross-examination, whether he had been convicted of burglary five years earlier. The court should rule, over an objection by defense counsel, that this question is most likely:

(A) improper, because burglary does not involve dishonesty or false statement.

(B) improper, because of the Best Evidence Rule.

(C) proper, if the court finds that the probative value for impeachment will outweigh any prejudice to the suspect.

(D) proper, because the burglary conviction is irrelevant.

Question 59

A caterer sued a client for failure to pay for a bar mitzvah she had catered for the client's son. At trial, the caterer plans to testify that she personally supervises every affair, and plans to explain the amount of money expended on the bar mitzvah by testifying as to how much food was served, the rental cost of the ballroom, and the cost of hired help. The client objects on the ground that the caterer regularly records all this information in the plan book in her office. The caterer's testimony is:

(A) inadmissible because it violates the Best Evidence Rule.
(B) inadmissible, as hearsay.
(C) admissible, because it is based on firsthand knowledge.
(D) admissible, as a business record.

Questions 60–61 are based upon the following fact situation.

A driver injured a jogger with his automobile at an intersection. The jogger's wife was with him and witnessed the accident, as was a pedestrian, who happened to be walking by. The pedestrian called the police, who sent an officer to investigate.

Question 60

The officer testified, "I brought the pedestrian to the police station about an hour after the accident, and as soon as I questioned him, he started screaming about the driver running the light. I included his statements in my notes." The trial judge should rule the officer's testimony:

(A) admissible, as a present sense impression.
(B) admissible, as an excited utterance.
(C) admissible, as a public report.
(D) inadmissible, as it is hearsay not within any exception.

Question 61

The jogger seeks to allow the officer's testimony that the driver told him, "I was driving about eighty-five miles an hour." The trial judge should rule this testimony:

(A) admissible, as a party admission.
(B) inadmissible, because it is hearsay.
(C) inadmissible, because the driver does not qualify as an expert in determining automobile speeds.
(D) inadmissible, as an opinion.

Question 62

A patron sues a restaurant for injuries he says he suffered after eating an allegedly contaminated bowl of soup. The restaurant testified that more than forty other customers ate the same soup and none of them

got sick. The patron called a doctor who testified, "I treated six patients for stomach ailments. All of them had eaten the same kind of soup at the restaurant on the same day that the patron did." The trial judge should rule the doctor's testimony:

(A) admissible, as long as other testimony linked the stomach ailments to contaminated soup.
(B) admissible, as long as the doctor is accepted as an expert.
(C) inadmissible, because the patients' statements to the doctor are hearsay.
(D) inadmissible, because it is not relevant.

Questions 63–64 are based on the following fact situation.

A pedestrian sued a homeowner for injuries sustained when the pedestrian slipped on the homeowner's negligently maintained sidewalk. The homeowner denies that the pedestrian suffered any injuries.

Question 63

A doctor offers to testify for the pedestrian that the day after the accident, the pedestrian came to see him in his office and said, "I fell on a sidewalk that was all cracked and uneven." The doctor's testimony would be:

(A) inadmissible, because it states a fact not in issue.
(B) inadmissible, except the portion of the statement that the sidewalk was cracked and uneven.
(C) admissible, in full.
(D) admissible, but only as to the cause of the injury.

Question 64

The fourteen-year-old mentally incompetent brother of the defendant is called to testify. The trial judge should rule the brother's testimony:

(A) admissible.
(B) inadmissible because of the brother's age.
(C) inadmissible because the brother is mentally incompetent.
(D) inadmissible because he is the defendant's brother.

Questions 65–66 are based upon the following fact situation.

A driver's car collided with a truck owned by a trucking company. The driver's car slid beneath the truck's trailer, crushing the roof of the car and causing the driver severe head injuries. The driver sued the truck's manufacturer alleging that his injuries were caused by their negligent design, since the truck did not have a protective device to prevent cars from driving under the trailer. The manufacturer answered that it would be impossible to design a trailer with equipment to prevent a car from driving under it.

Question 65

The driver seeks to introduce evidence that two days after his accident, the manufacturer's engineers began to work on a bumper that would wrap all around the truck's trailer, at the same height as a car bumper. The bumpers became standard equipment on all of the manufacturer's trucks within two years later. The trial court should rule this evidence:

(A) inadmissible, because public policy is to avoid discouraging remedial measures.
(B) admissible, to show the prior design was negligent.
(C) admissible, to show the manufacturer was aware of the need to take precautionary measures.
(D) admissible, to refute the manufacturer's argument that the protection was impossible to design.

Question 66

The driver offered as evidence a pamphlet put out by a government regulatory agency. The manufacturer objected. The trial judge should:

(A) sustain the objection, because the document was not properly authenticated.
(B) sustain the objection, because of the Best Evidence Rule.
(C) overrule the objection, because the document is a statement against interest.
(D) overrule the objection, because the pamphlet is an official publication.

Questions 67–68 are based on a defendant's trial for robbing a diamond store.

Question 67

The prosecution seeks to offer evidence, obtained in a valid search of the defendant's apartment, showing he was heavily in debt from an illegal gambling habit. This evidence should be:

(A) inadmissible, because the defendant did not put his character at issue.
(B) inadmissible, because the prejudicial effect will outweigh its probative value.
(C) admissible, to prove the defendant's motive to rob the diamond store.
(D) admissible, to prove the defendant's motive to commit crimes.

Question 68

On direct examination, the defendant testified that he does not know how to drive cars with manual transmissions. The car used to escape the scene of the crime was recovered by the police, and it had a manual transmission. The defendant's counsel asked him, "What did you tell the police on the day of the crime?" The defendant's answer was, "I do not drive a manual transmission."

The defendant's answer is:

(A) inadmissible, as hearsay not within any exception.
(B) inadmissible, because the defendant's answer helps his case, giving him a motive to lie.
(C) admissible, only as a prior consistent statement.
(D) admissible, only to prove that the defendant does not know how to drive a manual transmission.

Question 69

A motor company was sued in a product liability action when the axle of one of its cars broke. The company asked an assembly line worker to tell the motor company's counsel exactly how the axle is assembled. The worker said to the lawyer, "Quite frankly, I was drunk a lot last year and luckily nobody noticed." The plaintiff asks the counsel to testify about his conversation with the assembly line worker.

The trial judge should rule that:

(A) the counsel may be forced to testify because the conversation is relevant.
(B) the counsel may be forced to testify because the assembly line worker is only a factory worker.
(C) the counsel cannot be forced to testify because of the attorney-client privilege.
(D) the counsel cannot be forced to testify because the assembly line worker is not an expert.

Questions 70–71 are based upon the following fact situation.

A patient went to a doctor to treat his cold. The doctor erroneously prescribed a drug known to have severe side effects and generally used only by terminally ill patients. The patient had a high fever for the next three days, then suffered a heart attack and died. The doctor's records were admitted into evidence.

Question 70

An expert, another doctor, carefully examined the doctor's records. He was asked, "In your opinion, could the medication have caused the patient's heart attack?" The expert's opinion should be ruled:

(A) inadmissible, because an expert may not be asked a hypothetical question based on prior testimony.
(B) inadmissible, because an expert may not be asked a hypothetical question based on a party's records.
(C) admissible, as a response to a hypothetical question.
(D) admissible, since he is an expert and is in a position to weigh the evidence.

Question 71

The pathologist who performed the autopsy on the patient seeks to state his opinion as to the cause of the patient's death. His opinion is based upon his examination of microscopic tissues that were prepared by an assistant in his office and not admitted into evidence.

The trial judge should rule the pathologist's testimony:

(A) proper, if such tissues are reasonably relied upon by physicians.

(B) proper, as a record of regularly conducted activity.

(C) not proper, unless the slides were admitted into evidence.

(D) not proper, because the pathologist did not prepare the slides himself.

Question 72

A defendant was present with his counsel at a preliminary examination where a codefendant was being questioned under the suspicion that he had been an accessory after the fact in a bank robbery case. The codefendant testified, "The defendant jumped into my back seat with a bag full of cash." The defendant was charged with armed robbery. The prosecution was unable to locate the suspect to testify at the defendant's trial, so they moved to admit the suspect's pretrial testimony.

The trial judge should rule this testimony:

(A) admissible, as a past recollection recorded.

(B) admissible, as former testimony.

(C) inadmissible, as hearsay not within any exception.

(D) inadmissible, because the codefendant is a codefendant and has a right against self-incrimination.

Questions 73–74 are based upon the following fact situation.

A plaintiff sued for injuries sustained in a shopping mall when he tripped over a broken step and fell. The defendant, the landlord, maintained that the lease for a restaurant provided it with complete responsibility for the condition of those steps.

Question 73

The plaintiff brought a witness who testified that he was hired by the defendant on the day after the accident to fix the steps. The court should rule this testimony:

(A) inadmissible, because the law seeks to encourage repairs and prevent injuries.

(B) inadmissible, because of the confidential relationship.

(C) admissible, because the repairs are relevant to prove that the prior condition constituted negligence.

(D) admissible, as relevant to the issue of who maintained control over the steps.

Question 74

The defendant offered the testimony of its employee who said, "Hundreds of people use those steps every day, and I have no knowledge of any accidents." This evidence should be:

(A) inadmissible, because the employee's testimony is not relevant.

(B) inadmissible, because the testimony is not relevant to the issue of due care.

(C) admissible, because it tends to prove proper maintenance of the steps.

(D) admissible, because it has no bearing on the issue of due care.

Question 75

A dealer and his employee, a mechanic, were both sued by a purchaser for damages incurred when his brakes failed. An attorney was retained to defend the dealer and his mechanic. The three had a conference; the only other person present was the attorney's secretary, who took notes.

The purchaser seeks to have the mechanic testify to what was said at the conference. The trial judge should rule the testimony:

(A) admissible, because the conference was attended by persons other than the attorney and client.

(B) admissible, as an admission against interest.

(C) inadmissible, as violating the Best Evidence Rule.

(D) inadmissible, because of the attorney-client privilege.

Questions 76–77 are based upon the following fact situation.

A driver was driving his car and listening to the radio when he suddenly crashed into another car. A sheriff arrived approximately one hour later.

Question 76

The second driver sat in the sheriff's car and answered questions for a police report. At one point the second driver said, "I most likely did jump the light." The first driver seeks to admit the sheriff's testimony of the second driver's statement.

The trial judge should rule the testimony:

(A) inadmissible, as hearsay not within any exception.

(B) inadmissible, unless the second driver's confirms the statement.

(C) admissible, as a written recollection.

(D) admissible, as an admission.

Question 77

The first driver seeks to testify that the second driver had offered him a new car if he would agree to drop the suit. The trial judge should rule this evidence:

(A) admissible, as a party admission.
(B) admissible, on the issue of liability, but not on the issue of damages.
(C) inadmissible, because a settlement offer is not relevant to liability or damages.
(D) inadmissible, even though relevant, due to legal policy.

Question 78

In 1986, a buyer brought a suit to challenge the validity of a conveyance made by a seller in 1973. The buyer, alleging the seller's incompetence, offers valid affidavits by two of the seller's neighbors, stating that they have observed the seller hanging from a tree branch by his legs for hours at a time. The affidavits further allege that the seller had walked around the neighborhood during a snowstorm clad only in his underwear.

These affidavits should be:

(A) admissible, as a record of documents affecting an interest in property.
(B) admissible, as ancient documents.
(C) admissible, as official documents.
(D) inadmissible, since they are hearsay not within any exception.

Question 79

A suspect was charged with murder and testified on his own behalf. The prosecutor seeks to impeach the suspect by admitting the suspect's thirteen-year-old conviction for voluntary manslaughter and his two-year-old conviction for perjury.

The trial judge should rule:

(A) both the manslaughter and perjury convictions admissible.
(B) only the perjury conviction is admissible.
(C) only the manslaughter conviction admissible.
(D) neither the perjury conviction nor the manslaughter charge admissible.

Question 80

On cross-examination, a plaintiff was asked about a tape of a conversation he'd had with a convicted child molester who was planning a drug deal. The plaintiff objected on the grounds that the content of his conversation with the drug dealer was obtained by an improper wiretap and had been excluded in a prior criminal trial.

The question about the taped conversation is:

(A) proper.

(B) proper, to impeach the plaintiff's veracity, but not to prove that the plaintiff was a drug dealer.
(C) proper, to prove that the plaintiff was a drug dealer, but not proper to impeach him.
(D) not proper.

Question 81

A plaintiff sued a defendant for injuries suffered in an automobile accident. The defendant asked a witness at the scene of the accident if she thought the plaintiff had been speeding. The plaintiff's counsel objected. The trial judge should:

(A) sustain the objection, because the witness may not provide an ultimate conclusion.
(B) sustain the objection, because a proper foundation has not been laid.
(C) overrule the objection, because it is not proper.
(D) overrule the objection, because a lay witness is permitted to judge if a car is speeding.

Questions 82–83 are based upon the following fact situation.

A bus driver collided with a driver's car. The bus driver claimed the car driver's left headlight had not been on, causing her to think the car was a motorcycle.

Question 82

The bus driver seeks to introduce the testimony of a bystander, a disinterested witness who had heard the mechanic who worked for the car driver say, "I told you yesterday that broken headlight would be trouble." The trial judge should rule the testimony admissible only if:

(A) the bus driver proves that the mechanic is an agent of the car driver, his statement was within the scope of his employment, and he is unavailable to testify.
(B) the bus driver proves that the mechanic is an agent of the car driver and is unavailable to testify.
(C) the bus driver proves that the mechanic is an agent of the car driver, is unavailable to testify, and produces evidence that the bulb was out for at least one day.
(D) the bus driver proves that the mechanic is not available to testify.

Question 83

The bystander testified that she heard the car driver reply to the mechanic, "It's your fault you were supposed to fix it." The car driver objects to a bystander's testimony. The trial judge should:

(A) sustain the objection because it is hearsay not within any exception.

(B) sustain the objection because the car driver was the principal, not the agent.
(C) overrule the objection only if the mechanic is unavailable.
(D) overrule the objection, as an admission of a party.

Question 84

A woman filed suit against a church for breach of contract. A witness testified in favor of the church. On cross-examination, the woman asked the witness, "Is it not true that you are a member of the church in question?" The trial judge should rule this question:

(A) proper, to show bias.
(B) proper, despite the Best Evidence Rule.
(C) not proper, because leading.
(D) not proper, because religious beliefs may not be introduced to prove veracity.

Question 85

A pedestrian brought an action against both a bus company and the bus driver, an employee of the bus company, to recover for damages he allegedly suffered when hit by the bus the bus driver was driving for the bus company. The pedestrian found a witness who testified that the bus company is known in the community to hire reckless drivers. The witness also testified that the bus driver has a reputation in the community as a flagrant violator of traffic laws. The trial judge should rule the testimony:

(A) admissible, as tending to prove the accident was caused by the negligence of the bus company and of the bus driver.
(B) admissible, because the issue of character was raised by one of the defendants.
(C) inadmissible, because the issue of character was raised by a defendant.
(D) inadmissible, to prove negligence.

Question 86

A plaintiff sued a company for injuries she claims she suffered from an accident in the company's department store. An employee completed a standard form provided by the company's attorney in order to assist him in defending the company. The plaintiff requests that the report be submitted into evidence.
The trial judge should rule the report:

(A) admissible, as a statement against interest.
(B) admissible, as recorded recollection.
(C) inadmissible, as hearsay not within any exception.
(D) inadmissible, because the report is a privileged communication between client and attorney.

Question 87

A plaintiff was involved in a medical malpractice suit against a doctor. A second doctor was called as an expert and asked on direct examination, "In your opinion, could a mistake like the one made by the doctor cause the symptoms exhibited by the plaintiff?" The defendant objected.
The trial judge should rule the question:

(A) proper.
(B) not proper, because leading.
(C) not proper, if the opinion is based on facts not submitted in evidence.
(D) not proper, because the ultimate opinion should be left for the trier of fact.

Question 88

A defendant is on trial for putting razor blades inside candy bars and giving the candy to children on Halloween. A six-year-old boy answered "yes" when asked, "Did a man in a yellow convertible call you over and give you candy that made your mouth hurt?"
Over proper objection, the boy's answer should be ruled:

(A) admissible, as an answer to a proper question.
(B) admissible, only if corroborated by an adult.
(C) inadmissible, because the question was leading.
(D) inadmissible, because the boy's age prevents him from being a competent witness.

Question 89

A plaintiff sues a defendant for breach of contract. A witness is called to testify on behalf of the plaintiff. The defendant cross examines the witness.
Which of the following questions should the trial judge rule improper?

(A) "Isn't it true you are the plaintiff's cousin?"
(B) "Weren't you convicted of larceny three years ago?"
(C) "You just testified that the two parties sealed the contract with a handshake. Didn't you testify during the pre-trial deposition that the parties did not shake hands?"
(D) "Isn't true everyone in your hometown knows you are an alcoholic?"

Question 90

A defendant is on trial for drunk driving. When the defendant was booked at police headquarters, a police officer made a videotape of the defendant showing him to be dizzy, rude, and garbling his words. Assuming proper authentication, is the judge likely to admit this evidence?

(A) No, because specific instances of conduct cannot be proved by extrinsic evidence.

(B) No, because it is hearsay not within any exception.

(C) Yes, because it is an admission.

(D) Yes, because its value is not substantially outweighed by unfair prejudice.

Question 91

A defendant is on trial for conspiracy. A witness testified that she heard the defendant's conversation through a wall separating their hotel rooms. The defense denies that the voice she heard was the defendant's.

Which of the following would be the LEAST sufficient basis for admitting the testimony?

(A) The witness also listened to the defendant speak through a wall in the courtroom and identified it as the same voice.

(B) The witness was familiar with he defendant's voice, but had never heard the voice through a wall.

(C) The witness knew the defendant was staying in the room next to hers before she heard the voice.

(D) The witness shared a room with the defendant's mother, who had identified the defendant's voice.

Question 92

A plaintiff sued a defendant for injuries suffered when he slipped in a hallway outside the defendant's office. The defendant sought to admit evidence that he did not carry liability insurance for accidents occurring in the hallway.

This evidence should be ruled:

(A) admissible, to determine damages.

(B) admissible, to prove ownership of the hallway.

(C) inadmissible, because irrelevant.

(D) inadmissible, because of the Best Evidence Rule.

Question 93

A couple was involved in an automobile accident. A bystander happened to be carrying a camera and took several photographs. Before the photographs may be admitted into evidence, a proper foundation must include, as a minimum, testimony of which of the following?

(A) Possession of the photographs must be traced from the time they were developed until the time they reached the courtroom.

(B) Someone present at the scene of the accident must attest to the photos' accuracy.

(C) The photographer must testify.

(D) An expert must testify that the photos were not retouched.

Question 94

A plaintiff sued a defendant for damages to her automobile occurring when it was struck by an empty trash can on a windy day. The defendant denies ownership of the trash can and seeks to offer testimony that he puts his empty trash cans inside his garage when he returns from work in the evening. Both parties agree that the accident took place late at night. The trial judge should rule the evidence:

(A) admissible, as evidence of habit.

(B) inadmissible, as a conclusion.

(C) inadmissible, as a self-serving declaration.

(D) inadmissible, because propensity may not be proved by specific instances.

Question 95

A defendant hit a plaintiff over his head with a bat. Two witnesses testified to the event. A leading question will be permitted over objection in all of the following situations except:

(A) the plaintiff's direct examination of the defendant.

(B) the plaintiff's cross-examination of the first witness.

(C) the plaintiff's direct examination of the second witness.

(D) the plaintiff's cross-examination of a physician who testified as an expert witness.

Question 96

In the felony murder trial of a defendant arising out of an armed robbery, the defendant's father was called to testify. The prosecution objected to his father's testimony on the grounds that the father just completed a five-year prison sentence for manslaughter and is the defendant's father. The trial judge should rule the testimony:

(A) admissible.

(B) inadmissible, because of the father's relationship to the defendant.

(C) inadmissible, because of the father's manslaughter conviction.

(D) inadmissible, because of the father's manslaughter conviction and his relationship to the defendant.

Question 97

A drug dealer refused to testify during his trial for drug smuggling, claiming his right against self-incrimination. The prosecution called a witness who testified that he had incorporated a company for the drug dealer. The company's boats were later found to be carrying cocaine. The defendant moved to strike the witness' testimony.

The trial judge will rule the testimony:

(A) admissible, under the "business record" exception to the Hearsay Rule.

(B) admissible, because the witness is merely stating the general nature of the legal services rendered.

(C) inadmissible, because it is hearsay not within any exceptions.

(D) inadmissible, because of the attorney-client privilege.

Question 98

A defendant on trial for robbery took the stand and testified in his own behalf. On cross-examination, the prosecuting attorney asked the defendant whether he had embezzled money from his previous job. The defendant replied, "That's a lie, I never did." In rebuttal, the prosecuting attorney called a court officer to testify that the defendant admitted embezzling money from his company. The court officer further testified, however, that the defendant was granted immunity from prosecution in exchange for his testimony against others.

The court officer's testimony is:

(A) admissible, as bearing on the defendant's credibility.

(B) admissible, as bearing on defendant's guilt.

(C) inadmissible, because the court officer's testimony is extrinsic evidence.

(D) inadmissible, because the court order is the best evidence.

Questions 99–100 are based on the following fact situation.

The defendant was charged with the murder of a local club owner, who died from a beating he received during the course of a robbery in which his wallet containing $1,000 in cash and his gold wine glasses were stolen. The police found the club owner's body floating in a shallow pond near the defendant's apartment.

Question 99

The prosecution called a grocery store clerk, who testified that he had received certain $5 bills from the defendant on the day after the killing. The prosecution showed that these bills had been in the club owner's possession on the day of his murder. Under cross-examination, defendant's attorney asked the store clerk, "Is it not true that you committed false pretenses?" Upon objection by the prosecuting attorney, the trial judge should rule this question:

(A) proper, because it shows that the witness is biased.

(B) proper, for attacking the credibility of the witness.

(C) improper, since a foundation must be established for attacking a witness's credibility.

(D) improper, as a collateral matter.

Question 100

Assume for the purpose of this question only that the objection is overruled and the store clerk is directed to answer the question. The store clerk denies having ever been arrested for false pretenses. Then the defense attorney offers the store clerk's arrest record into evidence. The trial judge should rule this evidence:

(A) admissible, under the public records exception to the hearsay rule.

(B) admissible to impeach the store clerk's credibility.

(C) inadmissible, since such extrinsic evidence may not be introduced to impeach the credibility of a witness.

(D) inadmissible, since the store clerk's reputation is not in issue.

Questions 101–102 are based on the following fact situation.

The defendant was prosecuted for assault and battery after he admitted striking a friend with a bottle of whiskey during a bar room argument. The defendant claimed he acted in self-defense after he was attacked by his friend, who was drunk and belligerent, with a bottle of vodka.

Question 101

As his first defense witness, the defendant calls his next door neighbor to testify that the defendant is a good neighbor. The neighbors testimony is:

(A) admissible, because it is relevant to show the improbability of the defendant's having committed an unprovoked attack.

(B) admissible, because it is relevant to support the defendant's credibility.

(C) inadmissible, because it is merely the opinion of a character witness.

(D) inadmissible, because it is not directed toward a pertinent trait of the defendant's character.

Question 102

On cross-examination of the neighbor, the prosecuting attorney asked the witness if he had heard that the defendant had often engaged in fights and brawls. Upon objection by the defendant's attorney, the trial judge should rule this question:

(A) proper, because it tends to show the neighbor's knowledge of the defendant's reputation.

(B) proper, because it is relevant to prove the defendant's violent propensities.

(C) not proper, because it puts into evidence separate and unrelated offenses.

(D) not proper, because character cannot be proved by generalities.

Question 103

A realty estate company occasionally hires temporary workers from a temporary employment agency. During an especially busy month, the company needed an accountant to assist in its financial data operations. The realty company contacted the temporary agency and requested an administrative assistant for temporary employment. The realty company and the temp agency then entered into a contract in which the temp agency promised to provide an administrative assistant "who was honest, trustworthy, and efficient."

A short time later, the temp agency sent over a woman who was placed in the administrative position. The woman worked at the real estate company for one week when she was fired for stealing money. The real estate company then brought suit against the temp agency for misrepresentation. During the trial, the temp agency denied having any knowledge that the woman was dishonest and untrustworthy.

Thereupon, the real estate agency proffered evidence to show that two months before the temp company referred the woman to the real estate company, she had been terminated from a previous temporary employment job for theft.

Upon objection by the temp agency, the proffered evidence is:

(A) admissible, because specific instances of conduct may be admitted for the limited purpose of impeachment.

(B) admissible, as proof of the woman's character trait for dishonesty.

(C) inadmissible, because character can only be proved by reputation and opinion evidence.

(D) inadmissible, because specific instances of conduct are an improper means of proving character.

Question 104

A woman accuses the defendant of assault and battery while at a dance club, whereby the defendant pushed her and broke the woman's arm when the woman was dancing with the defendant's boyfriend.

At trial the prosecution calls the patron at the dance club who witnessed the accident to testify as an eyewitness. The patron, who is 23, did not have his glasses on at the time because he didn't want to lose them when he spun around on the floor and landed in splits, as was his usual routine. Without his glasses, the patron's eyesight is severely affected.

Which of the following is true regarding the patron's eyesight?

(A) It disqualifies him from testifying.

(B) It may be proved to impeach him as a witness.

(C) It has no bearing on either his competence or his credibility.

(D) It must not be referred to because it is unfairly prejudicial.

Question 105

In a trial for an embezzlement scheme, the defendant claims not to have been part of the scheme. The prosecution calls a witness to testify concerning the defendant's involvement in the embezzlement scheme, but the witness instead testified that the defendant was not involved and claimed that he never stated that the defendant was involved. The prosecution now calls a second witness to testify that the first witness had told him, while the two were playing golf, that the defendant was in fact involved in the embezzlement scheme.

Is the testimony of the second witness admissible?

(A) No, because the second witness may be biased against the first witness.

(B) No, because it is hearsay not within any exception.

(C) Yes, for the limited purpose of impeaching the first witness only.

(D) Yes, both for impeachment and its truth.

Evidence

Answer 1

(C) The Multistate Exam often contains questions that draw from different subjects. This question requires knowledge of the law of both evidence and contracts. In a court action based on a contract between a buyer and a seller, if the seller is a merchant, the UCC rule controls the outcome in this question. "The express terms of an agreement and an applicable course of dealing or usage of trade shall be construed whenever reasonable as consistent with each other; but when such construction is unreasonable, express terms control both course of dealing and usage of trade and course of dealings controls usage of trade" (UCC 1-205(4)). In accordance with this provision, the court should admit evidence of customary business practices to aid in interpreting the contract between the broker and computer designer (A) is not correct, because the broker's copies are not a past recollection recorded. A past recollection recorded is a written record made by a witness unable to remember the facts. (B) is not correct because Federal Rule of Evidence (FRE) 1003 provides, "A duplicate is admissible to the same extent as an original unless (1) a genuine question is raised as to the authenticity of the original or (2) in the circumstances it would be unfair to admit the duplicate in lieu of the original." (D) is not correct because of (C).

Note that the broker's copies should be admitted under the business records exception of the FRE.

Answer 2

(B) Although the driver's statement is hearsay as an out-of-court statement, it is admissible under FRE 803(3) as a then-existing physical condition. The driver's declaration will be admitted to prove his symptoms, including pain and suffering, but not to prove the actual injury itself. (A) is incorrect because statements of past symptoms are admissible under FRE 803(4) if made to a doctor to assist in his diagnosis, but a then-existing physical condition is a separate exception. (C) and (D) are not correct because declarations of a then-existing physical condition are admissible even if they are made to a non-physician.

Answer 3

(C) Under the Best Evidence Rule, the law requires that when writings are introduced as evidence in a trial, the original writing must be produced as the "best evidence." The term "writing" has been liberally interpreted to include photographs, X-ray, and films. Note that for photographs and film, this could be construed to mean negatives, not prints, as they are the true "original." The rule applies in two situations: (1) where the terms of the writing are legally dispositive in the issue at bar (not collateral documents or issues); (2) where the witness's sole knowledge of a fact comes from having read it in the document.

For material terms, the original writing must be produced unless it is shown to be unavailable for a reason not attributable to the fault of the party seeking to admit the evidence. The plaintiff's counsel's question violated this rule because the original report was available. (A) is not correct because the Business Exception Rule (FRE 803(6)) is an exception to the Hearsay Rule to allow a business record into evidence. No attempt was made by the plaintiff's counsel to enter any record into evidence. (B) is not correct because the plaintiff's counsel's question calls for information in the report, not for the witness's personal knowledge.

Answer 4

(B) A witness's statements will not be admissible because their probative value is substantially outweighed by the danger of unfair prejudice they create. (A) "Self-serving declaration" is a frequently used Multistate Bar Exam choice. It is rarely correct. (C) is not correct because such a question is proper for impeachment purposes only. One may introduce evidence of a prior statement that is inconsistent with present testimony. The question would not be proper if set forth for another purpose. (D) is not correct because while the statement may be unfairly prejudicial, it does not mean that it bears no relevance.

Answer 5

(B) The Best Evidence Rule requires that when writings are introduced as evidence in a trial, the original writing must be produced as the "best evidence." In federal practice, however, any exact copies of the original carry the same legal weight as the original unless their authenticity is in question.

The term "writing" has been liberally interpreted to include photographs, X-rays, and films. Note that for photographs and film, this could be construed to mean negatives, not prints, as they are the true "originals." The rule applies in two situations: (1) where the terms of the writing are legally dispositive in the issue at bar (not collateral documents or issues); (2) where the witness's sole knowledge of a fact comes from having read it in the document.

In this question, the best evidence available would be the tape recording, not the witness's recollections. (A) is incorrect because recounting defamatory statements is not hearsay. The words are not set forth to prove the content of the statements, but merely to establish that the defamatory statements were made. (C) is relevant only to determine if a suit should be brought for libel or for slander. (D) would have been correct under the reasoning set forth in (A), but the best evidence issue makes the objection sustainable.

Answer 6

(D) Both the taxi driver's log and the secretary's writing are hearsay. The friend's statement regarding her husband is hearsay within hearsay. FRE 805 provides, "Hearsay included within hearsay is not excluded under the Hearsay Rule if each part of the combined statements conforms with an exception to the Hearsay Rule. . . ." In other words, each component of the hearsay must meet an exception to the Hearsay Rule. The secretary's phone log entry will be considered a business record and is admissible on its own as a "business record" exception to the Hearsay Rule. However, the friend's statement about her husband that was written in the log was hearsay and inadmissible because the friend did not have personal knowledge of her husband's plans after he arrived at the airport. As a result, the secretary's notation in the log book would be inadmissible. The taxi driver's log is admissible under the "business record" exception to the Hearsay Rule.

Answer 7

(D) Although the witness's testimony is an of out-of-court statement, FRE 804(b)(1) gives a hearsay exception for former testimony if the declarant is unavailable (the witness's refusal to testify makes him "unavailable" under FRE 804(a)(1)), the testimony was given by the declarant as a witness in another proceeding, and the criminal defendant (or a "predecessor in interest" in a civil case) had an opportunity to develop cross-examination. All the above listed conditions have been met and both transcripts are admissible.

Answer 8

(B) Although the witness's statement to her husband constitutes hearsay not within any exception, it will be ruled admissible for the limited purpose of impeaching the witness. It will not be admissible for substantive purposes (i.e., for its truth). Students should note that when evidence is being admitted for substance, this means it is being admitted for its truth. FRE allows hearsay statements to be admitted that do not fall within any exception or that do not fall within non-hearsay to be admitted for the limited purpose of impeachment only. (D) is not correct because there is no written document whose contents are being offered for their truth, as is required for a past recollection recorded.

Answer 9

(B) A statement made by the co-conspirator of a party during the course and in furtherance of the conspiracy is admissible under the "admission by a party opponent," which is considered non-hearsay (FRE 801(D)(2)). If this statement was not made in furtherance of the conspiracy it will be inadmissible as hearsay. Read the question carefully. It asks under what circumstances the court will rule for the president solider to disallow the testimony by using the double negative "will not rule against." (A) is incorrect because if the statement was made during the course and in furtherance of the conspiracy, then the court would rule against president solider. (C) is incorrect because the statement does not have to be made directly to a party opponent.

Answer 10

(B) Evidence must be relevant to be admitted. This is the initial threshold to admitting evidence. Relevancy will be established if an item tends to prove or disprove a fact at issue. The color of the passenger's shirt was not related to the plane crash in any manner. The testimony was hearsay (Choice A), but the first test for the admissibility of any evidence is its relevancy, making (B) a better answer. This is a classic example of why one should always ask about relevancy first and foremost, and prevent oneself from getting caught up on a more difficult answer. (C) is not correct because the term *res gestae* refers to excited utterances or present sense impressions. (D) is incorrect because one does not have to be an expert to testify about car speed.

Answer 11

(B) Answering this question requires a mastery of the fine-line distinction between two hearsay concepts. The owner's statement to his friend was not hearsay because it is based on the owner's inspection, not on a statement the owner heard from another party. The owner's friend's testimony regarding the owner's statement was hearsay because she was recounting the words of the owner. Students must be able to make the distinction between the "admission" and "declaration against interest." Admissions by a party-opponent are considered non-hearsay under the Federal Rules, and the declarant must be a party to the action or in privity with such a party. The owner's statement did not meet this requirement, but it did qualify as a declaration against interest, which is an exception to the hearsay rule. In addition, the declarant must be unavailable for the declaration against interest exception to apply, and the owner is not present at trial.

Answer 12

(C) All four choices involve exceptions to the Hearsay Rule. Under (C), the "former testimony" exception requires that the declarant be unavailable and, in this choice, he was available. The declarant was unavailable in (A), satisfying the requirements to admit a "dying declaration." Had the witness recovered, the exception would still apply as long as he believed he was about to die at the time the statement was made and he was unavailable to testify. The declarant must also be unavailable for the "statement of pedigree" exception (B) to the Hearsay Rule. Under the "family record" (D) exception, the availability of the declarant is immaterial.

Answer 13

(D) The testimony concerning where the author lived, along with the woman's mother's mail, are admissible because the postal worker had personal knowledge. This type of evidence is admissible. (A) is not correct because the Best Evidence Rule applies when the terms of a writing are at issue, which is not the case in this question. The postal worker's testimony of the author's statement is hearsay, making (C) incorrect, because the testimony is admissible under the "pedigree" exception that provides, "Reputation among members of his family by blood, adoption, or marriage, or among his associates, or in the community, concerning a person's birth, adoption, marriage, divorce, death, legitimacy, relationship by blood, adoption or marriage, ancestry, or other similar fact of his personal or family history, are not excluded by the Hearsay Rule even though the declarant is available as a witness" (FRE 803(19)).

Answer 14

(D) The employee's testimony is not hearsay because it is not set forth to prove the truth of the matter asserted. The testimony seeks to establish that the employee was lacking the requisite *mens rea* to commit embezzlement. Remember that hearsay is an out-of-court statement offered to prove the truth of the matter, and here, it is not, thus (B) is incorrect. (A) and (C) are both irrelevant.

Answer 15

(A) If a witness testifies that he recognized the voice of a speaker, this will fulfill the requirements of authentication under the Federal Rules. Here, the neighbor is a party-opponent per FRE 801(d)(2)(A), and his statement would be ruled an admission. Hence, the statement will come in.

Answer 16

(B) The employee's statement was within the "statement against interest" exception to the Hearsay Rule if the employee is unavailable, and because the employee was an agent of the neighbor's company it could be an admission as well. In the absence of voice recognition, the witness can authenticate the speaker's voice by showing that he (the witness) dialed the number assigned and if the number is a business number, that the speaker identified himself and purported to act for the company called. It will be presumed that the speaker was allowed to act on behalf of the company (FRE 901(B)(6)(A)).

Answer 17

(D) The witness is testifying from her memory and she contains the personal firsthand knowledge to do so. She is not attempting to testify as to the content of the trucker's notes. Therefore, the Best Evidence Rule does not apply. The rule requires that the terms of a writing be proved by producing the document. The witness is not concerned with the writing. (C) is inapplicable to this question because it is a hearsay exception and the witness's statement does not contain hearsay. (B) is irrelevant.

Answer 18

(D) If one remains silent when accused, the silence may constitute an admission. The test is whether the reasonable person would have felt compelled to answer in a similar situation. Hence, note the operative word "if," which renders the answer more complete than (A). (A) assumes the student can answer the question based on the facts, and (D) gives the student the additional language he or she needs.

Answer 19

(C) Prior testimony of a witness under oath and in a judicial-like proceeding may be used for impeachment and as substantive evidence (i.e., for its truth). It may be brought in for its truth if designated non-hearsay under the FRE.

Answer 20

(C) Leading questions can be asked on direct examination to further a child's testimony. FRE 611 provides the court with control over the permissibility of leading questions to further ascertain the truth.

Answer 21

(C) A lay witness may not express an opinion as to the mental health of another. Only a qualified expert may express such an opinion. The mental health of a witness is relevant to his veracity.

Answer 22

(D) FRE 608(2) states that evidence of truthful character is admissible only after the character of the witness for truthfulness has been attacked by opinion or reputational evidence or otherwise. Since the first witness was not cross-examined and his truthfulness was never questioned by the prosecutor, the defense may not introduce what is essentially a new issue.

Answer 23

(D) Evidence of a pertinent trait of his character may be offered by the accused (FRE 404(a)(1)).

Answer 24

(C) The defendant's perjury conviction can be brought into evidence under FRE 609(a)(2) since the crime of perjury involves dishonesty or a false statement, regardless of the punishment. Generally, specific instances of a witness's conduct may not be proved by extrinsic evidence unless the specific conduct was a felony conviction (FRE 609) or unless the conduct is directly probative of the witness's truthfulness or lack thereof and resulted in a conviction (FRE 608(b)). Note that if the defendant was simply accused of perjury or arrested for perjury and not convicted, this would not be able to come in via extrinsic evidence as a prior bad act. (D) is incorrect because the crime of perjury is relevant to the defendant's veracity and not to the issue of whether he actually murdered his mother.

Answer 25

(A) Anyone familiar with a person's handwriting may authenticate that person's signature. It does not matter that a substantial time has elapsed since the person seeking to authenticate has seen the other's writing.

Answer 26

(B) Under the Best Evidence Rule, "A duplicate is admissible to the same extent as an original unless (1) a genuine question as to the authenticity of the original is raised or (2) in the circumstances, it would be unfair to admit the duplicate in lieu of the original" (FRE 1003). Since these exceptions do not apply to this question, the photocopy is admissible.

Answer 27

(B) The wife's testimony is hearsay because it is an out-of-court statement that is being offered to prove the truth of the matter. However, the testimony is admissible as an "excited utterance" (FRE 803(2)). It is not necessary to show that the declarant is unavailable under the exceptions set forth in FRE 803.

Answer 28

(A) The statement is admissible as an admission, and is considered non-hearsay under the Federal Rules.

Answer 29

(D) "A statement is not hearsay if the declarant testifies at the trial or hearing and is subject to cross-examination . . . and the statement is inconsistent with his [prior] testimony" (FRE 801(d)(1)(A)). (A) is not correct because FRE 607 affirmatively permits a party to impeach its own witness.

Answer 30

(D) Although FRE 408 excludes the defendant's $10,000 settlement offer from being admitted, the rule does not require the exclusion of other evidence that would otherwise be discoverable. Therefore, the defendant's statement about the "fifteen-year-old kid" is admissible under FRE 801(D)(2) as an "admission by party opponent."

Answer 31

(C) The prosecution may not open the door as to the character of the defendant until and unless the defendant has placed his character in issue.

Answer 32

(A) An accused may offer evidence of a pertinent trait of his character for the purpose of proving he acted in conformity therewith on a particular occasion (FRE 404(a)(1)). Compare this with the above question; the difference is who is trying to introduce the evidence.

Answer 33

(D) In order to admit a photograph, the witness must know about the facts that are portrayed in the photo. The witness need not have taken the actual photographs. (A) is incorrect because then-existing physical condition applies to a statement made by the declarant regarding his physical or mental condition. (C) is incorrect because the witness can testify that the photos are accurate representations of the scene, notwithstanding the time element involved.

Answer 34

(A) The first passenger's statement is introduced to prove the truth of the matter — the car's speed. In addition, it is an out-of-court statement, therefore it is hearsay. It will be ruled admissible under an exception to the Hearsay Rule, as an excited utterance (FRE 803(2)).

Answer 35

(D) FRE 404 states that evidence of a person's character or trait, such as safe driving, is not admissible to prove that he acted in conformity therewith. The driver's reputation will not be admissible to show that he did not act in a negligent manner in this instance unless provided for through the exceptions in FRE 404 and 607, 608, and 609.

Answer 36

(D) The pedestrian testified about another's statement. That is a classic example of hearsay. The statement does not qualify under the "declaration against interest" exception to the Hearsay Rule nor does it qualify as an "admission of party opponent" excluded from FRE 801(d).

Answer 37

(B) The pedestrian's testimony is introduced to prove that the windshield wipers were actually not working; therefore the pedestrian's testimony is hearsay. It will be admissible under the "present sense impression" exception to the Hearsay Rule (FRE 803(1)), or possible excited utterance. The availability of the declarant (A) is immaterial under all 803 exceptions.

Answer 38

(D) FRE 609(a)(2) allows evidence of a witness's past crimes to be admitted if they involve dishonesty or false statements. Since embezzlement is such a crime, and resulted in a conviction (a suspended sentence still means that he was convicted), it may be inquired into on cross-examination and it may also be proved by extrinsic evidence. (A) is incorrect because convictions of felonies may be proved by extrinsic evidence. (B) is incorrect because if the misdemeanor conviction was one that involved truth or falsity, it can also be proved by extrinsic evidence. (C) is incorrect because inquiry into the witness's arrest record is not admissible unless he was being asked specifically about a particular arrest involving dishonesty; and even then, the prosecutor would be bound by his answer since it did not result in a conviction.

Answer 39

(B) The court in U.S. v. Napier, 518 F.2d 316 (9th Cir.), *cert. denied*, 96 S. Ct. 196 (1975), ruled that a startling event satisfying the exception to the Hearsay Rule may occur weeks after the actual crime. In that particular case, the declarant was startled by seeing a photograph of the perpetrator. Availability of the declarant is immaterial under the "excited utterance" exception to the Hearsay Rule.

Answer 40

(D) FRE 804(b)(2) states that a statement made by a declarant, the friend, is admissible if it was made while believing that his death was imminent and concerned the cause of what he believed to be his own impending death. (A) is incorrect because the dying declaration exception does not permit the friend's statement to be admitted as evidence that the robber killed the friend.

Answer 41

(B) The witness may not be impeached on a collateral matter; however, the salesman's testimony would be admissible to prove the robber had a motive to steal (to repay the loan), as provided for under FRE 404(b).

Answer 42

(B) The accused, in all criminal cases, may produce evidence of his good character as substantive evidence of his innocence. It is merely circumstantial evidence bearing on the probability that the accused did or did not commit the act with the required intent. Here, this may be done by reputation or opinion evidence, and it must be relevant. (C) is incorrect because the rule stated in this choice applies only to negligence cases.

Answer 43

(A) A cross-examiner may ask a character witness whether he has "heard" or "knows" of other particular crimes of the accused as a form of impeaching the witness, provided the question is asked in good faith.

Answer 44

(B) FRE 411 allows evidence of whether or not a person was insured to be admitted to prove agency, ownership, control, or bias, but not to prove that the person acted negligently, which is why (C) is incorrect. (A) is incorrect because even though it may be an excited utterance, it still has to jump through ALL hurdles, meaning that even if evidence of insurance is said excitedly, it still has to pass the requirements of 411, so (A) is incorrect because it does not tell you the entire story. (D) is incorrect because it COULD be an excited utterance, and we know it CAN come in to show ownership. (A) is not the correct choice because this exchange between the two drivers does not resemble a startling event that would trigger the "excited utterance" exception (FRE 803(2)).

Answer 45

(A) A criminal conviction is admissible in a civil suit arising from the same action in order to prove the defendant's behavior during the occurrence in dispute (here that the defendant was intoxicated), but not to prove character.

Answer 46

(D) Subsequent remedial measures are inadmissible as evidence of negligence on public policy grounds. We do not want to discourage people from taking precautions if they feel that it will make them look liable. Subsequent remedial measures are admissible, however, to show ownership or control.

Answer 47

(A) The statement made to the witness by the victim is hearsay, not within any exception. However, such a statement can be admitted for impeaching the victim's earlier statement, but not for substance (i.e., not for its truth). The jury can only weigh it as being inconsistent with the victim's first statement.

Answer 48

(A) FRE 901(b)(2) allows anyone familiar with the handwriting of a given person to supply authentication testimony, in the form of an opinion that a writing or signature is the handwriting of that person.

Answer 49

(A) Prior crimes are admissible for the purpose of determining length of sentence during a sentencing hearing.

Answer 50

(B) Any person who has acquired sufficient familiarity with a voice may identify that person. The rules requiring the other person to identify herself, etc., only apply when the voice is not familiar (FRE 901).

Answer 51

(B) The statement is considered non-hearsay as an admission. (A) is incorrect because the then-existing mental condition exception, FRE 803(3), is generally applicable when the declarant is describing his mental condition during the time he is feeling it. And since this is clearly an admission, a non-hearsay answer, if applicable, is always stronger than a possible hearsay exception.

Answer 52

(B) Although religious beliefs are not admissible to prove veracity, they may be admitted for another purpose, if relevant. Here, since the defendant did not eat shellfish, this evidence is relevant to show that he would not likely be found in a clam bar.

Answer 53

(B) is the only correct answer because the report does not fit within any hearsay exception. It is not admissible under FRE 803(6) as a business record because the report is not truly made in the course of regularly conducted business. The business of the spa is not to fill out accident reports when they happen, but rather to offer spa services. In addition, the accident report could have been biased in favor of the spa since the spa is being sued for negligence, making the record untrustworthy. (C) is not correct, because a recorded recollection is used only to enable a witness who has sufficient recollection to testify fully and accurately.

Answer 54

(D) Evidence of a guilty plea, later withdrawn, or of statements made in connection with the plea, are not admissible either in a civil or criminal proceeding against the person who made the plea (FRE 410).

Answer 55

(C) The driver's conduct in attempting to bribe the witness is probative as to the driver's negligence and is therefore considered an admission by conduct. Do not confuse this with an offer to settle. A settlement offer is also probative, but is not admissible due to public policy to encourage settlements.

Answer 56

(D) The pedestrian is not attempting to submit the diary as evidence, he is merely attempting to use the diary to help the witness's memory. Because it is not being offered into evidence, or rather "for the truth of the matter," hearsay is not at issue, and therefore (B) and (C) are incorrect. (A) is inapplicable because it does not make sense since the diary was written directly after the accident.

Answer 57

(C) Evidence of a person's character or a trait of character is generally not admissible except, under FRE 404(a)(1), if the defendant first "opens the door."

Answer 58

(C) Since the burglary is a felony conviction, it is admissible under FRE 609(a) if the court determines it will not prejudice the defendant. (A) is not correct since a felony conviction may be inquired into on cross examination for the purposes of impeachment, and even proven by extrinsic evidence. (B) is inapplicable since no writing is being offered into evidence. (D) is wrong because felony convictions are considered relevant under the FRE and are a proper method of impeaching a witness.

Answer 59

(C) Since the caterer is testifying based on firsthand knowledge, her testimony is admissible even though the same information is written down. (A) is incorrect because the Best Evidence Rule only applies where the contents of the writing are being directly proved from the writing itself. (B) is not correct because there is not an out-of-court statement at issue here.

Answer 60

(D) An excited utterance must be made "while the declarant was under the stress of excitement caused by the event or condition" (FRE 803(2)). Since the pedestrian did not tell the officer about the accident until an hour later, the law assumes he had time to plan his outburst and does not fit this into an exception to the Hearsay Rule. A present sense impression must be made "while the declarant was perceiving the event or condition, or immediately thereafter" (FRE 803(1)).

Answer 61

(A) A statement is considered a non-hearsay admission if the statement offered against a party is his own (FRE 801(d)(2)(A)).

Answer 62

(A) The doctor's testimony is relevant to determine if the soup was contaminated. The doctor is relating the statements of others, which would ordinarily be hearsay, but in these facts the statements qualify under the "statements for purposes of medical diagnosis or treatment" exception to the Hearsay Rule (FRE 803(4)).

Answer 63

(D) FRE 803(4) permits statements to be admitted if they were for purposes of medical diagnosis or treatment, but such statements should not include statements as to cause. (B) is incorrect because statements as to fault are not admissible under FRE 803(4).

Answer 64

(A) Infants, interested persons, and incompetents are valid witnesses. Facts may be introduced as to matters of weight and credibility, but not admissibility.

Answer 65

(D) Although evidence of subsequent remedial measures is not permitted to show negligence (FRE 407), such evidence may be admitted to rebut a claim that the precaution was impossible. The evidence is admissible here to controvert the manufacturer's answer that it was impossible to design a trailer with proper equipment. Evidence of subsequent remedial measures can also be used for purposes of impeachment and to prove ownership or control.

Answer 66

(D) Extrinsic evidence of authenticity is not a condition precedent to admissibility with respect to books, pamphlets, or other publications purporting to be issued by public authority (FRE 603).

Answer 67

(B) "Although relevant, evidence may be excluded if its probative value is substantially outweighed by the danger of unfair prejudice" (FRE 402). In this situation, the fact that the defendant has an illegal gambling habit may prejudice the jury and distract them from the real issue at hand, and the probative value of the defendant's gambling is small when compared to its prejudicial effect.

Answer 68

(A) A prior statement of a party is only admissible if offered against that party, not in favor of that party. The reasoning behind this is that when a party speaks against himself, the statement is usually inherently reliable. However, when speaking in favor of himself, the statement is inherently unreliable because the declarant can easily lie to protect himself.

Answer 69

(C) For the purpose of the attorney-client privilege, "client" is a person, public officer of a corporation, association, or other entity. The privilege extends to lower-echelon employees of a corporation.

Answer 70

(C) An expert opinion may be offered in response to a hypothetical question where assumed facts have been previously offered into evidence. (D) is a generally correct statement, but is not as specific as (C) is in directly answering the call of the question.

Answer 71

(A) "If a type is reasonably relied upon by experts in the particular field, in forming opinion or inferences upon the subject, the facts or data (i.e., the microscopic tissue) need not be admissible in evidence" (FRE 703).

Answer 72

(B) Under the "former testimony" exception to the Hearsay Rule, a witness's testimony may be admitted, providing the witness is unavailable and the party against whom the testimony is being offered had an opportunity to cross-examine the witness (FRE 80(b)(1)).

Answer 73

(D) "Evidence of subsequent measures is not admissible to prove negligence or culpable conduct in connection with the event. This rule does not require the exclusion of evidence . . . for another purpose, such as proving ownership" (FRE 407). (A) is correct policy, but (D) gives us the legal standard.

Answer 74

(B) The fact that many others passed without injury does not prove the owner exercised due care in maintaining it.

Answer 75

(D) A communication remains confidential and within the attorney-client privilege if a secretary, or other person necessary to assist the attorney in preparing the case, is present.

Answer 76

(D) The sheriff's recollection of the second driver's statement is admissible as an admission.

Answer 77

(D) The policy of the law is to encourage settlement negotiations; therefore, courts will not allow testimony of the actual negotiations.

Answer 78

(D) Choices (A), (B), and (C) are not correct because the buyer seeks to introduce the neighbor's testimony, which are all out-of-court statements offered to prove the truth of the matter asserted, that the seller was not competent. In addition, there are no exceptions that would fit, so the correct answer is (D).

Answer 79

(B) FRE 609 provides that any crime involving dishonesty or false statement is admissible to impeach a witness. The crime is admissible via extrinsic evidence since it resulted in a conviction. Felony convictions punishable by more than one year in prison are admissible to impeach a witness and may be offered via extrinsic evidence if the punishment was less than ten years ago, and the prejudicial effect is substantially outweighed by the probative value. Since the manslaughter crime is more than 10 years old, it will not be admissible. Hence, (B) is the correct answer.

Answer 80

(B) Illegally obtained evidence may not be admitted as substantive proof of guilt, but may be used to impeach credibility (U.S. v. Havens, 100 S. Ct. 1912(1980)). Note that it does not matter whether the party is attempting to impeach testimony given on direct or cross.

Answer 81

(D) A witness does not need special qualifications to determine the speed of an automobile. (A) is incorrect because it only gives half of the rule, that witnesses may not draw conclusions on matters of law. (B) is incorrect because no foundation is necessary, and (C) is incorrect because there does not seem to by any evidence that this is an improper objection.

Answer 82

(A) If an agent makes a statement within his agency, contrary to the principal's interest, this statement qualifies as a "statement against interest" exception to the Hearsay Rule (FRE 804(b)(3)). In addition, 804 requires that the declarant be unavailable. So, all of the requirements for statement against interest are met in (A).

Answer 83

(D) By blaming his agent, the driver has in effect blamed himself and made an admission.

Answer 84

(A) Although religious beliefs may not be introduced to prove credibility, they may be introduced for other reasons. Here, the witness's membership in the church is relevant to show possible bias in the church's favor.

Answer 85

(D) One's reputation may not be offered to show he acted in a negligent manner in a specific situation (FRE 404).

Answer 86

(D) The attorney-client privilege applies to written as well as oral communications, as long as it was intended by the parties to be confidential.

Answer 87

(A) An expert witness may base his opinion on facts not admitted into evidence. The opposing party may ask about these facts on cross-examination (FRE 704). The questions may be leading and hypothetical in form.

Answer 88

(A) Leading questions are permitted when the witness needs aid due to immaturity. Here, the witness is only six years old, and hence the leading question would be allowed.

Answer 89

(D) One may not question a witness about his addiction to alcohol because it is not considered to have bearing on veracity. The witness may be impeached by prior inconsistent statements.

Answer 90

(D) FRE 403 excludes evidence if it is unfairly prejudicial, but there is little danger of that here because the tape fairly shows the state of the defendant as being intoxicated. (A) is not correct because the tape does not seek to impeach the witness on a collateral matter as required by the rule against impeachment by use of extrinsic evidence regarding specific instances of conduct. (C) is not correct because it is unlikely his acts equal an admission, and there is not a hearsay problem in this question. An admission against a party opponent is considered non-hearsay under the federal rules.

Answer 91

(D) In this choice, the witness' testimony is hearsay because it is an out of court statement offered for the truth of the matter. The prosecution should call the defendant's mother to the stand.

Answer 92

(B) Evidence that one is insured is not admissible to prove liability or damages, but is admissible to prove ownership or control (FRE 411).

Answer 93

(B) A foundation witness must attest that a photograph accurately portrays what it purports to depict. The photographer need not testify, so (C) is incorrect. In addition, there is no chain of evidence issue, making (A) incorrect.

Answer 94

(A) Evidence of the habit of a person is relevant to prove that the conduct on a particular occasion was in conformity with the habit of routine practice (FRE 406).

Answer 95

(C) Leading questions should be permitted on cross-examination and when a party calls a hostile witness or adverse party (FRE 611(C)).

Answer 96

(A) Convicted felons and relatives are competent witnesses. A conviction for a felony or a crime involving dishonesty or fraud is a basis for impeaching the witness (FRE 609), as is bias.

Answer 97

(B) The court, in U.S. v. Mackay, 405 F. Supp. 854, (E.D. N.Y. 1975) held that an attorney could be compelled to testify he was an incorporator because the attorney-client privilege does not apply to testimony concerning the general nature of legal services rendered, making (D) incorrect. Also, there is no out-of-court statement being testified to, so (A) and (C) are incorrect.

Answer 98

(C) The court officer's testimony here is extrinsic evidence. On cross-examination, a witness may be impeached by prior bad acts bearing on credibility by *inquiry only*. Once the witness answers, all questioning must stop and no extrinsic evidence may be used to further impeach the witness. (D) is incorrect because the court order still would have been extrinsic evidence.

Answer 99

(B) Here, the defense attorney is cross-examining the prosecution's witness about a *prior bad act*. Note that the fact pattern does not say that it is a conviction. As stated above, a witness may be impeached by prior bad acts bearing on credibility, so this question is proper.

Answer 100

(C) Once the witness answers, all questioning must stop, and no extrinsic evidence, by way of testimony of another witness or documents, may be used to further impeach the witness.

Answer 101

(D) All evidence must be relevant. Just because the defendant may bake cookies for his neighbors, doesn't mean he isn't a violent bar room brawler who doesn't have problems with his liquor and using it as a deadly weapon. Always keep in mind that evidence must be relevant as the initial threshold to admissibility.

Answer 102

(A) A witness may be impeached by showing that he has a *lack of knowledge* of the defendant's reputation. The prosecutor may do this by asking the witness on cross about specific instances of bad conduct by the defendant as long as it is relevant to the specific character train testified to by the witness, which it is here.

Answer 103

(B) This question has the real estate company suing the temp agency for knowing about the woman's sticky hands. The temp agency has denied knowing about the woman's character trait for dishonesty, so now the real estate company may ask the temp agency on cross about specific instances of conduct by the woman to demonstrate that the woman has the character trait of dishonesty. (A) is wrong because the evidence was not offered for the limited purpose of impeachment (even though this may in fact impeach the temp agency regarding their knowledge of the woman's character). The evidence is admissible to show that the woman has a character for dishonesty.

Answer 104

(B) A witness may be impeached by showing that his capacity to observe, remember, or narrate events correctly has been impaired. In this case, the witness may be shown to have such poor eyesight that he couldn't have seen what he claims to have seen. It does not, however, disallow the witness from testifying, as (A) states. Impeachment by a sensory defect goes to the weight of the evidence, not the admissibility.

Answer 105

(C) Prior statements made by the witness that are inconsistent with the witness's current testimony may be used to impeach the witness. Since this prior statement was not made under oath, it may not come in for its truth, as (D) states.

Property

Property

Question 1

A landowner divided his plot of land into two parts, Eastacre and Westacre. He then built a house on each. A buyer purchased Westacre and the owner kept Eastacre. In the course of construction, the owner had run plumbing for Eastacre through Westacre. The pipes were underground and not apparent to the casual observer. One year later, the buyer decided to put a swimming pool in his yard. The buyer's contractor discovered the owner's pipes, which obstructed the area for the pool. The buyer asserted an action to force the owner to remove his pipes from Westacre. Who will most likely prevail?

(A) The buyer, because the owner's pipes trespassed on his land.

(B) The owner, because he owned an easement by implication.

(C) The owner, because he owned an easement by prescription.

(D) The buyer, because the owner violated the covenant against encumbrances.

Question 2

Which of the following conveyances would be altered by the Rule Against Perpetuities?

(A) A grantor conveyed his chain of video stores to his son "on the condition that he does not rent X-rated movies. Should the son rent X-rated movies, the grantor or his heirs have the right to reenter the premises."

(B) The grantor conveyed his chain of video stores to his son "for as long as X-rated movies are not rented from the stores."

(C) The grantor conveyed his chain of video stores "to my son then if my daughter is living upon my son's death, to my daughter; upon my daughter's death to my grandchildren who have reached the age of twenty-five."

(D) The grantor conveyed his chain of video stores "to my son for life; remainder to my son's children for life; remainder to my daughter's children and their heirs."

Question 3

A retired physician without children owned his former office, which was part of a professional condominium complex. The physician rented out the office, but he wanted to give it to one of his nephews to ensure that someone would follow in his footsteps. One of the physician's nephews was in medical school and had chosen psychiatry as his specialty. As a proctologist, the physician couldn't understand why his nephew wanted to waste all that good education to deal with nuts. The physician's niece was a high school sophomore who did well in science class and seemed interested in proctology.

The physician decided to convey his condominium "to my nephew for life, then, if my niece should be awarded the degree 'Doctor of Medicine' and complete a residency, to my niece and her heirs as long as the office is used for the practice of medicine."

Which of the following choices is NOT correct?

(A) While the niece is in college she holds a contingent remainder in fee simple determinable.

(B) If the niece completes her residency in medicine she owns a fee simple determinable upon the nephew's death.

(C) The physician's interest at the time of the conveyance is best described as a possibility of reverter.

(D) If the niece becomes a florist and never goes to medical school, possession will eventually return to the physician without the fee simple determinable ever being invoked.

Question 4

In 1916, a grantor executed a deed conveying Blackacre "to my son for life, upon my son's death, to his children or their respective estates." His son lived on Blackacre all his life. He had three children.

A creditor of one of the grantor's grandsons asserted an action to attach the grandson's interest prior to the son's death. Can the creditor succeed?

(A) Yes, because a remainder may be attached by creditors.

(B) Yes, because a vested remainder may be attached or sold by creditors.

(C) No, because neither a vested nor a contingent remainder may be attached or sold by creditors.

(D) No, because the grandson's interest was a contingent remainder.

Question 5

A grantor owned a parking lot in fee simple. When the grantor died his will provided, "I leave my wife a life estate in my parking lot. After my wife's death, the lot shall pass to my only son, to use and manage in his lifetime. After my son's death, the parking lot shall pass in fee simple to the heirs of his body."

The grantor's wife died. Some years later, his son died intestate, married, and without issue. In a common law jurisdiction, the parking lot will pass:

(A) to the son's wife in fee simple by the rules governing intestate succession.

(B) to the son's long lost sister.

(C) to grantor's estate.

(D) to grantor's wife's estate by reversion.

Question 6

A seller sold his home to a buyer with full covenants. The house, resting on a half acre of land, had three bedrooms and a two-car garage. Two years later, the buyer conveyed the house to a second buyer by a quitclaim deed.

Which of the following choices is correct?

(A) The second buyer can successfully assert an action against the seller if at the time the seller sold the home a logging company owned the rights to all the timber on the property.

(B) The second buyer can force the seller to take further action within his power to perfect title to the home when her next-door neighbor argues that her fence is on his property.

(C) The second buyer can enforce the seller's guarantee to the first buyer that the land is free from easements that diminish its value.

(D) The second buyer can enforce a covenant against encumbrances made by the seller to the first buyer.

Question 7

State Water is a public utility that supplies the city with water. A man owned a large amount of vacant land in the city. State Water calculated that it could save $400,000 by running its pipes across some of the man's land rather than crossing a public highway. After months of negotiations the man granted State Water an eight-foot-wide strip of land under which to bury its pipes and use in perpetuity for consideration of $200,000.

Which of the following choices best describes the rights State Water acquired?

(A) profit

(B) easement in gross

(C) easement appurtenant

(D) real covenant

Question 8

In 1922, a minister and strong supporter of Prohibition conveyed a ten-acre farm he had inherited from his father "to my son and his heirs so long as this farm is not used to sell, produce, or warehouse alcohol or assist the alcohol industry in any manner." The son died in 1925 whereupon the property passed to his two children. In 1965 they sold their interest in the property to a buyer. The children died in the early 1970s, each leaving three children and a spouse. Both spouses eventually remarried. Kentucky Bourbon purchased five of the ten acres in 2000 and constructed a whiskey distillery.

What should the status of the land be now?

(A) The land will remain in Kentucky Bourbon's possession because the anti-alcohol clause violated the Rule Against Perpetuities.

(B) The land will revert to the minister's heirs because the anti-alcohol clause created a valid fee simple subject to condition subsequent.

(C) The land will revert to the minister's heirs because the anti-alcohol clause created an indestructible fee simple determinable.

(D) The land will revert to the minister's heirs only in a minority of states that have not enacted statutes of limitations applicable to fee simple determinables.

Question 9

A grantor owned a lovely beach home in fee simple, and he had grown very attached to it. When he purchased a new and much larger house for his growing family, the grantor could not bear to part with his old home. So, he decided to grant a life estate in the house to his cousin, who had very little money and a family of his own to provide for. The grantor left himself the remainder of the life estate.

The cousin lived in the house for a little while, but then realized he could have a nice income if he rented it out. He decided to grant an attorney a ten-year lease on the house. The attorney agreed to pay $2,000 per month for the first year, with an increase each subsequent year tied to the local inflation rate.

Who can be said to have seisin after the attorney occupies the house?

(A) the grantor

(B) the cousin

(C) the attorney

(D) none of the above

Question 10

A lawyer was besieged by friends, relatives, and acquaintances seeking free legal advice. The lawyer's cousin, one of the cheapest men in North America, purchased a house without retaining counsel. He stopped by the lawyer's house on a Sunday, pretending to be in the neighborhood, and said, "Hey, I happen to have the contract to my house. Why don't you take a look at it as a refresher in contract law."

The lawyer looked at the contract and told his cousin, "Your agreement provides for 'usual covenants.' You should have insisted on 'full covenants.'"

The difference will be important if the cousin wants to assert an action against the person who sold him the house based on the covenant:

(A) for quiet enjoyment.

(B) of general warranty.

(C) for the right to convey.

(D) for seisin.

Question 11

In which of the following cases is the easement NOT valid and/or enforceable?

(A) A rancher owned a 10,000-acre ranch that was divided by a river and a county highway into three distinct sections. One section had become known in the neighborhood as "The Flats." Out of affection for his business partner, the rancher signed a writing granting an easement to his partner to "have full recreational use of, and all pleasure rights to, the part of my ranch known as 'The Flats.'" The business partner recorded the easement pursuant to a local recording act.

(B) A lyricist owned a house with a large yard. After living in the house for twenty years, sky-rocketing real estate prices, followed by a large rise in taxes, began to deplete his bank account. The lyricist decided to sell one-half acre of his property to his brother, a composer, who built a house on it. The only access from the composer's house to a public road was over the lyricist's property. The composer received no confirmation, written or otherwise, of an easement to drive over his brother's property, and he did not make any official recordings.

(C) A runner jogged along a path on his neighbor's property every day for twenty-one years. The neighbor, tired of hearing his wife nag him because the runner was active and healthy while he only sat around smoking and getting fat, asserted an action to prevent the runner from using the path. The runner claimed he had an easement by prescription. The statute of limitations was fifteen years.

(D) A grantor, the owner of a three-story house with a view of the beach, paid his neighbor, the owner of a neighboring parking lot, for a written easement assuring that "no structure blocking the grantor's light and air will be built on the neighbor's property."

Question 12

An heir, a fifty-year-old bachelor, inherited a 200-acre estate that had been in his family's possession for more than a century. Since he did not have a family of his own, he decided he would be lonely living there. He had also never worked a day in his life and needed some cash. The heir decided half the land would be enough for his own use. He only needed sufficient acreage on which to ride his horses. The heir sold one-acre lots pursuant to a contract that contained the clause "Heir agrees to reserve ten acres of land to be used as a private park for the exclusive use of residents of the ninety one-acre plots. The purchaser of this lot agrees to erect no building taller than two stories. Such structures may be used for residential purposes only." The heir kept two of the one-acre lots. He took a long trip abroad with his new-found money. While the heir was abroad, a homeless person moved into his mansion and remained in exclusive, open, notorious, continuous, and hostile possession for twenty-one years. Shortly before the heir returned from abroad, the homeless person was granted title to the 100-acre estate in fee simple. A contractor purchased one of the one-acre tracts from a seller, who had purchased from the heir. The contractor filed a building permit to construct a house three stories high.

Will the homeless person succeed in collecting damages from the contractor for constructing her house?

(A) Yes, because a common development scheme had been established for the entire subdivision.

(B) Yes, because the restrictive clause ran with the land.

(C) No, because the homeless person received "new title" and should not be considered to have privity of estate with the contractor.

(D) No, because the restriction was not enforceable.

Question 13

On July 7, Alpha conveyed Rockacre to Beta. The deed provided for a "general warranty." Four years later on February 22, Beta conveyed Rockacre to Gamma. The deed contained the same language as the Alpha-Beta deed. In which of the following lawsuits will Gamma most likely prevail?

(A) Six months after purchasing Rockacre, Gamma was notified by a neighbor that a real covenant prevented any construction on the property. After researching the relevant law, Gamma determined that he was bound by this covenant. Gamma sued Alpha for damages.

(B) Six months after purchasing Rockacre, Gamma was notified by a neighbor that he was occupying her land. She had just been awarded title to Rockacre after a year of litigation. Gamma asserted an action against Alpha.

(C) Six months after purchasing Rockacre, Gamma was notified by the local bank that it held a mortgage on the property. Gamma was subsequently told that the mortgage was taken out eight years previously. He asserted an action against Alpha.

(D) Gamma will not succeed in any of the above actions.

Question 14

A tenant had one year remaining on a twenty-four month, $400 per month, apartment lease. A sublessee and the tenant signed the following agreement on January 1:

"The sublessee agrees to sublease from the tenant apartment 13A in the building known as 'Lake View Manor,' for $420 per month. This sublease shall expire on December 31."

The sublessee paid his rent in a timely manner for six months. The tenant did not pay any rent to the landlord. The tenant and her husband were forced into bankruptcy by their creditors in November.

The landlord asserted an action against the sublessee to recover six month's rent. Is the sublessee likely to prevail?

(A) Yes, because there is no privity of estate between a lessor and a sublessee.

(B) Yes, because otherwise the sublessee would be paying his rent twice.

(C) No, because a sublessee is liable to the landlord for rent.

(D) No, because the tenant transferred to the sublessee the rights for the complete remainder of her tenancy.

Question 15

Macre was next to Pacre and to its west. The owner of Macre was granted an easement by the owner of Pacre to cross his property in order to reach the train station. Several years later, the owner of Macre acquired Lacre, which lay on Pacre's east side. May the owner of Macre use his easement to pass between Macre and Lacre?

(A) Yes, if the traffic is similar to the traffic passing to the train station.

(B) Yes, if passage is the most economical means of transport.

(C) No, because it is not an easement by necessity.

(D) No, because the owner of Macre's easement limits use of the servient tenement to only the dominant tenement.

Question 16

B transferred an apartment complex to C and his heirs with the proviso that "C and his heirs shall not have the right to convey or transfer title to the complex." C conveyed the property to D "for a period of thirty years, in exchange for payment of $10,000 a month to be increased by the greater of the cost of living increase or prime lending rate increase." C then conveyed the complex "in fee simple to G or her heirs upon termination of D's interest and upon payment of $1,000,000."

Which of the following choices is NOT correct?

(A) G's interest will still be valid despite B's disabling restraint.

(B) B's conveyance to C is void because the restriction was to last longer than a life in being plus twenty-one years.

(C) D's heirs have a valid contingent remainder and their interest is not a violation of the Rule Against Perpetuities.

(D) C created a valid interest in D and a valid interest in Elyse and her heirs.

Question 17

Red owned a commercial fish pond. Harvesting the pond became unprofitable when demand and prices for catfish suffered a prolonged slump. Yellow used the pond for weekend recreational fishing. Blue owned a commercial fish pond adjacent to Red's. One day, Blue told Red, "I'm fed up with this pond. It's been losing money for years, and it will always lose money. You can fish in my pond from now on."

"Great, can you put that in writing so the bank will finance me?" Red asked.

Blue executed a proper writing expressing his promise to Red. Since fishing both ponds together was more economical than the cost of fishing both separately, Red was able to earn a healthy profit.

Red sold his property to Green. Will the right to fish in Blue's pond pass to her?

(A) Yes, because there was privity between Red and Green.

(B) Yes, because the economic benefit of Blue's pond is tied to Green's land.

(C) No, because the benefit to Red was personal.

(D) No, because the agreement between Red and Blue was an affirmative easement.

Question 18

H and N owned abutting farms. N's farm was adjacent to a public highway. H's farm was surrounded by water and dense woods wherever it did not border N's farm. H's farm had two easements to cross N's property when he first acquired it. One allowed passage to a public highway, and the other allowed passage between two of H's fields.

In 1922, N granted H a written contract that expanded his previous easements with the right to use motorized vehicles on them. From 1922 to 1960, H drove his pickup truck and tractor over the easements. In 1961, H decided to build a racetrack on his farm. One corner of the track ran across N's property, but only on the easement that used to connect two of H's fields. The track was used for races every Friday night. The race cars were very noisy and emitted toxic fumes. N asserted an action against H, hoping to enjoin all use of the easement. The court will most likely rule that:

(A) H has forfeited his right to one of the easements.

(B) H could continue to use the easement for reasonable farm use, but not as a race track.

(C) both easements were extinguished by blatant excessive use in an unintended manner.

(D) use of the race track was proper, as long as it was within the guidelines of the original writing.

Question 19

A seller conveyed three acres of land to a buyer, who intended to build twelve single-family homes on the land. The deed contained the clause, "All usual covenants are included, as this is a general warranty, subject to deed restrictions and easements of record."

Several months later, the buyer found out that a neighbor owned an easement to drain his property via a tiny stream that ran across the buyer's land. The easement prevented the construction of two homes. The neighbor was able to enforce his easement despite never having recorded it.

If the buyer asserts an action against the seller for breach of a covenant, she will most likely:

(A) prevail, because discovery of any easement is a breach of the covenant against encumbrances.

(B) prevail, because this easement was unrecorded and an unknown defect in the title.

(C) not prevail, because the language of the deed excludes easements that could be discovered.

(D) not prevail, because it is a personal covenant.

Questions 20–21 are based on the following fact pattern.

Ann granted an easement for a right of way to Barbara. The grant, in the form of a deed, was properly recorded. Ann sold the property to Cory, who sold it to Denise, who then sold the property to Elaine. Cory, Denise, and Elaine recorded their deeds without mentioning the right of way.

Smith, Elaine's attorney, examined title to the property and told Elaine, "It's all yours." Two days later, Elaine conveyed the property to Francine with a covenant against encumbrances. Francine learned of Barbara's easement shortly thereafter.

Question 20

If Francine asserts an action against Smith to recover for the lower property value of the land due to the easement, is she likely to prevail?

(A) Yes, as a third-party beneficiary, in states that recognize the duty of an attorney to the intended beneficiary of their services.

(B) Yes, because the title was guaranteed.

(C) No, because Smith did not owe a duty to Francine.

(D) No, unless Francine can prove Smith was negligent.

Question 21

If Francine asserts an action against Elaine to recover for the lower property value of the land due to the easement, is Francine likely to prevail?

(A) Yes, because Elaine did not satisfy her contractual agreement.

(B) Yes, because Elaine was negligent.

(C) No, because Elaine relied on Smith.

(D) No, because a purchaser must conduct her own title search.

Question 22

A grantor owned Cacre, an undeveloped tract of land, in fee simple. He conveyed a quitclaim deed to a buyer in exchange for fair value. The buyer never recorded the deed.

Two years later, the buyer executed and delivered to his niece a warranty deed to Cacre in exchange for the niece's secretarial services. The niece recorded the deed two years later. Neither the niece nor the buyer have occupied Cacre. The jurisdiction has a pure notice recording act and requires that a junior claimant, to have priority, act in good faith and pay consideration of sufficient value. In an action between the buyer and the niece for title to Cacre, which of the following is the best answer?

(A) The outcome will be determined by whether the niece gave consideration of sufficient value to the grantor.

(B) The buyer will not prevail because she did not record the deed.

(C) The buyer will not prevail because she obtained a quitclaim deed.

(D) The outcome will be determined by whether the buyer gave consideration of sufficient value to the grantor.

Question 23

A buyer contracted with a seller to purchase a bullet-proof house. The contract stated that the seller would provide a general warranty deed. The agreement had to be closed in a hurry because the seller was moving to Europe for business. The buyer did not notice that the seller had given her a quitclaim deed.

In an action by the buyer against the seller, the seller should argue that:

(A) the quitclaim deed was not materially different from a warranty deed.

(B) a deed is controlling when it conflicts with a contract.

(C) the buyer does not have a cause of action until she actually loses title.

(D) the buyer's only remedy is for damages.

Question 24

Wildacre and Overgrownacre are both undeveloped plots of land bordering the highway in a remote area. A buyer purchased Wildacre in 1977 and received permission to cross Overgrownacre from his neighbor, its owner. By crossing Overgrownacre, the buyer could more easily reach the highway from certain parts of Wildacre. In 1987 the neighbor purchased Wildacre from the buyer. In 2000, the buyer purchased Overgrownacre from the neighbor.

Did the buyer own an easement to cross Overgrownacre in 2001?

(A) Yes, because the original easement was still in effect.

(B) Yes, because it should be inferred that the easement was sold back with the property.

(C) No, because the easement had been extinguished.

(D) No, because the Statute of Frauds was not satisfied.

Question 25

A sister and brother obtained title to Blackacre as tenants in common in 1970. The sister began constructing a house on Blackacre in 1973 and has occupied the house continuously since it was completed in 1977. The brother has never seen Blackacre. In 1995, the sister asserted an action to obtain title to Blackacre in fee simple. A local ordinance provides that the period to satisfy adverse possession is twenty years. Is the sister likely to prevail in her action?

(A) Yes, because the sister's occupation of the land for the purpose of adverse possession began in 1973.

(B) Yes, because building a house establishes a claim of right.

(C) No, because the sister did not occupy her house until 1977.

(D) No, because the sister's occupation of Blackacre was probably not adverse.

Question 26

A buyer purchased a house from a seller by signing a valid written contract. The contract did not specify the kind of title to be transferred. The buyer paid the contractual price and accepted the deed from the seller. A third party came along and filed a successful suit to claim the title. In a suit between the buyer and the seller, which of the following factors will LEAST influence who prevails in the suit?

(A) the terms of the deed

(B) the intent of the various parties

(C) the good faith of each party

(D) the kind of title owned by the previous owner

Question 27

A seller and a buyer signed a valid agreement whereby the seller agreed to sell Whiteacre to the buyer. Two weeks before the scheduled closing, the seller died. The seller's will provided that Whiteacre should pass on to her son, and all other property should pass to her daughter. Neither the seller nor the buyer breached their contract.

Which of the following choices is the best answer?

(A) Unless the contract specified otherwise, the seller's death terminated the agreement.

(B) The son is entitled to the property.

(C) After closing, the daughter will receive the proceeds of the property.

(D) The son and daughter will each own a share in the property.

Question 28

Alpha owned 2,000 acres of mountain land. Beta paid Alpha a yearly fee for the right to build and use a road that crossed the mountain land. Beta built a small wooden bridge to cross a small stream as part of the road. The parties did not specify who was to be responsible for maintenance of the road or bridge. One day, Alpha went jogging across the mountain land. Alpha passed over the bridge Beta built. The bridge collapsed, causing damage to a garden that belonged to Alpha. An expert determined that improper maintenance caused the bridge to collapse. If Alpha asserts an action against Beta for damage to her garden, should Alpha prevail?

(A) Yes, because the possessor of an easement is strictly liable to a servient estate.

(B) Yes, because the owner of an easement is obligated to maintain the easement.

(C) No, because the parties did not delegate duties.

(D) No, because Alpha should have known the condition of the bridge, so she was contributorily negligent.

Question 29

A grantor's will provided that "in gratitude for twenty years of past service, I leave $100,000 to my personal housekeeper." The grantor did not leave any property except for the Avenue Motel he owned with his cousin as tenants in common.

Will the housekeeper's service constitute sufficient consideration to bind the grantor?

(A) Yes, if the housekeeper performed services beyond his contractual duty before the will was written.

(B) Yes, because the grantor received material benefit.

(C) No, because the housekeeper was a paid employee.

(D) No, because the bequest was made after the services were performed.

Question 30

A grantor conveyed Lakeacre to a university "so long as the university uses Lakeacre as a practice field for its football team, then to J and his heirs." The local jurisdiction has adopted the common law Rule Against Perpetuities. What is the grantor's interest in Lakeacre after the above conveyance?

(A) a fee simple absolute

(B) a reversion

(C) a possibility of a reverter

(D) she has no interest

Question 31

A grantor executed a will whereby she left a life estate in an apartment building to her daughter. The will further provided that the building should pass to the grantor's daughter's children in joint tenancy upon the daughter's death. A clause prevented any of the grantor's grandchildren from mortgaging, selling, or otherwise alienating their interest.

If challenged, what will be the status of the grantor's attempt to devise the apartment in her will?

(A) The devise is wholly valid and enforceable.

(B) The devise will be void due to the Rule Against Perpetuities.

(C) The devise will be void as a restraint on alienation.

(D) The clause against sale or mortgage will be held invalid, but the grandchildren's remainder will be held valid.

Question 32

A grantor conveyed his farm "to the farmer for so long as the farmer does not grow tobacco or marijuana on the farm."

Which of the following choices best describes the farmer's interest in the house if she does not grow tobacco or marijuana?

(A) fee simple subject to a condition subsequent

(B) fee simple determinable

(C) fee simple subject to an executory interest

(D) fee simple determinable subject to an executory interest

Question 33

A grantor executed a will that said, in part, "I hereby devise the house on Tree Street that I own in fee simple to be shared by any of my grandchildren that reach the age of twenty-one. If none of my grandchildren reach the age of twenty-one, the house should revert to my estate." The grantor's only child at the time the will was written was her daughter, age twenty-nine, and she had a six-year-old daughter.

Will the grantor's conveyance be held valid?

(A) Yes, because the grantor had a grandchild at the time the will was executed.

(B) Yes, because the grantor's daughter (or any other child born to the grantor) can be the measuring life.

(C) No, because of the Rule Against Perpetuities.

(D) No, because the will is too uncertain.

Question 34

A landlord rented a two-bedroom apartment to a tenant. The apartment was modern and in good condition, except that one of the showers had spewed scalding hot water from its handle on two previous occasions. The landlord forgot to tell the tenant about the shower. Two years after moving into the apartment, the tenant was severely burned by hot water spewing from the handle. If the tenant asserts an action against the landlord for damages sustained in the shower, judgment should be for:

(A) the landlord, because a landlord is under no duty to deliver the premises to a tenant in a good state of repair.

(B) the landlord, because the tenant had ample opportunity to inspect the apartment.

(C) the tenant, because a landlord is strictly liable for injuries sustained on the premises.

(D) the tenant, because the landlord did not disclose the defect.

Question 35

Furst purchased a house from Secund in 1919 that was completely surrounded by property owned by Secund. Furst's only access to a public highway was via a dirt path that ran across Secund's property. Furst used the path from 1920 to 1960. In 1960, Furst sold his house to Thurd. In 1966, Thurd sold the house to Secund. Secund sold the property he purchased from Thurd to Furth in 1990. Twenty years is the time required to satisfy adverse possession in the jurisdiction.

If Secund asserted an action in 1925 seeking an injunction ordering Furst not to enter upon his land, judgment should have been for:

(A) Secund, because Furst was using the path less than twenty years.

(B) Secund, because he revoked an express or implied grant.

(C) Furst, because Secund had impliedly given him a license to use the path.

(D) Furst, because his land was entirely surrounded by Secund's property.

Question 36

A musician, owner of Purpleacre, granted a singer an easement to cross Purpleacre in 1991. The singer did not record the easement. The musician conveyed Purpleacre to a model in 1992. The model promptly recorded the deed, which contained a reference to the easement. In 1993, the model conveyed Purpleacre to an actress, who paid value but had no knowledge of the easement. May the singer force the actress to honor his easement?

(A) Yes, because an easement may not be defeated by lack of notice.

(B) Yes, because the actress is considered to have notice.

(C) No, because the singer did not record.

(D) No, because the actress did not have knowledge of the easement.

Question 37

An owner of a 200-year-old castle built on a mountaintop enjoyed a spectacular view of a valley, river, and sea of mountains beyond. Unfortunately for the owner, many insects entered his castle through the windows. In 1980, the owner had screens installed on the windows. The screens had to be custom made because of the unusual shape of the windows. They were then soldered to the window frames. A buyer purchased the castle from the owner in 1996. Must the owner leave the screens for the buyer?

(A) Yes, because the screens were custom made.

(B) Yes, because these screens are fixtures.

(C) No, because screens are generally not part of a building.

(D) No, because the screens are not permanently attached to the building.

Question 38

An elderly widow owned a small house and several personal possessions. The widow had trouble supporting herself, but desperately wanted to remain in her home. She orally contracted with her neighbor that if the neighbor took care of her, the neighbor would inherit her house. The neighbor quit law school and diligently cared for the widow until she died seven years later. The widow's daughter showed up at the funeral. The widow had not seen her daughter since the 1960s when her daughter ran away. The daughter was the widow's only heir and demanded the widow's entire estate since the widow died intestate.

The neighbor will most likely receive title to the widow's house under which of the following legal theories?

(A) A state statute provides that the Statute of Frauds is inapplicable where part performance has made the party's intentions obvious.

(B) The neighbor's action of quitting law school will support her claim to the house.

(C) A state statute provides that the Statute of Frauds is inapplicable where part performance will result in irreparable hardship.

(D) The widow's obvious break with her daughter will prevent her daughter from recovering.

Question 39

AB and CD signed a written valid agreement with EF to lease EF's seventy-acre farm. EF delivered possession of the premises. The lease provided that AB and CD were to use the farm to grow corn. EF was to receive half of the profits earned by the farm. The lease further provided that "any attempted assignment, subletting, or transfer by AB or CD without EF's written permission is null and void." With GH, CD signed a written agreement to sublet his share of the farm and to take his profits, without consulting EF.

If AB asserts an action to prevent CD's assignment, should AB prevail?

(A) Yes, because one may not assign an interest in real property without the consent of all parties involved.

(B) Yes, because of the clause prohibiting assignment.

(C) No, unless AB can show he will suffer pecuniary loss or other damage from the assignment.

(D) No, because he may not enforce the clause restricting assignments.

Question 40

An alumnus conveyed a three-acre tract to his alma mater, a university, by a deed specifying that "the university shall own this land in fee simple provided a theater for the university's Music Department is erected by 1990." The university constructed a theater on the land conveyed by the alumnus, and this theater was used by the Music Department from 1921 to 1999. In 1999, a "theater in the round" was built for the Music Department, and the old theater on the land donated by the alumnus was transferred to the university Ballet Department.

If the alumnus asserts an action demanding the return of the three acres, will the alumnus succeed?

(A) Yes, because the deed had the effect of creating a remainder in the alumnus.

(B) Yes, because the university's change in the use of the building violated a condition subsequent.

(C) No, because the university fulfilled the requirements of the deed.

(D) No, because use of the building for ballet substantially fulfilled the requirement.

Questions 41–42 are based upon the following fact pattern.

A tenant was a life tenant of a large house. A substantial mortgage had been owed by the grantor on the house.

Question 41

Which of the following choices is correct?

(A) The tenant will be liable to pay the principal owed on the mortgage but not the interest.

(B) The tenant will be liable to pay the interest on the mortgage but not the principal.

(C) The tenant will be liable for both the interest and principal on the mortgage.

(D) The tenant will be liable for neither the interest nor the principal on the mortgage.

Question 42

Which of the following choices is correct?

(A) The tenant will be liable to pay taxes on the house but not insurance.

(B) The tenant will be liable to pay insurance on the house but not taxes.

(C) The tenant will be liable to pay both insurance and taxes on the house.

(D) The tenant will be liable for neither insurance nor taxes on the house.

Question 43

On April 1, D conveyed title to Blackacre to J, who paid full value. J did not know that Blackacre was still owned by B on April 1. On May 1, B conveyed Blackacre to D for full value. D then conveyed Blackacre to K, on June 1, for full value. In a suit between J and K to obtain title to Blackacre, K's most persuasive argument is:

(A) one cannot purchase an interest from someone who doesn't possess the interest.

(B) J was never in the chain of title.

(C) K could not have discovered D's recording.

(D) equitable estoppel should control.

Question 44

S owned 2,000 acres of undeveloped land in an isolated and remote area. S decided to develop the land into a retirement village called "Wetland Estates" and built 6,000 residential apartments. Due to the remoteness of the village, S also built a health club, medical offices, a golf course, and retail stores. The remaining undeveloped land was left available for the use and enjoyment of the residents. F purchased an apartment from S. The contract provided that F could occupy the apartment indefinitely but would not own the apartment. F was given a share in a corporation that owned the 6,000 apartments. He was obligated to pay a fee of $62,000 and a share of maintenance costs. F's share was freely transferable. The contract further provided that the offices, sports facilities, and stores would continue to be used for their current purposes.

Which of the following devices will best guarantee that the open areas of "Wetland Estates" will remain undeveloped?

(A) leasehold

(B) covenant

(C) zoning law

(D) easement

Questions 45–46 are based upon the following fact pattern.

A grantor owned a 5,000-car parking lot outside a sports arena. The jurisdiction's Recording Act provided: "Every conveyance of real property must be recorded in the county recorder's office. In the case of a conveyance not recorded, the conveyance is void as to a subsequent bona fide purchaser for value who does not have notice of the first conveyance." On April 1, 1995, the grantor conveyed the parking lot to Brothers, Inc., at fair value. Brothers, Inc., did not record the deed until May 1, 1995. The grantor then mortgaged the lot on April 5 to Park N' Lock, Inc., who had no notice of the April 1 transaction. Park N' Lock promptly recorded the mortgage. The grantor then conveyed a warranty deed on April 13 to his son, who did not pay value. The son promptly recorded the deed. The son then conveyed by general warranty deed his interest in the parking lot to Dollar Park on May 15. Dollar Park paid full value and promptly recorded.

Question 45

If Dollar Park loses in a suit brought by Brothers, Inc., it will be because:

(A) the son recorded before Brothers, Inc.

(B) the first deed prevails in a dispute among deeds.

(C) the son did not have constructive or actual notice of Brothers' rights.

(D) the son was not a purchaser for value.

Question 46

If Brothers, Inc. asserts a suit against Park N' Lock to quiet title, who should prevail?

(A) Brothers, Inc., because the consideration furnished by Park N' Lock was not sufficient to be considered "full value."

(B) Brothers, Inc. because mortgagee and purchaser are not the same.

(C) Park N' Lock, because Park N' Lock's transactions were without actual or constructive notice of Grantor's conveyance to Brothers, Inc.

(D) Park N' Lock, because Park N' Lock recorded first.

Question 47

D and G purchased a house as tenants by the entirety. They used the home, located near a ski resort, as a weekend retreat. D conveyed her right in the house to H.

The conveyance will be effective:

(A) because D and G were tenants in common.

(B) because G was never in the chain of title.

(C) if D and G were not married.

(D) because D was the sole owner.

Question 48

Grantor conveyed Appleacre, a beachfront condominium, to "P for the remainder of his life, remainder to M and E as tenants in common." The condominium had a substantial unpaid mortgage held by H.

Which of the following choices will describe the mortgage obligations of the various parties if Appleacre is occupied by P?

(A) P must pay the interest, but M and E must pay the principal.
(B) M and E must pay the interest, but P must pay the principal.
(C) P must pay both the principal and interest.
(D) M and E must pay both the principal and interest.

Question 49

G agreed, in writing, to maintain the road between his property and C's property. C gave G his car in return for G's promise to maintain the road for G, his heirs, his successors, and his assigns. G sold his property to W. C sold his land to J. W refused to maintain the road. J asserted an action for damages against W for failure to maintain the road.

The court should rule in favor of:

(A) J, because burdens run with the land.
(B) J, because the properties of G and C shared a common border.
(C) W, if G did not buy his land from C and C did not buy his land from G.
(D) W, because he was not a party to the original agreement.

Question 50

On March 1, a lawyer sold property to a general for value. The general did not record the deed until March 4. The lawyer sold the property to a writer, on March 3, for value. The writer did not record the deed until March 5. Under which of the following statutes will the court award title to the writer?

(A) pure notice recording act
(B) race-notice recording act
(C) race-race recording act
(D) pure race recording act

Questions 51–52 are based upon the following fact pattern.

Isaac owned 100 acres of undeveloped land. Isaac decided to subdivide the land into 200 plots of land. One hundred twenty plots were sold pursuant to a deed providing that "all parties, their successors, and heirs agree to construct no more than one single-family home on each lot. The land may not be occupied by trailers or other temporary structures." The remaining eighty lots were unsold for many years. Isaac finally sold all the remaining lots to the speculator without any restrictions. The speculator then also sold the remaining lots without any restrictions.

Question 51

Suppose the speculator decided to build two homes on each lot. If an owner of one of the original lots asserts an

action to prevent the building of more than one home on a lot, which of the following factors will be most crucial?

(A) Whether the local government can provide services for housing of such density.
(B) The local zoning ordinances.
(C) Whether a common scheme of development had been established.
(D) Whether a contract takes precedence over a deed.

Question 52

If a successor to an owner of one of the original lots asserts an action against a successor of the speculator to prevent installation of a mobile home, the speculator's successor should assert which of the following defenses?

(A) Time has made the two developments separate and independent entities.
(B) The totality of the facts presented establish that a common development scheme was not used for all the land.
(C) The speculator did not have notice of the restrictions.
(D) The plaintiff has not established pecuniary damages.

Questions 53–54 are based upon the following fact pattern.

A granted a right of way to Waterco to run a pipe across the yard behind his house. The grant was in the form of a written deed that was properly recorded by Waterco. A sold his house to B, who sold it to C, who sold the house to D. B, C, and D recorded their interests without mentioning the right of way. D asked his attorney to examine the title to the house. The attorney researched the title and told D, "It's all yours, the title is clean." Relying on his attorney's title search, D conveyed the house to E with a covenant of warranty and a covenant against encumbrances. E, who paid full value, learned of Waterco's rights and was furious.

Question 53

If E asserts an action against the attorney for damages, should E prevail?

(A) Yes, because the attorney guaranteed the title was good.
(B) Probably, because she was a third-party beneficiary of the attorney's contract with D.
(C) No, because the attorney owed a duty only to D.
(D) Probably not, unless she can show the attorney was negligent.

Question 54

If E asserts an action against D for damages, should E prevail?

(A) Yes, because D was negligent in hiring the attorney.
(B) Yes, because D did not fulfill his obligations to E.

(C) No, because E should have searched the title on her own.

(D) No, because D relied on his attorney.

Question 55

A sheriff and a deputy owned adjacent plots of land. The sheriff agreed to allow the deputy to cross his property. The property of both the sheriff and the deputy bordered on public highways. After crossing the sheriff's property for a month, the deputy was told by the sheriff, "I don't like you anymore, so stay off my land." Will the sheriff be able to prevent the deputy from entering his land?

(A) Yes, because the permission to enter the sheriff's land was revocable at will.

(B) Yes, because there was not an implied easement.

(C) Yes, regardless of whether the deputy paid any consideration.

(D) No, because the deputy had relied on the sheriff's promise.

Question 56

A producer leased his store for 30 years to an actress. The parties orally agreed that if the actress made all of her payments, the producer would give her title to the store at the end of the 30 years. The actress kept the premises in immaculate condition and was never a day late in making her payments. After 20 years, the actress spent $100,000 to redecorate the store. At the end of 30 years, the producer notified the actress that her lease was being terminated because the producer was leasing the building to someone else. "What about our agreement that I get title after 30 years?" asked the actress. "I don't recall any agreement," said the producer, an octogenarian suffering from Alzheimer's disease. The actress asserted an action for specific performance and brought two witnesses to her oral agreement with the producer. The producer asserted the Statute of Frauds as a defense.

Which of the following statements will help the producer most?

(A) Although the producer knew about it, he never approved the $100,000 remodeling.

(B) The producer will not benefit in an unconscionable manner when his relationship with the actress is looked at as a whole.

(C) The actress's expenditures were not unusual for a tenant during a long-term lease.

(D) The producer should have been excused due to his age and mental state.

Question 57

A grantor conveyed his home "to the Town of Tinyville to be used as a community center; however, if the premises shall ever cease to be used as a community center, title shall pass to the First Church of Tinyville."

Which of the following choices best describes the interest owned by the Town of Tinyville as long as the grantor's house is used for a community center?

(A) None, the conveyance should be held void due to the Rule Against Perpetuities.

(B) Fee simple subject to a condition subsequent.

(C) Fee simple subject to an executory interest.

(D) Fee simple determinable.

Question 58

A tenant rented a house from a landlord for five years. The tenant, a professional photographer, installed dark room equipment and studio lights. Toward the end of the fifth year, the landlord sold the house to his niece. The tenant was not notified of the sale of the house, but the landlord promptly recorded the transaction. At the end of the lease, the niece declined to renew and would not allow the tenant to remove the dark room equipment and studio lights.

Which of the following choices will be the tenant's best argument if she asserts an action to be allowed to remove the equipment?

(A) A tenant may remove anything she installs in rented premises.

(B) None of the installed equipment could be considered fixtures.

(C) The nature of the equipment shows it was installed for the tenant's benefit in the conduct of her trade.

(D) There was a lack of privity between the niece and the tenant.

Question 59

A grantor conveyed his house to his daughter on March 1 as a birthday present. He did not tell his daughter that, the same day, he had conveyed the house to his mistress for value. The daughter recorded on March 2. The mistress did not record until March 5. In an action between the daughter and the mistress for title of the home, the daughter will prevail under which of the following statues?

(A) pure notice recording act

(B) race-notice recording act

(C) pure race recording act

(D) more than one of the above statutes

Question 60

A forester owned several thousand acres of land used for logging. His will provided, "I leave all of my land to my son for his life, then to the arborist." The son took possession of the land and proceeded to remove many trees for his lumber business. If the arborist asserts an action against the son to enjoin removal of the timber

(A) The arborist will prevail, because the son is exploiting the land's natural resources.

(B) The arborist will prevail, because the son is committing waste.

(C) The son will prevail, because he is committing ameliorative waste.

(D) The son will prevail, because the forester used the land for logging.

Questions 61–62 are based upon the following fact pattern.

A buyer purchased a house from a seller. The seller conveyed a deed to the buyer that contained a warranty of title and a right to quiet enjoyment. The buyer received physical possession of the deed, but did not record.

A corporation owned an easement behind the buyer's new house. The easement allowed access to a mine two miles away. The mine has been abandoned for some time and could not be detected by visual inspection.

Question 61

Which of the following choices is the best answer?

(A) The house was not legally transferred to the buyer because of the easement.

(B) The house was not legally transferred to the buyer because she did not record.

(C) The house was not legally transferred to the buyer because the warranty was not satisfied.

(D) The house was legally transferred to buyer.

Question 62

If the corporation uses the easement to store coal, which of the following choices is the most accurate?

(A) The coal may be stored on a temporary basis only.

(B) The buyer will recover from the seller for breach of a covenant.

(C) The buyer may sue the corporation for damages only.

(D) The buyer may obtain an injunction requiring removal of the coal.

Questions 63–64 are based upon the following fact pattern.

A suburbanite owned 2,000 acres of land just outside the corporate limits of a city. He decided to divide the land into two parcels. The southern 900 acres bordered the city he called Suburbanvillage. The suburbanite named the northern portion, also 900 acres, which was located further from the city, Suburbantown. Suburbanvillage and Suburbantown were subdivided into many small lots. Purchasers of lots in Suburbanvillage and Suburbantown signed deeds containing express provisions binding their grantees, heirs, and assigns. The Suburbanvillage deeds provided that the land was to be used for residential purposes only. The Suburbantown deeds also provided that the land was to be used only for residential purposes, that only one house could be built on each plot, and that twenty feet of open space must remain between every two houses.

Question 63

A buyer purchased three lots in Suburbantown and decided to build a row of attached houses. An outraged Suburbantown homeowner was filled with fright that the neighborhood would deteriorate and filed suit against the buyer. Will the contractual restriction be enforceable?

(A) Yes, because any present owner of a lot in Suburbantown may enforce the restriction.

(B) Yes, if the local zoning laws restrict the land use to detached, single-family homes.

(C) No, if the buyer was not the original owner.

(D) No, because limiting the use to detached houses is the equivalent of a "taking."

Question 64

If the land not originally designated as part of Suburbantown is sold, will the owners be obligated to limit construction to detached houses?

(A) Yes.

(B) Only if the zoning laws so provide.

(C) Yes, if the new land is deemed part of this common development scheme.

(D) It cannot be determined from the above fact situation.

Question 65

A seller agreed in writing to convey title to his sixty-acre farm to a buyer. The farm was properly identified, as was the price. The contract was valid and complete except for the lack of any agreement regarding the quality of title to be conveyed. Will the contract be enforceable?

(A) No.

(B) Yes, and the seller will be required to convey whatever interest in the farm he owns.

(C) Yes, and the seller will be required to convey marketable title.

(D) Yes, and the seller will be required to convey a warranty title.

Questions 66–67 are based upon the following fact situation.

In 1962, a seller granted an easement to Railroad Company to build and operate railroad tracks through a specific twenty-foot strip at the north end of a 2,000-acre farm that he owned in fee simple. Railroad Company promptly recorded the easement. In 1992, the farm was subdivided and several houses were built. A buyer purchased the lot with the easement. His deed was properly recorded but did not refer to the easement. The buyer built a house and swimming pool on the lot. In 1995, Railroad Company notified the buyer that it intended to run railroad tracks across the part of his property where his pool was located.

Question 66

If the buyer attempts to secure an injunction to prevent the rail line from crossing his property, might he succeed?

(A) Yes, because the statute of limitations extinguished Railroad Company's rights.

(B) Yes, because his deed did not mention the easement.

(C) No, because Railroad Company is entitled to use its easement.

(D) No, because a railroad is more important than a swimming pool.

Question 67

If the buyer seeks monetary compensation from Railroad Company, might he succeed?

(A) Yes, because Railroad Company possessed an easement, not title in fee simple.

(B) Yes, because the statute of limitations extinguished Railroad Company's rights.

(C) No, because a railroad is more important than a swimming pool.

(D) No, because Railroad Company is entitled to use its easement.

Question 68

The owner of Blackacre in fee simple executed a gift to her daughter of a section of the property. The section was described in the conveyance as "one-eighth of my interest in Blackacre, the western half of the northeast corner of the property."

The description of the land to be conveyed:

(A) is not sufficient, because the transfer was gratuitous.

(B) is not sufficient, because it is vague.

(C) is sufficient because it satisfied the requirements of seisin.

(D) is sufficient because it can be located.

Question 69

The eleven homeowners on Tree Street in the resort area of Ocean Beach signed an agreement, in 1920, stating that "all homeowners agree that no stables are to be erected on their premises. The homes may not be occupied or owned by persons less than the age of eighteen. The homes may not be sold without including the terms of this agreement on the purchase agreements." E, one of the original parties to the agreement, had two of her

great-grandchildren spend the summer of 1995 with her. Both great-grandchildren were below the age of eighteen. L, who owned a house on Tree Street since 1915, brought suit to enjoin further occupancy by the children.

E's best argument will be:

(A) one may use her own property as she sees fit.

(B) the terms of the agreement are obviously obsolete.

(C) enforcement would violate the Equal Protection Clause of the Fourteenth Amendment to the U.S. Constitution.

(D) the agreement is unconscionable.

Question 70

A property owner executed a gift to his girlfriend. The gift was described as "The property I own in fee simple on Route 8, which was known as Car Company plant before I purchased it. This conveyance is to include the abandoned factory and the twelve acres of land surrounding it." The owner owned only eleven acres of land on Route 8. The description of the real property is:

(A) sufficient despite the inconsistency.

(B) insufficient because of the inconsistency.

(C) insufficient because of the absence of metes and bounds.

(D) insufficient because the description does not satisfy the Statute of Frauds.

Questions 71–72 are based upon the following fact pattern.

A grantor owned an entire square block of vacant land. He orally agreed to sell the northeast corner of the land to a buyer for $85,000. The grantor's counsel prepared the contract. The grantor signed it and mailed it to the buyer. The buyer called the grantor because the size of the lot was not stated. "Just write 150 × 85," said the grantor. The buyer wrote 150 × 100 and recorded the deed. Three weeks later, the buyer sold the land at slightly below its market value to another buyer.

Question 71

Assume for this question only that the grantor sought to rescind the contract the day after the buyer recorded it. The buyer's most persuasive argument will be that:

(A) a recorded deed cannot be questioned.

(B) the grantor should bear the consequences of his carelessness.

(C) the difference is not material.

(D) an oral agreement cannot alter the written contract.

Question 72

Assume for this question only that the first buyer sold the land to the second buyer before the grantor learned of the terms the first buyer wrote into the contract. If the grantor seeks to prevent the second buyer from obtaining title, the second buyer's best argument will be that:

(A) the grantor should be estopped from asserting an action against a bona fide purchaser.
(B) a recorded deed may not be challenged.
(C) the Statute of Frauds is not satisfied.
(D) public policy demands the respect of all recorded deeds.

Question 73

T and B signed a lease whereby B agreed to pay monthly rent to T until March 1998. T and his wife owned the land concurrently in fee simple. B and C later signed a valid instrument whereby C agreed that she would occupy the premises until March 1998 in exchange for paying B's rent. B retained the right to re-enter the premises if C did not pay rent. B and C have created a(n):

(A) assignment.
(B) sublease.
(C) sublease because B did not convey his entire interest.
(D) reversion.

Question 74

In 1991, a grantor conveyed title to a large tract of land on J Avenue to his daughter "in consideration of my daughter's love and affection." The grantor delivered the land's deed to his daughter, but neither the grantor nor his daughter recorded the transaction. In 1996, the grantor and his daughter became involved in a heated argument. The daughter took the deed to the J Avenue land and burned it in her fireplace. The daughter then ran out of her house and was struck by a car. The daughter's heirs asserted an action demanding title to the J Avenue property. Which of the following choices is the best answer?

(A) The grantor's original conveyance to the daughter was effective, and the daughter never relinquished her title.
(B) The grantor's conveyance was void due to the failure of the parties to record.
(C) The grantor's conveyance to his daughter was effective as was the daughter's abandonment of the title.
(D) The grantor's conveyance to the daughter can be retracted due to a lack of consideration.

Question 75

In 1975, a farmer granted a life estate in his farm to a rancher, "provided the rancher continues to grow corn on the land." The farmer's conveyance provided that the land pass to a naturalist in fee simple upon the rancher's death or upon the rancher's failure to grow corn, whichever came first. The rancher planted, grew, and harvested corn from 1975 to 1995. In 1999, the price of oil skyrocketed and the rancher decided to drill for

oil on the land. A large oil deposit was discovered, and the rancher pumped 500 barrels a day from the ground.

The naturalist asserted an action seeking damages for removal of the oil and an injunction against future removal. Which of the following choices is the best answer?

(A) The naturalist will prevail because the rancher's life estate was terminated when he drilled for oil.
(B) The rancher will be enjoined and forced to pay damages.
(C) The rancher will be liable for damages, but an injunction will not be granted.
(D) The injunction will not be granted, and the naturalist will not recover damages.

Question 76

A grantor left a will providing that "my assets shall be divided among my children in equal shares." The grantor was survived by H, a daughter by his marriage that ended in divorce; D, a daughter from the wife to whom the grantor was married to at the time of his death; L, a step-daughter; E, a granddaughter; J, an illegitimate daughter; and R, a legally adopted daughter.

Which of the grantor's descendants might NOT receive a share of his estate?

(A) E, R, J
(B) E, L
(C) E, J, L
(D) E, J, L, H

Question 77

A traveler went to Europe for a month. He agreed to let a friend use his apartment while he was away. When the traveler returned from Europe, the friend refused to vacate the apartment. The traveler asserted an action to evict the friend; whereupon the friend claimed protection under a local ordinance that required a landlord to give ten-working-days notice before evicting a tenant.

The traveler's best argument to prove the statute is not applicable is that the friend is a:

(A) periodic tenant
(B) tenant at will
(C) trespasser
(D) licensee

Question 78

A seller entered into a valid written agreement to sell her house to a buyer. The parties agreed to close thirty days later, but did not specify who was to bear the risk of loss in the interim. After the seller and the buyer signed the agreement, but before closing, the house was struck by lightning, causing a fire and explosion. The house was totally destroyed. There is no local statute that specifies which party shall bear the risk of loss in the interim.

If the seller prevails in a suit against the buyer for specific performance, the most likely reason will be:

(A) the buyer should have taken out insurance on the property.

(B) the risk of loss follows possession.

(C) the doctrine of equitable conversion.

(D) the law will leave the parties where it finds them.

Question 79

A businesswoman purchased two tracts of land in an industrial park still in its planning stages. The businesswoman planned to build a hub for her air-freight business. She began construction of an airstrip on one tract of land and a warehouse on the other tract. The two tracts were to be linked by a road designated by the industrial park's developer, but not yet approved by the local authorities, as a public highway. The businesswoman sought to use the designated road immediately because the road was imperative to her ongoing construction. The developer refused to grant permission to use the land.

The developer should advance which of the following arguments?

(A) The Statute of Frauds.

(B) The developer would be forced to incur insurance costs without reimbursement.

(C) The businesswoman must wait for the local governmental authorities to designate a road because an easement by implication has not yet arisen.

(D) The businesswoman would receive something for nothing.

Question 80

S and K inherited property, which they divided and designated as Northacre and Southacre, as joint tenants. S and K orally agreed that S would own Northacre in fee simple and K would own Southacre in fee simple. S sold Northacre, took the proceeds to the casino, and lost it all at the blackjack tables. K built a house on Southacre. S asserted an action to determine ownership of Southacre.

If K is adjudged to be the owner in fee simple of Southacre, the most likely reason will be that:

(A) S's conduct estops her from claiming an interest in Southacre.

(B) the logical division was more important than any formalities.

(C) the oral agreement immediately terminated the previous ownership terms.

(D) S terminated the joint tenancy by selling Northacre.

Question 81

A tycoon owned an 800-acre peninsula in fee simple. The tycoon decided to divide the land and develop the area for single family homes. Realizing the houses would need access roads, the tycoon set aside some of the land for roads. He also set aside land on the part of the peninsula bordering a public highway to build a guardhouse and gate. The tycoon sold all the lots with a clause providing that the property may be used only for residential purposes. Another clause provided that the residents agree to pay annual dues for maintenance of roads and for hiring a security guard.

A buyer purchased a lot and built a house. The buyer refuses to pay the annual dues. Under which of the following theories will his neighbors be most likely to compel the buyer to pay dues?

(A) easement

(B) personal contract

(C) covenant

(D) equitable servitude

Question 82

A grantor conveyed title to his house, which he owned in fee simple, to a contractor, who paid full value. The contractor never recorded the transaction. Several months later, the grantor conveyed title to the same house to his daughter "in consideration for services provided by my daughter." The daughter promptly recorded. The grantor was retired and living out of state and had not occupied the house for several years. Neither the contractor nor the daughter attempted to occupy the house. The jurisdiction has a pure race recording statute requiring "good faith" and "value" in order for a junior claimant to obtain priority.

In an action between the contractor and the daughter for title to the house, which of the following choices is the best answer?

(A) The daughter will prevail because the contractor did not record.

(B) The daughter will prevail only if the contractor obtained a quitclaim deed.

(C) The outcome will be determined by whether the contractor gave consideration of sufficient value.

(D) The outcome will be determined by whether the daughter gave consideration of sufficient value.

Question 83

A man and a woman lived as husband and wife although they never formally married. They held themselves out to the community as husband and wife, signed contracts together, and had several children. They purchased a house together as tenants by the entirety and made payments on the house for twelve years. One day, the man told the woman he was leaving her. The jurisdiction does not recognize common law marriage. If the man seeks to partition the house will he be successful?

(A) Yes, because this tenancy is terminated by operation of law when the man and woman separate.

(B) Yes, because a tenancy by the entirety was never created.

(C) No, because a tenancy by the entirety may not be partitioned.

(D) No, because both parties must agree in order to partition a tenancy by the entirety.

Question 84

C and J purchased bordering lots from B, who owned a country club and had subdivided the club's land. A tennis court, left over from the country club, remained between C's and J's houses. Half the court was on J's property, half was on C's. C and J would like to sign an agreement whereby successor owners would be prohibited from partitioning or limiting access to the tennis court. C and J should agree to:

(A) each grant the other an express easement.

(B) a restrictive covenant against partition.

(C) a trust in perpetuity.

(D) a renewable lease.

Question 85

A skipper leased 400 acres of land from a longshoreman. The land bordered on a deep-water bay, and the skipper leased the land to dock his fleet of vessels. The skipper and the longshoreman enjoyed cordial relations for several years, each fulfilling his respective contractual obligations. Both parties were notified that the government decided to build a super-highway and was going to take all 200 of the longshoreman's acres bordering the water. The government reimbursed the skipper for the value of these 200 acres over the balance of the lease. The longshoreman was reimbursed for the value of the land. The skipper notified the longshoreman that the remaining land was of no value to him and refused further payments.

If the longshoreman asserts an action against the skipper, the longshoreman should:

(A) prevail, unless he knew that the skipper's intended use was related to the water.

(B) prevail, because the contract between the skipper and the longshoreman was not affected.

(C) not prevail, because the contract was void due to impossibility.

(D) not prevail, because the lease was breached.

Question 86

A collector devised his collection of antique cars to "my former trusted employee, remainder to my employee's children and their heirs and assigns." The employee, who was divorced three times, had only a forty-year-old childless son.

The remainder "to my employee's children" is:

(A) a possibility of a reverter.

(B) indefeasibly vested.

(C) vested and subject to a condition subsequent.

(D) vested, but subject to open.

Question 87

In 1908, a groomer and a jockey decided to build a stable between their houses. They also erected a fence around a field, half of which was owned by the groomer, the other half by the jockey. Each kept a horse in the stable and allowed it to graze in the fenced-in area. The groomer and the jockey exchanged written easements allowing each to use the land surrounded by the fence and stable in perpetuity. The easements were properly recorded.

In the 1920s, the jockey and the groomer no longer used the stable or field because they replaced their horses with cars. The stable and fence remained standing. In 1982, the groomer notified the jockey that he could no longer use the field. The jockey objected because his grandchildren liked to occasionally play football there.

If the groomer asserts an action to prevent the jockey from using the field, should the groomer prevail?

(A) Yes, because the purpose of the easement had terminated.

(B) Yes, because an easement may be terminated at the option of a party in interest when use becomes sporadic.

(C) No, because an end to the necessity for an express easement does not terminate it.

(D) No, because the fence and stable were still erect.

Question 88

A tenant rented an apartment from a landlord. Her lease provided that she pay $250 by the fifth of every month. The tenant, who was compulsive, always paid her rent at least a week before it was due. The landlord made a sexual advance that the tenant refused. The landlord decided to punish the tenant by circulating a rumor in the apartment complex that the tenant was "loose." The landlord maintained the apartments very poorly, and the tenant circulated a petition among the tenants that spelled out the poor maintenance of the apartment building. When the landlord learned the tenant was forwarding the petition to the housing authority, the landlord moved to evict the tenant.

Of the following choices, which will be the tenant's best argument?

(A) A tenant may not be evicted prior to the completion of the term of a lease.

(B) The tenant possessed a periodic tenancy.

(C) The tenant had an implied right to remain in her apartment.

(D) The doctrine prohibiting retaliatory eviction.

Question 89

In 1985, a grantor conveyed the State Building, which he owned in fee simple, to an art museum "as long as they use the building to promote the arts. If the building is used for other purposes, then to the architect, her heirs, and assigns." The grantor died in 1988. His valid will said, "I leave all my property to my only daughter."

In 1991, the art museum contracted to sell the building to a patron in fee simple. After a title search, the patron refused to perform.

If the art museum asserts an action based on breach of contract against the patron, should the art museum prevail?

(A) Yes, because the agreement with the patron was valid and enforceable.

(B) Yes, because the building was owned in fee simple by the art museum.

(C) No, because the architect had an interest in State Building.

(D) No, because of the daughter's interest in State Building.

Question 90

A buyer signed a valid written contract to purchase a house from a seller. The parties agreed that the seller would provide a general warranty deed. At closing, the buyer did not notice that the seller gave her a quitclaim deed. If the buyer asserts an action against the seller, the seller should argue:

(A) when a deed conflicts with a contract, the deed is controlling.

(B) a quitclaim deed is not materially different from a warranty deed.

(C) the buyer's only action is for damages.

(D) the buyer may assert an action only when she actually loses title.

Question 91

A seller owned Officeacre, a luxury downtown office building, subject to a $3,000,000 mortgage held by the Downtown Bank. The seller and a buyer entered into a written agreement stating that the buyer was to pay $10,000,000 on April 1, 1986, in exchange for clear title to Officeacre.

On April 1, the seller offered to tender title, but the buyer refused to make the agreed upon payment, citing the bank's mortgage as an imperfection in the title. The seller claimed he would use part of the $10,000,000 to pay the remainder of the mortgage.

The seller's best argument to compel the buyer to perform will be that:

(A) the buyer signed the agreement with full knowledge of the bank's mortgage.

(B) the seller has not breached the contract.

(C) the seller has an implied right to clear the title with proceeds from the building's sale.

(D) the contract implied that the buyer would assume the mortgage.

Question 92

A company owned a large warehouse. The company installed air conditioning units in several offices in the buildings. Large holes were made in the walls so vents could run between offices. The company sold the building to a buyer. The air conditioning units were not mentioned in the contract.

If the buyer asserts an action to include the air conditioners as part of the sale, judgment should be for:

(A) the company, because the units were not attached to the building.

(B) the company, because an air conditioner is not part of a building.

(C) the buyer, because the company planned to permanently improve the building with the system.

(D) the buyer, because air conditioning units are fixtures.

Question 93

A grantor conveyed three acres of land "to the Foundation for Flu Research; however, if the premises shall ever cease to be used for medical research, title shall pass to the Society for Cancer Research."

Which of the following choices best describes the interest owned by the Foundation for Flu Research?

(A) fee simple absolute

(B) fee simple subject to a condition subsequent

(C) fee simple subject to an executory interest

(D) fee simple determinable

Questions 94–95 are based upon the following fact pattern.

A grantor conveyed his home "to the grantee, but if the grantee should ever sell drugs on the premises, then the grantor or his successors shall have the right to retake the home."

Question 94

Which of the following choices best describes the interest in the house owned by the grantee if he hasn't sold drugs?

(A) fee simple subject to a condition subsequent

(B) fee simple determinable

(C) fee simple subject to an executory interest

(D) fee simple determinable subject to an executory interest

Question 95

Which of the following choices best describes the grantor's interest in the house, as long as the grantee does not sell drugs?

(A) reversion

(B) right of entry for condition broken

(C) possibility of reversion

(D) executory interest

Questions 96–97 are based upon the following fact pattern.

The owner of a large tract of land decided to develop the "Industrial Mall." The land, which was undeveloped, did not have any roads running through it, but it did border on a major state road.

The owner subdivided the land into twenty parcels and recorded it as such, leaving a strip of land large enough to build a four-lane highway in the middle of the property. Seven corporations each purchased a parcel from the owner, relying on the availability of the proposed highway. Each company signed a covenant providing, "No building taller than forty feet may be constructed in Industrial Mall." The owner sold the remaining thirteen parcels of land to a homebuilder. Coalco purchased the land the owner promised to reserve for a road. It planned to build a coal burning facility.

Question 96

If the homebuilder attempts to build an 80-foot condominium apartment building, will the landowners in Industrial Mall be able to stop him?

(A) Probably, because the real estate value will be lower due to the tall building.

(B) Probably, because the covenant it violates can be ruled to apply to all of Industrial Mall.

(C) No, because the homebuilder's deed did not contain the covenant.

(D) No, because the homebuilder purchased several lots.

Question 97

If the county decided to build a road on Coalco's plot and Coalco seeks to prevent the construction by the county, which party should prevail?

(A) Coalco, because it is the owner of the land.

(B) Coalco, because it purchased the land without reference to a covenant.

(C) The county, if it has made a dedication and acceptance.

(D) The county, because otherwise the other corporations will not be able to use their lands.

Question 98

A grantor relinquished control of a parcel of land by executing a deed in favor of a zookeeper. Grantor gave the deed to a friend on March 1. The friend delivered the deed to the zookeeper on March 15. On March 10, a poacher lost his leg to a wild animal while driving across the land.

If the poacher decides to assert an action for the loss of his leg, against whom should he file suit?

(A) The grantor, because the friend delivered the deed after the accident.

(B) The grantor, unless he can prove his intent was to extinguish ownership on March 1.

(C) The friend, because he held the deed.

(D) The zookeeper, if the grantor released all control over the land on March 1.

Question 99

A landowner owned five hundred acres of undeveloped land. She decided to subdivide the land into one thousand plots of land, one-half acre each. Six hundred plots were sold with a provision that "all parties and their successors agree to construct only one single family house on each half-acre lot." The contract for the sale of the lots further provided that the land may not be occupied by trailers or other temporary structures.

The landowner was unable to sell the remaining four hundred plots, and they remained idle for twenty years. Six hundred houses had been built on the lots the landowner sold previously. When real estate values in the area suddenly skyrocketed, the landowner sold the remaining lots to a developer without any restrictions.

If a successor to an owner of one of the original lots asserted an action against a successor of the developer to prevent installation of a mobile home, the developer's successor should NOT assert which of the following defenses?

(A) A declaration of subdivision was never filed by the landowner.

(B) The totality of the facts presented establishes that there was no common plan or development scheme for all 500 acres.

(C) Plaintiffs must establish pecuniary or other tangible damages.

(D) The developer did not have notice of the development.

Question 100

An uncle devised his collection of antique cars "to the children of my favorite niece." At the time of the uncle's death, his favorite niece had two children. A third child was born three years after the uncle's death. Is the third child entitled to a share in the uncle's estate?

(A) Yes, because the third child became a member of the class entitled to receive the estate.

(B) Yes, because the uncle's intent is clear and obvious.

(C) No, because the class was closed.

(D) No, because the uncle may not have liked the third child.

Question 101

An heiress owned 2,000 acres of land in fee simple. She had inherited the land in 1920 and had never visited the property. In 1923, a trapper asked the heiress if he could use the land to hunt and fish. The heiress assented, so the trapper hunted and fished on the land at least five times a week.

In 1960, the trapper sought to acquire title to the land, claiming an easement by prescription. The trapper should be:

(A) successful, because he did not renew permission to use the land.

(B) successful, because the use was adverse for the necessary amount of time.

(C) unsuccessful, because the type of use the trapper enjoyed was not of sufficient quality to satisfy the requirements for adverse. possession.

(D) unsuccessful, because of the trapper's request in 1923.

Question 102

J purchased a home at fair market value from D but did not record his deed. J moved into the house shortly after closing and has lived there ever since. Two years later, D conveyed the same house to F. F recorded her deed almost immediately.

In an action between F and J for title to the house, judgment should be for:

(A) J, because he was the first purchaser.

(B) J, because F was on inquiry notice of D's conveyance to J.

(C) F, because she was the first to record.

(D) F, but only if she paid fair value.

Question 103

A tenant leased a house from a landlord for 20 years in 1964. The house was located along a major highway. The area had been a sparsely populated farming and residential area, but in 1979 an interstate highway was completed, with an exit near the landlord's house. The area became inundated with fast food restaurants and gas stations. The tenant invested $75,000 to remodel the home and convert it into a tourist shop in 1980.

If, in 1984, the landlord opts not to renew the lease and asserts an action against the tenant for the cost of restoring the house to a residence, judgment should be for:

(A) the landlord, because a tenant may not substantially alter a tenancy.

(B) the landlord, because the tenant has committed ameliorative waste.

(C) the tenant, because the character of the area changed.

(D) the tenant, because he has not violated any housing code.

Question 104

A farmer owned a very small farm. A water company paid him ten dollars a year for the right to run a water pipe across the farmer's farm. The pipe was ignored by both parties for many years. The parties never agreed who was responsible for the maintenance of the pipe. One day the pipe burst, causing a major flood, and several of the farmer's pigs drowned. An expert determined that the pipe burst because it had not been maintained properly.

If the farmer sues the water company for his damages, should the farmer prevail?

(A) Yes, because one who possesses an easement is held strictly liable to the servient estate.

(B) Yes, because the owner of an easement is obligated to maintain the easement.

(C) No, because the parties did not delegate duties.

(D) No, because the farmer knew the pipe's location and condition.

Questions 105–106 are based upon the following fact pattern.

A millionaire owned an office and apartment building, in fee simple. The millionaire conveyed the property to "The apprentice, his heirs, and assigns, but if the apprentice should be found guilty of any felony, to the mayor, if the mayor has no less than three children by the time he is seventy years old. If the apprentice is convicted of a felony and the mayor has less than three children, then to me and my heirs in fee simple." The millionaire's only heir is a son.

Question 105

The clause "to the mayor, if the mayor has no less than three children by the time he is seventy years old" is:

(A) not valid.

(B) valid, because if it vests, it will vest within a life in being.

(C) valid only if the apprentice has already been convicted of a felony.

(D) valid, because the mayor's interest has already vested although it may later divest.

Question 106

Which of the following best describes the son's interest upon the millionaire's death?

(A) fee simple

(B) possibility of a reverter

(C) condition subsequent

(D) none of the above

Question 107

A and E owned homes built on adjacent lots. Both had scenic views of a lake from their living room windows. E often sat and knitted in the afternoons, enjoying the view and waiting for her children to come home from school. From her living room perch, E could see her children get off the school bus at the corner and walk home. A decided to erect a billboard in front of her house to provide the family with extra income. The billboard would block E's view of both the lake and the school bus stop. There are no applicable local zoning laws.

If E asserts an action against A to enjoin building the billboard, should E prevail?

(A) Yes, because the billboard will block E's natural rights to an easement for light and air.
(B) Yes, because the neighborhood's lack of billboards created a reciprocal negative servitude prohibiting them.
(C) No, unless E used the view for a period long enough to create an easement by prescription.
(D) No, because E did not have a covenant to protect her view.

Question 108

A farmer built a barn on her farm knowing that the barn extended two inches onto her neighbor's property. The farmer thought the infringement would go unnoticed because the neighbor owned 2,000 acres of undeveloped land, which she had not visited for several years. The land was very hilly and rocky and had no economic value since it was in the boondocks and unfarmable.

If the neighbor asserts an action against the farmer based on trespass and requests damages, should the neighbor prevail?

(A) Yes.
(B) No, because she has not suffered pecuniary damages.
(C) No, because no use of the land was affected.
(D) No, because the trespass was not material.

Question 109

A homeowner owned a house with a very large back yard. Property values skyrocketed throughout the neighborhood, and the homeowner decided to sell his back yard to a buyer. The homeowner forgot to tell the buyer that several pipes ran from the house to municipal pipes across the yard.

If the buyer demands that the homeowner remove the pipes, the homeowner should argue that he owns an:

(A) easement by prescription.
(B) easement by implication.
(C) easement by reservation.
(D) easement by solicitation.

Questions 110–111 are based upon the following fact pattern.

A mining company dug a mine on its property that was adjacent to a homeowner's house. The mine was operated in compliance with all local ordinances and was built in a careful and prudent manner. The mine came up to, but not over, the boundary between the company's and the homeowner's property. The homeowner's house developed a crack in the foundation and was severely damaged due to the company's mine. The property is in a common law jurisdiction.

Question 110

If the homeowner asserts an action against the company for damages to his house, is he likely to prevail?

(A) Yes, because the support to his land was damaged by the company.
(B) Yes, because the structural damage is evidence of the company's negligence.
(C) No, because a house is an artificial structure.
(D) No, because the company acted in a careful and prudent manner.

Question 111

Assume for this question only that an oak tree in the homeowner's yard collapsed due to the company's digging on its own property. If the homeowner asserts an action, should he prevail?

(A) Yes, if he can prove the company was negligent.
(B) Yes, regardless of whether or not the company was negligent.
(C) No, because one is not liable for damaging a tree.
(D) No, because the company acted in good faith.

Question 112

A dealer purchased a large tract of land from a townsperson. The dealer's land was completely surrounded by land owned by the townsperson, and the dealer's only access to a public highway was across the townsperson's land, by using an old driveway that the townsperson used to use.

The dealer will be allowed to pass across the townsperson's land under an:

(A) easement by implication.
(B) easement by prescription.
(C) easement by reservation.
(D) easement by necessity.

Questions 113–114 are based upon the following fact pattern.

A grantor owned an apartment building called "Town Gardens" in fee simple. The grantor conveyed the property to "The landlord, his heirs, and assigns, but if the landlord should not provide heat to his tenants then the producer shall have a right of entry, if the producer has two or more children before he reaches the age of sixty. If the landlord does not provide heat and the producer does not have children, then to myself and my heirs in fee simple."

Question 113

The provision "to the producer if the producer has two or more children before he reaches the age of sixty" is:

(A) valid, only if the landlord has not provided heat.

(B) valid, because the producer's interest has already vested even though it may divest at a later date.

(C) valid, because if it vests, it will vest within a life in being.

(D) not valid.

Question 114

Which of the following best describes the interest held by the grantor's children after his death as long as the landlord provides heat and the producer has no children?

(A) possibility of a reverter.

(B) fee simple.

(C) condition subsequent.

(D) none.

Question 115

A landlord leased an apartment to a tenant by written lease for two years, ending on the last day of April 2007. The tenant was to pay $1200 a month rent, and he occupied the entire apartment, promptly paying rent for the first fifteen months of the lease, until he moved to a new job in a new city. Without talking to the landlord first, the tenant let a friend move into the apartment and signed an informal writing transferring to the friend his "lease rights," until April 2007. The friend promptly made rental payments to the landlord for the first four months, but for the final five months, no one paid rent and the friend moved out the end of January 2007. The landlord was visiting family in Europe and did not notice until April, and decided to sue the tenant and the friend jointly and severally, for $6,000, or five months rent.

What is the likely outcome?

(A) Both the friend and the tenant are liable for the full amount, because the tenant is liable on privity of contract and the friend is liable on privity of estate as an assignee.

(B) The friend is liable for $2,400, on privity of estate, for the time he was there, and the tenant is liable for the rest on privity of contract for the time after the friend vacated.

(C) The friend is liable for the entire amount, and the tenant is not, because the landlord's failure to

object to the friend's payment relieved the tenant of liability.

(D) The tenant is liable for the entire amount, since he was in privity of contract and the friend is not liable at all, because a sublessee does not have personal liability to the original landlord.

Question 116

An investor purchased a tract of land, and used his business partner to help finance it. This loan was secured by a mortgage. The investor regularly made the installment payments to his partner for several years, but then decided to sell it to his neighbor subject to the mortgage. The mortgage contained a "due on sale" clause stating, "If mortgager transfers his/her interest without the written consent of mortgagee first obtained, then at the mortgagee's option the entire principal balance of the debt secured by his mortgage shall become immediately due and payable." However, without seeking his partner's consent first, the investor conveyed the land to a neighbor, the deed reading "subject to a mortgage to the business partner." The neighbor took possession of the land and started making mortgage payments, which the business partner accepted. However, neither the investor nor the neighbor has made any payments for the last few months, and the business partner wants her money. She has sued the neighbor for the delinquent amount.

How should the court render judgment?

(A) for the neighbor, because he did not assume the mortgage

(B) for the neighbor, because he is not in privity of estate with the business partner.

(C) for the business partner, because the investor's deed to the neighbor violated the due-on-sale clause

(D) for the business partner, because the neighbor is in privity of estate with the business partner.

Question 117

A grantor owned Blackacre in fee simple. He wanted the land to eventually pass to his oldest granddaughter. He devised the land as follows: "To my son for life, remainder to my son's widow for life, remainder in fee simple to their eldest surviving daughter." At the time the grantor died, his son was not married. Which of the following choices is correct?

(A) The remainder to the widow is void under the Rule Against Perpetuities.

(B) The son's widow will own Blackacre in fee simple.

(C) Title to Blackacre will revert back to the grantor's estate.

(D) The son owns Blackacre in fee simple.

Property

Answer 1

(B) The owner impliedly reserved himself an easement when he granted Westacre to the buyer. An easement implied from prior existing use arises when an owner of an entire tract of land creates an easement and then conveys part of the property that is burdened by the easement without mention to the buyer. Proof of the easement implied from preexisting use is established by three elements: (1) There was common ownership of the dominant and servient parcels and a subsequent conveyance of one of those parcels; (2) the use was apparent, i.e., readily discoverable by investigation, continuous and permanent; and (3) the claimed easement is necessary and beneficial to the enjoyment of the parcel conveyed or retained by the grantor. Although the pipes were underground, they will still be found to be discoverable by investigation, meeting the third element. An easement by prescription (C) is similar to adverse possession; the use must be open and notorious and continuous for the statutory time period (which is certain to exceed one year). The covenant against encumbrances wasn't violated (D) by the owner's implied easement. We don't know from the facts that the land was conveyed with such a covenant, and the overall point is that the buyer is charged with knowledge of the owner's easement. There is also no trespass (A) because the owner's easement gave him the right to maintain his pipes on the buyer's land.

Answer 2

(C) The Rule Against Perpetuities cannot defeat a vested remainder or a reversionary interest in the grantor. Therefore, (A), (B), and (D) are unaffected by the rule. (C) is correct because the remainder in the grandchildren is contingent upon their reaching the age of twenty-five. The very fact that the grandchildren must reach an age over twenty-one should put you on notice that the Rule has probably been violated. The daughter is the measuring life (because her life has a causal effect on the existence of the remainder), and twenty-one years after the daughter's death the class won't necessarily have vested or failed. To satisfy the Rule Against Perpetuities, the remainder must definitely vest or fail within a (measuring) life in being (at the conveyance or devise) plus twenty-one years.

Answer 3

(C) Until the niece fulfills the conveyance's requirements, the physician holds the remainder of the nephew's life estate (he really holds a reversion upon the nephew's death) as the niece has a springing executor interest. After the requirements are met, then the physician's interest becomes a possibility of reverter if the office is no longer used for the practice of medicine.

Answer 4

(B) A remainder vests when its holder is alive and any conditions precedent have been met. The grandson's interest had vested as soon as he was born since he was one of the son's children and there were no conditions precedent in the conveyance. Only a vested remainder may be attached or sold by a creditor, a contingent remainder may not be. A remainder is contingent if it is subject to a condition precedent or if it is in an unascertainable person. The vesting of the grandson's interest might have seemed contingent upon his outliving the son if the grantor's will had not provided that a deceased child's portion should go to the respective estate. Therefore, the grandson now owns a remainder even if he is deceased at the time he would have come into possession of Blackacre.

Answer 5

(A) The Rule in Shelley's Case applies in a state following the common law. It provides that when a grantor conveys a limited estate to a grantee and in the same instrument creates a remainder in the grantee's heirs (grantor must use the word "heirs"), the grantee takes the estate in fee simple.

Under the Rule, the son had acquired the lot in fee simple and it will pass to his wife upon his death.

Answer 6

(B) There are six covenants for title to real property, which are divided into "personal" (or present) covenants and "real" (or future) covenants. Personal covenants are usually breached (if at all) as of the time the deed was delivered. They may not be enforced by a remote grantee (the second buyer) against a grantor (the seller). These are (1) for quiet enjoyment, (2) of the right to convey, and (3) against encumbrances. In contrast, real covenants may be enforced by a remote grantee. These are (1) for seisin, (2) of general warranty, and (3) for further assurance. (B) is correct because it is an example of the covenant for further assurances. Profits (A) and easements (C) fall under the covenant against encumbrances, which is personal and unenforceable by a remote grantee. The second buyer has no legal rights against the first buyer to perfect title because a quitclaim deed makes no guarantees. The first buyer only purported to pass on to the second buyer whatever interest he actually possessed.

Answer 7

(B) An easement is the right of one to make specific use of the land of another. An easement in gross benefits its owner in the conduct of its business, general affairs, etc., and not for the sole benefit of an adjacent parcel of land. This easement benefits State Water in its business of supplying water to the city. An easement appurtenant benefits its owner's adjacent parcel of land at the expense of the land owned by another. The land that is benefited is called the dominant tenement, and the land used is called the servient tenement. For an easement appurtenant to exist, you must be able to identify a dominant and a servient tenement. With an easement in gross, there is a servient tenement but no dominant tenement. Once created, an easement automatically runs with its tenements and binds successors to the land. If State Water were to buy the rights to use a strip of land adjacent to its own land in order to run an electric cable that will power its water plant, that would be an easement appurtenant because the use of the adjacent land benefits State Water in the use of its own land. A profit (C) is the right to enter another's land to remove natural resources. A covenant (D) is a promise or a contract between landowners that binds their successors.

Answer 8

(D) In 1922, the minister granted his son a fee simple determinable with a possibility of reverter in himself.

The key is in the use of the words "so long as" modifying the condition of the grant. As soon as this condition is broken the land automatically reverts to the minister, or his estate if he is deceased. The son cannot convey any more than he owns; therefore, anyone who follows the son in interest takes a determinable estate. At common law, the determinable status could last in perpetuity, but most American states have enacted valid statutes of limitations on the number of years for which such a possibility of reverter will be effective. If this had been a fee simple subject to condition subsequent, language such as "but if this farm is used for alcohol production, I will have a right to re-enter" would have been used. The condition subsequent gives only a right of re-entry. The previous estate does not divest automatically, but the grantor holding the possibility of reverter must exercise her right to re-enter for the estate to divest.

Answer 9

(B) One has seisin of real property if one (1) has legal possession of that property and (2) has a freehold estate (fee simple, fee tail, or life estate). One does not have seisin when one holds a non-freehold estate, such as the various types of tenancies: a tenancy for years, periodic tenancy, tenancy at will, or a tenancy at sufferance. Transferring the right to actual possession during a life estate holder's lifetime does not cut short the ownership right in the property, as this transfer, a lease in this case, does nothing to the title. Since the attorney is a tenant with a tenancy for years, he has the right to actual possession, but he does not hold legal possession of the land or a freehold estate. The cousin, as the owner of life estate, has legal possession of the land until his death; therefore, he has seisin of the property despite the fact that the attorney is occupying the house. The grantor does not currently hold a freehold estate or legal possession; he owns only a future interest in the property.

Answer 10

(C) The six covenants for title to real property are (1) of the right to convey, (2) for seisin, (3) against encumbrances, (4) for quiet enjoyment, (5) of general warranty, and (6) for further assurances. If a deed provides for "usual covenants," only five will be included. A deed that provides for "full covenants" will include all six. Under the covenant of the right to convey, the grantor promises that he has the power to transfer the interest purportedly conveyed to the grantee. Although in most cases the same as the covenant of seisin, it might differ in cases where a life estate is burdened by an enforceable restraint on alienation or where the property is adversely possessed by another party. In such a case, the seller would have record title (seisin) but not the right to convey it.

Answer 11

(A) This easement is not enforceable due to the vagueness of its terms. The description of the usage granted and the area the business partner may use is too broad. (B) is a valid easement by necessity. The lyricist owned both parcels of land and granted one part with no access to a road; therefore, it is implied that the composer will have the right to travel over the lyricist's land. (C) is most likely a valid easement by prescription, especially because the runner jogged on a specified path. The runner could not acquire an easement to run all over the neighbor's land. If the neighbor had given the runner permission to use the path in the past, he might try to argue that the runner had a license that was revocable at will. (D) is a valid negative easement. The number of negative easements is limited, but they are valid for light and air. Usually a real covenant can be used more effectively to achieve the same purpose as a negative easement.

Answer 12

(C) This clause was a valid restrictive negative covenant that "runs with the land." To be an enforceable covenant, the following conditions must, at the time of the covenant's creation, be present: (1) a writing, (2) the covenant touches and concerns the land, (3) privity between the covenantor and the covenantee, and (4) the parties intend that the covenant run with the land. All of these conditions were satisfied until the homeless person acquired title by adverse possession. He cannot enforce the covenant because he was never in privity with the seller.

Answer 13

(B) Gamma cannot enforce a personal covenant against Alpha. He may only enforce a real covenant that runs with the land. The covenant against encumbrances ((A) and (C)) is a personal covenant, which he may only enforce against Beta. However, (B), the covenant for quiet enjoyment, may be enforced by a remote grantee. When the neighbor asserted paramount title to Rockacre and effectively "evicted" Gamma, the covenant for quiet enjoyment was breached.

Answer 14

(D) This question examines the fine line distinguishing a sublease from an assignment. A transfer by a tenant of all of her interest in a leasehold is an assignment, despite any words to the contrary. A tenant who has transferred less than all of her interest has created a sublease. In this example, the tenant could have given the sublessee the remainder of her tenancy less one day. This is a loophole used to avoid an assignment, but will not be effective in all jurisdictions. An assignment creates privity of estate between the landlord and the assignee. Therefore, the sublessee is liable to the tenant's landlord for rent, although the tenant was also liable as a surety. But now that the tenant is bankrupt, she's off the hook for her old debts. A sublessee is not in privity of estate with the landlord and, therefore, may not be held liable for the tenant's failure to pay the rent or fulfill other obligations.

Answer 15

(D) An easement that is tied to the use of adjacent land is a very specific right. The owner of a dominant tenement receives the benefit of an easement over the servient tenement for use by the dominant tenement only. The owner of Macre cannot add another dominant tenement (Lacre) to this arrangement because no party may unilaterally alter an easement. This answer does not need to address the intensity of the owner of Macre's use or the efficiency and the necessity involved. These considerations are irrelevant. In short, you cannot arbitrarily change the easement from benefitting one property to another.

Answer 16

(B) B's attempt to limit the fee simple is called a "disabling restraint," and the clause is void. Any provision that puts an undue restraint on the alienation of property will be deemed invalid by the courts. This usually applies when there is a penalty for conveying the property, such as when a person's interest is forfeited if she tries to convey it. The transfer itself is valid and will be construed as if it were written without the restriction. The net effect is a fee simple transfer. The Rule Against Perpetuities does not come into consideration because the clause is already void.

Answer 17

(C) Just as with easements, profits may be in gross (benefits the holder without a dominant tenement) or appurtenant (tied to the land and passing only with the land). For a profit or an easement to be appurtenant, it must be intimately tied to that land. In this instance, the profit was a business arrangement and the right to use Blue's land was personal to Red. Profits are usually in gross and freely alienable by their owners. Red could sell Green his profit, but it must be done separately from the sale of his land. However, it should be noted that it is assignable, separate from land, because it is commercial. Generally, noncommercial profits and easements in gross are not assignable. The majority of easements are affirmative; only a minimum of negative easements, i.e., for light and air, exist.

Answer 18

(B) One does not forfeit an easement due to excessive use. Although such use may exceed the use allowed by the easement, the original easement remains in force. N can prevent car racing but not normal use of the easement. (D) is false, which can be inferred from the facts of the question. (C) is simply incorrect. There is no reason for both easements to be extinguished.

Answer 19

(B) The easement was not readily discoverable and breached the covenant against encumbrances, where the seller promises that there are no encumbrances on the property, other than those that have been previously disclosed; therefore, it constituted a defect in the title. Had the easement been obvious, such as a paved road, the result might be different. (A) is a correct rule of law, but in the present case the deed disclaimed liability for recorded easements.

Answer 20

(A) Francine was a third-party beneficiary to the agreement between Smith and Elaine and she may, therefore, recover for a breach in this agreement. It is important that Smith knew that Francine wanted the title examined in order to sell it. However, this knowledge can easily be seen as implied in the request. (B) is incorrect because the facts make no mention of title insurance. (C) and (D) are false.

Answer 21

(A) Elaine executed a warranty deed and a covenant against encumbrances. Since the covenant was not satisfied, she will be liable to Francine.

Answer 22

(A) Cacre will be awarded to the niece because she bought the land without notice of the buyer's prior purchase, but only if she paid value for the land as required by the statute. The niece is the junior claimant because she was the second purchaser although the first to record. (B) is not the best answer because the buyer's failure to record will only cause her to lose the land if the niece qualifies for priority under the statute. A quitclaim deed (C) is one given without any warranties to title. This choice is irrelevant because it does not affect the validity of the buyer's purchase. (D) is incorrect because the statute only requires that a junior claimant pay value.

Answer 23

(B) The general rule is that when a deed and contract contain contradicting clauses, the deed is controlling. (A) is incorrect because a quitclaim and a warranty deed are materially different, in fact they can be considered opposites. (C) and (D) are false.

Answer 24

(C) The easement granted to the buyer from the neighbor was for his benefit in the use of Wildacre. This makes it an easement appurtenant to the land. Wildacre was the dominant tenement, and Overgrownacre was the servient tenement. Normally, when the dominant tenement is sold the new owner also gets the easement. You can think of it as Wildacre owning the easement. However, when the dominant and servient tenement are both owned by the same person, merger occurs and the easement automatically extinguishes. You cannot own an easement over your own property. Therefore, no easement existed over Wildacre once the buyer owned both Wildacre and Overgrownacre.

Answer 25

(D) The fact that one owner has maintained actual possession of a concurrent estate for the statutory time period will not be sufficient to give that owner sole title to the entire estate because adverse possession must be hostile. A concurrent estate gives all its owners the right to possession although they are not required to exercise that right. For the possession to be hostile the one owner must unequivocally notify all others that she intends to acquire sole possession. This requires more than simply an ouster. Since adverse possession is not applicable here, the other choices are irrelevant.

Answer 26

(D) The kind of title owned by the previous owner would be relatively unimportant. (A) is the most important factor in determining the quality of the title conveyed. The parties' intent and good faith, (B) and (C), will also be influential factors in determining which party would prevail. Only (D) would be relatively unimportant.

Answer 27

(C) The death of a seller will not terminate a contract (thus rendering (A) incorrect). Since the contract will be enforced, the proceeds will enter the estate and pass to the daughter. (B) is clearly incorrect, as is (D), due to the terms of the seller's will.

Answer 28

(B) The owner of an easement has the obligation to maintain the easement and avoid unreasonable interference with the servient tenement. Strict liability, (A), is not imposed. (D) assumes facts not in the question.

Answer 29

(D) "Past consideration is no consideration" and will not satisfy the requirement to render a contract binding on the parties. The housekeeper had not relied on the terms of the grantor's will when he performed the services; therefore, he cannot enforce the grantor's promise to leave him $100,000. And yes, this is a contracts question, but sometimes the subjects overlap. However, this does not mean the actual will should not be enforced, only the contractual promise.

Answer 30

(C) J's future interest will be held void because it is too remote and because it violates the Rule Against Perpetuities. What remains is land held by the the university as long as it is used for the football team. If it is not used for such purpose, it will revert to the grantor. Thus, the grantor's interest is a possibility of a reverter, which follows determinable fees. This should be distinguished from a reversion (B), which is created if the grantor transfers an estate of shorter duration than the one she holds. Keep in mind that the effects of the Rule Against Perpetuities differ in respect to determinable fees and fees subject to a condition subsequent. If the grantor had transferred a fee simple subject to a condition subsequent with an executory interest that was invalidated by the Rule, then the university would have a fee simple absolute.

Answer 31

(D) As a general rule, any restriction of a legal interest in property that prevents its free alienability is void. A disabling restraint provides that the grantee has no power to transfer her interest, and it will be voided. The property will then pass in fee simple. Hence, the grandchildren will obtain a fee simple interest. The Rule Against Perpetuities has not been violated because possession has vested within the required life in being (the grantor's daughter) plus twenty-one years.

Answer 32

(B) A fee simple determinable automatically terminates upon the happening of a certain event. Look for the key words, "for as long as," "while," "during," or "until." In contrast, a fee simple subject to a condition subsequent gives the grantor the power to terminate a grantee's estate upon occurrence of a condition. The key words indicating the estate is subject to a condition are, "but if" and "shall have the right to re-enter." An executory interest is one that divests a fee simple in favor of another grantee and not the original grantor.

Answer 33

(B) The "life in being plus twenty-one years" requirement was met. As it seems now, the grantor's daughter is the life in being and all of her children will turn twenty-one, if they reach that age at all, within twenty-one years after her death. If the grantor has more children, the one who lives the longest will be the measuring life in being. By its terms, the rule limits the period to at the latest 21 years after the death of the last identifiable individual living at the time the interest was created. This "measuring" or "validating" life need not have been a purchaser or taker in the conveyance or devise. The measuring life could be the grantor, a life tenant, a tenant for a term of years, or in the case of a contingent remainder or executory devise to a class of unascertained individuals, the person capable of producing members of that class. The fact that a grandchild exists (A) is irrelevant because the grantor's daughter could have additional children.

Answer 34

(D) Ordinarily, a landlord is under no obligation to deliver premises to a tenant in good condition (A). However, a landlord is obligated to disclose the existence of defects the tenant could not discover upon reasonable inspection if the landlord had actual knowledge or reason to know of such defects. Landlords will not be held strictly liable, in most jurisdictions, for conditions within an apartment.

Answer 35

(D) An easement by implication arises when the conveyee has no convenient means of access except across the land retained by the conveyor; the conveyor is presumed to have given the conveyee a right-of-way across the easement. An easement by implication is presumed where the conveyer has left himself totally landlocked, which requires an easement by necessity. In this instance there was a path in existence to demarcate the location of the easement. If there hadn't been a path, Secund would have the right to locate the easement (since it is on his land) within reason. Since the elements of an easement by implication were satisfied, whether the elements of an easement by prescription were fulfilled is not material.

Answer 36

(B) If a recorded instrument makes reference to an unrecorded transaction, a subsequent purchaser is bound to inquire into the nature of the unrecorded transaction. In the instant case, the court should rule the actress had inquiry notice of the singer's easement because she could have found record of it in a thorough title search.

Answer 37

(B) A fixture is a chattel that has been annexed to real property. It becomes part of the real property and passes with the property. Most courts will examine whether it was intended that the chattel be permanently attached to the building. A custom-made screen does not automatically become a fixture, but since these screens were not easily removable it seems that it was intended that they be permanent.

Answer 38

(C) The contract between the widow and the neighbor would ordinarily be void due to the Statute of Frauds because it is an oral contract for an interest in land. The neighbor's best chance will be under the facts enumerated in this choice. (A) seems like a good alternative, but it's not so clear that the neighbor's actions in caring for the widow will make the intentions of their contract obvious. (D) is not a good choice because it does not matter that the daughter and the widow have not spoken.

Answer 39

(D) The assignment clause was not written to benefit AB. Only EF may assert an action based on the clause. The lease simply prohibited an assignment without EF's permission; it did not prohibit assignments in general. AB's interests are irrelevant since EF was the beneficiary of the restriction.

Answer 40

(C) The requirement of the deed was to construct a theater for music within a certain time period. This requirement was met, and the university obtained the land in fee simple. Use of the building for music in perpetuity was not a condition of the conveyance.

Answer 41

(B) A life tenant is liable for interest that accrues on the mortgage of a tenancy but is not liable for the principal.

Answer 42

(A) A life tenant must pay the taxes on the property but will not be required to insure it.

Answer 43

(B) K's argument that J was not in the chain of title is the view in the majority of jurisdictions. J's interest might have been discoverable, but it would put a tremendous burden on the title searcher. Therefore,

K cannot be charged with notice of J's interest, and she will most likely be awarded possession. This is her most persuasive argument, although the other choices might be valid.

Answer 44

(D) An easement is the best method to secure the use of land. Easements bind the owners of land regardless of notice, touching and concerning the land, privity, etc. A covenant that runs with the land can remain in effect in perpetuity, but its enforcement will not be as secure as an easement's. A zoning law is not the best device because it can be legislatively changed.

Answer 45

(D) In this question it is important to examine the terms of the relevant statute. The statute clearly provides that one who records first without notice of a prior conveyance and pays value owns the land. Since the son hadn't paid value it didn't matter that he recorded his interest first. Remember that recording statutes only speak to "purchasers."

Answer 46

(C) The consideration furnished by Park N' Lock was sufficient to obtain title. They should be viewed as any other in the chain of title. Under most Recording Statutes, the status of mortgagee and purchaser are the same.

Answer 47

(C) A tenancy by the entirety may only be created between a husband and wife. A covenant by the entirety may not unilaterally convey his interest; it can only be done jointly. Therefore, the man and woman would have a true tenancy in the entirety with this restriction on alienability only if they were married. It is also effective if they have a common-law marriage.

Answer 48

(A) A life tenant is obligated to pay only the interest on a loan owed for the tenancy. The remainderman is liable for the principal. Further, a life tenant is liable to pay taxes on the property but not insurance.

Answer 49

(C) To be an enforceable covenant, the following conditions must, at the time of creation, be present: (1) a writing, (2) the covenant touches and concerns the land, (3) privity of estate between the covenantor and the covenantee, and (4) the parties intend that the covenant run with the land. This agreement resembles a covenant running with the land that benefits or burdens successors in interest to the original parties, but it will only be enforceable against W by J if C and G were in privity of estate, i.e., one of them had purchased his land from the other.

Answer 50

(A) A pure notice recording act protects a subsequent bona fide purchaser for value regardless of whether he was the first to record. To qualify as a bona fide purchaser for value, the purchaser must not have had actual or record notice of a prior conveyance at the time of buying the property and must pay value. A race-notice act would protect the writer only if he recorded prior to the general. A pure-race act would protect the writer if he recorded first — even if he had knowledge of the prior conveyance. (C) is nonsense.

Answer 51

(C) The courts will enforce a covenant against a buyer whose deed does not contain the restriction only if evidence shows that, when the sale of property began, the developer had a common scheme of development that included the lots in question. A common scheme has to be such that an observer would notice the covenant. This is justified under the doctrine of reciprocal or implied negative servitudes. Most states assume that the unrestricted buyer had constructive notice of the restrictions on the other deeds. However, some states will refuse to enforce any covenants without actual notice.

Answer 52

(B) The above rule applies to this question. If the speculator was bound under the doctrine of reciprocal negative servitudes, his successors in interest will be as well. Therefore, the best defense is to argue that there was not a common development scheme.

Answer 53

(B) E will most likely be considered a third-party beneficiary to the agreement between D and the attorney and she could therefore recover against the attorney for breaching his duty to D. (D) is incorrect because the attorney can bring suit regardless of whether the attorney was negligent, which makes (C) incorrect as well. (A) is incorrect because even though the attorney did guarantee the title, he did so to D, so we have to go a step further and figure out if E, not D, has any claim.

Answer 54

(B) D executed a covenant of warranty and a covenant against encumbrances. Since the covenant against encumbrances was not satisfied, D will be liable to E. (A) is incorrect because it is not relevant whether he was negligent in hiring the attorney; that is not the issue, and (D) is incorrect for the same reasons. (C) is incorrect because the covenants prevail over any issue of buyer beware.

Answer 55

(A) The Statute of Frauds requires that every conveyance of an interest in land of more than one year must be evidenced by a writing. Since there was no writing and no consideration paid, the deputy only had the sheriff's permission, i.e., a license, to enter his land. Licenses differ from easements because they are revocable at will. For an easement to be created there must also be an evident intention to create one. (B) is incorrect because, while it is true that the deputy had no rights to an easement by implication, it is irrelevant to the answer. (D) is incorrect because it does not apply to licenses, and it has already been determined this is a license.

Answer 56

(C) A way of satisfying the Statute of Frauds, aside from writing, may sometimes be part performance. Under this doctrine, there must be part performance by one party in detrimental reliance on the contract, while the other party has notice and sits idly by. This part performance should also clearly demonstrate the intentions of the parties to the contract. Therefore, the producer's BEST argument would be that the actress did not take any actions that a person with a long-term lease would not take, thus not relying on the option to buy, and therefore the elements of part performance have not been met. Keep in mind that the question is asking you for the producer's BEST argument. The actress's best argument is that she has satisfied part performance, but that is NOT what the question is asking. (A) might also help him, but (C) is still better, and once again, you are being asked for his BEST argument. (D) may be correct but would be very difficult to prove. (B) is wordy nonsense.

Answer 57

(C) Fee simple subject to an executory interest is an estate subject to divestment upon occurrence of a condition subsequent, and when the condition occurs the title will be given to another grantee rather than the original grantor. (D) is correct, the fee simple is determinable, but it's not the best answer because this fee simple is also subject to an executory interest. Although executory interests are rarely valid due to the Rule Against Perpetuities, in this case the "charity to charity" exception will apply. The "charity to charity" exception provides that the Rule Against Perpetuities will not void the executory interest of a charitable organization when it succeeds another charitable organization.

Answer 58

(C) If the fixtures were by their nature installed to benefit the tenant in the conduct of her business, she may remove them. This is an exception to the rules of fixtures to prevent a businessperson from losing an investment. (A) is an incorrect statement of landlord-tenant law. Proving (B) would be difficult. The general darkroom equipment may be easily removable, but the lights could be regarded as permanent attachments. (D) is false.

Answer 59

(C) Under a pure race recording act, a subsequent purchaser will prevail if she is the first to record, regardless of whether she paid value. Under pure notice (A) and race-notice (B) statutes, only a bona fide purchaser for value will prevail.

Answer 60

(D) A life tenant may not commit waste on the tenancy. When land has been previously used to exploit natural resources, it is assumed that the grantor expected the life tenant to do the same. However the son may not remove an inordinate amount of the timber because a life tenant does not have the right to impair the interest of the remainderman. Ameliorative waste (C) is that which changes the nature of the premises in a "good" way, i.e., one that increases its value.

Answer 61

(D) Title to real property is transferred when a deed is conveyed, despite the purchaser's failure to record. The purchaser may not be protected against subsequent bona fide purchasers for value who recorded first, however that does not mean the property is not transferred. In addition, the existence of an easement will not negate the transfer.

Answer 62

(D) The easement is for a right of way and not for storage. When an easement is granted, the holder may not exceed its "boundaries."

Answer 63

(A) The covenant was valid and runs with the land. (B) and (D) are incorrect because they deal with zoning laws that aren't of concern in this case.

Answer 64

(C) If the court determines that the land was part of a common development scheme, the newly developed land must be used in conformity with that scheme. Another method to have construction limited to detached houses is to enact a zoning ordinance (B), but zoning ordinances are less secure than common schemes because they may be changed.

Answer 65

(C) Under a contract for the sale of real property where the kind of title has not been specified, delivery of "marketable title" is implied. Not specifying title will NOT make the contract invalid.

Answer 66

(C) An easement is a non-possessory right one holds to use the land of another. An easement is of perpetual duration unless otherwise stated, and is not extinguished because of mere non-use. (A) is incorrect because traditionally easements were granted in perpetuity. However, an easement can be extinguished by hostilely cutting off access for the statutory time period or when abandoned by the owner, but remember, abandonment is NOT mere non-use. There has to be some action taken. (B) is incorrect because failure to mention an easement does not negate it and the buyer will most likely be charged with constructive notice of the easement. (D) is incorrect because whether the railroad or pool is more important is irrelevant.

Answer 67

(D) For the reasons stated in the answer above, monetary damages will not be available to the buyer. However, he might be able to collect monetary damages from the seller if his purchase was accompanied by a covenant against encumbrances.

Answer 68

(D) To be a proper conveyance, the deed and contract must identify the land precisely enough for anyone to locate it. Although this description is not given in metes and bounds, it is exact enough for a person to figure out where the plot of land lies. (A) is wrong because whether a description is adequate has nothing to do with consideration. (B) is incorrect because there is nothing inconsistent, and (C) is incorrect because, as already discussed, even though metes and bounds help, there is no requirement for them.

Answer 69

(C) The agreement can be viewed as an equitable servitude, which is a type of covenant that binds the successors of land. It is a subset of real covenants, but privity of estate is not a requirement to enforce it. An equitable servitude is enforceable through injunction only and will not give rise to monetary damages. However, this equitable servitude will not be enforced because it violates the equal protection clause. The servitude will not be invalidated, but no court will enforce it against homeowners with children. Although unenforceable in regard to children, the rest of the agreement remains valid.

Answer 70

(A) The nature of the property and the description are sufficient to identify the property. The mistake in acreage will not affect the conveyance; it will simply be reformed to represent what the owner actually possessed.

Answer 71

(D) The Parole Evidence Rule will prevent testimony of oral understandings to alter a written contract. This is a contracts and property overlap, and this is not uncommon since property and contracts issues often overlap in the practice of law. (A) is incorrect because recording a deed does not make it immune to attack, particularly since the error is merely computational.

Answer 72

(A) The second buyer is a bona fide purchaser who properly recorded. She will be able to obtain valid title to the land. However, the computational mistake that the first buyer made will most likely be rectified.

Answer 73

(A) A transfer by a lessee of his entire interest is an assignment, and a transfer of less than his entire interest is a sublease. Under the majority view, a right of re-entry is not a true reversion; therefore, B's transfer was an assignment.

Answer 74

(D) is correct because a court of equity will look into the adequacy of consideration when determining the ownership of land. The transfer to the daughter will most likely be considered a gift, which is not binding on the donor. Even at law, "love and affection" is not usually considered adequate consideration. (A) would be correct if the daughter had furnished consideration for the land.

Answer 75

(B) The rancher has committed waste, which is using a life estate to the full estate's detriment. A life tenant is not allowed to impair the interests of the remainder. By pumping this oil, the rancher has reduced the value of the land. The naturalist will succeed in recovering the value of the waste and preventing future waste. The rancher's life estate was not terminated (A), since he satisfied the condition of growing corn through 1995.

Answer 76

(C) A person's "children" are defined as children by all marriages and adopted children. The following are generally not defined as children: (1) step-children, (2) grandchildren, and (3) illegitimate children. But some states have enacted statutes that will include illegitimate children in the definition.

Answer 77

(D) License is merely permission. The traveler can argue that he gave the friend permission to live in his apartment but did not give him an interest in the apartment. A licensee is one with formal permission or authority to do something on the land of another. A licensor may terminate a license at will. (A) and (B) are incorrect since any type of tenancy will subject the traveler to landlord-tenant laws. The friend is not a trespasser, since he initially occupied the apartment with the traveler's permission.

Answer 78

(C) Under the doctrine of equitable conversion, the risk of loss is on the buyer when damage is caused by neither the buyer nor seller. The original contract is valid and enforceable. (D) is incorrect since such a remedy would effectively "undo" the contract. Though the buyer should have taken out insurance (A), the reason for doing so is that equitable conversion will place the risk of loss on him. Some states have abandoned this doctrine and determined that the risk of loss follows possession. If this standard had been applied, the seller would have been unsuccessful in her bid for specific performance.

Answer 79

(C) The developer must argue that he cannot manifest the granting of an easement prior to handing the property to governmental authorities.

Answer 80

(D) When two parties share a joint tenancy, they each own a one-half undivided interest in the whole. Severance of a joint tenancy occurs when one party alienates his or her share. When S conveyed Northacre, the court might find that she terminated the joint tenancy by selling her entire interest in the estate, thus resulting in a tenancy in common. Unlike a tenancy by the entirety, a joint tenancy can be severed by one party acting alone. Therefore, the estate has effectively been partitioned, and Southacre is K's alone in fee simple.

Answer 81

(C) The agreement to share expenses was an affirmative covenant. It can be enforced in a court of law for damages. An easement is a non-possessory interest allowing use of another's land, and an equitable servitude is a subset of real covenants that can be enforced by an injunction.

(B) is wrong because Cheepskate did not contract with his neighbors.

Answer 82

(D) The house will be awarded to the daughter, who was first to record, only if she satisfied the statute by providing consideration of sufficient value. This depends on the worth of the services she performed compared to the fair market value of the house.

Answer 83

(B) A tenancy by the entirety may only be created between a husband and wife. It requires five unities: time, title, interest, possession, and marriage. Since the local jurisdiction did not recognize common law marriage, a tenancy by the entirety was never created. Therefore, the property may be partitioned. Jurisdictions differ in interpretation of what type of tenancy is actually created when an unmarried couple attempts to obtain property through a tenancy by the entirety. Some will say that they have a tenancy in common and others will give them a joint tenancy because it better approximates their intention. All the unities necessary for a joint tenancy are already present. Both of these alternative estates are capable of partition.

Answer 84

(A) Since each party owns part of the tennis court, all they have to do is grant the other party an easement in writing. This option is the most secure. All of the other choices are contestable and must conform to specific requirements, such as privity for enforcement.

Answer 85

(B) When the government obtains title to part of a leasehold through eminent domain or condemnation, the tenant will take part of the award and then be held to the full contract. If the skipper wants out of the lease, his only redress is against the government. He can also sublet the land or assign his interest in the lease. If any other party had obtained paramount title to part of the land by purchasing it from the longshoreman and evicted the skipper from that portion, the covenant of quiet enjoyment within the lease would be breached. Quiet enjoyment is a dependent covenant; if the landlord breaches it, the tenant is not required to pay rent. Most leases currently contain a condemnation clause that provides that the agreement will be terminated and the landlord will receive all compensation from the government.

Answer 86

(D) The correct choice, "vested, but subject to open," means the same as vested and subject to a partial defeasance. Until the employee should have another child, the son owns the remainder alone in fee simple. If the collector has more children, the estate will be shared. The employee's son will still own a partial interest, but not the whole. Therefore, it is subject to open if the employee has additional children.

Answer 87

(C) An easement created in writing to last in perpetuity will not be terminated due to a lack of necessity. If this were an implied easement due to necessity, it would be terminated. Abandonment would be one way to terminate this easement, but the jockey still used the field. If the groomer had first told the jockey to keep off the land in the 1940s and the jockey then stayed away for the statutory period, the groomer could claim that the easement was extinguished adversely.

Answer 88

(D) In many jurisdictions, under the doctrine that prevents retaliatory evictions, a landlord may not raise rents or otherwise harass a tenant because she has sought to enforce her rights.

Answer 89

(D) The Rule Against Perpetuities will void the clause creating the architect's interest because it may not vest or fail to vest within twenty-one years. The daughter inherited the grantor's possibility of reverter and will own State Building in fee simple if it is not used for promoting the arts.

Answer 90

(A) When a deed and contract contain contradicting clauses, the deed is generally controlling. Since a quitclaim deed is one that makes no warranties, (B) is clearly false.

Answer 91

(C) A promise to deliver good title will be satisfied by clearing title of a previous mortgage shortly after the sale with the proceeds from the sale. When a defect in title is easily curable, the buyer must give the seller a fair opportunity to remedy it. The seller will not be in breach for failing to pay off the mortgage before receiving payment, but the buyer will be in breach for refusing to comply with the contract. (A) is irrelevant because a buyer can sign an agreement with full knowledge of a mortgage (i.e., defect in title) as long as it will be cured or is likely to be cured by the closing date (or in this case, shortly after the closing date).

Answer 92

(C) A fixture is a chattel that has been permanently annexed to real property. It becomes part of the real property and passes with the sale of the property. To determine if a chattel becomes a fixture, the courts look at the manifest intent of the owner at the time of installation. The greater the degree of annexation of the chattel to realty, the stronger the inference of its being a fixture. Since these air conditioning units required a significant alteration of the building, it seems that they were meant to be permanent. (D) is incorrect because air conditioners are not fixtures by nature, it depends on the relative circumstances.

Answer 93

(C) Fee simple subject to an executory interest is an estate subject to a divesting condition subsequent, which, if the condition occurs, will vest title in a third person rather than the grantor. Although executory interests are subject to the Rule Against Perpetuities, the "charity to charity" exception to the Rule will apply in this question and allow the Society for Cancer Research's interest to remain valid indefinitely. This fee simple is also determinable (D), but (D) is less specific and not the best answer.

Answer 94

(A) A fee simple subject to a condition subsequent is an estate where the grantor has the power to terminate a grantee's estate on the happening of a specified condition subsequent (i.e., the sale of drugs). This estate differs from a fee simple determinable in that it does not revert until the grantor exercises his right of re-entry, whereas under a fee simple determinable the estate automatically reverts.

Answer 95

(B) The right of a grantor under a fee simple subject to a condition subsequent is called "right of entry for condition broken." (C) is incorrect in the most part because the proper term is "possibility of reverter."

Answer 96

(B) Under a subdivision plan deemed a common development scheme, most courts will enforce the provisions of a covenant even though it is not contained in the violator's deed. The court will assume the homebuilder has "inquiry notice" of the restriction.

Answer 97

(C) The act of recording a designation for the road will cause the property to vest in the county. (B) is incorrect because the court will probably assume that Coalco had constructive notice of the covenant.

Answer 98

(D) When a grantor delivers the deed to a third person as an intermediary, the conveyance will be effective if he has surrendered all control over the property conveyed.

Answer 99

(C) The courts will enforce a reciprocal negative servitude or covenant if the evidence shows that when the sales began, the developer had a common scheme of development that included the lots in question. Whether there are resultant damages is irrelevant.

Answer 100

(C) Under the rule of convenience, a class closes when some member of the class can call for a distribution of his share of a class gift. Upon Uncle's death, the favorite niece's children have the right to receive their distribution. (B) is incorrect because, if Uncle intended to benefit the third child, he would have used more explicit language.

Answer 101

(D) An easement by prescription is acquired through a process similar to adverse possession and has many of the same requirements. The main distinction lies in that exclusive use of the easement is usually not required. Since the heiress had knowledge and granted permission to use the land, the trapper's use wasn't "hostile to the rights of the true owner"; therefore, a necessary element for adverse acquisition of an easement was absent.

Answer 102

(B) A title search is incomplete until the possession of the land has been examined. If the record does not explain who is in possession, the purchaser must inquire further. Since it is presumed that the buyer conducted a diligent title search, F will be charged with inquiry notice that J owned the home. The fact that J occupied the house for two years simply furthers his rights.

Answer 103

(B) Ameliorative waste is usually an improvement in the character and nature of the premises. Courts will not allow recovery for ameliorative waste if the change increases the value of the premises, the tenant was in possession of the premises for a long time, and the change reflects a change in the character of the neighborhood. In this instance, the tenant may have increased the value of the house for someone who wants to sell souvenirs, but he has reduced the value for residential purposes; therefore the landlord will be able to recover. (A) is generally correct since waste usually lessens a property's value. (C) alone does not entitle a tenant to change the character of the premises.

Answer 104

(B) The owner of an easement has the obligation to maintain the easement and to avoid unreasonable interference with the servient estate. Strict liability (A) is not imposed and hence is an incorrect statement of law.

Answer 105

(B) This clause is valid in all respects. It does not violate the Rule Against Perpetuities because all conditions will or will not be fulfilled during the time of a life in being.

Answer 106

(B) "Possibility of a reverter" is a future interest left in a grantor who conveys a fee simple determinable. The millionaire has conveyed a determinable fee because the estate will divest in his favor upon the happening of certain events. If these conditions are not satisfied at some point subsequent to the millionaire's death, the estate will revert to the millionaire's heirs.

Answer 107

(D) E's use of the view did not provide her with an easement or any other rights to prevent the construction of the billboard. Negative easements have traditionally existed only for rights to light and air and must be in writing. If she had anticipated a neighbor blocking her view, she could have attempted to enter into a valid covenant that would have prohibited the erection of billboards and the like, but since she hadn't, she had no enforceable rights. An implied reciprocal negative servitude can only be created in residential subdivisions, which are not present in this fact pattern.

Answer 108

(A) Construction on the property of another gives rise to a cause of action regardless of the magnitude of the transgression or condition of the land. Trespass gives rise to liability regardless of actual damage. The farmer's only defense would be a bona fide boundary dispute or that she had acquired the strip through adverse possession. Remember, trespass is a tort, therefore a plaintiff may receive nominal damages with nothing else except proof of trespass.

Answer 109

(B) When an owner sells a portion of his property, the existence of a prior use over that portion may give rise to an easement by implication, even though no reference is made to the continuation of that use. (C) is not correct because an easement by reservation can only be created with an express clause in the deed.

Answer 110

(C) A landowner has no obligation to provide support to artificial structures on his neighbor's land; however, he will be liable for negligence. Structural damage alone (B) does not prove Goldco acted negligently.

Answer 111

(B) A landowner may bring an action for damage to the natural condition of his property caused by the removal of the lateral support of his land. Though a landowner has no obligation to provide support for artificial structures on his neighbor's land, there IS a duty to provide support for the land, or things coming out of the land, such as trees.

Answer 112

(A) An easement by implication, which allows a grantee to use the land of a grantor for access to the grantee's own land, arises when the grantor sells a part of his land that has no outlet to a public road except over the remaining portions of his property. This is similar to an easement by necessity, but it does not HAVE to be necessary, only meet the requirements laid out above.

Answer 113

(D) This clause violates the Rule Against Perpetuities because the producer was given an executory interest, which does not technically vest until it becomes possessory. The intention of the grantor was to give the producer the right to re-enter Town Garden if the landlord should fail to provide heat for the tenants, but since the landlord and his heirs and assigns might fulfill this condition for longer than a life in being plus twenty-one years, the producer's interest is voided by the Rule. The portion of the clause requiring that the producer have at least two children before he turns sixty is valid on its own because it must vest or fail within a life in being, but not following the rest of the grant, so (C) would be correct if it was just that provision on its own. (A) is incorrect because who owns the property may shift depending on whether heat is provided, but that alone will not validate or invalidate a clause of a grant.

Answer 114

(A) Possibility of a reverter is a future interest left in a grantor who conveys a defeasible fee simple estate. The grantor conveyed a fee simple subject to an executory interest to the landowner when he attempted to give the producer the right to re-enter upon the happening of certain events. Unlike fee simple determinables, when an executory interest following a fee simple subject to condition subsequent is invalidated by the Rule Against Perpetuities, it will usually transform the grantee's (the landowner's) interest to a fee simple absolute. But in this instance, the grantor's last clause granted himself and his heirs a possibility of reverter and maintained the estate's defeasibility.

Answer 115

(A) is correct, since the friend and the tenant created an assignment when the tenant transferred the entire remainder of the lease. Had he only transferred a portion of the lease, it would be a sublease. When an assignment is created, both the original tenant and the assignee, in this case the friend, are liable for rent. The rest of the answers are incorrect for the reason stated above.

Answer 116

(A) is correct, because even though the neighbor made payments, he only took the deed subject to the mortgage, he did NOT assume it. When you assume a mortgage, you take on the personal responsibility to pay it when you take land subject to a mortgage, it means only that your property has the mortgage attached, but the buyer is not personally liable. (B) misstates the reason why the neighbor will prevail, as privity of estate is irrelevant here, which also

makes (D) incorrect. (C) is incorrect because the business partner would have a cause of action for Investor for the due on sale clause, not the neighbor.

Answer 117

(C) Under the Rule Against Perpetuities, no interest is good unless it must vest, if at all, no later than twenty-one years after some life in being at the creation of the interest. In this scenario, while the possibility that the son could have a widow is addressed in the grantor's will, the widow is not an identifiable life in being at the creation of the interest, the grantor's death. As such, there exists the possibility that she will be born after the time the gift was made, marry the son and then outlive him so that vesting in their children could occur more than twenty-one years after the death of the measuring life, the son. Thus, the transfer to the son's eldest daughter then living violates the Rule as her status cannot be determined to vest or fail twenty-one years after the measuring life and Blackacre will eventually revert to the grantor's estate. Had the transfer said to the children of the son, then those children could have been determined upon the son's death and the provision would have been good under the Rule.

Torts

89. Indirect Cause
90. Defamation
91. Parent's Liability for Torts of Children
92. Defamation
93. Nuisance
94. Parent's Liability for Torts of Children
95. Intentional Infliction of Emotional Distress
96. Invasion of Privacy

97. Defamation
98. Product Liability
99. Intentional Infliction of Emotional Distress
100. Negligence
101. Battery
102. Negligence
103. Negligence

Torts

Question 1

A medical college operated a clinic where students, under the supervision of the school's faculty, examined and treated patients with foot problems without charge. The school included in its clinic's advertisements that "appointments are recommended but not necessary." A commuter saw the advertisement on a public bus one morning and decided to go to the clinic to have his bunion treated. Since he didn't have an appointment, the commuter sat in the waiting room for two hours. As he stood up to get another magazine from the coffee table, a piece of plaster fell from the ceiling and landed on his foot. He immediately sat down because he was in so much pain. The falling plaster severely aggravated his bunion. The commuter sued the school. Is he likely to prevail?

(A) Yes, if the school knew or should have known about the possibility of falling plaster.

(B) Yes, but only if an agent of the school knew the plaster was a hazard.

(C) No, because the commuter did not have an appointment.

(D) No, because the school's treatment was to be gratuitous, and gratuitous landowners never have a duty.

Question 2

A shopper purchased a jar of peanut butter at the local grocery store. She made a sandwich for her son, whose mouth began to bleed profusely after the first bite. After carefully examining the product, she discovered several shards of glass and peanut shells in the peanut butter. The peanut butter was manufactured by a manufacturing company, and placed in jars supplied by a local glass factory. The peanut butter was then sold to a wholesaler, and the grocery store purchased it from the wholesaler. In a product liability suit brought by the shopper, on behalf of her son, against the manufacturing company, which of the following will the shopper NOT need to prove for the manufacturing company to be held strictly liable for the injuries?

(A) The product was not altered from the time it left the defendant's control until it reached the plaintiff.

(B) Privity existed between the plaintiff and defendant.

(C) The defendant was a commercial supplier.

(D) The product's defect was the actual and proximate cause of the plaintiff's injuries.

Question 3

A security guard at an airport was on his way home from a wild evening at the local watering hole on Cedar Road. Realizing he was drunk, the security guard drove home in his truck well within the citywide speed limit of twenty-five miles per hour. The security guard relaxed at the wheel once he was within a mile of his home. He made a left turn onto Warrensville Center Road northbound where he mistakenly drove on the wrong side of the double yellow line.

A mechanic worked for a nearby garage. After work, he customized cars for profit and pleasure. He decided to "see what his latest project could do." This latest project was a hot pink car that was not yet completed and had only two out of its four brakes installed, but the mechanic assumed he would be safe because the roads were usually deserted at 2 A.M. He drove the car southbound on Warrensville Center Road at eighty miles per hour.

Just as the mechanic approached Cedar Road, the security guard turned his truck and came straight at him. The mechanic could have stopped had his car been equipped with four brakes. The cars collided. The mechanic suffered $4,000 in damages. The security guard's damages were $3,000. After a full and fair civil litigation, both the security guard and the mechanic were judged to be negligent by a jury of their peers, the mechanic 60 percent and the security guard 40 percent. Which of the following choices best represents their respective liability?

(A) If the jurisdiction has a pure comparative negligence statute, the mechanic will have to pay the security guard $200.

(B) If the jurisdiction follows the last clear chance doctrine, the security guard will recover $18.

(C) The mechanic assumed the risk and will not recover in any jurisdiction.

(D) The mechanic will recover $1,600 in a contributory negligence jurisdiction.

Question 4

A doctor was a world-famous heart surgeon who pioneered a life-saving heart bypass treatment. Throughout his distinguished career, he performed hundreds of operations, almost all of them successful. His bedside manner, on the other hand, was less than pleasant, and he frequently alienated patients.

One patient, a cantankerous, sixty-three-year-old widow, was referred to the doctor, who recommended the now routine bypass surgery. Although she sailed through the operation, the patient felt that the scar on her chest was "more unsightly than average." The doctor responded by telling her, not so tactfully, that if she lost 100 pounds, the scar would fade. The patient, after conducting extensive research on the subject, found that the average scar in such a case was a half-inch shorter than hers. She sued for malpractice, and the jury found for the doctor. However, the doctor felt that his brilliant reputation was seriously tarnished. Without explanation, several patients canceled their scheduled surgeries a few days after the patient instituted the malpractice suit. If the doctor brings a common law suit against the patient for defamation, which of the following is the best answer?

(A) The doctor will win the action if he can prove that the patient's suit was lacking probable cause and resulted in actual damages.

(B) The doctor will win his action if he can prove that the patient was motivated by an improper purpose in bringing her action, and the suit resulted in actual damages to him.

(C) The doctor will not prevail because her statements were oral, and did not result in any special damages.

(D) The doctor if the patient believed she had reason to bring a malpractice suit.

Question 5

In which of the following situations has the court erred?

(A) A plaintiff became severely ill after eating popcorn flavored with rancid butter. The plaintiff, who purchased the popcorn at a multiplex theater, brought a product liability action against the theater alleging strict liability. The trial judge ruled in favor of the multiplex theater on the grounds that since the sale of popcorn was subsidiary to the theater's primary business activity of showing movies, it was not a commercial supplier.

(B) A plaintiff, while on a tour of a cannery, is injured by an exploding boiler and brings a product liability action against the owner alleging strict liability. The trial judge dismissed the action because the cannery cans pineapples and does not supply boilers.

(C) A plaintiff, injured in a plane crash, brought a product liability action alleging strict liability against the airline. The trial judge dismissed the case.

(D) A plaintiff, injured in a plane crash, brought a product liability action alleging strict liability against the airplane manufacturer. The trial judge instructed the jury that the plaintiff need not prove negligence.

Question 6

In which of the following four cases will the plaintiff most likely not prevail?

(A) The defendant's convertible stalled on an isolated highway. Sensing an imminent thunderstorm, he broke the window of a nearby shack that appeared abandoned and climbed through for shelter from the dangerous storm. The plaintiff, owner of the shack, asserted an action to recover for the damage to his shack.

(B) The defendant loaned $1,000 to the plaintiff, who did not repay the loan when it was due. The defendant complained to the plaintiff one day when they happened to meet on Main Street. The plaintiff had his toy poodle with him on a leash. The defendant's tone was so hostile that the plaintiff's dog became upset, growled, and barked at the defendant. The defendant struck the plaintiff's dog with his newspaper, causing a slight cut. The plaintiff brought an action against the defendant based on trespass to chattels.

(C) The plaintiff's employee took home a stereo system from the plaintiff's warehouse without paying for it, used it for a week, and then sold it to the defendant. The defendant, the owner of the electronics store, was unaware that the plaintiff's employee did not rightfully own the stereo system. The defendant sold the system at 20 percent less than his usual price for comparable equipment during his "Annual Sale." The plaintiff brought an action against the defendant based on conversion.

(D) The defendant assaulted a victim in the plaintiff's full sight. The defendant thought the plaintiff was a mere passerby while the plaintiff was, in fact, the victim's brother. The plaintiff brought an action against the defendant based on intentional infliction of emotional distress.

Question 7

A defendant, a driver, will be most likely to succeed in his appeal of which of the following four verdicts?

(A) The victim was injured in a traffic accident caused by the defendant's negligence. The victim was in excruciating pain due to a compound fracture of his right leg. The ambulance driver did not properly set the victim's leg before rushing him to the hospital. The doctor in charge of the emergency room was also negligent in her treatment of the victim. The leg became gangrenous and had to be amputated at the hip. The jury found that the ambulance driver's negligence alone would have resulted in the victim's leg being amputated at the knee. The amputation at the hip was due to the doctor's negligence. The trial judge ruled the defendant must compensate the victim for the loss of his entire leg.

(B) The victim's car was immobilized after a collision with the defendant's car caused by the defendant's negligence. The victim could have walked away to safety, but instead she stood in front of her car on the well-lit road and waved a flag to prevent further damage to her car. The victim was struck by a car while waving the flag. After three weeks in the hospital, doctors concluded that the victim, steadily recovering, would not suffer any permanent disability. Several days later, the victim contracted pneumonia because of her weakened condition. She died several weeks later of pneumonia-related complications. The jury found that the victim had acted completely without negligence, and the trial judge ruled the defendant should be held civilly liable for the victim's death.

(C) A hunter holding a gun and walking along a country road was so startled when a car, negligently driven by the defendant, crashed into a nearby tree that he accidentally fired his rifle. A bullet from the rifle struck the victim, the hunter's son, in the leg. Two weeks later, the victim fell while walking with the help of crutches and broke his other leg. The trial judge ruled the defendant was liable for the damage to both of the victim's legs.

(D) The defendant struck and knocked down a telephone pole due to his negligent driving. The victim was forced to sit in traffic with his car because the pole had blocked the state highway on which he was driving. The victim's car was struck by lightning while waiting, and the victim was electrocuted. The victim was rushed to the hospital, where he received an emergency blood transfusion. The victim recovered from the electrocution, but died ten years later of AIDS contracted from the transfusion. The trial judge ruled the defendant civilly liable for the victim's death.

Question 8

On October 1, 2001, a patient had his appendix removed by a doctor at the hospital. Three days after the operation, the doctor told the patient to rest, drink plenty of water, eat lots of ice cream, and go home. On October 1, 2002, the patient visited the doctor and complained that ever since the operation he felt a sharp pain in his stomach. "Oh, I wouldn't worry about it," said the doctor. The patient moved 100 miles away and never saw the doctor again. The pain did subside, and he completely forgot about it until October 15, 2006. That was the date when the patient went to another doctor for a routine check-up. An X-ray showed that the patient had been carrying a surgical tool in his abdominal cavity. The patient brought an action against the doctor, who moved to dismiss the case due to the statute of limitations. The

jurisdiction where the surgery was performed allows five years to commence a malpractice action and follows the majority position as to when the statute begins to run. Which of the following statements is the best answer?

(A) The case should not be heard because the statute begins when the malpractice occurs.

(B) The case should be heard because the statute begins when the doctor-patient relationship terminates.

(C) The case should be heard because the statute begins to run when the malpractice is actually discovered or reasonably should be discovered.

(D) The case should be heard because the statute begins to run at the time the object left inside the body is discovered.

Question 9

A truck driver had thirty years' experience and had been awarded several company commendations for safe driving. The truck driver drove down a street, passing a sign that warned him to take a detour due to demolition work in the area. The truck driver did not take the detour and was injured by debris falling from a building in the process of being demolished. If the truck driver brings an action against the demolition company, which of the following is most accurate?

(A) The truck driver will recover because demolition is an ultra-hazardous activity.

(B) The truck driver will recover under strict liability.

(C) If the truck driver's ignoring the warning sign is considered negligent, he will not recover.

(D) If the truck driver read the sign, he may be found to have assumed the risk of injury.

Question 10

A driver knew Friday, June 22, was going to be a rough day, but it was even rougher than he expected. At 3 P.M., the driver waited apprehensively behind the steering wheel of his school bus as the young students chanted, "No more pencils, no more books, no more teachers ugly looks" and sang songs.

The driver drove off, realizing it was useless to ask the students to be seated or to be quiet. The celebrations began relatively innocently with the emptying of loose-leafs out the windows of the bus into the dry and warm June breeze, but then progressed further, culminating with many students breaking windows and lights, ripping seats, and causing whatever damage their juvenile strength could muster and their minds could conjure up. After destroying everything that they could get their hands on, the contented children returned to singing. The driver decided to pass three scheduled stops and take the children to a nearby police station.

A passenger seated in the rear of the bus was so engrossed in reading that she did not even notice the commotion. The passenger sued for false imprisonment.

The driver's best defense will be:

(A) public necessity.

(B) private necessity.

(C) self-defense.

(D) justification.

Question 11

A boss dictated a letter to his secretary that contained the following sentence: "In sum it seems quite obvious to me that your client's dealings have been consistently dishonest and certainly unethical, and his character makes him a bad risk for a loan from your bank."

After dictating the letter, the boss thought for a moment and then told his secretary, "Do me a favor. Destroy the letter I just dictated. There's no reason to type it. Why should I help out the bank? They charge me eight dollars to certify a check."

The letter was never typed, and no one other than the bank's client found out about the letter's contents. If the client asserts a defamation action against the boss:

(A) the action will fail because of the absence of publication.

(B) the action will fail because the client has not suffered damages.

(C) an action based on slander will succeed, but a similar action based on libel will fail.

(D) an action based on libel will most likely fail due to privilege.

Question 12

A homeless middle-aged woman lived on a sidewalk heating vent on an exclusive upper class street. Formerly a secretary for ten years, she became homeless when she decided that she preferred the outdoor life to the comfort of having four walls and a roof. The woman consistently refused offers of assistance and shelter from city officials. Late at night, she found plenty of good hot food to eat by sorting through the garbage of the area's fine restaurants. The woman decided to spend the night at a shelter one evening after word had spread among the street people that the police were about to go out with psychiatrists to pick up deranged homeless people and take them to a hospital for psychiatric testing.

The shelter was owned and operated by a nonprofit corporation. It relied on private donations and federal grants. As the woman waited to speak to a social worker, a scaffold, used to change light bulbs, collapsed on top of the woman, causing her serious injury. A company, an independent contractor, was engaged in the business of changing the light bulbs in all the shelters. The company had a reputation in the city as a dangerously sloppy company. The city knew of this reputation but was politically motivated to retain the company because the company president had once been homeless.

If the woman asserted an action against the city for injuries sustained, which of the following choices is the best?

(A) The trial judge should dismiss the action because the city is a nonprofit organization.

(B) The woman will prevail if the city could have known of the danger through reasonable inspection.

(C) The city will prevail because an employer is not responsible for the negligence of an independent contractor.

(D) The woman will prevail because she was an invitee.

Question 13

An employee was employed as a laborer by a firm that maintained the lawns and gardens of homeowners residing in affluent suburbs. The employee resented his employer. He felt his work was extremely difficult even for a man as talented as he. He was especially bitter that his employer paid only the minimum wage without a health plan or any other perquisites. The employee found this to be insufficient compensation when he had to endure a daily commute and support a family. He also believed that the employer operated at a high profit margin. They required their clients to sign yearly contracts, but did not provide any services in the winter months.

One day, the employee decided he would make sure that he received his due share. Instead of reporting to work that day, the employee knocked on the doors of the employer' clients and explained that, as an added convenience, they could pay him in cash instead of mailing a check to the employers. The company found out about the employee's activities after failing to receive $22,000 worth of checks from their customers. Which of the following is true?

(A) The employee cannot be liable for conversion because intangibles may not form the basis for a conversion suit.

(B) The employee will be liable to the employer for embezzlement.

(C) The employee will be liable to the employer for conversion.

(D) The employee will be liable to the employer for interference with contractual advantage.

Question 14

A bank was chartered to operate in 1869. Deposits were insured by a loan corporation. The president of the bank had assets of five billion dollars. The bank was poorly managed, but its banks were all nicely maintained, and its slick advertising campaigns helped the bank keep a favorable public image.

An entrepreneur owned seven video stores. In 1978, she borrowed $3,000 from her aunt to buy some movies and rent them from a six-foot counter located in a candy store. Business was so brisk she rolled over her receipts to buy more tapes. Within six months, she needed much more space and rented her own store. The store performed extremely well, and because it was the town's first video store, she was able to rent tapes for five dollars per night. She opened one store at a time, filling new stores with tapes that no longer rented at other locations because they had been on the shelves for months or years.

By 1984, the entrepreneur had a total of 13,200 movies in the inventories of her seven stores. The movies had cost the entrepreneur a total of $686,400 and had an estimated wholesale market value of $377,520 Used tapes were in great demand because video stores were opening all over the country and new store owners tried to stock their inventories with used movies to save costs. The entrepreneur was acutely aware of the value of her movies. She made a practice of selling copies of tapes she no longer needed to used tape dealers. These dealers, who brokered used tapes, had surfaced with the video boom.

In 1984, the entrepreneur decided to open four new "super stores," each stocking five thousand movies. She felt that consumers would prefer to rent from stores that had a wider selection. She was also convinced that these stores would intimidate competitors with less capital to lay out.

She requested a loan of $350,000 from several banks, deciding to use her personal savings for the balance of the investment. The banks wanted collateral, and the entrepreneur offered her inventory. Each banker she consulted checked a little book, and all the books stated that video movies were to be valued at three dollars per movie. The entrepreneur explained that her movies were worth much more, and she offered to prove their value, but all she received was sympathy.

Finally, the entrepreneur decided to put up $350,000 in bearer bonds to secure a loan from the bank. She handed the bonds to the president to be held until she paid back the loan on January 2, 1988. On that date, the entrepreneur made her last payment and asked for her bonds. The president could not find the bonds, for which no record of ownership is kept. The president had, in fact, accidentally used the bonds to house-train his puppy in 1984. If the entrepreneur brings a tort action against the bank, the court should rule the bank, through the president as its agent, is liable for

(A) trespass to chattels.

(B) conversion.

(C) negligence.

(D) nothing that will give rise to liability.

Questions 15–16 are based upon the following fact situation.

A married couple went to a comedy club where they saw several up-and-coming talents. It was a cold winter night toward the end of February. The husband was bundled up in his new white fox fur coat and matching hat. The husband had such a good time that they stayed for hours and enjoyed several acts. The club showcased some known comedians, one of whom had recently appeared on many national talk shows, and two men the couple recognized from a beer commercial. The couple consumed more than the club's minimum of two drinks. The husband is a big guy; his blood alcohol level was below that which would seriously impair his judgment.

When he left the club, the husband mistakenly took someone else's hat.

Question 15

Assume for this question only that the husband did not realize the hat was not his own until three months later. After realizing his mistake, the husband immediately returned the hat to the comedy club's "lost and found." The husband will most likely be liable to the hat's owner for:

(A) trespass to chattels.

(B) conversion.

(C) neither trespass to chattels nor conversion, because the hat was returned to its rightful owner.

(D) neither trespass to chattels nor conversion, because the husband acted in good faith.

Question 16

Assume for this question only that the husband knowingly took the wrong hat. As he crossed the street, he changed his mind and returned it. The husband will most likely be liable to the hat's owner for:

(A) trespass to chattels.

(B) conversion.

(C) neither trespass to chattels nor conversion, because he returned the hat right away.

(D) both trespass to chattels and conversion.

Question 17

A landlord owned a store on the boardwalk that he had rented to a tenant for twenty-three years under a tenancy at will. The tenant ran a retail salt-water taffy operation in the space he leased. When gambling became legal, the landlord notified the tenant that he was going to triple the store's rent. The tenant was happy to pay the increased rent because the added traffic more than tripled his volume and the new breed of tourist paid for taffy without looking at the price. The landlord received many offers from developers interested in purchasing his store, but he refused to sell. The landlord's wife begged him to accept the offers, some of which were for more money than the landlord ever dreamed he would have, but the landlord was convinced that the value of the property would continue to increase.

A casino wanted the landlord's store because they had secretly acquired several nearby properties. After the landlord refused an offer of $3 million in cash, the casino sent one of their employees to visit the tenant.

The employee, a huge man wearing a pinstripe suit, black shirt, and white tie, walked into the salt-water taffy store carrying a violin case. He told the tenant about a retailer who stayed longer than he was welcome when the casino wanted his store: "The man died a slow, painful death." The tenant called the landlord as soon as the employee left and told him he was retiring. The landlord should assert an action against the casino based upon:

(A) interference with prospective advantage.

(B) interference with existing contract.

(C) interference with business relations.

(D) intimidation.

Question 18

A homeowner lived in a little house surrounded by a white picket fence. The homeowner's house was not the kind of place that impressed her friends and family, but the homeowner loved it. After a hard day's work, she found it an ideal environment in which to relax with her puppy.

When she came home one day, a man introduced himself as her new neighbor. The neighbor asked the homeowner to go to dinner, and she agreed because she thought he was cute.

After that first date, the neighbor asked the homeowner to dinner again, but she refused. She decided that he was a creep. The homeowner had paid for the entire dinner because the neighbor forgot his wallet. The neighbor refused to accept the homeowner's rejection and kept calling her. At first, he called every few days, but later the calls became more frequent, often several times a day until long past midnight, and they were often threatening. The homeowner was extremely disturbed by these calls. They also prevented her from getting eight hours of sleep each night. She lost her job one day when she fell asleep at her desk. The homeowner has grounds to assert an action based on:

(A) private nuisance.

(B) intentional infliction of emotional distress.

(C) invasion of privacy.

(D) all of the above.

Question 19

A farmer hated the railroad. Several times a day, he stopped his tractor, took a cigarette break, and watched a noisy train spewing black smoke as it passed his farm. The farmer was convinced that the noise, vibrations, and especially the smoke from the train damaged his organic crops.

On November 1, a strike idled all trains passing the farmer's property, and the farmer was in ecstasy. His neighbor, another farmer, was not pleased. He had ten thousand bushels of apples loaded on an idled train, and the apples had begun to rot. On December 6, the strike was settled. The first farmer, having become accustomed to the peace and quiet, hated the trains more than ever, and, out of anger and desperation, blocked the railroad tracks with an old car. The train carrying the second farmer's apples struck the car and derailed. The accident caused the second farmer's apples to be delayed an additional six days.

In a suit asserted by the second farmer against the first farmer, the second farmer should:

(A) not recover, because the farmer is not responsible for the strike.

(B) not recover, because of the alternative causes doctrine.

(C) recover the part of the loss due to the farmer's actions.

(D) recover the difference between the value of the apples when delivered and the value had the apples not been spoiled.

Question 20

A shopper could not find a parking spot in his grocer's lot. He decided to park his car in a nearby driveway because he was in a hurry. A car was already in the driveway that the shopper pulled into, but he simply left his car at the beginning of the driveway, blocking the sidewalk. He didn't think anyone would be inconvenienced. Since all he needed was a container of orange juice, he planned to be gone for less than a minute.

While the shopper was in the store, a child rode toward the shopper's car on his tricycle. He could not pass because the sidewalk was blocked. The child rode into the street to get around the car and was struck by an automobile negligently driven by a driver. The child received nothing more than bruises and cuts, but he was rushed to a hospital where an intern confused him with another patient and brought him into surgery to have his spleen removed. While recovering from the surgery, the child died from an overdose of a sedative administered by the attending anesthesiologist.

Which of the following choices is NOT correct?

(A) The shopper's parked car was a cause in fact and a legal cause of the car's striking the child.

(B) If the child's estate asserts an action against the shopper for the death of the child, the estate will prevail.

(C) The anesthesiologist's mistake was a superseding cause.

(D) The driver-child accident was a foreseeable consequence of the child's actions.

Questions 21–22 are based upon the following fact situation.

A seven-year-old boy was nervous and full of aggression. The boy's father, a psychiatrist, encouraged the boy to vent his anger. "If someone or something bothers you, let them have it," the boy was told by his father. The boy followed his father's advice, wrecking property and bruising his friends on several occasions. One day, the boy was in an especially bad mood because he had struck out four times in his little league baseball game. He smashed two large window panes of a bank while walking home. "Why did you do that?" asked the boy's best friend. The boy proceeded to break four of his best friend's front teeth.

Question 21

If the bank asserts a claim against the boy's parents, is the bank likely to prevail?

(A) Yes, because parents of a minor are strictly liable for the torts of their minor child.

(B) Yes, because the boy was encouraged to vent his anger.

(C) No, because a parent is not liable for the torts of his child.

(D) No, because the boy was too young to form the requisite intent.

Question 22

If the best friend brings suit against the boy, is he likely to prevail?

(A) Yes, because the boy was of sufficient age to understand that his actions were wrong.

(B) Yes, because the boy intentionally harmed his best friend.

(C) No, because the boy's parents were solely responsible for his action.

(D) No, because a child the boy's age cannot be liable in tort.

Question 23

A customer was severely inebriated. He walked into a store and asked questions in a loud and abrasive manner. The salesman, an employee of the storekeeper, told the storekeeper, "This guy is drunk as a skunk." The customer was insulted and said to the salesman, "If I wasn't in such a good mood, I would flatten your face." The customer then prodded the salesman's shoulder with his index finger. The storekeeper called over two other employees and told them to "take care of this bum." The employees shoved the customer into the storekeeper's car over the customer's protests and dropped him off on a state road. The customer wandered into the middle of the road and was hit by a bus just five minutes after having been thrown out of the car.

If the salesman brings an action against the customer, his best cause of action will be for:

(A) assault.

(B) battery.

(C) defamation.

(D) intentional infliction of emotional distress.

Questions 24–25 are based on the following fact situation.

A fifteen-year-old girl was staying at a neighbor's house for a week while her parents were away on vacation. She went back to her own house after school one day and took the keys to her father's car. The minimum legal driving age of the state in which the girl lives is sixteen. The girl opened the garage door, got behind the wheel of her father's new sports car, started the engine, and cruised over to a local strip of road perfect for drag racing. The girl revved her engine, floored the accelerator, and within seconds reached a speed of ninety miles per hour. She watched with amazement as the speedometer's needle disappeared. The girl's town had enacted a statute prohibiting people from driving in excess of sixty miles per hour on any of its roads.

The girl did not slow down as she approached a railroad crossing. She knew that the crossing was equipped with flashing lights that signaled whenever a train was passing. No lights were flashing as the girl approached the tracks. The lights had malfunctioned. The girl drove across the tracks while a train was rapidly plowing through. The train struck the back of the girl's car. The tiny sports car flipped over three times. The girl emerged remarkably with only minor cuts and bruises, but she was a hemophiliac and bled to death from her apparently minor cuts. Her estate filed suit against the company that was the owner of the train, track, and signal lights. Subsequent investigation showed that the signal had been malfunctioning for three weeks.

Question 24

What effect will the girl's age and lack of a driver's license have on her estate's action?

(A) It proves she was contributory negligent.

(B) It makes her a trespasser on the state roads; therefore, the company's only duty was to refrain from willful and wanton conduct.

(C) It does not release the company from any liability.

(D) It prevents the girl from invoking the doctrine of last clear chance.

Question 25

Assume for this question only that the railroad company is found liable for the girl's injuries. Will the railroad company also be held responsible for the girl's death?

(A) Yes, because the railroad company should have known that fatalities are the foreseeable result of the broken signals.

(B) Yes, despite the fact that death is not a common result of an accident that causes minor cuts and bruises.

(C) No, because hemophilia is a rare disease.

(D) No, because an ordinary person would have suffered minor injuries.

Questions 26–27 are based upon the following fact situation.

A homeowner purchased a lawnmower from a retail store. The mower had the following cautionary statement printed on it in large red letters: "Warning, this lawnmower has exposed blades. Keep children away. It can be very dangerous." The homeowner left his mower outside on the lawn. He was about to mow the grass, but first he went inside his house to refresh himself with a drink of lemonade. The homeowner's five-year-old son was curious about the inner workings of a lawn mower and stuck his hand inside the mower. The blades were whirring. Two fingers on the son's right hand were severed and chopped up so badly that no surgeon could attempt to save them. A small piece of one bone was shot out of the mower, striking the son in his left eye and causing him a permanent partial loss of vision.

Question 26

If a product liability suit is brought on the son's behalf based on manufacturer's strict liability, the son must establish that:

(A) the blades' shield conformed with the design standard prevalent in the community.

(B) the mower was negligently constructed.

(C) the mower had a design defect that made it unreasonably dangerous.

(D) the warning was insufficient.

Question 27

If the son brings a strict liability action against the retail store, he must establish that:

(A) the mower had not been substantially altered after purchase.

(B) his parents were in privity with the retail store.

(C) the retail store was involved in the design.

(D) the retail store was aware, or should have been aware, of the hazardous design.

Questions 28–29 are based on the following fact situation.

A customer thanked the garage for repairing his car's steering column, paid him, and drove away. The garage forgot to tell the customer that he had not found time to repair the car. The customer saw an employee, one of the garage's mechanics, walking home, and offered him a ride. The employee knew that the customer's car had not been repaired. He also knew that the customer thought it had been fixed, but he kept this information to himself because the employee and the customer were good friends, and the employee didn't want to ruin the customer's day.

It was a beautiful spring day. The customer was driving with his windows open, well within the speed limit, casually appreciating the smell of the early evening air, when a driver opened the door of her parked car. She had seen the customer's car approaching, but reasoned that, if she moved quickly, she could close her door in plenty of time. The customer tried to swerve out of the way of the open door, but his wheel locked because of the malfunctioning steering column. Both the employee and the customer were seriously injured. Had the steering column been repaired, the collision could have been avoided.

Question 28

If the employee asserts a claim against the driver in a pure comparative negligence jurisdiction, will the employee recover?

(A) Yes, but only a percentage of his damages as calculated from the relative negligence of himself and the driver.

(B) Yes, if the employee's negligence is determined to be less than 50 percent.

(C) No, because the collision was caused by the defective steering column.

(D) No, because the employee had the last clear chance.

Question 29

If the customer brings suit against the driver, is he likely to prevail?

(A) Yes, because the customer reasonably believed the car was repaired, and the driver was negligent in opening her door.

(B) Yes, but the amount of the recovery will be reduced because the employee was also negligent.

(C) No, because the negligence of the garage and the employee superseded the driver's negligence.

(D) No, because the driver did not assume the risk that his steering column would malfunction.

Questions 30–31 are based upon the following fact situation.

A construction worker was in a designated hard hat area. According to state statute, construction workers must wear protective helmets in designated hard hat areas. The construction worker was eating his lunch and took his helmet off to use it as a seat.

A teenager decided to sneak into a city club located next door to the construction site. The teenager was not a member of this club and was technically not permitted to be in the building. A city ordinance established that to enter a private club without proper authorization was a misdemeanor. The teenager took an elevator up to the club's rooftop lounge, sat down on a lounge chair by the pool, sipped a can of soda pop that the porter brought him, and enjoyed the spectacular view of the city from 400 feet above the street.

After the teenager drank half the can of soda pop, he had quenched his thirst. The teenager nonchalantly tossed the can over the protective gate that ran along the roof's perimeter. The can plummeted 400 feet to the street by the construction site, grazing the construction worker's shoulder. The impact was so slight that a typical person would not have been seriously injured, but the construction worker was in the midst of recovery from a serious bone fracture. The bones of his shoulder were held together by surgical pins. The can shattered the surgical work in the construction worker's shoulder. The pain was so great that the construction worker lost consciousness, toppled into a heap on the ground, and smashed a watch that he kept in his pocket. It was a precious family heirloom worth $5,000. A city ordinance provides that it is illegal to throw objects from a rooftop. Another ordinance makes it illegal to litter. The construction worker brought an action against the teenager.

Question 30

The fact that the teenager violated the city ordinance policing illegal entry to a club:

(A) will disqualify him as a witness.

(B) will not affect his liability to the construction worker.

(C) makes the teenager absolutely liable.

(D) makes the teenager liable as a trespasser.

Question 31

Assume for this question only that the teenager is found liable for throwing the can of soda pop that grazed the construction worker's shoulder. Is the teenager liable for injuries sustained by the construction worker because his shoulder was especially sensitive?

(A) No, unless a non-sensitive person occasionally had a similar reaction.

(B) No, because shoulders held together with pins are unforeseeable.

(C) Yes, because the teenager could have predicted the results of his actions.

(D) Yes, regardless of the injury's foreseeability.

Question 32

An auto store buys wrecked cars, disassembles them for their parts, and rebuilds them. The auto store obtains most of his additional parts from junkyards, but he occasionally needs to buy new parts. The owner of a transport company purchased a van that the auto store rebuilt from a wreck. The owner informed the auto store that the van's snow tires were acceptable for her purposes because, though the treads were almost bare, the van was to be driven in a warm climate where it does not snow.

The auto store agreed to install four brand new radial tires purchased from a tire mark and manufactured by a tire manufacturer. The tire manufacturer had recently received an award from an association for its exemplary inspection procedures.

Two days after putting the van into service an employee of the transport company, was involved in an accident with the van during which he sprained his right ankle. The van was fixed within two hours, but the employee was unable to drive for three days. The owner of the transport company could not find another driver. Assume that the trier of fact concluded that the accident was caused by the van's front axle falling out. The owner of the transport company brought a product liability action based on strict liability in tort against the auto store for her loss of income due to the employee's injury. Will the owner of the transport company prevail?

(A) Yes, because the auto store was aware that the van was to be used in the transport business.

(B) Yes, because the auto store was in effect the manufacturer and, therefore, was the legal cause of the accident.

(C) No, because there was no privity of contract between the auto store and the employee.

(D) No, because the compensable damages will not include loss of income due to an employee's injury.

Question 33

A traveler was scheduled to fly on an airline. She was leaving home for a year to study abroad and had many valuables in a bag that she was planning to carry onto the plane. An employee of the airline decided to hassle the traveler out of a demented hatred for people with red hair. The employee alerted the traveler that she was suspected of carrying explosives in her bag and asked her several brief questions at the check-in counter. The employee told the traveler that her bag would have to be searched at a nearby office and she could watch if she wanted, or she could leave and pick the bag up before boarding the plane. The traveler decided to watch the bag being searched. The employee searched the bag and then put it aside. The traveler politely reminded him that her flight was scheduled to leave in five minutes. "Go on the plane, we'll send the bag to you," he replied. The traveler decided to stay with the bag and missed the flight.

If the traveler asserts an action for false imprisonment against the airlines, will the traveler prevail?

(A) Yes, if the employee held the bag with the intent of forcing the traveler to stay.

(B) No, because the traveler was free to leave at any time.

(C) No, because the traveler was never confined.

(D) No, because only the traveler's bag was inspected.

Question 34

A restaurant owner owns an exclusive restaurant set in a tranquil wooded area along a river. The restaurant offers views of the river, and the restaurant owner sets up tables outdoors in the summer. A privately owned utility owns a nuclear reactor a mile upstream from the restaurant owner's restaurant. The utility uses the river to cool its reactors. The water temperature further upstream from the reactor averages 65 degrees in the summer; below the reactor, the water temperature sometimes reaches 95 degrees because of the heat generated by the power plant. Thousands of trout and other fish swimming downstream were killed by the heat. Many of the dead fish floated behind the restaurant owner's restaurant. The restaurant owner tried cleaning them up, but to no avail. His restaurant smelled like dead fish, and his business dropped so quickly that he was forced to close down. The restaurant owner lives with his wife and eleven children in an apartment above the restaurant. He must keep his windows closed all year round to partially eliminate the smell.

If the restaurant owner asserts an action based on private nuisance against the utility, the restaurant owner will:

(A) prevail, if he can prove that the utility's actions unreasonably interfere with the restaurant owner's use and enjoyment of his property.

(B) prevail, if he can prove that the power plant interferes with the restaurant owner's business and restaurant.

(C) not prevail, because the plant was so far away that the damages must have been unintentional.

(D) not prevail, because the value of a restaurant is inconsequential when compared to a billion dollar power plant.

Questions 35–36 are based on the following fact situation.

A driver drove a 1967 car without a third brake light in the rear window. The driver's left rear brake light was functioning, and a police officer pulled him over and warned him to fix the light. A week later the driver's neighbor, who owns an identical car, stole the driver's right rear brake light to replace a broken light of her own. The driver was completely unaware that the light was stolen since the driver's neighbor had carefully replaced the light's red encasement. He still had not fixed the left light. Later in the day the driver stopped short in the middle of a highway to prevent hitting a grasshopper. Since neither of the driver's tail lights worked properly, a second driver who was driving behind the first driver did not realize he should stop until it was too late. He collided with the first driver. Both sides agree that the collision would not have occurred if either of the lights were properly functioning.

Question 35

If the second driver asserts a civil claim against the first driver's neighbor, the likely result is that the first driver's neighbor's actions will be found to be:

(A) neither the legal nor actual cause of the second driver's injuries.

(B) the legal but not actual cause of the second driver's injuries.

(C) the actual but not legal cause of the second driver's injuries.

(D) both the actual and legal causes of the second driver's injuries.

Question 36

If the first driver brings an action against the second driver and the second driver argues that first driver was contributorily negligent for driving without taillights, second driver's best argument is that:

(A) the first driver had an absolute duty to maintain his tail lights in good repair.

(B) the first driver is strictly liable for harm caused by defective tail lights.

(C) the first driver was negligent for driving with a light out for a week.

(D) the first driver is the legal cause of the injuries.

Questions 37–38 are based on the following fact situation.

A manufacturer makes a home coffeemaker. A retailer purchased several hundred coffeemakers under an arrangement whereby the retailer was responsible for shipping the merchandise from the manufacturer's factory to his stores.

While loaded with coffeemakers, one of the retailer's trucks skidded on a highway and careened into a guardrail. The appliances were thrown about the truck, toward the front of the cargo area.

A consumer purchased a coffeemaker from the retailer at a reduced price because the box was damaged. The consumer had no reason to assume the appliance inside was damaged as well. A guest at the consumer's home turned on the coffeemaker to make a cup of coffee in the morning. The machine exploded. The guest suffered third-degree burns on his face. The explosion was caused by a defect created in the truck's accident.

Question 37

Will the guest prevail in an action for her injuries against the consumer?

(A) Yes, because the consumer was the owner of the appliance.

(B) Yes, but only if the consumer's conduct was malicious and wanton.

(C) Yes, if the consumer was negligent.

(D) No, because the guest was a social guest.

Question 38

Will the guest recover in an action against the retailer?

(A) Yes, under strict liability in tort.

(B) Yes, under res ipsa loquitur.

(C) No, because there was no privity of contract.

(D) No, because the retailer did not imply any warranty.

Questions 39–40 are based on the following fact situation.

A college student wanted to join a fraternity at school, so he went to a party sponsored by a fraternity house. The college student overheard a fraternity brother whisper to his friend about him, "That guy seems like a real jerk." The college student picked up a cake knife and said to the fraternity brother, "If I was a little more angry, I would slice your throat with this." The college student put the knife down, while pinching the fraternity brother's neck with his fingers. The fraternity brother ordered two pledges to take the college student in their car and drop him off in the woods. The college student was taken to a spot ten miles from the nearest house. The temperature was less than eight degrees Fahrenheit. The college student lost eight fingers and two toes from frostbite and exposure.

Question 39

The college student wants to bring an action against the fraternity brother and the two pledges. The college student will be most likely to succeed if the action is for:

(A) violating a civil rights statute.

(B) strict liability.

(C) negligence by aggravating the college student.

(D) false imprisonment.

Question 40

On what theory would the college student most likely recover for his frostbite damages?

(A) The fraternity brother and his friends acted negligently by placing the college student in peril.

(B) Battery, as the fraternity brother and his friends caused the injuries by touching the college student when they put him the car.

(C) The fraternity ensures the safety of all those present at its parties, and thus had a duty to the college student.

(D) False imprisonment, since he sustained the injuries after being confined in their vehicle.

Question 41

A group of four friends, all minors, stood on the edge of a dock, watching boats enter and depart from the bay. They decided it would be fun to throw rocks at passing vessels. To show off his superior rock-throwing skills, one minor picked up a large rock and tossed it. The rock smashed through the windshield of a yacht. Shards of broken glass entered a yacht owner's left eye, causing a permanent loss of vision.

If the yacht owner asserts a claim against the minor's parents, the yacht owner will:

(A) prevail, because the minor's parents are strictly liable for any tort he commits.

(B) prevail, if they encouraged him to throw rocks.

(C) not prevail, because as a minor he was not able to commit a tort.

(D) not prevail, because parents are generally not liable for their children's torts.

Question 42

A boy and a girl had been close friends since elementary school. The boy was constantly finding himself in dangerous situations from which the girl would save him. Frequently, when the boy would yell for the girl to come help him, she would faithfully run to his rescue. Finally, she got fed up and told the boy that, from now on, he was on his own. Several days later, after eating lunch, contrary to his mother's warnings, the boy went swimming too soon. The boy got a cramp and was struggling to keep his head above the water. The girl was standing on a bridge above him with a rope she was carrying home. The girl would be obligated to throw the rope if:

(A) she heard him ask for her help.

(B) she could save the boy without risking harm to herself.

(C) she caused the boy's perilous situation.

(D) the boy's own negligence did not place him in his perilous situation.

Question 43

A childless widower owned a small house in a neighborhood with many young children. The house was surrounded by a three-foot-high picket fence. A large cashew tree grew in the widower's front yard. One day, an eight-year-old girl climbed up over the fence, then climbed the tree and plucked a few cashews. When she jumped from the tree, she landed on a broken beer bottle, severely lacerating her foot. The girl's parents asserted a claim against the widower.

Which of the following is the most significant in the girl's suit against the widower?

(A) The tree was visible from the street.

(B) The tree and glass were a public nuisance.

(C) The tree and glass were a private nuisance.

(D) The children could have been kept out of the yard at a minimal expense by raising the height of the fence.

Question 44

A law graduate passed the bar exam and filed an application to be admitted to the state bar. He was required to submit a letter of good conduct from every company that had ever employed him. One company wrote a letter stating that the graduate occasionally stole eggs from them when he had been employed as a truck driver. The allegations turned out to be false, but the graduate's application was delayed for more than a year while the investigation was pending.

If the graduate brings a defamation suit against the company, will the graduate prevail?

(A) Yes, because he has proved the statements were false.

(B) Yes, because the statements caused the graduate real and actual harm.

(C) No, if the company reasonably believed that the graduate had stolen the eggs.

(D) No, if eggs were actually stolen while the graduate was on duty.

Question 45

A pilot took his friend for a ride in his private plane. A dense fog set in just before the plane took off, and the airport had been closed. The pilot took off anyway. The pilot was unmoved by the friend's high-pitched screams. The pilot flew the plane, which was manufactured by a company, at speeds twice as fast as those at which the plane was designed to fly. The friend pointed out that the gauges indicated the plane was overheating, but the pilot called her a "party-pooper" and ignored her.

"The engine's on fire," screamed his friend. "Relax," said the pilot, looking over his shoulder at the flaming engine. The pilot proceeded to make a perfect landing in the ocean, one mile from shore. The two climbed out of the cockpit and grabbed the two lifeboats that automatically inflated, and which were made by a manufacturing company and sold with the plane. The pilot and the friend climbed into the lifeboats and paddled away from the sinking plane. The friend's boat had a manufacturing defect and, all of a sudden, sank. As the pilot was rowing over to let the friend climb into his lifeboat, a shark ripped off the friend's left leg.

If the friend brings an action against the manufacturing company of the lifeboat, how will negligence on the part of the pilot affect the action?

(A) It will prevent the friend from recovering from the pilot because the pilot's dangerous flying was a superseding cause.

(B) It will prevent the friend from recovering from the company if the pilot's actions contributed to the friend's injuries.

(C) It is irrelevant because the friend was not injured in the crash landing.

(D) It is irrelevant since the manufacturing company is strictly liable for any defects causing the lifeboat to sink.

Questions 46–47 are based upon the following fact situation.

A tourist was enjoying a camping trip sponsored by a corporation. The trip was scheduled to last seven days and cover 400 miles of wilderness. The tourists were transported in a large luxury bus. At night, they set up tents to sleep in. On the third day of the trip, the bus driver came to a fork in the road. He paused for a moment, but was embarrassed to say he was unsure of which road to take, so he guessed and ended up choosing incorrectly. The driver drove hours out of the way into a very remote area. Several hours after the bus passed the fork, it ran out of fuel. The nearest gas station was seventy-five miles away.

After six hours of sitting in the parked bus, the tourist began to panic. He was worried that he would either starve or freeze to death. The tourist decided to get out of the bus and try to walk to the nearest town. The other passengers decided to wait in hope that another vehicle would pass. Approximately one hour after he left the bus, a bear came along and ate the tourist's entire left leg. The tourist filed a suit against the corporation based on negligence.

Question 46

If the corporation raises the defense of assumption of the risk, who is most likely to prevail?

(A) The corporation, because the other passengers did not venture out.

(B) The corporation, because the tourist should have recognized the danger of leaving.

(C) The tourist, because the group was stranded due to the negligence of the corporation's driver.

(D) The tourist, if a reasonably prudent person would have ventured outside in search of assistance.

Question 47

If another passenger, brings an action under false imprisonment, is he likely to prevail?

(A) Yes, because being confined to the bus is the equivalent of being imprisoned.

(B) No, unless he can prove mental anguish.

(C) Yes, because the driver was negligent.

(D) No, because the driver's mistakes were not made with the intention of sequestering the passengers.

Question 48

On a cold rainy day, a student was riding a bus to her home. The bus was owned by a private company.

The windshield fogged up, limiting the driver's visibility. The company had provided the driver with an extra-quick defogger, a new product it purchased from a retailer. The product, which contained a defogging chemical in an aerosol can, was manufactured by a manufacturing company. The driver carefully read the instructions, which said, "Danger, this product contains isopentanol, a chemical that is extremely toxic if swallowed. Keep out of the reach of children."

Moments after the driver sprayed the defogger, the passengers began coughing. Many of them, including the student, suffered severe burns of the internal respiratory tract.

Isopentanol is a dangerous chemical extremely caustic to the outside layer of internal human membranes.

If the student asserts a claim against the retailer for injuries sustained, will she recover?

(A) Yes, unless she entered the bus without paying the fare.

(B) Yes, if she can recover against the manufacturer.

(C) Yes, unless the retailer altered the spray in any way.

(D) No, unless she can prove retailer was negligent.

Question 49

A professional snake charmer toured the country, performing at county fairs. The snake charmer took several precautions to ensure the safety of his act. All of his snakes were operated on by a doctor so that they would not be able to secrete poisonous venom. Each time he performed, the snake charmer built a fence around himself and posted signs that said, "Warning: these snakes are dangerous."

A spectator at one of the snake charmer's performances bragged to his girlfriend, "It's easy. I could do the same thing." The spectator jumped the fence and grabbed the flute. The snake bit the spectator's leg, causing a localized permanent paralysis. It turns out that the snake was capable of producing venom.

If the spectator brings suit against the snake charmer, is he likely to prevail?

(A) Yes, because a professional snake charmer should have control of the snake at all times.

(B) Yes, because snakes are not domesticated animals.

(C) No, because the snake charmer took reasonable precautions to prevent injury.

(D) No, because the spectator was a trespasser.

Questions 50–51 are based upon the following fact situation.

An employer owned a very large meat packing plant. One day, the employer summoned a longtime employee to her office. The employer accused the employee of being infected with hepatitis and demanded that the employee resign from her job. The employee did not, in fact, have the disease, nor did the employer have any reason to suspect that the employee was ill. In fact, the employer wanted the employee to leave the job so she could hire a recent immigrant at a fraction of the cost. Several of the employee's co-workers overheard the employer's charges against the employee, and they told the employee they did not believe the statements.

Question 50

In an action brought by the employee against the employer, based on defamation, the employee:

(A) must prove she could not find comparable employment.

(B) must prove special damages.

(C) must prove the statements adversely affected her social life.

(D) need not prove special damages.

Question 51

Assume for this question only that the employee was the only person to hear the employer's statements. Which of the following statements is most correct?

(A) The employee will win an action based on defamation if she can prove she suffered severe emotional distress.

(B) The employee will win an action based on defamation if she can prove the employer's statements were made so that she could hire cheap labor.

(C) The employee should base her action on intentional infliction of emotional distress.

(D) The employee will have no cause of action.

Questions 52–53 are based upon the following fact situation.

A business owner is in the business of installing and reconditioning elevators. A statute, enacted for safety reasons, provides that elevators must have a safety device to absorb the impact caused when an elevator travels too fast toward the bottom of a shaft. The business owner regularly purchases this safety device from a retailer. The business owner conducts its own tests on the safety devices.

A company contracted with the business owner to install six new elevators in a tower that the company recently purchased and refurbished.

An employee of the company operated the tower's freight elevator, which was also installed by the business owner and is identical to the other elevators in the building, except that it must be manually operated.

On one occasion, the employee negligently let the elevator drop to the basement at high speed. The safety device, which should have prevented the passengers from being injured, failed. Two passengers suffered serious injuries, as did the employee. The employee would have suffered the same injuries even if the safety device had worked properly because he had been leaning on the drive shaft. Subsequent tests showed that the metal in the safety device was defective. The business owner had performed these same tests before installing the elevator.

Question 52

If the passengers bring a tort action based on products liability against the retailer, which of the following will be the most likely result?

(A) The retailer will prevail, because there was no privity of contract.

(B) The retailer will prevail, because the retailer had a duty to perform the test.

(C) The passengers will prevail, if it is proven that the metal was defective.

(D) The passengers will prevail, unless they put a warning on the safety device.

Question 53

If the passengers bring a negligence action against the business owner, to establish a prima facie case it is necessary that they prove that:

(A) the safety device failed.

(B) the safety device failed and had not been inspected by the business owner.

(C) the safety device failed and the business owner inspected it, but did not discover the defect.

(D) the safety device was defective and would have been discovered had the business owner exercised reasonable care.

Question 54

A college student borrowed his roommate's electric razor. The roommate forgot to warn the student to ground the razor since the razor had some bare wires inside of it that were not visible to the casual user. The student received a severe shock while shaving, causing permanent paralysis in his right arm. If the student asserts a claim against the roommate, he will most likely:

(A) prevail under strict liability in tort, because the shaver was defective when lent by the roommate.

(B) prevail in negligence, because the roommate knew the razor was defective and likely to cause injury and did not warn the student of the danger.

(C) not prevail, because the roommate fulfilled the duty of a gratuitous lender.

(D) not prevail, because the roommate was a gratuitous lender.

Questions 55–56 are based upon the following fact situation.

A man owns a baseball team. At times, the team's fans throw objects out of the stands onto the playing area. During one game against an opposing team the players engaged in a fight that inspired the fans to throw all sorts of objects from the stands. When the opposing team came to town again, the team owner ordered that extra precautions be taken. Fans were searched for cans and bottles as they entered the stadium. Beer was not sold at the stadium concessions. A spectator managed to smuggle a can of beer into the stadium by hiding it in the lining of his jacket. He threw the full can at the opposing team fan in the back row. The can missed the fan, sailed out of the stadium, and landed on a policeman who was patrolling the parking area.

Question 55

If the policeman sues the baseball team owner for damage, he will most likely:

(A) prevail, because an owner is strictly liable to licensees for any hazardous conditions on his property that result in injury.

(B) prevail, because the baseball team owner was on notice that violence may occur.

(C) not prevail, because the baseball team owner was on notice of danger to players only.

(D) not prevail, if the trier of fact determines that the baseball team owner took reasonable actions to prevent injuries.

Question 56

If the policeman asserts a claim against the spectator based on battery, is the policeman likely to prevail?

(A) Yes, because the doctrine of res ipsa loquitur would apply.

(B) Yes, because of the doctrine of transferred intent.

(C) No, because the spectator was lacking the requisite intent.

(D) No, because the policeman was never under any apprehension or fear.

Question 57

On a snowy night, a driver was driving his pickup truck down a state road. He happened to notice a car parked strangely on the side of the road and decided to investigate. Five severely inebriated people were sleeping in the car. The driver opened an unlocked door and tried unsuccessfully to wake the car's occupants. Fearing they would die of exposure, the driver locked his own truck, which was too small to transport the drunks, and started the parked car. He shifted the car into reverse. The driver was unaware that the car's transmission was not working and the car lurched forward instead of going backward, causing it to slide down a ravine. All the occupants suffered serious injuries.

If the passengers assert a claim against the driver, they will most likely:

(A) recover, because they were placed in greater peril when the car was moved.

(B) recover, because the driver did not have any right to move the car.

(C) not recover, because they were inebriated at the time of the accident.

(D) not recover, if the driver acted reasonably.

Question 58

A mugger walked over to a victim, who was standing at a bus stop, and stared at him for a while. The mugger then told the victim, "I am going to slice your throat and then cut you up limb by limb." The victim was afraid for his life and used his talents as sprinter to run away.

If the victim asserts a claim against the mugger, based on assault, is the victim likely to prevail?

(A) Yes, if the victim was under a reasonable apprehension of harmful or offensive contact.

(B) Yes, because the mugger had the requisite intent to bring about the victim's apprehension.

(C) No, because the victim should have known a sprinter could outrun almost anyone.

(D) No, because the mugger did nothing more than talk big.

Questions 59–60 are based upon the following fact situation.

An owner placed an advertisement in the local gazette that stated he was looking for a waitress, fifteen to seventeen years of age. A fifteen-year-old girl called the owner and expressed interest in the job. The girl hesitated when the owner told her she would have to make deliveries atop the many construction sites in the downtown area. The girl met the owner at the foot of a forty-story office building under construction. "I am scared to death, but I need the money for my baby," said the girl. The owner said, "Don't worry, my restaurant always coaches people on how to do this." He then ordered the girl to walk along a steel beam, four hundred feet above the street, and hand a man a can of soda. The girl was afraid for her life, but she made it.

On the way down in the elevator, the girl asked, "Did I get the job?" the owner answered, "I was only kidding. There's no job. I am a construction worker. I do this all the time for kicks." The girl had a nervous reaction that required a six-month hospital stay. The girl then brings a civil suit against the owner.

Question 59

If the owner argues that the girl consented, girl's best argument would be that:

(A) she is a minor.

(B) the owner did not have a restaurant that coached people on how to walk on steel beams.

(C) her consent was obtained by duress.

(D) one cannot consent to a life-threatening activity.

Question 60

If the girl sues the owner for assault, which of the following will be the most relevant evidence of his intent?

(A) The owner knew the walk was dangerous.

(B) The owner had intended for the girl to fall.

(C) The owner wanted to fool the girl.

(D) The owner knew that the girl thought she might fall.

Question 61

A driver parked his car at a bus stop, in violation of a city ordinance, because he had to use a nearby restroom. He had planned on leaving the car for less than two minutes and turned on his hazard lights to warn approaching vehicles. The driver admits he violated a city ordinance that makes it unlawful to park at a bus stop or at any curb painted with a yellow line. A second driver was driving at a safe speed along the same street when a dog ran in front of his car. The second driver managed to avoid the dog by veering right and crashing into the driver's car. A pedestrian, who was standing on the sidewalk waiting for a bus, was hit by the front of the car, which also knocked down a "No Standing" sign.

If the pedestrian asserts a claim against the driver for injuries sustained from the collision, she will most likely:

(A) prevail, because the driver violated a statute.

(B) prevail, because the driver's actions were negligent per se.

(C) not prevail, because her injuries were not of the type the statute sought to prevent.

(D) not prevail, because the statute gives rise to a criminal, not a civil, action.

Question 62

A developer was the developer of a seventy-story luxury condominium complex in a city. She hired a builder, an independent contractor, to build the steel frame of the building. The builder was given carte blanche from the developer to handle all technical matters concerning the construction of this frame.

A week after the frame was completed and the developer had paid the builder, a steel girder fell from the top floor. The end of the girder fell on the building inspector and caused him severe leg injuries.

The inspector brought suit against both the developer and the builder, who both admit that the girder fell because the builder had not followed the standard procedures of the construction industry in building the frame.

In the suit brought by the inspector against the builder, the builder's best argument is that:

(A) the developer's architect provided the specifications for the frame.
(B) the developer assumed all liabilities upon tendering payment.
(C) the structural failure was not due to any lack of care of the builder.
(D) the work was performed on behalf of the developer.

Questions 63–64 are based upon the following fact situation.

A doctor is a surgeon in a very small town. In a routine operation, the doctor removed a victim's gallbladder, but left a pair of scissors in the victim's abdomen. The doctor admitted he left the scissors in and offered to remove them for free. The victim filed suit against the doctor for negligence.

Question 63

To establish a breach of the duty by the doctor, the victim:

(A) must provide an expert from the town to testify that the doctor's conduct was negligent.
(B) must provide an expert in abdominal surgery to testify that the doctor's conduct was negligent.
(C) can rely on the common knowledge of the jurors to decide whether there was negligence.
(D) can rely on the judge to advise the jury if there was negligence.

Question 64

Besides proving negligence, to recover the victim must also prove that:

(A) she would have recovered fully and rapidly had the scissors not been left in her abdomen.
(B) she suffered a loss or detriment due to the scissors.
(C) she suffered permanent injuries due to the doctor's negligence.
(D) she was not guilty of contributory negligence.

Question 65

A mechanic repaired a customer's car pursuant to a written contract and drove the car to her home. The mechanic rang the front doorbell, but the customer did not answer. Assuming the customer had an extra set of keys to the car, the mechanic left his set of keys in the ignition and locked the car's doors. An hour later, a thief broke the car's window and drove away. If the customer brings a claim against the mechanic for damages for the loss of the car, is she likely to prevail?

(A) Yes, because the repair was pursuant to a written contract.

(B) Yes, because by leaving the keys in the ignition, the mechanic created a substantial risk of theft.
(C) No, if the customer told the mechanic that she would be home when the mechanic brought the car.
(D) No, because the act of the thief was a superseding cause.

Question 66

A shopper shopped around for the lowest price on a new compact disc player. He decided to buy one from a very large dealer. The CD player is manufactured by a very reputable electronics manufacturer. Excited with his purchase, the shopper rushed home to use it. On the way home, the bus the shopper had taken was stuck in a terrible traffic jam for more than two hours. Luckily, the shopper had something to read, the CD player's instruction manual, which he read carefully seven times. When he finally got home, the shopper carefully connected the CD player to his stereo. When he turned it on, he received severe burns on his right hand. The manufacturer had pointed the laser beams in the wrong direction, and this mistake caused the burns.

If the shopper brings suit against the manufacturer based on strict liability in tort, will the shopper recover?

(A) Yes, because the product was defective.
(B) Yes, because the shopper would not have an action against the dealer.
(C) No, because there is no evidence that the manufacturer failed to exercise due care.
(D) No, because there was a lack of privity.

Question 67

A driver knew his car's brakes were in poor condition, yet he drove the car anyway. He was driving toward an intersection and did not see the stop sign. By the time he noticed the sign it was too late to stop. Had his brakes been in proper order, he could have stopped in time. A teacher was also driving toward the intersection and saw the driver. The teacher could have stopped, but did not. They had a minor collision. If driver asserts a claim against teacher, driver will most likely:

(A) prevail, for all his damages, if he can prove that the teacher had told a bystander, "I could have stopped, but I wanted to teach that dude a lesson."
(B) prevail, for all his damages, if a comparative negligence statute is in effect.
(C) prevail in full, if a last clear chance statute is in effect.
(D) not prevail, if the motor vehicle code requires that brakes be inspected once a year.

Question 68

A person is under a legal duty to rescue a victim if:

(A) the victim is the person's aunt.

(B) the victim was placed in peril by a stranger.

(C) the victim was placed in peril by the person's negligent actions.

(D) the victim was placed in peril by her own negligent conduct.

Question 69

An art dealer went to a public tag sale conducted by a seller, who was disposing of the furniture and belongings of her late parents. When the seller saw the dealer staring at a painting above a fireplace, she walked over to him and said, "We just had this painting appraised; it is a very old Italian oil. Its value is $6,000. We'll sell it for five," The dealer recognized the painting as a genuine Da Vinci, worth at least a million dollars. He wrote out a check for $5,000 and took the painting to his gallery.

If the seller seeks to recover the painting and asserts an action based on misrepresentation, will she prevail?

(A) Yes, because the dealer's silence in the face of the seller's statements amounted to fraud.

(B) Yes, because failure to disclose material facts can also be a misrepresentation.

(C) No, because the seller was negligent in selecting a bad appraiser.

(D) No, unless the dealer told the seller the painting was worth $6,000.

Question 70

A private company owns and operates a subway system. The subway has a staff of safety engineers who examine the system to ensure the passengers' safety. For the past seven years, the system has been using the X-1, an air-conditioned subway car complete with the latest technological advances.

A forty-year-old blind woman has been riding the subway to work for almost twenty years. When the train pulls into her station she waits for the doors to open and then pokes for the opening with her walking cane. Upon feeling an opening, she steps onto the train. One morning, a train made of X-1 cars pulled into the blind woman's station. As always, the blind woman felt with her cane. The design of the X-1 left a space as large as an open door between the cars. The blind woman mistook the space for an open door and stepped forward. She fell to the tracks and received severe electrical burns from the third rail. A subsequent investigation revealed that twelve blind people had made the same mistake and fallen to the tracks.

If the blind woman asserts a claim against the private company, she will most likely:

(A) prevail, because, as a common carrier, the private company ensured the blind woman's safety while she was on its property.

(B) recover, if the private company could have taken reasonable steps to prevent blind persons from walking onto the tracks.

(C) not recover, because the blind woman assumed the risk.

(D) not recover, because the private company does not insure the safety of its passengers.

Questions 71–72 are based upon the following fact situation.

A famous rock star was constantly followed by a freelance photographer. The rock star brought several unsuccessful actions to prevent what he called harassment by the photographer. The rock star went jogging every morning, and the photographer followed him on a bicycle. One morning, a sudden rainstorm interrupted the rock star's run. He hailed a cab to get back home. The photographer took a photo of the rock star getting into the cab. A large advertisement for a guitar company was affixed on top of the taxi. The photographer sold the photo to a company who sold it to the guitar company. The guitar company used the photo in a major advertising campaign without determining whether the rock star had given consent. As a result of the ads another guitar company canceled its million-dollar-a-year fee to the rock star to endorse its guitars.

Question 71

In an action by the rock star against the first guitar company for invasion of privacy, the rock star will most likely:

(A) prevail, because he is a public figure.

(B) prevail, because the first guitar company accepted the photo without making any attempt to determine if the rock star had granted permission.

(C) not prevail, if the first guitar company determined that the photo was not defamatory.

(D) not prevail, if a reasonable person would conclude the photo was not defamatory.

Question 72

In an action for invasion of privacy by the rock star against the photographer, photographer will most likely:

(A) prevail, because the photograph was taken without the rock star's authorization.

(B) prevail, because the photograph was used for profit.

(C) not prevail, because the rock star was on a public street.

(D) not prevail, because he is a public figure.

Question 73

A former all-state swimmer was walking over a bridge when he heard screams from below. The swimmer looked over the side of the bridge and saw a woman, who screamed, "Help! I have a cramp, and I may not make it to the shore." The swimmer shouted some words of encouragement and walked away. A few moments later, a man, driving his motorcycle at more than twice the speed limit, crashed over the side of the bridge, landed on the woman, and killed her.

In a suit by the woman's estate against the swimmer, the estate will probably:

(A) prevail, because the swimmer was an expert swimmer, and a reasonable man with such skills would have saved the woman.

(B) prevail, because the swimmer's skills created an obligation to save the woman.

(C) not prevail, because the swimmer did not in any way affect the woman's struggle.

(D) not prevail, because the woman assumed all liability by swimming in unsupervised waters.

Question 74

A buyer purchased a brand new car, manufactured by a manufacturing company, from a car dealership. The car was sold as part of a year-end promotion that excluded dealer preparation. The buyer took the car to a service station that performed the preparation. The sales contract provided a thirty-day warranty for parts and labor. Thirty-seven days after purchasing the car, the buyer and his wife were driving along a freeway when the car stalled. The buyer managed to push the car to the side of the road. Since the buyer had no knowledge of car mechanics and the wife did, the wife checked under the hood. The service station forgot to install a gas filter and the gas line was clogged up. The wife repaired the car. She left the hood open while the buyer started the car to make sure all was well. The car started, but a blade from the fan flew out and hit the wife in the face. The blade was defectively manufactured by the manufacturing company. If the wife makes a claim against the manufacturing company for damages based on strict liability, she will probably:

(A) recover, because the manufacturing company is responsible for proper dealer preparation.

(B) recover, because the manufacturing company did not properly manufacture the car.

(C) not recover, because she assumed the risk.

(D) not recover, because there was no privity of contract.

Question 75

A water commissioner testified before a city council committee. "The plumber has bilked the city out of $2 billion. This man's business is corrupt in every aspect. No one should ever do business with this plumber," said the water commissioner. If the plumber asserts a claim against the water commissioner for defamation, is the plumber likely to prevail?

(A) Yes, if the statements were false and the water commissioner knew the statements were false.

(B) Yes, if the statements were false, and the water commissioner would have discovered the falsity had he exercised reasonable care to investigate the charges.

(C) No, if the statements were true.

(D) No, regardless of the truth of the statements.

Questions 76–77 are based upon the following fact situation.

A pedestrian was struck by an automobile driven negligently by a driver. The pedestrian suffered a fractured right hip and required two weeks hospitalization. Three months later, her hip apparently cured, the pedestrian resumed her daily five-mile run. One day, approximately one month after resuming jogging, the pedestrian ran across a busy street at the crosswalk. Ordinarily, she would have made it across with plenty of time to spare, but this time, her hip froze, an after-effect of being hit by a driver. The pedestrian could not move once her hip froze, and she was hit by a car.

If the pedestrian is able to bring a successful action based on negligence against the driver, will she be able to recover for injuries from the second accident?

(A) Yes, if the driver's negligence is found to be a proximate cause of the second accident.

(B) No, because the second accident was not a foreseeable result of the driver's negligent action.

(C) No, because the pedestrian decided to jog and assumed the risk that her hip would freeze.

(D) No, if the pedestrian's physicians pronounced her in good health.

Question 77

If the driver asserts the defense of contributory negligence to the claim arising from the second accident, is it likely to be accepted?

(A) No, because the pedestrian was not negligent.

(B) No, but only if the driver's conduct in the first accident is deemed reckless and wanton.

(C) Yes, because the driver will be able to assert the defense of contributory negligence only with respect to the first accident.

(D) Yes, because in her condition the pedestrian should not have been jogging.

Question 78

A famous actress was the subject of a weekly tabloid. The actress had recently called a press conference to announce that she had AIDS and had been an intravenous drug user for many years. The tabloid wrote that the actress's mother, an octogenarian residing in a nursing home, became sexually active at the age of fourteen and was hospitalized for alcoholism more than twenty-seven times.

If the actress asserts a claim against the tabloid based on invasion of privacy, for the statements about her mother, she will:

(A) not prevail, if the tabloid can prove that the statements about the mother are true and that the newspaper acted without malice.

(B) not prevail, because the actress is a public figure and invited inquiry into her personal life by making the announcement.

(C) not prevail, because the right to privacy is personal.

(D) prevail, because the statements hold the actress up to ridicule and contempt.

Question 79

As part of a promotion, a department store had its employees stuff chocolate bars in the pockets of pedestrians passing the store. A passerby was surrounded by four employees who stuffed chocolate in his jacket pockets. The passerby testified, "I saw them coming at me from across the street, and I thought they were going to mug me. When they reached toward me, I tried pulling out my wallet to give it to them." The passerby desires to bring suit against the employees. The best action for him to bring should be:

(A) battery.

(B) assault.

(C) false imprisonment.

(D) none of the above.

Questions 80–81 are based upon the following fact situation.

A driver was driving along a two-lane road with a passenger in the passenger seat. In the lane going in the opposite direction a car was passing a truck and did not see the driver's car. Facing a potential head-on collision, the driver drove his car off the road, through a barbed wire fence, and into a farmer's tomato patch.

The farmer was furious and drove his tractor as fast as he could toward the driver and the passenger to scare them. He was planning to swerve out of the way at the last moment, but his tire went flat, the tractor went out of control, and it hit a passenger.

Question 80

In an action by the farmer against the driver for the damaged tomatoes, the farmer should:

(A) prevail, because the driver did not have any privilege to enter a farmer's land.

(B) prevail, because the driver damaged the tomatoes.

(C) not prevail, because the driver entered a farmer's property to avoid serious injury.

(D) not prevail, because a farmer threatened the driver with injury.

Question 81

If passenger brings suit against the farmer for battery, he should:

(A) prevail, because the farmer would be liable under strict liability.

(B) prevail, because the farmer tried to scare the passenger.

(C) not prevail, because the farmer did not authorize the passenger to enter his property.

(D) not prevail, because the famer intended to scare, not injure, the passenger.

Question 82

A man and a co-worker were sitting quietly in a bar. The man casually mentioned that he thought a certain football team was lousy. The co-worker stood up and threatened to knock the man's teeth out. The man responded by punching the co-worker. The man continued to beat his co-worker until a customer happened to walk into the bar. The customer pulled out a knife, held it to the man's neck, and said, "Let go of him or you are a dead man." In a suit for assault against the customer, the man is likely to:

(A) prevail, because the threat was real and imminent.

(B) prevail, unless the knife had a dull blade.

(C) not prevail, because the man was the first aggressor.

(D) not prevail, because the customer was just trying to prevent the man from injuring the co-worker.

Question 83

A trespasser often jogged on a golf course near his house. He ignored repeated warnings to leave the area by the groundskeepers. In fact, he taunted the employees when they fertilized the golf course each month. The trespasser would jog alongside the tractor that was spraying fertilizer, forcing the workers to turn the machine off. One day, one of the workers said, "Let's teach this jerk a lesson and leave the machine on." The trespasser was sprayed with toxic chemicals and was severely burned. To prevail in a suit based on battery, the trespasser must establish that:

(A) the toxic chemicals caused severe emotional distress.

(B) his taunting was not the cause in fact of his injuries.

(C) the toxic chemicals constituted a harmful or offensive contact.

(D) he suffered severe injuries.

Question 84

A burglar broke into his neighbor's garage, opened the hood of the neighbor's car, and tried to start the engine. He managed to start the engine, but also caused the car to lunge forward. The burglar was pinned between the car and the wall. The gas tank ruptured and gas spilled all over the garage floor. A passerby heard a burglar screaming for help and ran to assist him. A passerby grabbed a crowbar and managed to free the burglar. The crowbar caused severe cuts in the passerby's hand. "Thanks, you saved my life," said the burglar. "You're welcome," the passerby replied, as he lit a cigarette and threw the match on the floor. The match ignited the spilled gas. Both the burglar and the passerby suffered severe burns.

If the burglar asserts a claim against the passerby for injuries sustained in the fire, the burglar may:

(A) prevail, because the passerby was negligent.
(B) prevail, because the passerby assumed the risk.
(C) not prevail, because the passerby acted gratuitously and was under no duty to rescue the burglar.
(D) not prevail, because the burglar assumed the risk of the passerby's competence by calling him for help.

Questions 85–86 are based upon the following fact situation.

A traveling salesman was driving through a coastal community 500 miles from his home during the beginning of a hurricane. While approaching a flooded intersection, the salesman decided it would be best to abandon his car and seek refuge in a nearby public library. He parked his car on top of a hill to reduce the chances of the car being flooded. The hill belonged to a property owner, who came out screaming as soon as the salesman parked his car. The property owner demanded that the salesman remove his car, but the salesman refused, explaining that the car would likely be damaged by the storm if parked elsewhere. The property owner jumped into the salesman's car, put it in neutral, and rolled it down the hill, causing $4,000 worth of damages.

Question 85

In a suit by the property owner against the salesman for trespass, a necessary element to determine whether the salesman is liable is:

(A) whether a reasonable person would have known the land belonged to the property owner.
(B) whether the salesman knew the land belonged to the property owner.
(C) whether the salesman had a reasonable fear his car would be damaged by the storm.
(D) whether the salesman was on notice to inquire regarding the ownership of the land.

Question 86

In a suit by the salesman against the property owner for damages to his car, should the salesman prevail?

(A) Yes.
(B) No, because he became a trespasser as soon as he entered the property owner's property.
(C) No, because he became a trespasser the moment he refused the property owner's demand that he remove his car.
(D) No, if the property owner proves that the car would have damaged his property.

Question 87

A constructor was building a single-family home on a previously empty lot in a middle-class area. The constructor had a fence built around the lot, but it was often left open after construction hours. Early one evening, a six year-old boy walked through the unlocked fence and played in the house. Intrigued by a strange noise, the boy went up to the top floor and discovered the carpenter cutting wood with an electric buzz saw. A carpenter was unaware of the boy's presence because of the noise created by the saw. The blade of the saw broke loose and struck the boy in the eye. The carpenter had just repaired the saw the day before at the saw repair shop. The boy's guardian filed claims against the constructor, the carpenter, and the saw repair shop.

Concerning the boy's suit against the constructor, the boy should:

(A) prevail, because the constructor should have made sure the gate was locked after hours.
(B) prevail, because construction is an ultra-hazardous activity.
(C) not prevail, because the repair shop's faulty repair acts as an intervening cause.
(D) not prevail, because the duty owed to a trespasser is to merely refrain from inflicting willful and wanton injury.

Question 88

Two attorneys had their offices next door to a shipping company. One attorney constantly complained that trucks making pickups and deliveries at the shipping company blocked the sidewalk. Virtually all of the trucks were owned by the shipping company, who ignored the attorney's requests to keep the sidewalk clear. One day, the second attorney was forced to back out of their driveway without checking for oncoming traffic, because the box company's trucks blocked the view. The shipping company had been cited, on several occasions, for violating city ordinances.

If the first attorney brings suit against the shipping company based on public nuisance, praying for injunctive relief and alleging that he is currently unable to walk past the shipping company's store, the shipping company will most likely prevail if he argues that:

(A) monetary damages are the only remedy available at law.
(B) the attorney consented to the trucks by allowing them over the years.
(C) there was no claim of unique damage.
(D) the attorney should have used abatement by self-help.

Question 89

A pedestrian was hit by a car driven by a driver. Both parties agree that the pedestrian was in a crosswalk and the driver drove past a red light. A bystander tried to stop the bleeding in the pedestrian's leg, but actually aggravated the injury. The pedestrian was rushed to the hospital where he was treated by the doctor. A licensed doctor in the jurisdiction, a graduate of an unaccredited medical school, forgot to put disinfectant on the wound. The pedestrian's leg subsequently became infected, and the pedestrian was forced to walk with a cane. Two months after the injury, while the pedestrian was crossing the street, a passerby grabbed the pedestrian's cane and hit the pedestrian over the head with it. The pedestrian asserted an action based on negligence against the driver.

Will the pedestrian be able to recover damages from the driver due to the passerby's actions?

(A) Yes, because the passerby's actions were a foreseeable intervening cause.
(B) Yes, because one who is negligent is responsible for all results of that negligence.
(C) No, because the passerby's actions were a superseding intervening cause.
(D) No, because the passerby could have assaulted the pedestrian with other weapons.

Question 90

A senator was the subject of a series of stories in the town's newspaper. The newspaper reported that the senator was addicted to cocaine and that this addiction motivated his behavior in office. The newspaper further alleged that the senator used his influence to steer construction contracts to companies controlled by organized crime. The article claimed that "reliable sources" had provided the information. The reporter believed that the story was true.

The senator lost his bid for reelection and suffered severe bouts of depression that caused him to be hospitalized. The senator brought suit against the newspaper based on defamation. Should he prevail?

(A) Yes, because the sources cited are not sufficient for such allegations.
(B) Yes, if he can prove the story was absolutely false.

(C) No, because the newspaper was not aware that the story was false and it did not publish the story with malicious intent.
(D) No, if the newspaper exercised ordinary care to determine the truth or falsity of the statements.

Question 91

A mother was hosting a charity benefit for the local church. Thirty minutes before the guests were scheduled to arrive, she realized she would need much more ice. She sent her sixteen-year-old son to get the ice from the local supermarket. The son, a licensed driver, drove through the residential neighborhood at speeds over eighty miles per hour. He decided he would take his chances and keep going when he came upon a red light. Unfortunately, a car driven by a driver was legally entering the intersection at the same time. The cars collided, causing serious injuries.

If the driver asserts a claim against the mom for injuries suffered, the driver will most likely prevail because:

(A) parents are vicariously liable for torts of their children.
(B) of the doctrine respondeat superior.
(C) she was negligent.
(D) the son was acting as an agent of the mother.

Question 92

A popular disc jockey is on a local morning radio show. One morning, he said over the air, "Those of you running late in this county, hit the pedal to the floor. You can pay off any cop in the county for less than ten dollars." A class action based on defamation was brought by the county patrolmen's association on behalf of six hundred law enforcement officers. The disc jockey will probably:

(A) prevail, because it is obvious he was only joking.
(B) prevail, because a group of six hundred is too large to be collectively defamed.
(C) not prevail, because the language was defamatory and damaged the reputations of the plaintiffs.
(D) not prevail, unless his statements were read verbatim from a script.

Question 93

A farmer raised chickens on a remote farm. His nearest neighbors were 20 miles away. A neighbor bought 20,000 acres of land approximately a half-mile from the farmer's farm and began removing the top layers of soil to recover coal.

The farmer filed written complaints on several occasions, demanding that the neighbor use a brand-name tractor instead of the ordinary tractors being used. He claimed that the brand-name tractors were 80 percent quieter and made fewer vibrations. The farmer had evidence showing that his egg production had been cut in half since the mining began. He personally suffered migraine headaches from the noise.

The neighbor responded with a letter stating that it would cost an extra $14 million per year to use the brand-name tractor and that the company did not feel that the expense could be justified.

In 2005, the farmer's egg sales amounted to $13,000, his best year ever.

In an action by the farmer for personal injuries from the neighbor based on nuisance, the neighbor will most likely:

(A) prevail, if the farmer's injuries were caused by an unreasonable interference with the use of his land imposed by the neighbor.

(B) prevail, because the neighbor is engaged in ultra-hazardous activities.

(C) not prevail, because the expense involved in purchasing the brand name is prohibitive.

(D) not prevail, because the vibrations are a public nuisance.

Question 94

A father received a stun gun as a gift from his wife. The gun emitted an electric charge that could paralyze a person for up to ten minutes. His twelve-year-old son begged his father for weeks to allow him to borrow the gun. Finally, the father relented. The son brought the gun to school and shot a teacher whom he hated for giving too many homework assignments. The teacher fell down on his head and suffered severe neurological damage. If the teacher asserts a claim against the father for injuries sustained, he will most likely prevail because of the rule of:

(A) respondeat superior.

(B) negligence.

(C) non-delegable duties.

(D) caution.

Question 95

A man despised men with long hair. Another man had shoulder-length hair. Every afternoon the second man's wife would drive her car to the front gate of a university and wait to pick up her husband. One day, the first man ambushed the second man while he was walking across the university's campus. The first man held a knife against the second man's neck to instill some fear in him and proceeded to cut the second man's hair with a pair of scissors. The second man's wife saw the entire incident while sitting in her car approximately 100 yards away. Ever since the incident, she has not been able to sleep, forcing her to quit her job.

If the second man's wife asserts a claim against the first man for intentional infliction of emotional distress, the second man's wife should:

(A) prevail, because the first man's actions were extreme and outrageous and would shock the person of average sensibility.

(B) prevail, because the first man's actions were the proximate cause of the wife's injuries.

(C) not prevail, because the first man was unaware of the wife's presence.

(D) not prevail, because the wife was outside the zone of danger.

Question 96

A famous movie star starred in dozens of movies. She often appears on television shows. A tabloid decided to capitalize on the star's popularity and placed her picture on the newspaper's cover. Research has shown that the newspaper's sales tripled after publication of the issue in which the star was featured on the cover. If the star asserts a claim against the tabloid based on invasion of privacy, the star will most likely:

(A) prevail, because her picture was appropriated for the tabloid's commercial advantage.

(B) prevail, because a magazine cover story interferes with one's solitude.

(C) not prevail, because commercial advantage may be taken of a public figure.

(D) not prevail, because the tabloid may use the star's picture for profit in this manner.

Question 97

A lawyer was depressed over not being offered a job at a prestigious law firm. His anger was fueled when he found out who got the job. The lawyer wrote a letter informing the law firm that the associate at the firm enjoyed having sexual relations with sheep and sent a copy of the letter to the State Bar Ethics Committee. Neither the law firm nor the committee made the contents of the letter public. Upon learning of the letter, the associate became clinically depressed. His condition required several months of hospitalization. The associate brought suit against the lawyer based on defamation. Proof that the statement is true will:

(A) not be a defense.

(B) be a defense only if the lawyer was sure his letter was true at the time he wrote it.

(C) be a defense only against punitive damages.

(D) be a defense.

Question 98

A buyer purchased an auto from a car dealership. The car was manufactured by a car manufacturing company. The buyer ordered an option called "ultimate cruise," which regulated the car's speed and was set by the driver. "Ultimate cruise," manufactured by a cruise control manufacturing company works by automatically controlling the gas pedal and brakes to keep a constant speed. The brakes were manufactured by a brakes manufacturing company. The gas pedal system was manufactured by a gas pedal manufacturing company.

A week or two after the buyer bought his car, he decided to go for a long drive with his family. He drove out to the country, where, for the first time, he was able to use the "ultimate cruise." The buyer did not know that there was a malfunction in the system. The "ultimate cruise" signaled the gas pedal to the floor. To prevent the car from going too fast, the brakes were signaled to be used for three hours straight. When approaching a toll plaza, the buyer turned the "ultimate cruise" off and stepped on his brake to stop. Since the linings were completely worn down, the buyer could not stop the car in time, and he slammed into a toll-collecting machine. The buyer, his wife, and his three children all suffered serious injuries. The buyer's six-year-old son asserted claims against the car, the cruise control, the brakes, and the gas pedal manufacturing companies, based on strict liability in tort.

The buyer's son should prevail against:

(A) the brake manufacturing company, because the brakes failed.

(B) the cruise control manufacturing company only, because the "ultimate cruise" was defective.

(C) the brake and the cruise control manufacturing company, because the "ultimate cruise" and brakes combined to cause the injuries.

(D) the brake, the cruise control, and the gas pedal manufacturing companies because the "ultimate cruise" system comprised all three systems.

Question 99

A woman and her younger sister had despised each other ever since their mother died and litigation concerning the estate began. The older sister knew the younger sister had a pathological fear of burglars. One night the older sister dressed up in black and walked across the younger sister's living room, after gaining entry through an open door. The younger sister was in the shower at the time, but her fiancé saw the older sister in the living room and chased her out. The fiancé ran upstairs to tell the younger sister what had just happened. She passed out and cracked her skull when the fiancé told her.

If the younger sister asserts a claim against the older sister based on intentional infliction of emotional distress, the fact that the fiancé told her of the "burglar" will:

(A) relieve the older sister of liability, because the fiancé's actions made the younger sister's reaction foreseeable.

(B) relieve the older sister of liability, because the fiancé was the immediate cause of the injury.

(C) relieve the older sister of liability, because the fiancé acted as a mitigating circumstance.

(D) not relieve the older sister of liability, because she intended to frighten her sister and her intent was achieved.

Question 100

A dairy farm owner was notified that the inspector for the Department of Agriculture would be inspecting her farm. "Go right ahead, look around," said the dairy farm owner when the inspector arrived. The inspector walked to the area used to milk cows. He stood in the area specifically designed for the cows, and not for people. He put his hand inside the machine used for milking. The cows were all out to pasture, having already been milked that morning. Someone suddenly turned the machine on, and severed three of the inspector's fingers. Upon later inspection, it was found that the milking machines and their switches were all in proper working order. If the inspector brings suit against the dairy farm owner based on negligence, he will:

(A) recover, because the dairy farm owner or an employee was negligent.

(B) recover, because the dairy farm owner is strictly liable.

(C) not recover, because the inspector assumed the risk.

(D) not recover, because the inspector was a licensee.

Question 101

A passenger is flying on a commercial airline in the dreaded middle seat. Another flyer is seated next to the passenger, and the flight attendant serves the other flyer a total of six drinks in an hour. The passenger attempts to avoid conversation with the other flyer, despite the flyer's best attempts to engage him. The passenger could have moved, but did not, as he was already settled. After the passenger repeatedly rebuffs the flyer, the flyer becomes enraged and hits the passenger over the head with his laptop.

If the passenger sues the airline for battery, what is the likely result?

(A) The passenger will not prevail because he assumed the risk.

(B) The passenger will prevail because the contact with the laptop was intentional and offensive.

(C) The passenger will not prevail because the other flyer is not an agent of the airline.

(D) The passenger will prevail if the flight attendant acted with reckless disregard in serving the other flyer the rinks.

Questions 102–103 are based upon the following fact situation.

A driver decided to take his brand new car out for a spin. He had just bought it yesterday, brand new from a dealership. As he came upon a stop light, he tried to break, but the breaks failed and he rear-ended a hockey fan, who was on his way to the game.

The two exchanged insurance information, and despite the fact that the hockey fan's neck and back were sore, he continued on to the game. While at the game, he slipped and fell on a puddle of beer. That fall caused him to break his back and be paralyzed.

Question 102

If the hockey fan asserts a negligence claim against the driver, will he prevail?

(A) Yes, because accidents like this do not normally happen but for negligence, and the driver was in complete control of his car.

(B) Yes, because a reasonable driver would have know his breaks were in need of repair.

(C) No, because the driver in no way breached his duty to the hockey fan.

(D) No, because the car manufacturer should be liable.

Question 103

If the hockey fan sues the hockey arena for negligence, what effect will the previous accident have on his recovery?

(A) His recovery will be barred, since the hockey arena had nothing to do with the prior accident.

(B) It will have no legal effect.

(C) His recovery will limited to just what an average person would have been injured, had they slipped and fallen.

(D) His damages will exclude those caused by the prior accident.

Torts

Answer 1

(A) The commuter was an invitee. An invitee is generally a patron of a business open to the public. The invitor has a special duty to an invitee because the invitee is considered to have entered the invitor's premises in response to an express or implied invitation. There is an affirmative duty to protect the invitee against all dangers of which the invitor is or should be aware. (B) is incorrect. Actual knowledge is not required; the school will be charged with constructive knowledge if it should have known about the hazard by reasonable inspection. (C) and (D) are irrelevant because the commuter was an invitee. Whether he was in invitee does not hinge on his appointment status, nor does it hinge on whether he paid for the services received.

Answer 2

(B) A manufacturer who sells a product in a defective condition that is unreasonably dangerous to the foreseeable user is strictly liable for injury if (1) the manufacturer is in the business of sales to the general public (C), (2) the product reaches the consumer in substantially the same condition in which it was sold (A), and (3) the product's defect was the actual and proximate cause of injuries (D). (B) is the correct answer. The requirement that the injured party be in privity with the manufacturer to sustain a product liability action has been abolished in all jurisdictions. Remember that the question is asking what need NOT be proven, so you have to think about what is required for products liability and eliminate those as "wrong" answers.

Answer 3

(A) Comparative negligence statutes allow recovery based on relative degrees of fault when both parties were negligent. The recovery of each party is based on the damages incurred. A pure comparative negligence statute requires that each party pay for the percentage of damage that he caused. The mechanic's $4,000 in damages will be reduced by his 60 percent of fault, to equal $1,600. The security guard's $3,000 damages are reduced by 40 percent to total $1,800. From these calculations, the security guard owes the mechanic $1,600 and the mechanic owes the security guard $1,800; the security guard has a net recovery of $200. A modified comparative negligence jurisdiction will not allow a party who was more than 50 percent at fault to recover. The mechanic would be liable to pay for the security guard's entire sum of damage ($3,000) in such a jurisdiction. (B) is incorrect because the last clear chance doctrine provides that the person who had the last clear chance to avoid the accident, but failed to do so, is wholly liable. Last clear chance is used by the plaintiff as a defense to contributory negligence. It would not apportion the damages. (C) is incorrect because a plaintiff may be denied recovery under the Assumption of Risk Doctrine on the theory that the plaintiff knew the situation contained a risk and then voluntarily assumed that risk. Since neither party in our case knew of the other's reckless driving, this doctrine does not apply. (D) is incorrect because contributory negligence is a defense that completely bars the plaintiff from recovery if he is at all negligent. The inequitability of this doctrine led to the adoption of comparative negligence statutes.

Answer 4

(D) The suit will not prevail unless there was negligence on the part of the patient. If she believed she had a claim, there would be no negligence. (A) is incorrect because whether her suit was lacking probable cause will have no bearing on the defamation claim. (B) is incorrect because even if the action was motivated by improper purposes, the patient was not necessarily negligent in telling people she was bringing a malpractice suit. (C) is incorrect because although it is a correct statement of law, here there would be special damages if the doctor can prove that he lost clients.

Answer 5

(A) The elements that must be present to support strict liability in a product liability tort case are (1) an absolute duty owed by a merchant or commercial supplier to the user, (2) a breach of this duty (a defect), (3) the defect actually and proximately causes injury, and (4) damages. The multiplex is a "popcorn merchant" because its business includes the regular sale of popcorn. This merchant-supplier requirement is meant to exclude a casual one-time seller from strict liability, such as one who sells his personal washing machine. There is no requirement that the sale of the particular good must be the defendant's primary business activity. The rancid butter constituted a defect in the product. (B) is incorrect because the cannery is not a merchant or a supplier of boilers. The plaintiff may have prevailed on a theory that the cannery owed its visitors a duty that the plant was free from hazards, but this is different from products liability. Pay careful attention to what claims are being brought in both the fact patterns and the answers. (C) is incorrect because the airline uses planes, but does not make or sell them. Again, we are dealing with the wrong claim. You might feel that the airline was negligent, but that is much different from products liability. The instructions given in (D) are appropriate, since strict liability does not depend on fault.

Answer 6

(D) The elements of intentional infliction of emotional distress are (1) an extreme and outrageous act by defendant, (2) intent by defendant to cause plaintiff severe emotional distress, (3) causation, and (4) damages. The plaintiff must establish that the defendant intended to cause the plaintiff emotional distress. Such intent requires, at the very least, that the defendant know that there is a very high probability that his actions will cause the plaintiff emotional distress. The defendant did not have the necessary intent since he did not know that the plaintiff was the victim's brother. Although the defendant in (A) could use the defense of private necessity to a trespass action, he is still liable for the actual damages he caused. In (B), the defendant's purposeful beating of the plaintiff's dog rendered him liable for trespass to chattels. Since the dog was on a leash, the defendant doesn't seem to have a valid claim of self-defense. The plaintiff will most likely prevail on his conversion suit in (C). Conversion is the intentional exercise of control over a chattel that interferes with the true owner's right to dominion over it. To establish liability, it is only necessary that the defendant intend to control the chattel, but the defendant need not know the chattel belongs to another.

Answer 7

(D) All four choices deal with the issue of intervening causes. An intervening cause occurs after the negligence of the defendant and adds to or causes the damage. The issue related to intervening causes is at what point the defendant should be relieved of liability. The rule is that the defendant will be liable for the entire damage if the intervening cause was foreseeable. This rule provides that if a defendant should have reasonably foreseen that the resultant injury might occur in the due course of events, the court will find that the defendant has proximately caused the injury and is liable. If the intervening action was unforeseeable, then the defendant's negligence will have been superseded, and the defendant will not be held liable for that damage attributed to the intervening cause. (A), (B), and (C) are generally considered foreseeable events by the courts and therefore are not superseding intervening causes. The defendant will be liable for causation of the entire injury. Extraordinary acts of nature are generally considered unforeseeable, which makes them superseding causes of injury. In this case, the victim was no more likely to be hit by lightning while waiting on the highway than if he were driving five miles away.

Answer 8

(D) In a medical malpractice case, the majority rule is that when a foreign object is left in the body, the statute begins to run at the time the injury is discovered. (B) and (C) are rules followed in other types of malpractice cases. (A) is the traditional rule, but is no longer followed in the majority of jurisdictions. (C) would normally be the correct answer, as with medical malpractice the general rule is that the statute of limitations begins to toll when the malpractice should have been discovered. However, there is an exception for objects left in the body, which is why (D) is the correct answer.

Answer 9

(D) If one knowingly, voluntarily, and unreasonably subjects himself to a risk, he has assumed the chance of injury. On this basis, the truck driver's recovery may be limited or denied. Once the truck driver read the sign, he knew that he was encountering a dangerous environment. (C) differs from the assumption of risk. It refers to the doctrine of contributory negligence, which provides that if the plaintiff was at all negligent he will be barred from recovery. (C) is not the best answer because most states abolished the contributory negligence defense in enacting comparative negligence statutes. (A) and (B) are incorrect because even though this may be considered an ultra-hazardous activity, and thus fall under strict liability, one can still assume the risk. Also, while demolition work would most likely be considered ultra-hazardous, the fact that it was "off the beaten path" works against strict liability.

Answer 10

(D) Justification is a "catch-all" defense to intentional torts, including false imprisonment. Although all the elements of false imprisonment were present in this question, the driver's defense of justification contends that since his actions were justified, he had a privilege to take such action. A court allowed the defense of justification upon similar facts by finding that the driver had a duty to take reasonable safety measures (Sindle v. New York City Transit Authority, 307 N.E. 2nd 245 (NY 1973)). Necessity is the privilege to harm a property interest during an emergency. The harm may be done for the public good (A) or for the private individual (B). A person is allowed to use self-defense when he believes he is in danger of imminent harm (C). Since there is no evidence that the children were going to harm the driver, justification is his best defense. There is a good chance that this question took you by surprise, as you may not have heard of the "justification" catch-all defense. This is quite common. However, now you know!

Answer 11

(D) Defamation encompasses the doctrines of slander and libel. Although the two sometimes overlap, slander is oral defamation and libel is printed, therefore (C) would be incorrect. For defamation to be actionable, there must be publication of the defamatory material, which is accomplished merely by communication to one person other than the plaintiff. The boss's dictation to his secretary will be treated by some courts as if he wrote the letter himself without an intermediary. However, most courts will consider it libel when the defamatory words are taken down by a third person, therefore (A) is incorrect. Restatement (Second) of Torts § 577 provides that dictation to a stenographer who takes notes is libel. Although these words were spoken, they would be treated as libel and not slander. An action for libel does not require that the plaintiff suffer actual damages. Therefore, answer (B) is incorrect. (D) is correct because of the privilege to make statements that the author reasonably believes to be true in settings where candor is encouraged, such as financial statements.

Answer 12

(B) The general rule is that an employer is not responsible for the negligence of an independent contractor (C). However, this rule does not excuse the employer from its own negligence. In our case, the city should have foreseen harm when it hired a contractor known to be incompetent. The knowledge of the company's incompetence created a duty in the city to reasonably inspect the safety of the company's work site. (D) is partially correct because the city also owed the woman a duty as an invitee, but the city has not breached this duty unless they had actual or constructive knowledge of the danger. The city will not be held strictly liable for the woman's injury. (A) is incorrect because charitable immunity has been abrogated in most jurisdictions and is filled with exceptions in where it remains in effect.

Answer 13

(D) The tort of interference with contractual advantage is committed by a person who induces someone to breach a contract he has entered with another. The clients breached their contracts with the employer by paying the employee instead of making their payments due to the company. The employee has not committed conversion (C). The taking of another's cash will not qualify as conversion because money is not a chattel. (A) is incorrect because intangible rights closely linked to a document have been recognized as the subject of conversion, but no such document was present in the employee's case. Embezzlement (B) involves the conversion of property entrusted to an employee by the employer. The employee was never entrusted with property by the employer.

Answer 14

(C) The elements of negligence are: (1) a duty, (2) breach of this duty, (3) proximately causing injury, and (4) damages. The president had a duty to hold the bonds in safekeeping. He breached this duty when he accidentally housetrained his puppy with them. The breach proximately caused injury to the entrepreneur and resulted in damages. He did not commit trespass to the entrepreneur's bonds (A) because he had the right to their possession. Conversion requires intent (B) to maintain dominion over the property. The president had no such intent.

Answer 15

(B) The owner of a chattel (personal property) may bring a tort action against someone who deprives him of use or possession of that chattel. Trespass to chattels and conversion only differ in the extent to which the plaintiff was deprived of property. The Multistate will often ask questions that require knowledge of the fine line distinction between these two torts. The elements of trespass to chattels are (1) an act interfering with plaintiff's right to possess his chattel, (2) intent to perform the act, (3) actual deprivation of property, and (4) damages. The elements of conversion are (1) wrongful possession of chattel of such serious nature or consequence to warrant that the defendant pay the rightful owner its full value, (2) intent to control the chattel, and (3) causation. To distinguish between trespass and conversion, the court will examine the time period of the deprivation, the extent of deprivation, the defendant's intent, the harm done to the chattel, the inconvenience to the plaintiff, and the expenses the plaintiff incurred as a result. The more significant the deprivation, the more likely it will be classified as conversion. (B) is the correct answer if a three-month deprivation of property is sufficient interference to qualify as conversion (Restatement (Second) § 222A, illus. 2). The rightful owner of the hat was deprived of the entire use of this expensive item for the rest of the winter and might have understandably replaced it.

Answer 16

(B) The husband's bad faith will present sufficient grounds for conversion despite the short period of deprivation (Restatement (Second) § 222A, illus. 4).

Answer 17

(A) Interference with prospective advantage is a tort committed when a person unlawfully interferes to cause another the loss of future income. It differs from the tort of interference with contractual advantage (B) in that it doesn't require deprivation of a contractual benefit, only the unlawful interference with a relatively certain economic return. (B) is not a basis for the landlord's action because a tenancy at will does not create a contract right. (C) and (D) are not names of torts.

Answer 18

(D) Private nuisance is the interference with one's use and enjoyment of land. Repeated telephone calls have been ruled private nuisance (Wiggins v. Moskins Credit Clothing Store, 137 F. Supp. 764 (EDSC. 1956)). The elements of a prima facie case for intentional infliction of emotional distress are (1) an extreme and outrageous act by a defendant, (2) intent to cause severe emotional distress, (3) causation, and (4) damages. Invasion of privacy can be based on one of four actions: (1) appropriation, (2) intrusion, (3) public disclosure of private facts, or (4) false light. Intrusion has been held to include persistent phone calls. Therefore, the homeowner may assert an action based on any of these three torts.

Answer 19

(C) When damages have been caused by two or more independent causes the plaintiff can recover from either or both. Pursuant to these facts, neither the railroad nor the farmer will be liable for that portion of damage caused by the other. With respect to the railroad's liability, the farmer's actions will be deemed a superseding cause of damage because intentional torts are not considered foreseeable. Since the farmer's actions were subsequent to the railroad strike, the second may only recover from the farmer that damage he actually caused. The second farmer must prove the decrease in value of his apples caused by the derailment. (A) is incorrect because even though the farmer is not responsible for the strike, he can still be held responsible for the damages caused by his actions. (D) is incorrect for the same reasons that (C) is correct, he can only be held responsible for the damages he actually caused. (B) is incorrect because it is irrelevant to the question.

Answer 20

(C) A defendant will usually be liable for all harm caused directly by his negligence and for all harm caused by foreseeable intervening events that would not have occurred in the absence of his negligence. Such foreseeable events include medical malpractice and a plaintiff's subsequent actions. A defendant will not be held liable for those further consequences caused by unforeseeable intervening events, also called superseding causes. (C) is the correct choice because medical malpractice has been ruled a foreseeable event, and not a superseding cause. (D) is an incorrect choice because the child was reacting in a reasonable manner to the situation the driver created, so his actions are considered foreseeable. In addition, (C) is the only answer that is "different," as in if (D) is correct, both (A) and (B) also have to be correct, and so forth. This is one way to determine how to eliminate answer choices. Also, please pay attention to the call of the question, which asks LEAST correct, so you have to reverse your thinking, so to speak.

Answer 21

(B) As a general rule, a parent is not vicariously liable for the torts of a child (and A is therefore incorrect). However, if a parent has knowledge of the child's proclivity to commit the specific tort, encouraged the behavior, or directed or ratified the child's tortious conduct, the parent will be liable. A young child is considered capable of forming the intent (D) required for an intentional tort. All that is necessary is that the child has knowledge to a substantial degree of certainty that the prohibited results will follow. (C) is incorrect because it is far too general: While a parent is not vicariously liable for the torts of the child, and not ALWAYS liable, similarly, they are not NEVER liable.

Answer 22

(B) Minors are held liable for assault and battery, trespass, conversion, defamation, seduction, deceit, and negligence (Prosser § 134). Prosser quoted Lord Kenyon, who said, "If an infant commits an assault or utters slander, God forbid that he should not be answerable for it in a court of justice." However, a child will not be held liable if incapable of forming the requisite intent. To prove intent, the best friend only needs to show that the boy knew to a substantial degree of certainty that by swinging his arm at his friend he would strike him and cause him harm. At age seven, and after having been encouraged by his father, the boy knew what he was doing and is thus liable for his torts. (C) is incorrect. Parents are not solely responsible for their child's conduct.

Answer 23

(B) The elements of battery are (1) harmful or offensive contact, (2) intent, and (3) causation. The little shove that the customer gave the salesman is enough to constitute a battery. The customer's actions are not nearly outrageous enough for intentional infliction of emotional distress (D). (A) is incorrect because he didn't put him in apprehension of a harmful contact, he actually made contact with him. (C) is incorrect because there was nothing defamatory said in the fact pattern regarding salesman.

Answer 24

(C) The accident was caused by the company's negligence. A car driving at any speed could have been hit by the train. The girl's age and lack of a driver's license were not factors in the accident and will not play a role in the case. "Last clear chance" (D), the doctrine providing that the party with the last opportunity to avoid the accident is wholly liable for the ensuing damages, is completely unaffected by whether the girl had a license to drive. In addition, (A) is too broad because it doesn't necessarily prove she was negligent. It MAY prove she was, but not necessarily. Be careful of overbroad statements. (B) is also incorrect, as she was not a trespasser.

Answer 25

(B) One is liable for all consequences proximately caused by his negligence whether foreseeable or not. This is because "the defendant takes the plaintiff as he finds him" (Watson v. Rinderknecht, 84 NW 9798 (Minn. 1901)). (C) and (D) are incorrect because it does not matter that hemophilia is rare, or that an ordinarily person would not have died. As stated above, you take the plaintiff as you find him, so if you cut a hemophiliac, and he dies, you are still responsible for that death.

Answer 26

(C) To recover under strict liability in a product liability suit, a plaintiff must prove (1) an absolute duty owed to users by a commercial supplier or merchant, (2) breach of duty (a defect), (3) actual and proximate cause, and (4) damages. The breach of duty will be established by showing that the product is defective. There are two types of defects: manufacturing and design. Manufacturing defects are easier to prove. They exist when the product deviates from its intended design in a manner that makes it unreasonably dangerous. Design defects exist when the product has been designed in an unreasonably dangerous manner. Restatement of Torts defines defective as "unreasonably dangerous" to users. (A) is an element that will help show the defective design, but it is not imperative that (A) be established. (B) is extraneous to a strict liability action. While an insufficient warning may be considered a design defect (D), a warning will not absolve the defendant of liability for an unreasonably dangerous product.

Answer 27

(A) To establish the strict liability of a retailer, a plaintiff needs to prove (1) sale by the defendant, (2) existence of the defect, (3) proximate cause, and (4) that the defect existed at the time the product left the defendant. Privity (B), involvement in the product's design (C), and knowledge of the hazard (D) are not necessary elements.

Answer 28

(A) Under a pure comparative negligence statute one recovers or pays damages based upon his percentage of fault, even if it is greater than 50 percent. Under a modified comparative negligence statute (adopted in a majority of jurisdictions), a plaintiff will recover only if he is less than 50 percent negligent (B). Make sure that the answer choice you choose, even if it is a correct statement of law, is also correctly answering what is being asked. Here, even though (B) is the correct statement of law as applied to modified comparative negligence, that is NOT what is being asked. Pay close attention to all facts, as well as the question stem. (D) is incorrect since the employee did not have the last clear chance to avoid the accident.

Answer 29

(A) Since the customer was not aware, and did not have reason to be aware, of any defect, he was not negligent. The driver was negligent in opening the car door and, therefore, will be liable. The employee's negligence (B) is irrelevant in a suit between the customer and the driver. A superseding cause would potentially relieve the garage of liability, not the driver (C). (D) does not absolve the driver of negligence. The mere fact that she did not assume a specific risk, does not excuse her otherwise negligent actions.

Answer 30

(B) The ordinance regarding trespassing is in no way related to the present action and will therefore not affect the outcome. The teenager is not absolutely liable (C) as a result of his trespassing; his negligence must still be proven. The teenager trespassed (D) on private property and will be civilly liable to the club's owners, but not liable under the criminal statute this question addresses. Violation of a statute will not prevent the teenager from acting as a witness (A).

Answer 31

(D) As long as the defendant's negligent act is the proximate cause of injury, the defendant is liable for the entire extent of the plaintiff's injuries, no matter how bizarre. The fact that the construction worker's shoulder was extra-sensitive is irrelevant.

The defendant can't choose his plaintiff; he takes him as he finds him. (C) is incorrect because liability attaches regardless of whether the teenager could foresee the potential consequences.

Answer 32

(D) A plaintiff suing under strict liability in a tort action is not entitled to recover for pure economic loss. The employee may sue for his lost income during his convalescence, but the owner of the transport company may not recover the loss her business incurred while she lacked a driver. She might recover this loss under an express warranty theory if the van had been expressly and unconditionally guaranteed. The auto store's knowledge of the intended use of the van (A) is irrelevant to a strict liability action. It will only be a factor in the determination of whether there exists an implied warranty of fitness for a particular purpose. (C) is irrelevant because privity is no longer a requirement in product liability cases. In a majority of jurisdictions, (B) is incorrect because a seller of used goods is not strictly liable for those defects not created by him. With used goods it is understood that the product has been altered between the time it left the manufacturer and the time it reached the salesman.

Answer 33

(A) The elements of false imprisonment are (1) an act that unlawfully confines or restrains a person to a bounded area against her will, (2) awareness of the confinement by the plaintiff, (3) intent, and (4) causation. To satisfy the first element, the restraint may be by acts or words. False imprisonment has been found where the unlawful act was directed toward a person's property. Although the employee said the traveler was free to go, she was restrained by his threat to deprive her of her property. Since she could only leave if she let the employee hold onto her bag of valuables, the traveler should win her action based on false imprisonment.

Answer 34

(A) An action for private nuisance arises when one party causes substantial and unreasonable interference with the use or enjoyment of another's property. (C) is not correct because intent is not an element of private nuisance. (D) is incorrect because, although the relative values of the restaurant and power plant are relevant in determining the form of the remedy, they are not relevant in determining whether the utility is liable for nuisance. (B) is incorrect because nuisance law protects a person's interest in the use and enjoyment of property. One use of property might be the conduct of business, but a business entity does not receive special protection in the absence of a property interest.

Answer 35

(D) Causation in negligence cases requires that the act be both the actual and proximate cause of the injury. One's conduct is considered the cause in fact of an injury if "but for" the act of the defendant the injury would not have taken place. This is called the "but for" test and is easily satisfied. Another test for causation in fact is whether the defendant's action was a "substantial factor" in bringing about the injury. The substantial factor test is useful when there are concurrent causes of injury. To establish liability, the conduct must also be the legal or proximate cause of the injury. Proximate cause is more narrowly drawn than cause in fact and is largely driven by policy considerations that seek to limit the defendant from infinite liability for his actions. An act will generally be considered the proximate cause of injury if no "superseding" acts have intervened. Since the second driver would have been able to stop if the driver had a functioning brake light, the first driver's neighbor's action was a "substantial factor" in the chain of events causing the injury. "But for" the first driver's neighbor's actions the accident would not have occurred. There were also no superseding acts subsequent to the first driver's neighbor stealing the light. Therefore, she is an actual and proximate cause of the injury.

Answer 36

(C) The second driver's best argument is that it is unreasonable to drive for a week without fixing a nonfunctional taillight. (D) may be correct, but it is not the second driver's best argument. The first driver's role in causing the accident is a conclusion that must be drawn from the facts. Remember you are looking for the BEST argument. This means there might be more than one accurate answer, but one will always be stronger than the other. In addition, courts do not impose strict or absolute liability for driving with a broken taillight (A and B).

Answer 37

(C) The consumer will be held liable if she was negligent. (B) is incorrect because the consumer would be liable not "only" for the malicious and wanton infliction of injuries, but also for negligence, etc. The word "only" makes the choice incorrect. (D) is incorrect. Hosts do have a duty toward their social guests

Answer 38

(A) A seller is liable under strict liability if (1) he is engaged in the business of selling such product, (2) the product travels from the seller to the consumer without substantial change, (3) the product is defective (unreasonably dangerous to the user or consumer), and (4) the defect causes injury. (B) might be an alternate avenue of liability, but strict liability in tort is much more certain of success.

This seller can be liable even though the manufacturer was not, because the goods were damaged while in the seller's possession.

Answer 39

(D) The fraternity brother and his boys had no right to throw the college student into their car. The college student was unlawfully confined to the car against his will. One important element of false imprisonment is awareness of the confinement. If the college student had been unconscious while he was in the car, he would be unlikely to succeed. (B) is incorrect because strict liability only applies to wild animals, products, and ultra-hazardous acitivites. A fraternity party, while it may HAVE wild animals, is not something that falls under strict liability. (A) is incorrect because there is nothing to indicate that any civil rights statute has been violated. The fact pattern only tells you there is a college student and a fraternity, so there is nothing to indicate that anyone was discriminated against based on race.

Answer 40

(A) Leaving someone out in the elements on a cold night constitutes negligence. When looking at a negligence claim, it must first be determined whether there is a duty. The fraternity brother and his friends had no general duty to the college student, but as soon as they forcibly took him into the woods, a duty was created. They breached this duty by leaving him out in cold temperatures, which a reasonable person would not do. This caused his injuries. (C) is incorrect because it is untrue. Remember, those statements that are too broad are usually incorrect. (D) is incorrect because it is not the correct statement of law. Remember that an answer is never correct if it only states part of the law.

Answer 41

(B) Parents are generally not vicariously liable for the torts of their children. However, there are exceptions to this rule, one of which is when the parent encouraged the tort. (C) is false; a minor can commit a tort. Note: This question illustrates a classic Multistate ploy. Read each choice carefully! You may be tempted to think that the yacht owner may not prevail because you learned that parents cannot be generally liable for the torts of their children, knocking out answer (A). However, remember that if the parents encourage such a tort OR have a reason to know of a tendency to commit such torts, they can be liable. Remember, sentences including words like "never" and "always" are rarely true.

Answer 42

(C) As part of the cause of action for negligence, the boy must prove that the girl had a duty to rescue him. Generally, no duty exists—even between friends—unless the defendant either causes the peril or actually commences a rescue attempt (in which case she is obligated to use reasonable care in finishing the rescue). (A) and (B) are incorrect because even if she did hear him ask for help, or could have helped, there is still no duty to save someone.

Answer 43

(D) These questions involve knowledge of the elements of attractive nuisance. An attractive nuisance is an artificial condition on one's property that may attract children and subsequently injure them. The elements are (1) a dangerous condition on one's land of which one should be aware, (2) the knowledge that children frequent the area, (3) children are unable to appreciate the risk, and (4) the expense of remedying the danger is slight when compared to the risk. Dorothy is most likely to prevail if a cost-benefit analysis tips in her favor. (A) is related to the likelihood that children will trespass on the widower's property, but will not be as significant as the cost of preventing the nuisance.

Answer 44

(C) The elements of defamation are (1) defamatory language, (2) concerning the plaintiff, (3) publication, (4) damage to the reputation, and (5) intent. Truth is an absolute defense, but that is not the case here. In addition, "qualified privilege" may be available to some indvidiuals, as a defense in circumstances where it is considered important that the facts be known in the public interest; an example would be public meetings, local government documents, and information relating to public bodies such as the police and fire departments. A letter to the board of bar overseers regarding a candidate would fall under qualified privilege, so the plaintiff will not prevail. In addition, for someone to prevail on a claim of defamation, if the plaintiff is a public figure he or she must prove that the defendant acted with malice. If the plaintiff is a private figure, as is he is here, he needs to prove that the defendant acted negligently. Here if the company reasonably believed the law student stole eggs, there was no negligence. (A) is incorrect because even with proof that statements were fault, the plaintiff would still need to overcome the burden of proving the defendant acted at least negligently. (B) is incorrect because even though it is factually correct, the plaintiff still need to prove the elements discussed above.

Answer 45

(D) Regardless of the cause of the plane crash, the manufacturing company may be held strictly liable as the retailer of a defective lifeboat that was an immediate and proximate cause of the friend's injuries. (B) is incorrect because a plaintiff may collect from defendants who are jointly liable.

Answer 46

(D) The dilemma was caused by the driver. The tourist did not assume the risk of his injury as long as he acted reasonably in departing for help. Justice Cardozo has written "danger invites rescue." Since the driver led the bus into a dangerous situation, it is reasonable to expect someone to venture for assistance. (C) alone will not support the tourist's claim if he was unreasonable to venture out of the bus. "Reasonable" does not mean that a majority of passengers have to think like the tourist (Choice A). Remember that to assume the risk the plaintiff has to do so knowingly and intelligently, which means the plaintiff has to be well aware of the risk.

Answer 47

(D) Intent is an element of false imprisonment. Mental anguish and negligence (B and C) are not elements of false imprisonment. In addition, (A) is incorrect because, as evidenced by the fact pattern, passengers were free to leave, thus not being confined. Remember that false imprisonment is an intentional tort, and intent is a required element, so you cannot negligently or accidentally falsely imprison someone.

Answer 48

(B) Under product liability based on strict liability in tort, a commercial supplier or merchant is held equally as liable as the manufacturer if the product is not altered. Therefore, the student can certainly recover against the retailer if she could have recovered against the manufacturing company. (C) is incorrect because the student would still be able to recover against the retailer if the retailer had altered the spray. (A) is incorrect because whether she paid or not is really irrelevant to her action against the retailer. (D) is incorrect because, as said above, product liability is based on strict liability, so she need not prove negligence.

Answer 49

(B) is correct. An owner of an animal generally considered undomesticated (or wild) is strictly liable for the harm that animal causes, even if the particular animal has been "tamed." The fact that the snake charmer exercised reasonable care (C) is not a defense to strict liability. (A) is incorrect because while it may be factually correct, it is not the reason why the spectator will prevail. (D) is incorrect because, although perhaps a trespasser at a show, that is not an appropriate defense to strict liability.

Answer 50

(B) Slander is spoken or oral defamation. Its elements require that the defendant (1) make a defamatory statement (2) that identifies the plaintiff (3) that is published and (4) intended by defendant to (5) harm plaintiff's reputation. Ordinarily, a plaintiff must prove special damages (that actual monetary loss ensued) to sustain the action. Slander per se provides four exceptions to that rule. When the defamatory statement concerns (1) plaintiff's professional reputation, (2) loathsome disease, (3) crime, or (4) the sexual misconduct of a woman, special damages need not be proved. In the past, the loathsome disease exception rendered allegations of incurable communicable diseases, which carried a strong social stigma, slander per se. Hepatitis does not qualify under this exception. This exception has also not been used successfully in the past century.

Answer 51

(C) An element of defamation is the publication of the defamatory language to a person other than the plaintiff. Since employer communicated the allegation only to the employee, the employee will not be able to sustain a cause of action for defamation. She may be able to pursue an action for intentional infliction of emotional distress, the elements of which are (1) an act of extreme and outrageous conduct, (2) intent to cause severe emotional distress, (3) causation, and (4) damages. Please note that the question does not ask whether the employee will prevail, but which of the statements is the most correct. In these types of questions be careful not to fall into the Bar Examiner's trap; they want to trick you into thinking about whether the plaintiff will prevail, and that is not the question.

Answer 52

(C) The passengers should bring an action in strict liability because it is easier to prove than negligence; they must merely show that the device was defective and was the proximate cause of the injuries. (D) is incorrect because a manufacturer cannot warn away a manufacturing defect. In addition, privity of contract (A) is unnecessary for a strict liability action, and (B) is incorrect because any duty that the retailer may have had does not absolve the manufacturer of their duty.

Answer 53

(D) The elements of a prima facie case of negligence are (1) a duty, (2) a breach of the duty, (3) causation, and (4) damages. It should be clear that the installer of a safety device has a duty to diligently inspect it. Breach of this duty (D) remains to be proved. The proximate cause of injury, for the purposes of this action, is the failure of the safety device (A) which is not in dispute. (B) is incorrect because mere failure of the business owner to inspect will not be enough to prove that he breached his duty. (D) is enough to prove he breached his duty since the answer goes further and speaks of reasonable care. (C) is incorrect because had he taken reasonable measures to inspect, and still not discovered it (but the inspection was what a reasonable person would do), that would still not establish a breach of the duty.

Answer 54

(B) is correct. Although the roommate was a gratuitous lender, he was obligated to warn the student since he had knowledge of the defect and that it created an unreasonable risk of harm. (A) is incorrect because strict liability, as applied to products, only applies to those in the chain of production, i.e., manufacturer, distributor, wholesaler, etc. It would not apply to a lender of the product. (C) is incorrect for the reasons stated in (A); yes, he was a gratuitous lender, but he still had a duty to warn. (D) is incorrect for the same reasons.

Answer 55

(D) A licensee is one who enters an owner's property for the owner's benefit or with the permission of the owner. The owner must exercise reasonable care in ensuring the safety of licensees. (A) is incorrect because an owner will not be held strictly liable. Remember that strict liability only applies to ultra hazardous activities, wild animals, and products. This does not apply to this situation. (B) is incorrect because even if he was on notice, that is not enough to make him liable and (C) is wrong for the same reason.

Answer 56

(B) Battery is an intentional tort. However, the spectator may not argue that he is not liable because he did not intend to hit the policeman—the important fact is that he intended to hit someone. Under the law, this intent will be transferred from his chosen victim to whomever was actually harmed. In other words, if one acts with the intention of unlawfully harming someone, he is liable for the resulting harm to another, unintended victim. (A) is a doctrine for proving negligence, and (D) is an element of assault, not battery. Make sure the answer you choose matches the question being asked.

Answer 57

(D) The driver was most likely correct in determining that the passengers were in danger. In general, one has no duty to take affirmative action to benefit others. However, one who does act is under the duty to act in the manner of a reasonably prudent person. The driver acted properly if he reasonably assumed he could drive the passengers to safety. (A) is incorrect because under ordinary circumstances the driver's actions would not have placed

the passengers in any greater danger. (B) and (C) are incorrect because they are just not relevant to the question. Look for answers that do not deal with the elements of the tort being asserted, as they are sometimes easy to eliminate.

Answer 58

(A) A threat coupled with the apparent present ability to carry it out is sufficient to create the reasonable apprehension of harmful or offensive contact necessary to legally establish assault. Although the mugger did not brandish a knife in the victim's face, he may very well have had one available. Words alone are not enough (D), but the mugger seems to have inspired a reasonable apprehension of an imminent battery in the victim. (B) is incorrect because although intent is one element, there still needs to be a reasonable apprehension. (C) is incorrect because even if the victim, as a sprinter, COULD outrun anyone, that does not necessarily negate apprehension, as fear and apprehension are not the same.

Answer 59

(B) The girl could not have consented, because the assurance of safety she accepted was based on false pretenses. Consent is invalid if it was (1) obtained by duress, (2) induced by fraud (as in this question), (3) given by mistake, or (4) given by one without capacity to consent, e.g., a mentally incompetent person. Although children are generally not considered capable of consenting (A), a fifteen-year-old would probably be deemed capable. (C) is incorrect, because the owner did not unlawfully threaten the girl to obtain her consent and (D) is incorrect because it is not legally true.

Answer 60

(D) Assault is the reasonable apprehension of imminent harmful or offensive contact inspired intentionally by the defendant. To prove assault, the girl must prove the owner knew she was afraid of falling.

Answer 61

(C) The purpose of the statute is to allow buses to stop without impeding the flow of traffic. This accident was totally unrelated to the purpose of the statute. It was caused by the second driver's actions, not by the driver's. The accident with the pedestrian could not have been foreseen by the reasonable person in the driver's position, and he is not liable to the pedestrian. (A) is incorrect for the reasons just stated above; a violation of a statute will not be enough to prove negligence, there also needs to be an injury that was the type of injury the statute was designed to prevent. (B) is incorrect because all the requirements of negligence per se are not met, as stated in the above explanations. To prove negligence per se there must be a (1) safety statute, (2) a violation of that statute, and (3) the type of injury to the type of plaintiff that the statute was designed to protect against.

Answer 62

(C) An independent contractor is liable for damages incurred due to negligence involved in his work. The builder's best argument is that he was not negligent and exercised due care. (A) is incorrect because the fact pattern specifically states that builder made all the decisions concerning the frame. (B) is incorrect because there is nothing in the fact pattern to indicate that it is true. In addition, even if developer had assumed liability, that would be a contract between the builder and the developer and would not preclude the inspector from bringing a claim. Lastly, (C) negates an element of negligence, which is always a better answer than a defense (B). (D) is incorrect because that fact alone will not negate liability on the builder's behalf, and again, (C), which eliminates an element of negligence, would still be better than a defense.

Answer 63

(C) Traditionally, the plaintiff had to provide expert testimony from the same community to prove malpractice (A). This would usually be shown by a deviation from the local custom or standard of care. Modern courts have modified this standard to make it national. However, it is considered apparent, even to the layperson, that leaving an object inside a patient is a significant deviation from the reasonable standard of care; therefore, expert testimony is unnecessary to establish negligence in this question.

Answer 64

(B) Mere breach of duty is not sufficient; actual damages must be proved before a recovery is allowed. (C) is incorrect because the victim needs only to prove a loss or detriment, not permanent injury. In addition, (A) is incorrect because although proving that would help prove that there was an injury, the injury does not need to be that specific.

Answer 65

(B) It was foreseeable that the car would be stolen if the keys were left in the ignition; therefore, the mechanic is liable. The act of the thief is not a superseding cause. It is the foreseeable result of leaving one's keys in the ignition of a car. (A) and (C) are incorrect because they imply that the customer assumed the risk of having her car stolen — which she did not.

Answer 66

(A) The elements of strict liability in tort were fulfilled. They are (1) a duty owed by a commercial supplier, (2) breach of the duty (i.e., a defect) (3) that caused the injury, and (4) damages. This might seem simple, but do not let that throw you. Remember that the MBE often tests relatively straight forward legal concepts, so do not skip an answer because it seems too simple. (D) is incorrect because privity does exist between the buyer and the manufacturer. (C) is irrelevant to strict liability, and (B) is incorrect and irrelevant in a claim against the manufacturer. As a supplier in the chain of sale, the dealer will be strictly liable for the damage caused by a defective product that he sold.

Answer 67

(C) Under the last clear chance doctrine, a plaintiff may recover despite his own negligence. The party who had the last clear chance to avoid the accident will be held liable for all damage. Under a comparative negligence statute, each party is able to recover based on his percentage of negligence. (B) is therefore incorrect. Because the driver's actions were also a cause of the accident, he would not recover for all of his damages in a comparative negligence jurisdiction. (D) assumes more information than was in the fact pattern. Remember, do not infer too much, only use the facts that they have given you. We do not know the last time the driver's brakes were inspected. (A) is incorrect because intent is not required in a negligence claim, so the answer choice is irrelevant. Be careful not to choose answers that go outside the scope of the question, or assume facts that you have not been given.

Answer 68

(C) One is generally under no duty to rescue another. However, a duty to rescue will exist in someone who either intentionally or negligently places another person in danger.

Answer 69

(D) The elements of intentional misrepresentation are (1) misrepresentation, (2) knowledge of falsity, (3) intent to induce reliance, (4) causation, (5) reliance, and (6) damages. Silence (non-disclosure) can be held to be a misrepresentation (B), but in this fact pattern, the dealer did not make any representations at all, either by his silence or by his actions. (A) is incorrect for the same reason (B) is, the fact that the dealer was silent does not amount to misrepresentation. (C) is incorrect because it would not matter, had the dealer made a misrepresentation.

Answer 70

(B) If the private company had notice of the danger (by virtue of the past twelve occurrences) and could have taken reasonable steps to prevent the injury, the blind woman will most likely prevail in an action for negligence. (A) is incorrect because although common carriers are generally held to a high standard of care, they are not strictly liable and they are not insurers for all individuals on their premises. Posting barriers between cars and/or warning blind commuters are examples of such measures. (C) is incorrect because "assuming the risk" is rarely the correct answer. Comparative negligence statutes have made assumption of the risk considerations largely unnecessary. (D) is incorrect for the same reasons that (B) is correct

Answer 71

(B) Use of a person's picture or name for commercial advantage, such as in an advertisement, requires consent. Unauthorized use will give rise to liability for invasion of privacy. The first guitar company was obligated to determine if the rock star had consented to the use of the photograph. This is a separate cause of action from defamation. Defamation requires defamatory language and will not be satisfied by the publication of a picture (C and D). (A) is incorrect because even though public figures may sustain an action for invasion of privacy, it is not enough to say that he is a public figure. There needs to be more, as stated above.

Answer 72

(C) The photographer may take anyone's picture he pleases if that person is out in public at the time. (B) is incorrect because, although the photographer sold the picture for a profit, the tort of invasion of privacy is generally limited to instances where the picture is used by the defendant in advertisements (such as the above question). (D) is incorrect because whether he is a public figure or not is not relevant to this tort. It is an element of defamation, not invasion of privacy.

Answer 73

(C) There is generally no duty to aid one in peril unless you create the peril. (A) is incorrect because even if you are an expert, it does not create a duty to rescue. (B) is incorrect for the same reason. (D) is incorrect because assuming the liability is irrelevant here, the answer centers around whether there is a duty, which his addressed in answer (C).

Answer 74

(B) The wife will recover in her product liability action against the manufacturer under strict liability. A manufacturer will be held strictly liable for an injury caused by a defect in its product if the product contained the defect when it was sold. This product had a manufacturing defect that caused her injury.

The gas filter and dealer preparation were immaterial. (C) is incorrect because one does not assume the risk of such an accident by opening a car's hood. "Assuming the risk" is usually an incorrect choice. (D) is incorrect because privity is not required in product liability actions.

Answer 75

(D) Governmental executive officials have an absolute defense to defamation actions. All statements reasonably related to an executive matter are privileged. (C) is incorrect since, even though it would be a defense (truth is always a defense to defamation), (D) is the better answer because even if the statement is NOT true, the fact that as a governmental official the defendant has an absolute defense is a better defense. (A) and (B) are needed to prove defamation, but they ignore the fact that governmental officials have immunity.

Answer 76

(A) For the driver to be liable, he must have been the proximate cause and the cause in fact. (A) assumes that the driver was a proximate cause. The best approach to judge whether he was also the "cause in fact" is to apply the "but for" test. But for the driver's negligence, the second accident would not have occurred. Therefore, he may be held liable for the second accident because it is also foreseeable. This may seem unfair, but remember when you injure someone, it is always foreseeable that the injury will cause other injuries or accidents.

Answer 77

(A) The driver's defense of contributory negligence will fail because the pedestrian was not at all negligent. As far as she knew, she was capable of jogging safely.

Answer 78

(C) The right to privacy is personal and does not extend to family members. (A) is incorrect because truth and lack of malice are not defenses to invasion of privacy. (B) is incorrect because facts disclosed about a public figure that are so "intimate" that they outrage the average person are not privileged. (D) is incorrect because ridicule and contempt are not requirements to assert an invasion of privacy claim. (D) skips the issue; be careful that when you choose an answer, it addresses the issue, which in this case is whether the right to privacy extends to family members.

Answer 79

(D) None of the above. Assault is the apprehension of immediate physical harm (B). It is not satisfied in this question because it requires intent on the part of the defendant to arouse apprehension. (A) is incorrect because there was no offensive touching. (C) is incorrect because its intent element is also missing. These are all intentional torts, and the employees had innocent intentions.

Answer 80

(B) One is permitted to enter the land of another if necessary to avoid injury, i.e., in the case of private necessity (this makes (A) incorrect), but the person is liable for any damage he or she causes. (C) is incorrect for the same reason. (D) is irrelevant to this question. Remember that both parties can be liable for a tort, and just because one party is a tortfeasor does not mean the other party cannot also be a tortfeasor.

Answer 81

(B) Since the farmer intended to scare the passenger, he is liable for battery for all consequences of this action. Strict liability (A) would not apply in this question since the farmer's actions would not be deemed ultra-hazardous. (Remember there are only THREE instances where strict liability applies: wild animals, products, and ultra-hazadous activities. Do not let the bar examiners trick you into thinking there are more scenarios where strict liability will apply.) (D) incorrectly applies the "intent" element of battery. (C) is irrelevant; the farmer's actions were not privileged by self-defense.

Answer 82

(D) The elements of assault are (1) an act, (2) intent to do the act, and (3) causation. Although the customer's acts satisfied these requirements, the customer might claim that he was acting in the co-worker's defense. Someone who intervenes to save another may legally use the amount of force the other person was privileged to use in self-defense. Remember when a torts question asks you whether someone will prevail, think first about whether the elements of that tort are met, THEN think about whether there are any applicable defenses. (D) does not come right out and state "he acted in self defense" but that is essentially what the answer choice is stating.

Answer 83

(C) The elements of battery are (1) harmful or offensive contact, (2) intent to do the act, and (3) causation. (C) is one of the elements of battery. (A) and (D) are not necessary to establish battery. The trespasser need not prove (B), but may have to rebut the allegation that he instigated the action if it is introduced by the workers.

Answer 84

(A) One has no legal duty to rescue another, but if he does decide to volunteer in a rescue attempt, he

must act in the manner of an ordinary, prudent person. In this question, the passerby did not act reasonably when he lit a cigarette and through the match down, and is liable for the damage caused by his negligent behavior.

Answer 85

(C) If the salesman's panic was reasonable, he had the right to protect his car from the storm by parking on the hill. The salesman had the right to assert the defense of "private necessity." A person may interfere with the property of another where it is necessary to avoid injury and the threatened injury is more serious than the injury to be caused by the trespass. In such a case, a person asserting the defense of private necessity is liable for actual damages caused to the other party's property.

Answer 86

(A) Since the salesman was justified in parking on the hill, the property owner will be liable for damages to the car.

Answer 87

(A) With minimal effort and expense, the constructor could have made sure the gate was locked; therefore, his failure to do so constitutes negligence. Here, the answer hinges on the duty to act as a reasonable person would have under the circumstances. (B) is incorrect because it is doubtful that construction would be classified as ultra-hazadrous. (D) is incorrect because it is not the correct standard that landowners owe to trespassers.

Answer 88

(C) One of the elements that the plaintiff must prove in a claim based on public nuisance is that he suffered a special or unique damage different from that of the general public. The attorney is suing to clear a sidewalk. Since every member of the public has a right to use the sidewalk, the attorney will not be able to show a special damage. Note: Abatement by self-help (D) is the right of one to enter the property of another and use as little force as possible to end the nuisance. (B) is incorrect since the attorney repeatedly asked the shipping company to move his trucks. (A) is not true; monetary damages in this case will be inadequate.

Answer 89

(C) Criminal acts and intentional acts of third persons, if not foreseeable, are superseding intervening causes that break the chain between the initial wrongful act and the ultimate injury. In this fact pattern, it doesn't seem as if the act of the passerby would be foreseeable (which is why (A) would be incorrect) to the original tortfeasor. (D) is incorrect because the nature of the weapon really isn't relevant. (B) is incorrect because although it is the general rule, a tortfeasor will not be held liable for intervening cause, as stated above.

Answer 90

(C) Since the senator was a public figure, actual malice must be proved in addition to falsity. For this reason (D) is incorrect. For all defamation claims, a bare minimum of negligence must be proven. However, when dealing with public figures, it needs to be shown that the person making the statement was acting with malice, not merely negligent. (B) is incorrect because merely proving falsity is not enough, as stated above. (A) is incorrect because while it might be factually correct, it is not enough to prove malice. Make sure the answer choice you pick does not just repeat facts.

Answer 91

(D) Parents are generally not liable for the tortious conduct of their children. One exception is when the child is acting as an agent for his parents. Also, remember what the question is asking: "IF she prevails, it will be because . . ." The only way the mother would be liable for the son's actions is if he were acting as her agent, given the choices in the question. (A) is incorrect because, as stated above, parents are not generally liable for the torts of their children. Parents can be responsible for their own negligence, that is, breaching a duty to be a reasonable parent, but they are not automatically responsible for the actions of their children. (B) is incorrect because that doctrine does not apply to parents and children. (C) is incorrect because there is nothing in the facts that indicate that the mother was negligent.

Answer 92

(B) If a defamatory statement refers to an overly large group, no member of that group will fulfill the element that the defamation be "of or concerning" the plaintiff. (A) is inapplicable since "only joking" would not be a defense to defamation. (C) is irrelevant because of the size of the group. (D) is incorrect because whether the statements were read from a script or not is irrelevant.

Answer 93

(A) is the correct answer. Pay close attention, as the answer choice says, "If he has suffered an unreasonable loss." For the farmer to recover, the interference has to be unreasonable. However, you do not have to decide if the farmer has indeed suffered because of an unreasonable interference since the answer choice makes that clear for you (i.e., if you were debating as to whether the interference was unreasonable or not, answer A takes care of that debate by stating IF it was unreasonable he will recover). (B) is incorrect because it is not factually accurate, and (D) is not correct because the nuisance only seems to affect the farmer, and perhaps a few other neighbors, which his not enough to constitute a public nuisance. (C) might be tempting, but while expense can be one factor, it is not the only factor to consider in a nuisance claim, and if the interference is unreasonable, there may be still be a nuisance, even if the expense to cure that interference is indeed prohibitive.

Answer 94

(B) A parent is not vicariously liable for the torts of a child. An exception is when a parent negligently allows the child to perform a dangerous act (for example shooting a stun gun). In such an instance, the parent may be liable for his own negligence in permitting the child to act in such a manner. (A) describes a doctrine regarding employers and employees, and doesn't apply to parents and children (C) is a term used in contract law, and (D) is not a legal rule.

Answer 95

(C) The elements of intentional infliction of emotional distress are (1) an act of extreme and outrageous conduct, (2) intent to cause severe emotional distress, (3) causation, and (4) damages. In the instant case the first man could not possibly have fulfilled the element of intent, because he was not aware of the wife's presence. This is a common way that the bar examiners set up intentional infliction of emotional distress, and it is easy to get wrong since the first man's actions seem quite extreme and outrageous and emotional distress was indeed suffered. But always remember you can not intend to cause someone severe emotional distress if you do not know he or she is present.

Answer 96

(D) Appropriation of one's picture or name for commercial advantage is actionable as an invasion of privacy. However, this action is limited to advertisement or promotion of product or goods. A one-time magazine cover will not qualify. The mere fact that the tabloid used the star's picture to boost its sales will not make it liable under invasion of privacy, and is merely a red herring to get you to think of the "commercial advantage" standard. As it was not an advertisement, (A) is incorrect. (B) is incorrect because it is far too general and sweeping, and (C) is incorrect because, as just stated above, you cannot use a person's image for commercial advantage.

Answer 97

(D) Truth is an absolute defense to defamation, no matter how damaging. Note: Defendant has the burden of proving the statement's truth. (A) is incorrect because it is the opposite of the rule of law, as just stated above. In addition (B) and (C) are incorrect because of the fact that truth is an absolute defense.

Answer 98

(B) The cruise control manufacturing company built the mechanism that sent the signals to the accelerating and braking systems. This mechanism was the only component to malfunction. The brakes wore out because of overuse. They were not defective; therefore, the brake manufacturing company will not be held liable.

Answer 99

(D) The elements of intentional infliction of emotional distress are (1) an act of extreme and outrageous conduct, (2) severe emotional distress, (3) causation, and (4) damages. The younger sister's injuries were not only foreseeable, but were also the intended outcome of the older sister's actions. Whether the older sister's actions are extreme and outrageous might be debatable, but that element is not addressed in any of the answer choices, so you do not have to waste time debating with yourself as to whether her actions meet that requirement. (A) is incorrect because the answer does not make sense, legally. Make sure the answer you choose actually answers the question, and is relevant, in some way, to the claim being brought. (B) is incorrect because, while it may be true factually, it does not release the older sister of liability if the elements of intentional infliction of emotional distress are met. (C) is a wrong choice for similar reasons to (B). The fiancé's actions might have caused the injury, but it was entirely foreseeable, on the part of the older sister, that the fiancé, or someone else in the house, could act in that fashion.

Answer 100

(A) The machine was operated under the exclusive control of the dairy farmer. It should not have been turned on when the cows were not being milked and this was the cause of the inspector's injuries. (B) is incorrect because strict liability is inapplicable since this is a negligence action. Remember that strict liability is only a correct choice if the fact pattern deals with wild animals (even if you thought a cow was a wild animal, and it's not, it wasn't the animal that caused the injury), abnormally dangerous activities (milking is probably not an abnormally dangerous activity) and products liability. Products liability does not apply here because the inspector wants to sue the dairy farmer, not the manufacturer of the milking machine, and even if he wanted to sue the manufacturer, the facts tell you the machine is in working order. (C) is incorrect because the inspector did not assume the risk of the machine's being turned on. You might have been tempted since the facts tell you that the inspector was where only cows venture, but there is nothing in the fact pattern that indicates he was aware of the risk. (D) is not relevant to this question.

Answer 101

(C) is the correct answer. It was the other flyer, not the airline, that committed the tort. For the airline to be held responsible for the other flyer's torts, the other flyer would have to be an agent of the airline, and also acting to benefit the agent. Here, the other flyer is not an agent and, even if he was, it would be doubtful that the other flyer was acting to benefit the airline. (A) is incorrect because there is no evidence that the passenger assumed the risk merely by staying in his assigned seat. (B) is incorrect because, although it states the correct elements for battery, it does not give a reason why the airline would be liable for battery. The question does not ask whether the other flyer would be liable for battery. If that was the question, the passenger would most certainly prevail against the other flyer in battery. (D) is incorrect because it gives a reason why the airline might be NEGLIGENT, not why they would be liable for battery.

Answer 102

(C) is the correct answer. The car was brand new, so even the most reasonable of drivers would not have thought to get the breaks on a brand new vehicle inspected. For this same reason, (B) is incorrect. (A) is incorrect because although the answer correctly states the rule for res ipsa loquitor, accidents like this DO happen without negligence. This is a perfect example of an accident where no one breaches a duty. It is possible that people get into car accidents when neither party is negligent. (D) is incorrect because although it seems here that the manufacturer SHOULD be liable, that would not eliminate the driver's liability had the driver acted negligently.

Answer 103

(B) is the correct answer. The prior accident will have no legal effect since you take your plaintiff as you find him or her. For this reason, the other answers are incorrect.